When the Soul Calls

Silvana Maria Pagani

UNIVERSAL LAWS AND PRINCIPLES

All Creation is governed
by the Laws of the Universe

Everything happens according to law

There is order in the universe

As above so below:
The natural laws that govern
this planet
have their origin
in the higher laws
of the spiritual realms

The essence of creation is light

Light carries Information

We leave spirit and go away
from God into form
with the original purpose
of profound soul growth
Once accomplished
we shall return to God

All is one
We are all connected
all bearing the seed of Divinity
This is the way we start and the way we end

The Universe means well for you

The Source of Light always knows
what is best for you

What goes up comes down
Ask for guidance and you shall receive

All Substance carries consciousness
All life forms are infused with consciousness

All sentient beings have the same basic needs

Everything is interconnected

Treat all Life forms with Respect
animals, plants, the Earth, the Sky,
the mineral kingdom, the Air, the Water

Like attracts like

What you send out
shall return to you

There is justice in the universe

The more you give out,
the more comes back to you

As within so without
As one thinks, so one becomes

The outer world is a mirror of
our inner world

You are the creator of your own Reality

The future is built of today's thoughts
dressed by emotion
and driven by action

THE THOUGHTS AND IMAGES WE HOLD
IN OUR CONSCIOUS AND SUBCONSCIOUS MINDS
WILL MANIFEST THEIR MIRROR LIKENESSES
IN OUR EXTERNAL CIRCUMSTANCES

TRUE WISDOM COMES FROM LISTENING WITHIN

ACT IN ACCORDANCE TO THE HIGHER GOOD
OF ALL

TREAT OTHERS FAIRLY AND
YOU SHALL BE TREATED FAIRLY

TREAT OTHERS AS IF THEY WERE YOU
TREAT THEM AS YOU WANT TO BE TREATED

WHAT YOU SOW YOU SHALL HARVEST
IT IS THE NATURAL PRINCIPLE
OF CAUSE AND EFFECT

EVERY CAUSE HAS ITS EFFECT
EVERY EFFECT HAS ITS CAUSE

THE CONSEQUENCES OF PAST ACTIONS
ARE ATONED THROUGH KARMA
LET GO AND TRUST THE UNIVERSE
TO TAKE CARE OF IT

LET GO AND LET GOD
YOU ARE NEVER ALONE

AT THE MOMENT OF COMMITMENT
THE UNIVERSE ASPIRES TO ASSIST YOU

STAY CLEAR AND FOCUSED
ON YOUR INTENTION
SO THAT THE UNIVERSE
CAN ASSIST YOU
IN MANIFESTING WHAT IS MEANT TO BE

IN ORDER TO CREATE YOU MUST FIRST
BE ABLE TO IMAGINE IT

FOR SOMETHING TO HAPPEN
YOU NEED TO FIRST
DO SOMETHING
ALL RESULTS REQUIRE FIRST AN ACTION

WHEN YOU COMMIT, COMMIT FULLY
ALWAYS GIVE YOUR ALL
YET STAY UNATTACHED
FOR YOU MIGHT LOSE IT AGAIN

KNOW WHEN TO LET GO
AND WHEN TO HOLD ON
KNOW THE DIFFERENCE

THE GREATEST PAIN WE CREATE
IS RESISTANCE TO CHANGE
THAT NEEDS TO HAPPEN

RATHER THAN A RIGID RESISTANCE
ACCEPT THE PRESENT MOMENT

STUMBLING BLOCKS CAN BECOME STEPPING STONES
PROBLEMS CAN BECOME OPPORTUNITIES

EVERYTHING SERVES OUR HIGHEST GOOD
IF WE MAKE GOOD USE OF IT

RELEASE AND FORGIVE
AND MOVE ON

PRACTICE A LEAP IN FAITH
WALK THE HERO'S JOURNEY
COME OUT OF A NEGATIVE SITUATION
STRONGER AND BOLDER

THERE IS NO GROWTH IN CONTRACTION

(CONTINUED ON PAGE 488)

When the Soul Calls

True Stories of Deep Healing and Transformation
Through the Wisdom of the Heart and Soul
Books 1 & 2

Silvana Maria Pagani

Silvana Maria Pagani

Website: www.HeartPathRetreat.com
Contact: Silvana@HeartPathRetreat.com

When The Soul Calls
True Stories of Deep Healing and Transformation
Through the Wisdom of the Heart and Soul
Books 1 & 2

© Copyright 2021, Silvana Maria Pagani. All rights reserved.
HeartPath Publishing

HeartPath
Publishing

Cover design: Michael Motley

Cover Photo: Silvana Pagani

Temple of the Living Goddess, HeartPath Retreat Center, Santa Fe, NM

Interior book design: David Christel

ISBN: 978-0-578-38747-5

The following trademarks and registrations are the sole property of Silvana Maria Pagani:
HeartPath Re-Alignment™
PowerLine™ Healing
PowerLine™ Workout
Maha Intensive™
TENSU Body Injury Trauma Release™

Disclaimer: Because I am not a trained psychotherapist, I do not follow the rules and guidelines of the
classical therapist, though rules concerning confidentiality are strictly honored.

All ancient art objects property of the Museum of the Ancient Mother Goddess, Santa Fe, NM, USA.

All art objects are property of Silvana Maria Pagani unless otherwise noted.

TESTIMONIALS

While working with an individual in her intense healing process, she gifted me with a representation she had formed in clay of me as Mother Goddess with a snake running up my spine. In one arm I am holding her Inner Child and my other hand is holding her head. Her headless torso stands in front of me.

Du schenkst neues Leben, Hoffnung, dass noch nicht alles verloren ist. In Deinen Armen hältst Du meinen Kopf. Das Gesicht ist mir verborgen, Dir zugewandt. Bitte, zeige mir mein wahres Gesicht!

English Translation:

YOU GIVE NEW LIFE AND HOPE THAT NOT EVERYTHING IS LOST
YOU ARE HOLDING MY HEAD IN YOUR ARMS
MY FACE IS HIDDEN, FACING TOWARDS YOU
PLEASE, SHOW ME MY TRUE FACE

"I cannot convey adequately how grateful I am for the very powerful healing you facilitated for me earlier this year. It was transformative. You led me to an extraordinary place of vulnerability, creating conditions for me to feel so totally safe. I could face a very, very deep, archetypal issue, and CLEAR it. My relationship with my most intimate Divine master Jesus was healed, and so much dross dropped away I'm surprised I didn't lose 29 pounds in the process.

You are a gift to the world, because you are clear enough and devoted enough to channel the great gift of Spirit right where it needs to go. Keep spreading the love."

~ Robert Hoffman, Santa Fe, NM
Pastor, Church of Antioch

"My life was forever changed during my first Maha Intensive. I gained deeper self-awareness and discovered why pain and struggle continued to have control over me. The Maha Intensive awakened a great power within me, and Silvana helped me to truly invoke higher consciousness and divine energies in my life. I know without her tremendous gifts as a healer I would not have become who I am today, living my dream and helping others to live theirs. I've completed seven Maha Intensives in the course of five years, and I am deeply devoted to sharing this life-altering and transformational work with others, because of how it's healed my own life.

There is nothing I can describe that compares to this training of the 2-Year Principal Training Program in the HeartPath Re-Alignment. It is the deepest, most intensive alternative healing work anyone could ever do. It provides a personal healing experience that breaks down all internal structures to only rebuild it, aligned with truth and one's soul purpose. In my daily life, I am now working with divine beings and masters of light, which is the ultimate gift of this training. I wanted to learn Silvana's work, so I could help change lives the way mine was completely transformed. With absolutely no prior experience, within two years, I learned to heal others through energy work, as well as dialogue with clients on the deepest level of their being – what other work teaches us how to fully heal the body, change negative mindsets, release any pain in the heart and know God. This training is for the true of heart, because to share Silvana's work with others is truly a life-changing experience for facilitators as well."

~ Anne Ruth, Atlanta, GA
Accountant, Warner Bros,
Certified Facilitator, HeartPath Re-Alignment

"The Maha Intensive was truly a profound and life-altering experience. The sessions were filled with love, compassion, grace, safety, revelation, caring, and patience. So many things happened inside of me, so much shifted, that it's near to impossible to describe the scope of impact on me and my life. I learned to trust myself and my intuition; and I learned to trust God. I feel aligned with the universe and know that I belong here. What has manifested is that even now, months later, I can honestly say for the first time in my life that I am truly happy and at peace; experiencing love, compassion, and connection every day on various levels. Thank you for this gift in my life."

~ Kristine Hutari, Santa Fe, NM
Sculptor / Professional ballroom dancer

"Hace algunos años tuve la oportunidad de tener una sesión de sanación con Silvana Pagani. Me es imposible resumir en este posteo de que se trató pero puedo tratar de explicar lo que significó para mí: regresé a mi infancia e indagué en la vida de mis padres y en lo que yo había mamado – consciente e inconscientemente – de ellos, cuestioné mandatos que no hacían más que limitarme, desenmarañé inseguridades heredadas y, sobre todo, vi la raíz de mi insatisfacción. No voy a mentir, la sesión fue durísima y las repercusiones fueron enormes; una profunda crisis existencial. Un año más tarde aparecería la idea de este año sabático, una suerte de 'botón de reseteo mental,' con la premisa de soltar todo para llegar a mi esencia. Un año más me costó juntar el coraje de hacerlo … y acá estamos en pleno proceso. Pasar por USA era interesante y divertido desde el principio pero se convirtió en mucho más que eso. Adrian se copó y juntos estudiamos con Silvana el PowerLine Healing y Workout, no solo para entender y continuar nuestro propio proceso de crecimiento si no también para poder guiar a otros a alinearse con su propia intensión de vida. Sigo entusiasmada con todo lo que esto puede generar. Gracias, Sil, por tanto!!" ♥

English translation:

"A few years ago I had the opportunity to have a healing session with Silvana Pagani. It is impossible for me to summarize what it was about but I can try to explain what it meant to me: I returned to my childhood and researched my parents' lives and what I had sucked – consciously and unconsciously – of them, I questioned commands that only limited me, uncovered inherited insecurity and, above all, I saw the root of my dissatisfaction. I'm not going to lie, the session was very hard and the repercussions were huge; a deep existential crisis. A year later would appear the idea of this gap year, a kind of 'mind reset button,' with the premise of releasing everything to reach my essence. One more year I had a hard time gathering the courage to do it... and here we are in the process. We studied with Silvana the PowerLine Healing & PowerLine Workout Training certification Program, not only to understand and continue our own growth process but also to be able to guide others to align with their own intention of life. I'm still excited about everything this can generate. Thank you, Sil, for so much!" ♥

~ Sara DiCarlo, Buenos Aires, Argentina
Textile Designer / Astrologer
Certified Facilitator, PowerLine Healing
Certified Instructor, PowerLine Workout

"Fue un tiempo muy intenso y movilizador. Me siento desafiado desde el idioma, lo escucho y lo físico. Trabaje con Silvana y me impacto la forma en que me ayudo. Desde este momento quize saber mas sobre su trabajo para poder crecer como persona. Sentí que la información del programa fue mucha pero clara. También hay una guía clara de como seguir. Comprendo mejor como interactuan las personas y porque. Me sirvió para entenderme y conocerme mas. Lo que me gusto lo mas del programa es la posibilidad de centrarme y reconociendo como estoy. Ahora me siento con todas las herramientas. Solo necesito practicar mas. En el futuro cercano no estoy planeando de abrir mi propia pratica de sanción. Ahora estoy planteándome la forma en que quiero vivir mi vida y en este momento hay mas dudas que certezas. La experiencia del curso con Silvana fue super agradable. Silvana tiene una forma de acompañar el proceso muy amorosa. Estoy muy agradecido. Entiendo que Sara y yo hicimos un proceso mas corto y intenso. Fue difícil por momentos trabajar con el material teorético tantas horas por dia. Y si, estoy interesado de continuar con mas aprendizajes."

English translation:

"The training was a very intense and mobilizing time. I felt challenged in the English language; having to concentrate in listening, speaking and writing; as well as the physical aspect of the program. When I originally worked with Silvana I felt struck by the way she helped me. From this moment on I wanted to know more about her work in order to grow as a person. I felt that the information of the training course was a lot but also clear. Furthermore, there is a clear guidance on how to follow. Now I better understand how people interact and why. This helped me to understand and get to know myself deeper. What I liked most about the program is the capability of focus while recognizing who and how I am. The course provided me with all the tools necessary; I just need to practice more. In the near future I am not planning to open my own healing practice because I am currently on a 1 -year sabbatical figuring out how I want to live my life. Right now there are more doubts than certainties. The experience of the course with Silvana was super pleasant. Silvana has a way of accompanying the process in a very loving way. I'm very grateful. I understand Sara and I did a shorter process and more intense. It was difficult at times to work with the theoretic material so many hours a day. And yes, I am interested in continuing to further my training and learn more."

~ Adrian Ferreira, Buenos Aires, Argentina
Master of Argentine Tango
Certified Facilitator, PowerLine Healing
Certified Instructor, PowerLine Workout

"Those drawn to Silvana's work, wisdom and devotion, are especially fortunate. My experience with the process that Silvana guided me through has been a life-evolving gift. During the process, I was not exactly sure of the direction I was going, but everything came together with wonder-filled resolution. The time that the process took gave me an opportunity to go inward in ways I had not before imagined. Through Silvana's unconditional loving presence and expertise, I accessed profound insights and appreciation for my life experiences. This was heart opening in that I became able to fully trust my knowing and move forward with clarity and purpose."

~ Teri Jo Summer, Whidbey Island, WA
Textile Artist

"During my process, I experienced that I am supported by forces that are beyond my understanding. I see now that my life can be very different from what I knew so far. I learned that I have not lived yet fully. The issues that I have suppressed came into the light of consciousness. I learned that I can trust that deeper knowledge / sources will guide me. I feel supported by Silvana's depth, deep being and integrity, love and warmth, the way she is. My soul recognizes the truth she makes available. Thank you! May you continue your work with the blessings of God and the whole Universe!"

~ Dr. Elisabeth Rimmele-Schick, Germany
Doctor of Dermatology

"Silvana's work is at the leading edge of healing. She has discovered a process to repair the split between us and the Divine. For her, 'the split from God' is the initial trauma of life. Healing this is such a profound, nurturing, and enlivening experience. She works you hard. You have to be willing to engage your fears. And the results are magnificent, glorious."

~ Martin Rutte, Prince Edward Island, Canada
Author of Project Heaven on Earth

"I am forever grateful that I've had the opportunity to work with Silvana in her TENSU Healing Sessions after my horse accident, which resulted in surgery on my spleen. I passionately believe that it was her help in healing the trapped energy and emotional trauma within me that has allowed for the significant results in my overall healing process physically. You must experience it for yourself because it is magical. 'What do I have to lose?' I thought to myself, only to find out that I had everything plus myself to gain. I experienced results from one TENSU session compared to what was only a hope with weeks of traditional physical therapy sessions."

~ Jayla Read, Santa Fe, NM

"This process has been intense! The healing session was direct, specific, and I felt guided and supported through the process. Silvana brought the process to subconscious beliefs, making them conscious, seeing where they began, and how it has affected me. It unraveled knots I have tried for years to undo. What we started, is continuing, even a week later as I write this. It is helping me address some underlying memories. New realizations emerge, freeing me to be more present. The HeartPath Re-Alignment is gentle, supportive, yet effective. I aim to practice gently and allow. Silvana is a beautiful soul, and a really good facilitator. She has aided the healing process in ways that surprised, challenged, and embraced me during a difficult process. Her strength is a testament to right living and an immense heart that she shares in this work, and her life. I recommend her HeartPath Re-Alignment. Thank you Silvana."

~ Ramona Lotti, California

THE DANCE OF LIFE: For Silvana with Love & Thanks

"She danced gracefully, her arms encircling an invisible lover in gentle embrace. She hummed as she spun slowly around the room, her skirts rustling as aspen in a soft summer breeze. She was alone but not alone, timid but eager for what was to come. The sun had settled in her being and she felt its power and loving grace radiating around her. She knew her aura to be a rainbow splash of colors, reaching into the universe to accept its rightful connection to home. She rejoiced in her own happiness. It had not always been like this. She had known times of intense pain and frustration. Times when she wondered if she would ever understand, the confusion seemed to run to the very core of her being, veiling every glimmer of truth. Each pain had been another climbed stair, each moment of frustration a doorway to understanding. This she knew to be true. She had been patient. Silvana had climbed many stairs and entered many doorways in her lifetime. Each time she had looked expectantly for the gold at the end of the rainbow. She had walked carefully through every room, peeking in closets and seeking under beds. Never had the holy word jumped out at her but she kept looking. She experienced many things as she searched. The world became a comfortable place for her, each culture her own, each language at her command. She came to understand the motivation, joys, and pain of those around her. With each experience, she studied the reflection. Her own picture grew clearer. Soon, a story grew with the pictures. Words became paragraphs and later whole chapters of self-knowledge manifested in her knowing places. With each step, the boulders, which rested as challenges in her pathway, chose to transform into pebbles, and her footsteps found surety. And so she came to dance. Dance for the joy of living, dance in thanksgiving for her inner and most divine teacher, dance for the new vistas ahead and experiences past, dance for herself."

~ Erica, Galisteo, NM

"It has been a rich experience working with Silvana, full of good will, caring concern, and inner guidance unfolding. I received the clarity I sought and reconnected with myself.

I loved my time with you, dear Silvana. I am so grateful for your kind listening presence, your healing imagination, your presence to the process. Blessings on you and your authentic work!"

~ Susan Hull-Walker

"My life task was validated and my outlook on life and myself has dramatically shifted. If you are seeking change and find yourself ready to take the big leap, I encourage you to get involved with the HeartPath Re-Alignment. Having been single for more than 12 years, I have now found fulfillment by attracting the right partner into my life. I did it – and so can you!"

~ Uli, Boutique Owner, Santa Fe

"I continue to tap into my vitality and aliveness as a result of working with you. Thank you so much for your time, energy, kindness, and most of all, your wisdom."

~ Melissa Weiner, Stray Dog Media
Publicist and PR Marketing

"Silvana has developed what I feel is a revolutionary fitness program. I've studied and tried many programs, however, the PowerLine Workout is superior. No matter what your fitness, the results that you are looking for – with core stability being a primary focus of the PowerLine – after the first session, I experienced increased vitality and found myself excited for the next session. IMAGINE having the toned physique you've always wanted, without spending hours at the gym. The PowerLine Workout will help you achieve your fitness goals."

~ Tyshawn Bryant, Los Angeles, CA
CEO, Green Regimen

"I am thrilled with Silvana's PowerLine Workout. What I most appreciate and have been searching for is that within this workout you are deeply connected to Spirit. Throughout the workout, I felt total connection and calmness. Plus, it is an amazing physical workout that strengthens, tones, and conditions the body."

~ Luren Bellucci, Santa Fe, NM
Professional Argentine Tango Instructor

DEDICATION

I bow to Seshat, ancient Egyptian goddess of writing,
knowledge and wisdom, and mistress of the House of Books;
divine scribe, measurer, and record keeper;
and daughter of Ma'at, goddess of truth and justice;
and Thoth, reckoner of time.

CONTENTS

Contents

BOOK TWO
The Path of Soul

PART VIII: DEEP REFLECTIONS

THE REALITY OF TRUTH

ALL THAT WAS HIDDEN
WILL COME INTO THE LIGHT

AND BY DOING SO
IT SHALL BE FREED
FOREVER

THERE IS NO SHAME,
BLAME OR GUILT

ONLY PURE LOVE
AND GRATITUDE

FOR A PRECIOUS
JOURNEY SHARED

SOME MIGHT BE UPSET
FOR TRUTH
REVEALED

TO THIS I SAY
THERE ARE NO SECRETS

SECRETS ARE AN ILLUSION

WHAT HAPPENED
CANNOT BE UNDONE

IT SERVED A PURPOSE
WHICH GOT FULFILLED

ALL IS CLEARLY VISIBLE
IN THE REALITY OF TRUTH

THE FOCUS IS TO FREE
WITH PURE INTENTION

Acknowledgments

This book has been long overdue. It was in the 1990s that Spirit instructed me to write down the stories of transformation and healing that I experience in my healing practice. But unfortunately — at the time being — I was fully absorbed in the building of the HeartPath Retreat Center, my healing practice, and the 14-day and 21-day trainings in Europe six times a year (part of the 2-year HeartPath Re-Alignment training certification program). What I did, though, was write a complex self-help guide called *The Split from God – Are You Living Your Dream And True Life Purpose Or Have You Settled For Compromise?* — a book unpublished to this day.

Now, standing at the crossroads of passing on the HeartPath Retreat Center to a new stewardship; to avail myself to my new given assignment from Spirit — healing still involved but no retreat center anymore — I find this might in fact be the perfect time to share with my readers some of the work experiences of my past thirty-one years.

Looking back at my life's journey, I can see how from the start my Soul had set the perfect scenario for me to learn and understand how my current life plan is a continuation of a mission started a long time ago, which may be — and maybe not — completed in this life. I am deeply grateful for all my life's experiences, the ones immensely beautiful like paradise and sweet like a fully ripened fruit. But also for the ones that have been like a bitter pill to swallow, a dark night of the Soul.

In deep reverence I shall forever remain in service of the Goddess and Jesus, the Christ, the master healer to whom my work is dedicated, as well as his consort Mariam of Magdala / Mary Magdalene.

Spirit is upholding and carrying me. I owe everything and all to Spirit. I am tremendously grateful for the bounty of the never-ending blessings and protection, and for the challenges and countless trials. They helped me grow in awareness and consciousness and advanced my understanding, which in turn have made me stronger and more resilient, to prepare me for my further tasks.

First and foremost, my gratitude goes to my parents who loved us children deeply, both of them in their own way. They taught us with their best intentions. I not only owe my very existence to them; they were my first teachers who provided me with the most important life lessons, many of them positive and, perhaps equally, many negative.

My mom, Olga, with her rare gift of unconditional love, in whose eyes there was nothing we children could do wrong. She allowed us to grow up liberally, hang out whole afternoons on the cherry trees laden

Marc and Philip

Marc and Lucas

with fruit and play until we came home dirty all over and covered in cow poop. Who all her life kept saying, "Your father is a very noble man" despite enduring not only verbal but also tremendous physical abuse.

Mom was a truly remarkable woman way ahead of her time. She was filled with curiosity, purity, and love for life. She was also a woman with no voice who lost her power when she married my dad. Doomed to an existence as a housewife and mother of three; forbidden to seek out her own career and live her creativity.

Dearest Mama, you were pure love and support with your never-ending source of giving and sacrifice. You taught me all I needed to know — and more. I live your heritage every day!

My dad, Emilio, a very successful, charismatic, sophisticated and refined, and handsome businessman who built an empire in export/import in the sausage and cold cut industry of Switzerland. Well versed in foreign languages, he also had deeply ingrained Catholic morals.

Dearest Papa, though you ridiculed me at first for my life's vocation as a Soul counselor and facilitator, yet, moving to the US, you supported me wholeheartedly, and financially allowed me to build the HeartPath Retreat Center. I thank you for so much, dearest Papa! As you have come to see, so many people are grateful to you for this gift!

My deepest love goes to my son whom I decided to have at the early age of seventeen as a single mom. My dearest Marc, I gave my life to you. And I did the very best I knew to do at the time. Please forgive me for any mistakes or wrongdoings I committed. You provided me with such rich experiences as a mom and with countless lessons I needed to learn. Sadly, you were afraid to follow your destiny as a healer in the lineage of your grandma and instead chose to become a businessman like your grandfather. Thus, you left this world far too early but not before leaving behind two marvelous grandchildren and their mother, all of whom I very much love.

Marc and Camila
in Santa Fe

Camila with
my grandsons,
Lucas and Philip,
in the Jemez
Mountains of
New Mexico

So much love I feel as well for my baby daughter whom I tragically lost at birth and whose spirit I feel is with my mom now. Much love to my very dear two brothers with whom I share countless childhood memories, very innocent and idyllic, as well as tragic ones. Carlo, whose life story in distant Australia sounds like one continuous party under the influence of recreational substances. Franco, who battled addictions for the greater part of his life, and who at forty-five became clean and later found his purpose by serving the elderly. I can feel my family's love and support from the other side as I remain the only one in body.

I particularly want to thank Barbara Ann Brennan for her tremendous service to mankind with her groundbreaking studies of the human energy field, which provided the framework upon which I could grow and develop my own healing modalities. And I thank Dr. Roseanne Farano, my former dean at the Barbara Brennan School of Healing, for her clarity and profound support. I am grateful to my first trainers Rachel Kaufman and Rick Philips at Deva Foundation. Furthermore, I owe my gratitude to Shirley MacLaine and her book *Out on a Limb*, which aligned me with my true purpose in life.

Such gratitude and love as well for the important love relationships in my life. For the rich abundance in romance, love and sex, as well as intimacy and companionship. And all the people who loved me very much and the ones with whom I share a very profound connection. Love always came easy and I could never complain about lacking marriage proposals. But mine has always been — and still remains — an untamed spirit; true to my name "the Wild One (Pagan > Pagani) from the Wilderness (Forest > Silvana)."

Then, of course, much gratitude to my loyal friends from long ago, as well as newer ones. You are part of my soul family; spread out on all the continents. To my former student and assistant, Anne, for your support and for sharing the love and devotion to the work. And for looking in the direction of the future of the HeartPath Re-Alignment.

Very special thanks to my editor David Christel for your knowledge, professionalism, and expertise. Working with you has been such a level of joy and inspiration. And thank you, dear David, for your compliance and determination in keeping to my plan of having this book in print before the end of February 2022, which makes it a blitz project. Written in less than three months, I can only fathom how long Spirit has waited for me to finally bring this body of work into material being.

In my list of acknowledgments I need to include my own lessons directly transmitted through my body. I am immensely grateful to my body that always signaled instantly when my life was offtrack. For all the tremendous physical and emotional pain I endured, I am truly grateful for it has made me an authentically compassionate healer. I do understand the nature of pain because I experienced it all in my own body. It has brought me understanding for suffering. Pain is not just a word or a concept to me. Pain is the language expression of a dying, suffering Soul, waiting to be heard. Listening with our Heart and Soul is all we need to do.

PAIN IS THE LANGUAGE EXPRESSION OF A DYING, SUFFERING SOUL WAITING TO BE HEARD

Last, but not least, my deepest gratitude goes to the countless individuals who bared their Souls for me to see, and who invested their trust in the work and the process of healing, some of whom I trained as well. I learnt everything and all from you. You are my testimony to the effectiveness of the HeartPath Re-Alignment. It is thanks to you that I am able to write this book, and hopefully in the course, your stories can inspire readers to see light where there is darkness, and gain trust where hope was lost.

BOOK ONE

THE JOURNEY OF HEALING

INTRODUCTION

When the Soul Calls is a book about healing. Not healing in an ordinary sense but the deepest kind of healing, healing on the level of the Soul. I shy away from calling myself a healer. One reason is that I find the word "healing" in our day and time misleading and misused. The other reason is that I have come to understand that each and every one of us holds the key to their healing within them. In this sense, we are our own best healer. If we have been able to make ourselves sick, we also have the capacity to cure ourselves from it.

In other words, we take an active position rather than dropping into a passive role and letting someone else do the healing for us.

My task as a facilitator and Soul counselor is to hold the space for the Divine to do its work, and to allow the individual to tell the story their Soul wants to reveal. I simply stay fully present in the healing space with them, listen deep, guide them where needed, and prevent the interfering mind from sabotaging.

I advocate that when a disease or a health issue ails us, we take self-responsibility for its manifestation, analyze and dissect it in order to understand its message, and then make amends by changing where change is needed. We then integrate the newly acquired lesson into our life. By taking self-responsibility for the manifestation of what ailed us and healing it, our life force can fully flow again where it was stuck and we reclaim our power. And move on from there rather than holding on to what ailed us.

This might sound strange or even funny, but I am serious about this point. Oftentimes, a childhood trauma, a disease or other painful intervening factors that hindered our natural and healthy flow provides us with an image we keep identifying with. We hold on to the power this image gives us in that particular identity, and keep behaving as if this is our main identity. Like the mother of a son with a life-threatening disease, we remain in the role so that others can pity us and accommodate us with special favors long after the boy passed away.

Our attachment to the power we receive in that role might govern us to stay stuck in the identification of the ailment or disease. Because, if we are healthy, we have to fully show up in our life. There are no more excuses we can use to justify the way we choose to live our life and for only showing up half the time or not at all.

Ever since I was a small child, I wanted suffering to stop. Growing up in Iran, I saw much suffering in my environment; physical suffering of the poor and underprivileged ones. When Mother Teresa picked up thousands of the poorest of the poor dying on the streets in India, she did so oftentimes only to provide them with dignity during the last hours of their life. She claimed she did so because in each and every one she saw her beloved Jesus Christ.

When she expanded her missionary work to the West, she exclaimed that the suffering of the Soul is far deeper than the physical suffering of the body. I am certain Mother Teresa saw with the eyes of her Soul.

Moving back to Europe and growing up, I started to witness the suffering of those I most loved: my immediate family members. Those painful circumstances provided the base for me to learn and grow.

When the Soul Calls is divided into two Books. Book One, *The Journey of Healing*, contains seven Parts that are as follows:

Book One

Part I: Contains my family background, the environment I grew up in, and some of my childhood memories into adolescence.

Part II: My life as a young mother and wife leaving Switzerland for Afghanistan, South America, and Africa; my return to Switzerland with my son Marc; and my life as a divorced mom. The circumstances my Soul chose to reveal my path that led me to my vocation as a facilitator and Soul counselor.

Part III: A journey back in time to the Neolithic age and the Matriarchate society. I elaborate in detail about the downfall of humanity by forsaking the Heart and explain the dynamic process of disease and the path toward wholeness. I also address our human heritage — Egyptian mythology — as the cradle of the Christian, Judaic, and Muslim religions. The process of the manifestation of disease in the physical body, the return to natural health, and reclaiming one's personal power. The various healing modalities I developed as a result of what I was learning.

Part IV: Description of general case studies: physical ailments, emotional trauma, mental conditions, and spiritual realizations.

Part V: Various themes and subjects with case studies: TENSU Body Injury Trauma Release Healing, the development of depression, the vicious cycle of victim / victimizer and rescuer, possessions and entity attachments, the dark powers of evil, projections & transferences, self-sabotage: the battle of the conscious vs sub-conscious intention, healing in the fifth dimension, communications with the ones beyond the veil, and the direct experience of union & galactic experiences.

Part VI: Case studies of childhood sexual abuse and observations of why that might have led to childhood sexual abuse.

Part VII: Development of the five different childhood woundings from birth to adolescence, which culminates with the description of the Luciferian Wound and the dangers of the Luciferian approach to life that threatens the continuation of our human race. I explain how humanity is divided into those who fear and those who trust, those who think with their mind and those who feel with their Heart, those who give in and those who question, those who follow blindly any dictate from an authority and those who follow their own inner guidance.

I dismantle the anti-Christ as a cold apparatus of misused technology and science in combination with the negation and disconnection from our Heart and Soul, leaving us bereaved from our true Self. I warn of the dangers to which too many people are falling victim by blindly succumbing to the comforts of modern life and ignoring the essential purpose of our existence. I bring to awareness the battles between good and evil that we are actively engaged in every day, and that we must fight the demonic powers by opening our eyes and remaining on guard.

PART I

THE CRADLE

Chapter 1

AN UNTAMED HEART

Both of my grandmothers passed long before I came into existence. My mom Olga was born in one of the heartlands of Switzerland; in the picturesque village of Urnäsch, in the hilly Appenzell, a place deeply rooted in agricultural and farming traditions. She grew up as a country girl together with two sisters in a little farmhouse filled with pungent cow smell. Typically, those old houses are built of wood with extremely low ceilings as the Appenzeller people are known to be quite small in stature.

My mom told me how much she revered her Mutti (mom) who lost her eyesight when Olga was an adolescent. For all her life, Olga stayed very connected to her heritage and people, their traditions, customs, rituals, and music and sometimes would play the harmonium when I was growing up.

My mom, Olga

My dad Emilio was born in the canton of Grison in Switzerland, the third oldest in a family of six siblings. Dad described his father as an honorable man who had first served as a boarder patrol in Campocologno in the valley of Poschiavo along the Italian / Swiss border and later became a school teacher. My dad's mother came from a family of means and his father felt inferior, because he was unable to provide the standard of living she was used to.

My dad, Emilio

Their life was simple and dad told me they only possessed Sunday shoes and walked barefoot to school. On cold days, they would jump from cow pat to cow pat to warm their feet. Dad was bright, ambitious, and eager to prepare himself for a higher standard of living. Pina, his youngest sister shared that on Sunday mornings, all the siblings cried because they had to wear Sunday clothes, whereas my dad only cried in the evening when he had to take them off again.

Emilio deeply loved his mother who died of liver cancer when he was a very young man.

My parents met in the town of St. Gallen in Switzerland, where my mom worked as a secretary for an egg distributor, Eier Lüchinger, and my dad studied economy at Europe's most renowned university for economics, the Handelshochschule St. Gallen. They both had rented a room in a pension above the restaurant Rosenburg and Dad fell in love with my mom when he first met her. Soon, they were dating, falling deeply in love, and planning their life together. My mom didn't mind living in a country far from her homeland and supported my dad's decision to move abroad.

Having received his PhD, my dad received a job offer at only $100 a month. So, he decided to leave Switzerland. In 1951 my parents drove together via Istanbul, Damascus, Beirut, Cairo, and Alexandria to Tehran. Having arrived, they married at the Swiss Embassy in Iran. Dad quickly learned Farsi, established beneficial business contacts, and built a tanning factory to export sheep intestines for the cold cuts industry in Switzerland. A university colleague of his stayed in Switzerland to build the infrastructure and distribute the products.

My two brothers and I were born in Tehran where we remained until I, as the oldest, was ready for kindergarten and school. I have many fond memories of our life in Tehran. Because my birthday is on the same day as the late Shah Mohammad Reza Pahlavi, there were millions of balloons floating down from the sky and small planes with banners wishing him happy birthday. My parents led me to believe this special celebration was all for me.

My dad and me

My dad worked very hard to build his business and left at 4:00 am when everyone was still asleep. One of the workers at his factory was a "little" person. He made an impression on me because I had never before seen a tiny body with a large head. His name was Reza. Whenever we went to visit my dad's factory, Reza served us incredibly delicious watermelon and hot tea. His wife was normal sized and dad told us that whenever Reza's wife was angry with him she just set him up on the windowsill from which he couldn't get down. Apparently, all the other workers found that amusing. My dad, too.

Our social life was vibrant as Mom organized many dinner parties and other social events. We belonged to a large circle of friends, Iranians, Swiss, and of other nationalities. My parents loved their life in Iran.

I remember one morning after a party, when the whole house was still asleep, I got up and stumbled into the garden. I was a three-year-old toddler. There was the aftermath of the party and a pear-shaped bottle on one of the low tables attracted my attention. It had three compartments — one yellow, one red, and one blue — with some liquid left in each. I drank them all. The liquid turned out to be banana liquor, strawberry liquor, and Curacao. My parents found me asleep beside the doorway, the empty bottle beside me.

Every day, all day long, I played with dolls, which I constantly bathed, dressed, and fed. During the week, I accompanied my mom to visit friends and socialize with them. Iranians love children and spoil them. I was gifted gold and silver jewelry.

Me and my brother, Carlo

My brother Carlo was born two years after me. My mom had been nursing me for a year and found out she was pregnant again. Baby Carlo almost died of cholera when he was a little over a year old. He needed much attention and I was aware of my parents' deep preoccupation.

Though he was fed intravenously, the doctors had given up on him because he was unable to retain any liquid. Then my mom had the brilliant idea to feed him with spoons of water and a couple of drops of gin in it. This saved his life.

Two years later, mom became pregnant again with my brother Franco. We now had a Swiss nanny named Rita. Every Sunday, the whole family went to the Catholic church. I so pitied the family of beggars in front of the church. All of them had a body part missing. For one, an arm missing, another had only one leg, one was blind, and yet another one's tongue had been cut out. My parents explained to us that parents inflict injuries on their children so that they're more successful beggars. I couldn't imagine parents who would do that. I kept asking endless questions of how and why.

My brothers and me with Santa Claus

Growing up, one of our favorite things was when our parents took us for a drive into the desert. We drove on bumpy dirt roads, which my dad tried to amplify. It was the most fun. There, we met nomads with their camels. To be seated on a camel and experience it getting up from the ground is for a little child a bit like a slow roller coaster ride. At my wedding many, many years later, my dad told the story that one camel owner offered his camel for me. He added jokingly that had he known how much trouble I would be, he would have gladly made the deal.

In 1960 we relocated for half a year to St. Gallen where I attended kindergarten. We then moved for two years to Hamburg, Germany for tax purposes where we lived in a villa on the Elbchaussee. In Hamburg, I mostly remember long strolls in very foggy conditions through parks with countless wild bunnies along the Elbe River.

Mom and us kids in front of our house in Hamburg

Returning to Switzerland, our new home became Schloss Watt (Castle Watt) built in 1271 by the abbot of Constance. It's a lovely historic building situated on a gently sloping hilltop in the village of Mörschwil that overlooks Lake Constance.

We lived in the residential part, which was huge and had two floors. Then there was the tower with a large clock, which separated the stable that housed sixty-four cows and Switzerland's biggest prize bull. I asked Toni, the stableman, one day what was in the low-hanging sack between its hind legs. Toni scratched his ear and responded: "Coffee."

Schloss Watt

I was intrigued. "Coffee?? Ground coffee or coffee beans?"

"Beans," he responded. I had my doubts and ran to my mom. She told me the truth, which made much more sense to me.

I attended grades 2-6 at the village school and later the first two grades of middle school in St. Gallen. In Mörschwil, I started to collect abandoned nests of birds and wasps. I also made Carlo wade into the nearby pond to get some tadpoles for me. My bedroom held an arsenal of animal material. The night the tadpoles lost their tails, I woke up with dozens of tiny, tiny frogs jumping around in my bed.

My best friend was a cat named Gräueli, "Little Grey." She slept with me, ate all meals at the corner of the table seated between my dad and me, walked me to school, waited in the meadow when I got out from school, and walked me home. The only exceptions were the two times a year when she gave birth to her kittens in the haystack above the stable. I would go search for her, she would lead me to her kittens, I would collect them in my skirt, and carry them into my bedroom to her cat bed. I am so grateful my mom never objected to me having all these cats. I had another cat, Luusbueb, "Little Menace." She was the best mouser, Toni the stableman reported, catching three mice at a time. When both cats had kittens, I had up to fourteen cats.

I always had at least one cat as a constant companion

One day, I was about nine years old, Little Grey was nowhere to be found when I arrived from school. Then I heard her meowing. She had climbed a thirty-foot fire ladder that had been placed by the stable to reach the top of the roof. There she was, unable to get down. Without a moment's hesitation, I climbed the ladder all the way up, placed her on my shoulder, and brought her down. Such was our bond. When much later, at age seventeen, I started my first job as an assistant in a home for children with special needs, Little Grey moved with me.

My favorite subjects in school were zoology and biology for I loved the animal kingdom and plant life. I knew every wild flower by name.

I had my little naughtiness, too. Our school path down the slope from Schloss Watt had a tiny creek, not more than sixteen inches wide. Every day, my classmate, Rolf, walked right on the edge as if asking to be pushed in. So I did him the favor day after day.

What a rich childhood we lived. I turned into kind of a tomboy. Hanging out in the trees, strolling the forests and playing in the creek with the boys. One day, while playing cops and robbers with a crowd of neighbor kids, Carlo climbed up a round grain warehouse and jumped down onto the roof, which caved in, and he fell eighteen feet onto the cement floor suffering a concussion. He was incredibly lucky because the cutting equipment with their sharp blades were usually parked there. But not that day.

Carlo had a number of such accidents. He fell badly while ice skating and suffered yet another concussion, broke his leg skiing, and so forth. Nothing ever happened to me. I don't remember my brothers and I ever fighting. Carlo and I usually had our gang of friends while younger Franco had his playmates.

One day, just as mom and I were about to leave for the hairdresser, Franco came running in and requested that mom buy a birthday present for Seppli, the little three-year-old son of our neighbors, the farmers.

Upon arriving back home, Franco again came running in and declared: "Mami, Seppli doesn't need the gift anymore — he's already dead." Poor little Sepp died on his birthday.

It was a tremendous tragedy. Seppli's father had his loaded shotgun leaning against the garage door ready for the drive to scare the birds off in the field. Little Sepp and two of his siblings were seated in the car waiting for their dad. Rudi, the six-year-old brother, took the gun in play and the gun went off killing his little brother. My mom tended to the farmer's wife, but must have gone through a nightmare, as she imagined it could have been one of us.

My mom possessed the rarest of gifts: she knew how to love unconditionally. She was wise, fun loving, never angry and always patient, tolerant, and immensely creative. Her love for life, people, and animals was intoxicating. Our doors were always open for our friends and everyone loved her.

She was naturally curious to explore and travel, readily available for any adventure. She was also an excellent host and passionate cook who prepared the most exotic meals from around the world. She sewed and knitted and always invented new games to play with us kids. Plus, she was a remarkable storyteller. When she told us stories, we kids paid close attention.

Sadly, my mom was also a woman with no voice, which was quite common in those times. She lived her creativity through motherhood since my dad didn't allow her to pursue her own career. Inside, she was dying but never spoke about it. My dad was traveling 3-4 months out of the year for his business in Iran and Afghanistan, as well as China, which then was still closed to general trade. I don't think mom ever knew exactly when dad was returning. Being alone for months at a time certainly was not easy for her, yet she never spoke about it nor did she ever complain.

My dad built the "Boot-e-Ahoo" shoe factory and founded the Afghan Swiss Trading Company, representing all Swiss companies that wanted to be represented in Afghanistan from the Brown Boveri Company to Electro Watt, to Schindler Elevators, to Swiss high-quality, brand-name watches, pharmaceuticals, chocolates, and more. Given the fact there was no Swiss Embassy in Afghanistan, his office in Kabul also became the Swiss Consulate.

Indeed, dad was a very successful, charismatic, sophisticated and refined handsome businessman who built an export/import empire. Very fluent in foreign languages, he had always been a well read, very educated, and cultivated man of the world. He was also a deeply critical and skeptical thinker, later in his life even bordering on cynicism and bitterness.

In my childhood he so tried to make me think yet apparently never succeeded. "Think, think, you have to think, you cannot just feel" was the constant mantra I heard when he desperately tried to stuff my head full of math. Poor dad, who didn't believe women worthy of an education, his plan for me was to marry a successful businessman and become a housewife just like my mom, or maybe devote my life to God in a monastery.

Dad was the archetypal patriarch. He didn't allow mom to work. He was the one who provided. Her job was to be the housewife and mother. He lived his life from fear rather than trust and faith. Dad's religion was a theoretical one. My mom was the opposite: she lived her life from trust. She was relaxed and joyful in all she did. My dad was tense except under the influence of wine when he loosened up.

I knew my mother was a healer when one day I came home from elementary school, and she excitedly led me to our dining room. She'd come in late that morning to close all the windows and there was a lynx sitting on the windowsill that didn't move and showed no fear of her.

Upon looking closer, she noticed the animal was wounded. She quickly went to fetch the first aid kit and removed from just above the eye a bullet while the animal was holding still. Having said that, she pulled out of her apron pocket the removed bullet. At that time, there were only three reported lynxes living wild in Switzerland. The lynx returned three times in the course of the next month, sitting on the windowsill for my mother to see, as if to thank her.

Mom only gave, she never took. It was a great joy for her to give. She not even once spanked any of us children and never scolded us, only supported. All children loved her for she was utterly different than any other mom. She also never made us kids feel that she was miserable when we were not home, or that she expected us to stay around or that she was living her life through us. I was unaware how free I felt as a child. I now know she was a woman way ahead of her time.

Sometime in 1963, our time in Mörschwil came to an end. For years, my parents plan had been to build their own house in Mörschwil. The architectural plans were in place and the lot site was purchased when they decided to buy a home in Herisau, in the Appenzell. Though the house was magnificent, I never liked the place. It was a very modern villa built on five different levels and featured in prestigious magazines for its architectural splendor. It was built on the top of a hill with views over the town of Herisau on one side and on the other side the largest mountain in the Appenzell, the Säntis.

While during childhood I had been the family diplomat seeking peace and harmony, in puberty, I became the family rebel. I rebelled against my dad's strict rules and his hypocritical behavior, my mom's misery, and the truths never spoken. At age sixteen, I left the church.

I became pregnant at seventeen and had my baby Marc at eighteen. I chose not to marry because I didn't feel ready for marriage, but I wanted my child. For the first four years of Marc's life, we lived at my parents' house in Herisau.

Marc and me, 1973

Me with baby Marc and my mom

Chapter 2

AWAKENING TO SPIRIT

I married my first husband, Peter, at twenty-three years of age. It was love at first sight. He had studied at the same university as my dad and was freshly graduated with his bachelor degree when I met him. At the time, Marc was four years old.

After we tragically lost our baby daughter at birth — due to anencephaly, a disease caused by folic acid deficiency, which could have been detected early had there been an ultrasound examination — my dad offered Peter the job of representing his company in Afghanistan, where we moved as a young family.

Apart from the fact that Afghanistan, a fundamentally Muslim country where proper dress code and behavior according to Muslim custom was required, we had lived a very happy, simple, and family-oriented life. We visited various parts of the country, which we enjoyed tremendously. Dari, the Afghan language, and the customs were easy for me because growing up in Switzerland we often had my dad's business partners staying at our home and they didn't speak any other languages.

We were also part of the diplomatic corps community, the United Nations, and various aid programs that consisted of Europeans, Americans, and a few Russians. Social life depended on private initiatives so all were very active in organizing parties and formal social events. Our life in Afghanistan was also filled with many unforeseen adventures.

One time, Marc and I were on board an Ariana Afghan International Airline flight, which everyone jokingly called Ariana Inshallah Airline. The Muslim say 'Inshallah' which means 'if God wills' because the planes were old and sometimes in questionable condition. We flew from Tehran to Kabul. Upon approaching Kabul airport, the pilot announced that one of the wheels was stuck and that he had to do an emergency landing. The face masks did not come down but the pilot did a very swift landing onto the desert sand just beyond the airport. All went smoothly except from one second to the next all windows were covered with sand and it got completely dark in the plane since the lights were also not working.

When flying with Ariana, one never expected food or drinks. The pilots and crew members were so poorly paid that for them every flight turned into a food feast. All the passengers could smell the aromatic Kabuli rice with chicken being prepared by the staff. But it got served only to the crew and never the passengers, which was okay considering the circumstances.

Peter's and my wedding and with little Marc.

Below is me with my dad and Peter.

Marc and me in the Afghanistan desert

Our primary concern was always only one thing: to arrive safely. Another time, Marc and I were sitting in the same row together with an Afghan who apparently had never flown before. He occupied the window seat and as soon as the take off procedure was over, he leaned over to me and requested that I help him open the window. Afghan tribal men often had livestock with them in their laps, a lamb or a few chickens to present to whoever they were meeting at the end of their flight.

Marc and me playing with
our lion cub in Afghanistan

While Marc was in kindergarten, I worked in the Swiss Consulate providing visas for Afghan nationals traveling to Switzerland, caring for Swiss hippies who ended up in prison for possession of drugs, and offering help to return the bodies of the unfortunate Swiss mountaineers who died climbing the high mountains of the Hindu Kush.

Every time we visited Switzerland, though, I experienced culture shock going from a so-called third world country into the civilized world — not vice versa. We remained in Afghanistan from 1975-1979 and experienced the Afghan / Russian coup, which wiped out the entire family of President Daoud Khan, and divided families and communities into communist versus capitalist.

While the coup was happening, a bomb, which was meant for the Ministry of the Interior next door, hit our swimming pool. We retreated to the backside of the house to the kitchen. It was a time of threat and panic. Yet I turned calm inside. I sewed a large Swiss flag out of a red bed sheet and a white one, which we pulled over the rooftop of our car and escaped in the middle of the bombing. We found rescue at the German Club, which was located in a less active part of the city.

Living under martial law was a traumatic time. One could only leave the house from 6 am – 6 pm. Marc was driven to school by an armed driver. The streets were occupied by many extremely young soldiers, recruited from up north, carrying Kalashnikov rifles. They were Uzbeks, Tajiks, and Turkmen who didn't speak Dari.

When my dad came from Switzerland, we went to the presidential palace, which had been completely destroyed. We were walking in the street when all of sudden, a soldier jumped in front of my dad with his gun in my dad's face. Without a moment's hesitation, I jumped in front of my dad and shouted, "I padare man ast!" (Dari / Farsi for "This is my father.") Startled, the young soldier lowered his gun.

In later times, my dad would sometimes remark on the incident. He said I behaved like a tigress. In no way do I count myself a courageous person. Yet, at times, this gut feeling comes over me and I do the unthinkable. It happens automatically. I can't explain it.

Every night, a brilliant, rotating light on a tower beamed its light right into our bedroom. Under the communist party of Nur Muhammad

Taraki and Babrak Karmal, there were nightly shootings. Soldiers went into the homes of democratic Afghans, pulled out the male house members, and usually shot them on the spot. We were regularly awakened by screams and gunshots. I constantly had disturbing visions that violent interrogations were taking place in the nearby Ministry of the Interior.

It was hard to stay confined to the house. At one point, when it got a little calmer, our friends Rolf and Sabine Truxa, teachers at the German school, organized a field trip and picnic. In six cars, we drove to a lake two hours from Kabul. Peter was unable to join because he had injured his knee. We all enjoyed a wonderful day on the lake.

Upon driving our boats back to our cars parked, we encountered a frightening sight. Two large military trucks filled with at least forty soldiers, awaited us with their guns pointing at us. Marc looked at me and said, "Mami, will we now die?" "No Marc," I responded calmly, even though it didn't look good for us. The soldiers took us in their convoy back to Kabul. We were all extremely concerned because, in general, a human life is worth nothing in a Muslim country, and even less so during times of war.

I have no idea where it came from but because we were on a narrow pass with cars passing us slowly, I wrote on a piece of paper:

PLEASE HELP!

CONTACT MY HUSBAND PETER BERNHARD, CONSUL OF SWITZERLAND.

TELL HIM TO MEET US AT THE MINISTRY OF DEFENSE AND THE MINISTRY OF THE INTERIOR.

Then I threw the paper into a passing car. Those good angels did just what I requested.

The trucks drove us to the Ministry of Defense where Peter was waiting for us. He had made arrangements for our driver to wait at the Ministry of the Interior in case we were driven there. Without comment, the soldiers let us all go — but it easily could have ended differently. We heard many stories of Afghans and foreigners disappearing and being killed.

Half a year later, in 1979, three weeks after we arrived in Venezuela, we read in El Diario in the only section written in English, titled "In Our Strange World" that our friends, the Truxa's had made another field trip

Marc and me in Switzerland
waiting for Peter to arrive
from Afghanistan

Peter, Marc, and me in
the Venezuelan Andes

to the countryside with friends. This time, everyone was shot right on the spot. It's a strange feeling to look death that close in the eye. We truly had been protected.

Living in a country at war with Marshall Law was no place for a small child. I left with Marc for Switzerland, until Peter, who represented the company as required by Muslim law, could follow as soon as my father went to Kabul to replace him.

Peter and I decided we didn't want to remain in Switzerland and chose to move to Caracas, Venezuela. Peter traveled ahead to find a job and home for us in time for when Marc and I arrived a few weeks later.

At the time, Venezuela was at the height of the oil boom with huge inflation rates and a very toxic city lifestyle where many hours every day were spent in traffic jams. Despite that, I fell in love with the Latin culture, its people, and the language. But just to give you a taste, in order for Marc to arrive at school by 7:30 am, we had to leave the house no later than 5:30 am. Had we left at 6:00 am, we would have arrived around 10:00 am.

We were in Caracas for eight months when business circumstances demanded Peter travel to Ecuador. He called and suggested I take Marc out of school for a few days and the two of us come and check out Quito. Ecuador became our country of choice.

We all loved it so much. We vowed to at least settle in Ecuador for the next five years. I established a "Galeria Cano" selling pre-Colombian gold reproductions, attending the shop while Marc was in school. There was only one problem: as Peter was building a business in trading coffee seeds from Ecuador in exchange for Alfa-Alfa seeds from Italy, he was fighting an inner battle of being financially dependent from my dad until business took off.

On the occasion of carrying my cat Mishou to her last resting place, sobbing uncontrollably, I had a vision. I saw Peter's and my life path up to that day aligned like a railroad track. Then I saw a new image: two paths leading into opposite directions. I was given the message that the time was nearing when Peter's life path would go in a different direction than mine and that the only way we could stay together, because of our love, was if he changed the track of his life path to join mine, or if I moved over to live his life path.

Eight months into our life in Quito, Peter awoke one day and spontaneously decided to travel to Switzerland to look for a job. Inside me, my world broke apart. I saw our life in shards. I didn't show it but rather supported Peter in pursuing what felt right for him to do. Within three days he got hired as the manager and part owner of a Swiss-owned beer and mineral water factory in Accra, Ghana.

When Peter left us so unexpectedly, for the first few days I felt very alone and concerned about what could go wrong. Ecuador was at the time a country where every day your child could get kidnapped, your business confiscated, and your house robbed. So I was very worried for Marc and myself.

Though I was not consciously aware of my connection to Spirit, I prayed nightly to the angels for protection. Prayer had worked when I was a child and was afraid on my walks home in the dark. Prayer had worked in moments of danger. I felt I had such a huge responsibility.

Within days, a peacefulness set in me and a heavy burden lifted from my shoulders, which I had been unaware of before. Everything felt effortless and light. Subconsciously, I had carried Peter's worries without having been aware of it. Instead of heaviness, I felt easy and light.

Meanwhile, on Sundays, Marc and I went to the soccer games in the stadium. Marc excitedly watched the arena while I was fascinated with the market-like activities in the audience.

But there was an incident with the cleaning lady's daughter and her boyfriend who had had sex in the guest room while I was out. I could tell something was wrong and ran upstairs to the guest room, quickly opened the closet door, and forcefully dragged the naked guy out. Where I had mustered the strength to do that, I had no idea.

Peter had hired that Indio woman but I had never trusted her. Ecuadorian law, though, did not permit firing someone, so I had to keep her. Within a month, our house was robbed. Two valuable pieces of my mom's jewelry were stolen, a down bedspread, and clothes. When I reported the incident to the police at the police station, I saw in the room adjoining the office a bed. I intuitively knew the cleaning lady's daughter had prostituted herself so her mother and she didn't have to go to jail. I inquired and found out they were indeed jailed. At least I was now rid of them and I never saw them again.

One time, when I flew back from Bogota where I had stocked up on more merchandise for my shop, I arrived at the airport late because the road had been blocked due to an accident. Within minutes, the plane was scheduled to take off without me. At check-in, I broke down crying at the thought of Marc not having me back at the promised time (Latins are compassionate when it comes to children). Without hesitation, I was guided through passport control and led to the plane, which let the stairs down so I could board. Once I was on the plane, I was greeted with cheers and smiles and within minutes, we took off. Apparently, the captain had filled everyone in on my arriving late. Latins are so cheerful and supportive when it comes to love and children.

There was also a man, divorced and with a boy the same age as Marc, who came to visit me every day in my gallery and gifting me with a

Chilean Granny Smith apple from a nearby fruit vendor. Roberto was a jeweler, originally from Spain, who had lived in South America for years. When he was a youth, he was on the Spanish gymnastic team for the Olympics.

We became good friends. Upon occasions when there was no gold available to buy at the national banks, I suggested that the four of us travel to the jungle where the Indians collected gold in the river. After carefully thinking it over, Roberto picked us up one very early morning at 3:30 am. The boys on the backseat stayed awake but did not speak for the first few hours. But after we stopped at a market and loaded up on fresh fruit, they talked nonstop.

By the time we arrived in Coca to board a narrow motorized canoe, the boys had fully bonded. In fact, so much so that Marc declared that he wanted to sleep in the same room with Georgy that night at the jungle lodge. I quickly responded, "Marc, impossible, I cannot share a room with Roberto." Marc's face dropped in disappointment. Roberto's, too. The next couple of days were filled with the exploring the jungle, shooting blow guns, and visiting the Indians.

The Indian women who wash the gold found in the river, do it every time before taking a trip to the market for essentials like salt and rice. They told us they only wash as much as they need in exchange for the merchandise they buy. They explained that this way, the river would still have gold in it when their great-grandchildren needed it. I was impressed.

Roberto with his son, Georgy

It was on that trip that I started to open my heart to Roberto, though I didn't show him at all and kept my distance. Roberto was the opposite of Peter's Nordic looks and tall stature. Roberto was Latin, and deeply male and sensuous. I observed this in the way he selected fruit at the market and in the way he instructed the boys.

We started to spend more time together. It took two months until Roberto and I became intimate. I thought I had known love but ours was a connection unlike anything I had ever experienced before, and ever since then. There was an indescribable harmony and synchronicity between us. I told Peter. He understood because it had been he who had broken our mutual agreement to stay in Ecuador for at least five years so that we could build a stable life for our family.

Me with Roberto

But Marc was jealous, which created an inner conflict for me. Like a mantra repeated over and over, I was constantly hearing in my ears, "You are a mother first and then a lover." I had no choice but to obey my inner duty. Deeply heartbroken, Roberto and I parted.

Many years later, once my Soul revealed my life path to me, it all started to make sense. Had I married Roberto, I would have been utterly fulfilled as a woman. But I would not have gotten connected to my inner calling and the path my Soul had planned for me.

Peter and I had always been excellent communicators. There were no secrets between us. Though I shared everything with him, all Peter wanted was to have me back.

Long story short, for the sake of preventing our family from falling apart, Marc and I lived in Ghana for one year. When Peter got transferred to Liberia, I was no longer willing to follow suit and subject Marc yet again to another school change.

When I left Peter after nine years and returned to Switzerland, I found my mom losing a long and painful battle to lymphatic cancer — while my dad and my brother Franco were in utter denial. It was all deeply challenging and disturbing. The word "cancer" was never spoken.

Lymphatic cancer = a deep secret is eating away at one's core.

I entered a very dark night of Soul. It was during that time that I experienced a re-occurring guiding dream that taught me to develop "Far Sense Perception," or what I also call "Long Distance Viewing."

Night after night I kept entering a pitch dark tunnel with only a pinpoint of light at its end. I was afraid of the dark but knew I had to cross the darkness in order to experience the light in the future. This was my first guiding dream. Many more such night visions would follow. Later on and further into my spiritual development, I started to understand that these dreams are messages from Spirit and my Soul guiding me through life.

The passing of my mom was extremely painful. Her suffering had been tremendous. I felt utterly helpless in being unable to adequately offer spiritual guidance through her transition.

During a visit to Switzerland, a year after our separation, Peter and I divorced. We walked hand-in-hand into the court room, presented our case, and then celebrated our union and marriage with champagne and a fine meal. We both wanted the best for each other. Because Peter offered minimal help financially, he got off far better than I. But I sincerely felt that we had enjoyed an abundant life together. I didn't want him to be dragged down by financial responsibilities because of how we had lived, but rather wished for him to be able to move on and create a new life for himself.

My dad wanted Marc and me to stay living with him and offered to bequeath his big villa to me. But I had never liked the location of that house nor the house. It had brought misfortune to our family, as if there were a curse. The initial owner who built the house went bankrupt and thus committed suicide in the attic. Plus, a construction worker was fatally hit by a large cement block when my parents built a garden hall. So, vehemently "No" to that house.

I told my father that I could see a new life for him, which happened shortly after when he met the woman who would become his wife for the next thirty years.

Roberto also came to visit with his son Georgy for fourteen days after my mom had passed away. Marc and I were still living in my parents' house. Everything between us was as it had always been. Marc was not jealous anymore. The four of us took many hikes into the Appenzell mountain region and the Toggenburg. We also played a lot of squash and cooked together. My dad really liked Roberto.

Roberto shared that when I left him, he fell into a deep depression. He said that I was still occupying his heart and during the two years after we separated, he had rarely dated anyone because there was no other woman he could imagine building a new life with.

On my part, the deep pain our separation had caused for both of us made it clear to me that I needed to raise Marc on my own. I told Roberto that if I could not give him what I most wanted to give him, then I wished for him to have it with someone else.

Upon separating, Roberto made me promise that within the month I would come and visit him in Quito, Ecuador. I bought a ticket. A couple of days before flying, I received a phone call from my dear friends in Ecuador. They told me that Roberto had just married. He had impregnated a woman before he came to visit me and as a result married her on his return. This came as quite a shock for me.

But I flew to see him anyway. I stayed with my friends at their home. The first day, upon walking on the main pedestrian street, the Avenida Amazonas, Roberto came walking towards me, smiling broadly. I was so mad at him that I had an outburst of anger. I barked at him, "Why did you not tell me?! Why in the world did you not let me know?! Tell me why!"

Roberto had his head deeply bent and looked like a dog with his tail between his legs. I had the image of a movie scene with Sophia Loren and Marcello Mastroianni. Unbeknownst to Loren, Marcello was married but had an affair with her anyway. When she found out, she passionately ran after him on the street and kept hitting him. He whined and said, "Oh, that hurts!" She felt sorry for hitting him, but kept hitting him again.

Roberto and I went into a nearby cafe and he told me that upon his return from Switzerland, he found out that he had impregnated the woman. Her family organized the wedding in Cuenca, where she was from, just as he returned home from out of town.

He was so happy to see me but I was so mad that he hadn't told me. I found his excuse of wanting to spare me lame. In my opinion, it hurt much more finding it out through a third party than if he had called and told me. It was, though, exactly what I had wished: for him to have with someone else what I was not able to give him.

By the way, it was all meant to be. He is still married to that woman. They have two daughters. As for me, during the entire time of living with Marc in Switzerland, I remained unattached.

Roberto and I continued getting together over the years. Usually, he came to Switzerland or we met in Spain or Paris. Every time we were together, we made endless love and both deeply cried. In 1988 I ended my relationship with Roberto.

I felt strongly that Marc and I needed our own life. We stayed with my dad a couple more months so Marc could finish his school term and then we moved into an apartment in Kilchberg on Lake Zürich, which belonged to friends who were living abroad. A little later, we found our own home in Rüschlikon, the village next to Kilchberg. It felt truly rewarding to be settling in and having our own life.

The day after moving in, I had a dream and awoke to an image. I saw two pairs of cupped hands opposite each other. One pair of hands belonged to my dad. The other pair were my husband Peter's hands. I saw myself in the hands of my father who was passing me into the hands of my husband. Then the image changed and I saw myself in my own hands. This became the day when I lost all pain in my back. For thirteen years, from pregnancy to that very day, I had been suffering from chronic back pain. Taking my life into my own hands, I was instantly released by coming into my life, into my own personal power, for the first time. I was now a woman in my own right.

Back pain = living a wrong life.

Within the month, I had another vision dream. I saw Marc and myself drifting in a small ship in the middle of the ocean. I was busy throwing everything unnecessary overboard. This marked the time when I significantly changed the relationship with my father. Even though we lived an hour away, my dad visited 3-4 times a week and called daily complaining about the behavior of my brother Franco. It was a nonstop litany of complaints. There was such negativity and a real heaviness about it all, hopeless, like a curse.

I felt sorry for my brother who did nothing right in my dad's eyes. Of course, Franco had shortcomings but his struggles were the ones of a lost and confused soul. I felt like a garbage bag. I wrote my dad a letter explaining that if he chooses to focus on Franco's shortcomings, all he will ever see is his shortcomings. But if he can aim to make it a practice to see the positive side of Franco, then those qualities would have a chance to grow.

Our small apartment on the top floor in Rüschlikon

For three weeks, my dad did not respond. Then he visited, with flowers. For the whole duration of his visit, there wasn't a negative word spoken about my brother. My father's behavior pattern had shifted, though I could see how much discipline he had to muster to be able to maintain it.

Marc and me in our yard

We lived in Rüschlikon for nine years. I at first worked various jobs and also completed a 3-month training at the School for Gymnastics in Zürich. I then opened a gallery / store again and hired a jeweler working in ancient methods, such as granulation. I specialized in Middle Eastern and pre-Columbian small archaeological artifacts, ancient jewelry, and beads. After four years, I closed my store to avoid the high maintenance costs and worked with my clientele from home. I also sold at antique shows and fairs and sometimes at the "Flohmarkt" (flea market) in Zürich.

While I was selling archaeological beads and ethnographic objects at an antique show in Munich, an Asian man came by my stand every day. He carefully picked up this object and that, or only just looked at pieces from all sides. He was humble and very kind, but for the life of me I could not figure out which particular objects he was interested in because every day he looked at some other pieces and he never asked me for a price.

On the last day, he introduced himself, gave his name, and told me that he was managing the Japanese restaurant Mifune for his dear friend, the actor Toshiro Mifune, one of the lead characters in the movie Shogun. He invited me to come and have dinner and said I should bring my colleague, a woman my age from Basel, Switzerland, who had her booth beside mine. So we went. He personally brought us plate after plate of delicacies and in the end did not allow me to pay. I thanked him kindly and that was that.

A week later, I got a call. It was the same gentleman who said he was in Zürich and wanted to invite me to dinner. He picked me up at my home and stopped by one of the premiere Japanese car dealerships. The entire staff came to greet him. He talked with them for a bit. Over dinner, he explained that he was the only son and that his parents lived in Hawaii. He said he was a Formula 1 racer and recently had an accident and that's why he limped. The conversation was courteous, formal, and he was kind.

Then, out of the blue he asked: "Would you marry me?"

I was flabbergasted and responded, "But I don't know you."

He responded with "I know you." I kindly declined and said we could be friends. But he didn't want that. I never heard from him again.

It was also during that time, I was offered a business partnership with a highly established antiquities dealer in St. Germain, Paris, France. I declined the offer because I intuitively felt something else was waiting for me — though I had zero idea what that could possibly be.

Shortly after that, for the first time ever, I heard of the "metaphysical." This was in the late eighties. Astoundingly, everything suddenly made sense. I had been attracted to psychology before but all the various approaches and opinions left me empty and unconvinced. Now, here it was — ancient scriptures and contemporary books were all pointing to the same facts. Different words and terms, yes, but nevertheless pointing to the same truth. I was completely sold.

We had lived a purely mundane life on four different continents, so I was only vaguely aware of spirituality. From childhood on, though, I had always been a "seer." The problem was that I saw what others didn't, which separated me from them. Plus, I had no idea that what I saw others couldn't see. From that young age, I always felt guided and protected by my Guardian Angel, and never did I not trust my strong intuition.

What a universe filled with magic and wonder opened up to me when I — finally — opened my eyes fully to spirituality. In hindsight, I am not surprised it was during my Saturn return that my old life had to die and my spiritual awakening come alive.

During a business trip around the globe to Indonesia, Japan, San Francisco and New York, I sold the main part of my inventory. Divine guidance led me to my first introductory training to become a facilitator in Psycho-Spiritual Therapy specializing in a 4-day intensive. Prior to leaving Switzerland for New Mexico, which was in late August of 1990, twelve clients signed up to work with me upon my return from the three-month training abroad.

PART II

THE BEGINNING

When the Soul Calls: True Stories of Deep Healing and Transformation

Chapter 3

ENTERING INTO SERVICE

I remember well my first client. He was a school teacher in his early forties, recently divorced, and father of three children. His wife had sucked him dry financially in their divorce settlement. She got their house and eighty percent of his salary. Apparently, she had grown tired of him and wanted out of the marriage. He followed suit to accommodate her demands — the classic victim. He ended up living in a 1-room studio having barely enough to make ends meet for himself, while his ex-wife maintained the same living standard they had while married.

His story broke my heart. The injustice, the pain of betrayal and abandonment, the separation from his children. His life looked so dark and hopeless. I had no clue how I could possibly help him except to stand by and hold the space for him to tell his story.

During his 4-day healing process, I did my utmost to connect him to his higher guidance, provide him with tools, and inspire him to give his life new meaning. One of his homework assignments was to get a flower pot and plant some seeds in it, place it on his dining table, and witness the seeds growing, see the sprouts break through the soil in order to connect with the light and then simply watch them grow into a flowering plant. I told him to feel the life force of the emerging plant and connect with the same life force within him. But when he left, I had to admit to myself a sunken feeling in my heart.

Poor man, my heart felt so deeply sorry for him. All the more was I surprised when within a month I received a hand-made card from him. On one side he had painted a huge, brightly shining sun and written the words "This light shines within me." On the other side he shared about the transformation in his life.

This man taught me the lesson that as healers, we are oftentimes like a gardener planting seeds not knowing whether what we plant will sprout and when. My task as a soul counselor and facilitator is to listen deeply and hold the space for healing to occur.

Another person stuck in my memory of my initial twelve clients was a woman, forty years old, happily married with three children. I shall call her Mary. Her presenting complaint was fear. Fear of life, fear of people, fear of situations. Life was deeply alienating to her and she felt only safe in the circle of her family. This was coupled with a huge amount of insecurity, a profound lack of self-love, being highly self-critical, and extremely dependent on others. Underneath it all, I recognized her deep spiritual longing to connect with Source, to find her way back to her true origin.

Working with her was like taking a child by the hand, encourage her to walk and guiding her home. She worked remarkably well and deep. And within the month signed up for the next 4-day session cycle. Her transformation was profound. In fact, so profound that after her first 4-day session cycle, when she asked the seller at a newsstand for a certain magazine and was handed the wrong one, she did what she had never done before: she requested the correct one. She reported to me that her daughter commented with, "Mama, was ist denn los mit Dir? Du bist ganz schön frech, Du wehrst Dich," which translates as, "Mom what's wrong? You behave naughty, you are speaking up."

Having completed the work with my twelve initial clients at the end of March 1991, I left for India for a 3-month training course in Cranio-Sacral Therapy at the Osho Institute in Pune, India. A friend of mine suggested I add the training to my skills because this form of therapy allows individuals to drop more deeply into their healing process.[1]

Quite immediately after my return from India I was introduced to a very successful practitioner in homeopathy who signed up for the 4-day session cycle. As a result of her healing transformation, she sent me all her patients, whom she was unable to help herself.

Within a short time, my healing practice was fully booked half a year in advance. My work experience took a huge leap forward as I witnessed tremendous transformations in the lives of my clientele: Patients whom doctors gave only a few more months to live with no further hope for life; individuals for whom the work with me provided their last strand of hope.

What astounded me most — even left me speechless — were the often miraculous cures that took place in patients with advanced cancer and aggressive tumors, adults and children for whom the work with me was their last possibility. I was utterly frustrated, though, with the fact that I had zero clue what exactly caused the miraculous healings. This needed to change.

I decided I needed to further my studies and signed up to train with Barbara Ann Brennan at the Barbara Brennan School of Healing in Long Island, NY. This was in 1991. Developing High Sense Perception plus her concept of the Human Energy Field and the various Character Defense Structures became a most valuable tool and set the frame for my own healing approach: the HeartPath Re-Alignment, which developed as a result of the work experience in my healing practice.

---

[1] Cranio-Sacral Therapy was developed by Upledger as a very subtle manipulative body therapy. It works with the spinal fluid that moves between the Sacrum and the Cranium.

Barbara, in her groundbreaking work, focuses on "chelations," a kind of Reiki though much further developed because energy is channeled from Source and from within the earth.

My work is different. I specialize in a dialogue process with the subconscious on the level of the Soul. My practice was quickly flooding with clients. When a patient called for an appointment stating that their doctors had given up hope for any chance of recovery, it was impossible for me to tell them my first opening would be in six months. Rather, I accepted them for the next week. This meant that during the two years of my healing practice by Lake Zürich, I worked with four clients every day, at least 16 hours per day, mostly seven days a week.

How in the world was I able to maintain this workload, plus fly five times a year to New York for a week for my training with Barbara Brennan and the required counseling sessions in Core Energetics[2] only Spirit knows. There was such demand for healing. Whenever I felt exhausted, I asked my angels to take over. I assure you it worked. As all healing sessions are word-by-word documented in writing, the continuous handwriting of fourteen and more hours a day affected the tendons of my right hand and arm to such a degree that when I finally dropped into bed, dead, ready to fall asleep, my arm kept painfully pulsating. After two years, my hand and arm would revolt if I tried to work such long hours.

I had found my life purpose and my mission. It felt strangely familiar as if I had been in service countless times before. My work deeply fulfilled me. I felt immensely grateful to my angels for guiding me, to Jesus Christ for being my master, and to my clientele for their trust in the work.

It goes without saying that I never claim ownership of the profound revelations and transformations due to my clients' experiences. On the contrary, I have always seen my task as the ability to simply hold space for the Divine to do its work while assisting the individual to drop deeply into the process and guide them, when they lost their way or when their mind took over.

I could very clearly see that just as we are able to manifest disease and emotional discomfort, we are also capable of creating health and emotional wellbeing. In other words, we are always holding the key to our own healing. What I also started to understand from working with my clients is that our body is functioning much like an immensely complex bio-computer linked to our emotions, thoughts, and our relationship to our spiritual nature. Whether we create health in our life or manifest disease is dependent on our relationship towards ourselves, our thoughts and feelings, and ultimately, our relationship to Source / God / the Universe.

---

[2] Core Energetics was developed by John Pierrakos and is a kind of body oriented psychotherapy.

I was not consciously aware back then that I had started to live the life of my Soul rather than the life of my ego personality. A few months after starting my practice, I had a vision dream and awoke to an image. I saw two hearts beaming with strong rays towards each other. Then the image changed and I saw my heart, but now it was beaming brightly in all directions like the sun. I understood that up to now my heart had been shining exclusively towards my great love and the people I loved most. But today, my heart had opened 360 degrees for all mankind. This marked the birth of my new life's vocation as a facilitator, healer, and soul counselor.

In this book, I will share my work with you. These stories are but a few of the many hundreds of healings I remember without digging deep through the many folders of my written documentation. To write them all would fill more than a few thousand pages. While the material is accurately described as it occurred, all names are changed to protect the identity of my clientele.

But before I do so, I shall explain in depth my healing modalities for you to get an insight into my work. I specialize in a deep Soul process called the 12-day Maha Intensive™ in the HeartPath Re-Alignment. Originally, when I started working in December of 1990, it was a process of 4 days, 3-4 hours in general, which over the years evolved into the 12-day Maha Intensive.

I need to also mention that while there are spiritual paths focusing primarily on mastering the mind, my work and teachings center on the Heart. The Maha Intensive is a profound 12-day, individual healing process, a dialogue with the sub-conscious on the level of the Soul. Each healing session may last approximately 3 to 5 hours or more every day. I carefully document each session, which is discussed and interpreted the next day.

The purpose of the review and interpretation is to decipher the language of the Soul and understand its journey on the deepest levels. In addition, reading, writing, listening, or drawing homework may also be assigned to the participant.

I shall elaborate on the relationship between healing and disease and how disease is manifested — any kind of disease — no exception.

Chapter 4

INITIATION, FIRST DIRECT TRANSMISSION

It was during the first year of my healing practice. Marc arrived home from boarding school for the holidays and we decided to invite his best friend Patrick over for dinner. I prepared Marc's favorite: Persian saffron rice, roasted tarragon chicken, and baked tomatoes.

Patrick arrived with a platter of home-made cookies. Gregorian chants were playing and we enjoyed a pot of tea after dinner, and each one of us had a cookie. Then the boys left for a night out with friends and I started to clear the table and carry the dishes to the kitchen. Walking back and forth, I soon had eaten the whole platter of vanilla-flavored cookies, so delicious they were. I was washing the dishes when all over sudden an immense wall appeared in front of me.

It was made up of countless small compartments. As I focused on one such compartment, it glided out towards me like a harmonium. I saw the reason why Marc and Patrick were so close. They had been brothers before. As soon as I saw this, the compartment pulled itself back in. I focused on another compartment and again, it glided out harmonium-like. I saw the reason why my dad never showed any attachment towards even very valuable gifts. He had been a spiritual dignitary in China who passed on all gifts he received to the monks for safekeeping. As these compartments kept gliding out towards me, I saw the consequences of possible future actions prior to the action.

By that point, I realized I was seeing the Akashic Records[3]. I was standing in the large entrance hall between the kitchen and dining room. Astounded, I burst out, "What is happening to me?" While looking up, I saw a circle of Light Beings smiling benevolently down at me. "You have passed all your tests," I was told. "From now on your wish is our command."

"What? I have been tested? When?!" They named all the most difficult cases I had been working with.

I responded with, "I want to build a healing retreat." They answered, "Go ahead, rely on us. We have the best architects up here."

"But I don't want to build it here. I want to move to Spain." They replied, "Anywhere you wish. Rely on us. We have the best real estate agents up here."

---

[3] The Akashic Records are a compendium of all universal events, thoughts, words, emotions, and intent that have ever occurred in the past, present, and future. They include all entities and life forms, not just humans.

By now, my heart was pounding strongly as if to jump out of my chest. I was worried I could have a heart attack and lay down on the floor of the corridor. Closing my eyes, I saw the image of the Native American in the movie Little Big Man with Dustin Hoffman, who retired to the mountains to die. I attempted to control my breathing to calm my heart but then thought that Marc should know I died having a God experience. This was prior to cell phone times, so I decided to call my friend, the homeopath, to pass on my message to Marc in case I didn't survive.

After that, I went to bed with my heart still racing like crazy. At some point, I fell asleep. I woke up in the morning without any heart symptoms. Getting up, I called my friend to report that I had survived the night and felt better. She had difficulties understanding my situation and kept asking questions as to what I had eaten, drunk, and so forth. The front door opened and Marc came in. He overheard the conversation and came quickly over and said, "Mami, those were marijuana cookies you ate." I had eaten twenty-three of them and had a God experience while Gregorian chants played.

Contrary to my brothers who were magnetically attracted to any kinds of substances, I never, ever felt drawn to recreational drugs. Even though we lived in Afghanistan, the Mecca of hashish, I never tried it. I have had a marvelous LSD experience, one Ecstasy experience where I felt nothing different from my usual self, and now the marijuana cookie experience that turned into a God experience for me.

Marc and me

Chapter 5

THE GIFT, SECOND DIRECT TRANSMISSION

Marc had started an apprenticeship at a bank in St. Gallen, where he now lived. This was the first time he was separated from me and in his own flat. Despite my over-booked healing practice, I managed three times to drive down to Spain to search for the place where I would settle and start my new life. Though I paid a visit to the island of Majorca, I felt a magnetic pull towards Andalusia, which I had already visited several times before due to my passion for Flamenco.

The rolling hills with vineyards on the outskirts of Jerez de la Frontera were lovely. I drove my car through the pathways of private properties to get closer and came upon a tractor driver who I stopped to ask if he knew to whom all these estates belonged. "Oh, yes, I know', he responded. "My father is the owner." He gave me a tour of three "Cortijos" (250 - 500-year-old hacienda-style groups of buildings surrounded by a wall with a central courtyard).

One, "El Cortijo Olivillo," I particularly fell in love with. The central courtyard was laid with cobblestones, the main house had six bedrooms, a large living area, a kitchen with an antique stove, and a separate building was the chapel. There were stables and barns and a sauna-like sweat house. The place was named for the olive tree in the middle of its courtyard.

Later, Gustavo introduced me to his father, an attorney in Jerez. I had found what my heart had been looking for. But his father told me that, unfortunately, El Cortijo Olivillo was their family weekend and vacation residence and, therefore, not for sale. I completely respected that and told them of my plan to build a healing retreat.

Gustavo's father arranged for some of his relatives to show me their properties. Yet, there was nothing else that touched my heart. A couple of nights later, Gustavo came to see me in my hotel and told me his father decided that because of my wanting to build a healing retreat, he agreed to sell. I was overjoyed. We met again and I received a set of plans and was told the asking price. I drove home as if with wings, so elated was I.

What followed was a period of two and a half years of profound spiritual trials. Throughout each day, I was filled with joy at the prospect of my upcoming move. During the night, however, I received visions and dreams that in the morning had me filled with doubt.

The message was always that I would be doing pioneer work in a foreign language and run into severe conflict with the church, though I would not burn at the stake again as I had in past lives. Like a sprinter at the starting gate, I was super ready to move ahead with my plan but I felt as if the front foot wanted to start running but the hind foot was preventing it from doing so. Where was the green light from Spirit?! This was the only thing missing.

Two and a half years passed in this way and I started to have severe self-doubt. My practice was flooded, the work magnificent, the transformations deep. But inside me there was this nagging feeling of self-doubt. Mind you, I am a doer rather than a talker. How come I was unable to get the green light from Spirit?!

I was in the second year of studying with Barbara Brennan. The course requirement included a biology and anatomy course in English. Because that was not available in Switzerland, I closed down my healing practice for a month and signed up at Boston College. My landlord wanted to renovate the apartment during my absence, but assured me it would be ready upon my return.

Arriving home, I had a sinking feeling when I walked past many cans of paint up to the third floor of the apartment. Entering my home, all rooms were sealed off with plastic drapes. After an eight-hour transatlantic flight, all I wanted was to run myself a hot bath, use the toilet, and enjoy a hot cup of tea.

I stood in the entrance corridor, utterly frustrated and burst out yelling, "That's it! I am moving! I'm moving to Santa Fe!"

I stood there flabbergasted. I could not possibly have said that! But there was no denying my having heard my voice yelling out those words, loud and clear. I looked up. And there "They" were again, the circle of Light Beings smiling benevolently down at me. This time, They said nothing, only smiled.

I surrendered to Their will and within three months, I was on my way to the US — but not before having organized a big farewell party in the forest for my family, friends, and clientele.

The month after the transmission, on the occasion of my next training course with Barbara Brennan, I flew to Santa Fe to meet with an immigration attorney and a real estate agent. I was clear that I was only interested in available properties between Santa Fe and Española. The agent showed me six properties, all of which didn't interest me. But she got a pretty clear idea of what I was looking for: a large piece of preferably empty land with water and big trees. She sent a video clip to me in Switzerland with the property that would become the Ministry of Angels / HeartPath Retreat Center.

Arriving in Santa Fe on June 13, 1993, I rented a little guest house on Cerro Gordo for five months. During the first two months, I slept eighteen hours a day. I had worked so hard and evidently needed to catch up on a lot of sleep. Whenever I awoke, I saw the image of my being cradled by the Universe.

I closed on the property on November 30 of 1993. Mike Martinez, a handyman, not a licensed builder, came recommended by Rick and Rachel, my former trainers and dear friends. Upon meeting Mike, I asked if he can build with adobe. "Nope, can't do it, I've never done it," was his answer. Nevertheless, together, we drew up all the plans, submitted them, and got the permits.

Altogether, we built five buildings in the course of seven years, with twenty-two crew members involved. Plus, we terraced the sloping land to prevent flash flood rain damage and also for a future vineyard. Furthermore, we improved the existing pond by adding an island for the water fowl, and mixed bentonite, a natural clay, to the soil to retain the water during all seasons. We created a stone circle, which I call "The Council of the Wise Elders." In all my actions I followed strictly and exclusively the guidance of Spirit.

Ours was an effortless flow as if divinely orchestrated. Only when we built "The Temple of the Living Goddess" in the center building with its big octagonal skylight did we involve an engineer to approve our plans. What an incredibly joyful and fulfilling time that was filled with wonder, creativity, and bliss.

One time, when I sat down at the bench in front of the shed, I asked Spirit *"How come this building process is such an effortless and joyful flow?"* The immediate answer I received was *"Because it already exists up here. All you are doing is bringing it down."* I understood and felt deep gratitude.

My dad, Mike Martinez, and me in Santa Fe

My dad, Marc, and me in front of the center building, Santa Fe

PART III

THE NATURAL SCIENCE OF WHOLENESS THE RELATIONSHIP BETWEEN HEALING AND DISEASE

"Though we are God's sons and daughters,
We do not realize it yet."

Meister Eckhart
1260-1328

Section 1

From Chaos to Order

Chapter 6

THE FORSAKEN

In order to explain what disease is, it is necessary to first understand what healing means. The Latin word for healing is "integer," which translates as complete, whole, holy. Being complete, whole, and holy reflects not being separate but "One" with the Source, united with God. As Mother Teresa stated, "It is nothing extraordinary to be holy; it is our birthright." Yet — in the long history of our Soul's evolution, we split ourselves off from our God Source and thus created separation.

We have forgotten that each and every single one of us has been created in the perfect image of God and that we were never meant to be separate from the sacred stream of Creator energy. Instead, we were meant to represent God on Earth, to be God's ambassadors in this world. We were meant to live the fullest glory of our Source energy. This is what we have forgotten.

We were meant to represent God on Earth, to be God's ambassadors in this world.

What, then, is disease? At its deepest level, disease points to separation from God, separation from the Source. Daskalos, the renowned 20th century healer and mystic on the island of Cyprus, whom I personally met with two years prior to his passing, once said: "We are all Gods, but we are not aware of it. We suffer from self-imposed Unconsciousness."

We are all Gods, but we are not aware of it. We suffer from self-imposed Unconsciousness.

The separation from our God Source is precisely the reason why life on Earth has become an existential struggle of misery for many of our human race. Pain and suffering seem predominant. For some, it is the nightmare of living in a country at war. For even more, it is the lack of food, battling natural disasters, loosing their homes, disease, famine and the dangers of relocation, elimination, and extinction.

THE MANIFESTATION OF DISEASE IN THE HUMAN AURA

Layer 7 of Aura: ➡   Wrong Relationship to Creator Source
Ketheric Body   Separation from Source
Divine Knowing

⬇

Layer 6 of Aura: ➡   Wrong Relationship to Creator Source
Celestial Body   Loves being separated from Source
Divine Loving   Denying Source

⬇

Layer 5 of Aura: ➡   Wrong Relationship to Creator Source
Etheric Template Body   My Will is separate from Thy Will
Divine Will   Ignoring Source

⬇

Layer 4 of Aura: ➡   Wrong Relationship to Humanity
Astral Body   Lack of Love for Self + Others
Loving

⬇

Layer 3 of Aura: ➡   Wrong Thinking / Wrong Beliefs
Mental Body   Confusion
Clear Thinking   Destructive Thought Patterns

⬇

Layer 2 of Aura: ➡   Wrong Feelings
Emotional Body   Fear / Anger / Grief
Authentic Feeling

⬇

Layer 1 of Aura: ➡   Block in Metabolism
Etheric Body   Unbalanced Energy System
Physical Existence

⬇

Physical Body   ➡   Disease

THE AURA OF THE HUMAN BODY WITH ITS SEVEN LAYERS, THEIR FREQUENCIES, AND THE NUMBER OF LOTUS PETALS ASSOCIATED WITH EACH CHAKRA

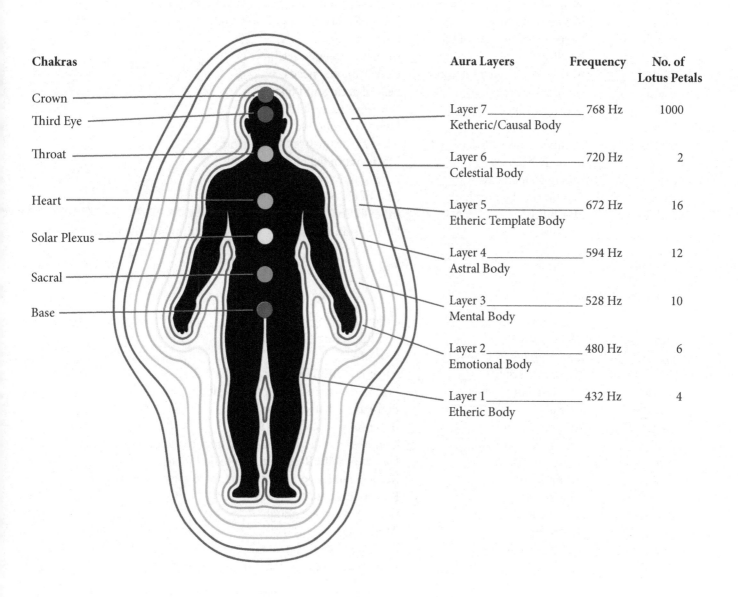

Chakras

Crown
Third Eye
Throat
Heart
Solar Plexus
Sacral
Base

Aura Layers	Frequency	No. of Lotus Petals
Layer 7 Ketheric/Causal Body	768 Hz	1000
Layer 6 Celestial Body	720 Hz	2
Layer 5 Etheric Template Body	672 Hz	16
Layer 4 Astral Body	594 Hz	12
Layer 3 Mental Body	528 Hz	10
Layer 2 Emotional Body	480 Hz	6
Layer 1 Etheric Body	432 Hz	4

Parts of the Body

Head _____ Ego personality _____ Headaches _____ Head breaks

Face _____ Face to the world _____ Fear of showing myself

Eyes _____ Seeing clearly _____ Fear of seeing _____ Past / Present / Future

Nose _____ Self-recognition _____ "I can't smell my life/that person" (German expression)

Mouth _____ Taking in nourishment _____ Fear of speaking out for self

Ears _____ Capacity to hear _____ Fear of hearing / Painful to hear / Listen

Throat _____ Swallowing / Expression _____ Fear of speaking truth / Can't swallow reality

Neck _____ Flexibility for life _____ Fears / Stubbornness / Inflexibility

Shoulders _____ Carrying the weight of life ____ Heavy burden

Arms _____ Holding life _____ Rejection to embrace life

Elbows _____ Ability to change directions ___ Defending my needs

Hands _____ Giving & taking _____ Fear of giving and taking

Chest _____ Feeling for life _____ Worries / fears of life

Back _____ Support of life _____ Living a wrong life

Abdomen _____ Intuitive power / Safety _____ Fears / Insecurities / Confusion

Hips _____ Being in balance _____ Life is out of balance

Legs _____ Moving apparatus _____ Fear of moving forward in life

Knees _____ Ego personality, pride _____ Fear of changing direction in life

Ankles _____ Flexibility _____ Inflexibility / Guilt

Feet _____ Standing safely _____ Fear of standing safely / Fear of stepping into the future

Organs of the Body

Brain _____ Thinking center _____ Control _____ Erroneous Thinking

Heart _____ Feeling center _____ Painful feelings, heartache

Lungs _____ Taking in life fully _____ Fear of life

Liver _____ Acceptance of life _____ Anger, resentment, rage

Kidneys _____ Fear of failure in life _____ Fear of criticism / Fear of losing love

Bladder _____ Releasing _____ Being pissed at someone

Gallbladder ___ Assimilating life _____ Bitterness / Condemnation

Stomach _____ Holds nourishment _____ Confusion, difficulty digesting circumstances

Genitals _____ Gender principles _____ Denial of self / Rejection of female / male

Colon _____ Assimilating waste _____ Refusing to let go / Holding on to the past

Spleen _____ Obsessions _____ Earthbound entity possessions

Pancreas _____ Sweetness of life _____ Life is not sweet enough

Skin _____ Protection _____ Attack, need to protect

Bones _____ Structure of life _____ Breaking down of structure

Blood _____ Free Flow _____ Feeling of being hindered in life

For a detailed reference, consult Louise Hay's book, *You Can Heal Your Life*

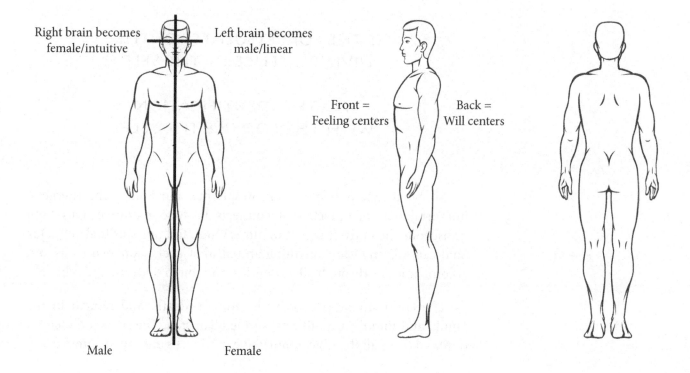

Feeling Centers =
Front side of the body

Will Centers =
Back side of the body

Right brain becomes
female/intuitive

Left brain becomes
male/linear

Front =
Feeling centers

Back =
Will centers

Male   Female

Despite the fact that we live in either a female or a male body, within us we have a female and a male side (the various attributes of female and male are described in the next chapter). A woman can primarily live her male qualities, and likewise a man may distribute predominantly female qualities. This has nothing to do with gender. It is dependent on the personality of the individual. All energy moves in a spiral, which is why the qualities on the level of the eyes shift, as well and female becomes male and visa versa.

- Right side / Male side: on eye level shifts to female → creative right brain

- Left side / Female side: on eye level shifts to male → rational left brain

- All Chakras: Feeling Centers = Front side of body

- All Chakras: Will Centers = Back side of body

For others — particularly in our hemisphere where materialism and power are at the top of the list to achieve — it is the loss of the Soul. It is the forgetfulness of the Divine essence of the Self and the identification with the body as the Self.

THE CAUSE OF OUR SEPARATION FROM SOURCE AND DISEASE INFESTING OUR BODY SYSTEM

IS THE FORGETFULNESS OF THE DIVINE ESSENCE OF THE SELF

AND THE IDENTIFICATION WITH THE BODY AS THE SELF

So, what exactly is our Soul? Simply put, our Soul is the energetic immortal part of ourself that connects us to our Source. Our Soul transcends the body, it is part of our essence and our spiritual Self. Our Soul carefully registers anything and all that ever happened to us and accompanies us through all our cycles from birth to death and rebirth.

The continuous cycle of birth, growth, death, and rebirth in the Hindu and Buddhist traditions is called Samsara. The scars inflicted on our Soul from all those accumulated experiences are called Samskara.

OUR SOUL IS THE ENERGETIC IMMORTAL PART OF OURSELF CONNECTING US TO OUR SOURCE

OUR SOUL TRANSCENDS THE BODY IT IS PART OF OUR ESSENCE AND OUR SPIRITUAL SELF

OUR HEART IS IN ALIGNMENT WITH OUR SOUL

We can deny our spirituality, as in fact many of us do, and we can ignore our Soul. We can claim ourselves to be atheists and live exclusively in our mind's structures. We can accumulate intellectual knowledge, wealth, and degrees and live our whole life without ever giving a thought to our Soul.

Nevertheless, none of us can deny that we are in our bodies. We have a body for as long as we exist on this Earth plane. Yet consider, before the body materialized, there was only energy or Spirit. We do come from Spirit. As the adage says, "We are spiritual beings temporarily inhabiting a body." Not vice versa. Spirit is our source. Spirit / Source and God are One.

Our Soul is like a thread connecting all our life experiences. Like each individual picture on a long movie roll, our Soul accompanies us from experience to experience, or for those who are familiar with the term "reincarnation," we are born and reborn again and again until we become one with Source, one with God. This is our purpose, to know our origin — Source — and become one with Source, one with Creator Energy. And by doing so, to know ourselves. All deeper mysteries of life can be accessed by knowing oneself. Self-knowledge is the basis of true knowledge.

We are spiritual beings temporarily inhabiting a body

Spirit is our source Spirit / Source and God are One

IT IS OUR PURPOSE TO BECOME ONE WITH SOURCE, ONE WITH CREATOR ENERGY

SELF-KNOWLEDGE IS THE BASIS OF TRUE KNOWLEDGE

The high path of all wisdom traditions is the practice of discovering that which transcends the body — the Soul — as well as becoming attached to that transcendent reality as the true Self rather than remaining attached to the physical body.

WE MUST BECOME ATTACHED TO THE TRANSCENDENT REALITY — SOUL — AS THE TRUE SELF RATHER THAN REMAINING ATTACHED TO THE PHYSICAL BODY

The spiritual life is the real life — all else is an illusion. Only those who are attached to God are truly free.

~ Mildred Lisette Norman

I personally feel our connection to Spirit must become our only interdependent relationship.

If we take into consideration the amount of power we have, we must admit that we managed to do a whole lot of damage. Mother Earth is our responsibility, and what can we show as a result? We've polluted nature, almost completely destroyed it. Many of us live in huge concrete jungles, an unworthy existence, and our lust for power and control drives us to conduct devastating wars. We prefer to invest money sources in rearmament and constructing more prisons and walls rather than devote ourselves to the wellbeing of our communities and fellow human beings. We are thinking of ourselves, accumulating for ourselves rather than thinking, feeling, and acting for the benefit of all mankind.

Let's start to think, feel, and act for the benefit of all mankind

Let's face it, humanity has deteriorated. We behave like Lucifer, the fallen angel, who prides himself in being superior. Due to our disease, we have contaminated our environment and poisoned our only physical home, planet Earth.

The revered Dalai Lama said about this:

> "In the world at present, there is not much concern for humane values; there is too much dependence on money and power. If human society loses the value of justice, the value of compassion, the value of honesty, we will face greater difficulties in the future. Some people may think that these sorts of ethical attitudes are not much needed in the areas of business or politics. I strongly disagree. The quality of our actions depends on our motivation.
>
> What we must do is balance external material progress with the sense of responsibility that comes of education and inner development. Spiritual practice involves, on the one hand, acting out of concern for others' wellbeing. On the other hand, it entails transforming ourselves so that we become more readily disposed to do so. To speak of spiritual practice in any terms other than these is meaningless."[4]

This is the sign of how far we have strayed from our original purpose as ambassadors of Creator Source, of becoming God-like through a life of virtue and by cultivating a life of Spirit. We have distanced ourselves far from our center and thus disconnected from our God Source. Being separated from our God Source creates disease. Instead of being united, we have created a split between ourselves and our Creator Energy.

WE HAVE DISTANCED OURSELVES
FROM OUR CENTER
AND THUS DISCONNECTED
FROM OUR GOD SOURCE

BEING SEPARATED FROM OUR GOD SOURCE
CREATES DISEASE

---

[4] This first paragraph is taken from a message the Dalai Lama wrote for the March 7, 2001 World Day of Planetary Consciousness. The 2nd paragraph is a series of excerpts from his book, *Ancient Wisdom: Modern World.*

INSTEAD OF BEING UNITED, WE HAVE CREATED A SPLIT BETWEEN OURSELVES AND OUR CREATOR ENERGY

We might feel blocked and suffer and most likely not understand why. Or maybe we are not even aware that we suffer. Because we fail to recognize the underlying dynamics at play, we cannot admit that we ourselves are the cause of it. We choose to ignore that our experiences are reflections of our own behaviors. Often, we are too unconscious and many times we blame God for our misfortunes. We make God responsible for our pain while we ourselves feel powerless, hopeless, senseless.

Instead of being at peace and in harmony, we feel out of balance. Our energy system is at war. We feel discomfort and pain and fail to acknowledge the cause. We do not recognize that the pain we feel is the language expression of our dying, suffering Soul, waiting to be heard. By disregarding the message of our suffering Soul, we are betraying our Heart.

We choose to ignore that our experiences are reflections of our own behaviors

PAIN IS THE LANGUAGE EXPRESSION OF A DYING, SUFFERING SOUL WAITING TO BE HEARD

BY DISREGARDING THE MESSAGE OF OUR SUFFERING SOUL, WE ARE BETRAYING OUR HEARTS

Chapter 7

BETRAYAL OF THE HEART

Discomfort is our simplest form of guidance yet, unfortunately, we often disregard it when we continually feel agitated or irritated. Nevertheless, it is a sign that our energy system is not at ease.

Discomfort is our simplest form of guidance

Therefore, dis-ease will ultimately set in. In this way, disease has a deeper meaning and a Soul purpose at its base. What we experience on the physical level as disease, though, is only a symptom, a warning sign, a signal that something got off track, a red flag that a part of our Self is not connected to the God Source anymore.

WHAT WE EXPERIENCE ON THE PHYSICAL LEVEL AS DISEASE IS ONLY A SYMPTOM, A WARNING SIGN, A SIGNAL THAT SOMETHING GOT OFF TRACK

Disease always carries an important message that needs to be heard and understood, a lesson that needs to be learned. Then, in very natural ways, health returns to the energy system while an expansion of consciousness takes place. In this sense, disease is never a curse but a blessing because it invokes spiritual growth. In psychotherapist Dr. Roseanne Farano's terms, it triggers Consciousness Growth.

Listen to your body when it whispers so you don't have to hear it scream

DISEASE ALWAYS CARRIES AN IMPORTANT MESSAGE THAT NEEDS TO BE HEARD AND UNDERSTOOD, A LESSON THAT NEEDS TO BE LEARNED

IN THIS SENSE, DISEASE IS NEVER A CURSE BUT A BLESSING BECAUSE IT INVOKES SPIRITUAL GROWTH

What we have forgotten we need to re-member. We need to recollect those lost parts and re-unite the different members of our Self. Most importantly, we need to integrate the Heart, because the Heart is our direct connection to God. And if we don't, but rather continue living life from the mind, we betray our Heart.

WE NEED TO RECOLLECT THE LOST PARTS
AND RE-UNITE THE DIFFERENT MEMBERS
OF OUR SELF
MOST IMPORTANTLY, WE NEED TO INTEGRATE
THE HEART
BECAUSE THE HEART IS OUR DIRECT CONNECTION
TO GOD

In Egyptian mythology, which is the root of Judaism, Christianity and Islam, we *find described in their Book of Going Forth by Day, also called the Book of Emerging Forth Into the Light,* the rite of passage called "The Weighing of the Heart and the Great Judgment."

THE ANCIENT EGYPTIAN BOOK OF *GOING FORTH BY DAY*

Oh my Heart which I had from my mother!
Oh my Heart which I had from my mother!
Oh my Heart of my different ages!
Do not stand up as a witness against me.
do not be opposed to me in the tribunal.
do not be hostile to me in the presence of the keeper
of the balance.
for you are my ka (creative and life-preserving power)
which was in my body.
The protector who made my members hale.
Go forth to the happy place whereto we speed;
do not make my name stink to the entourage who make men.
Do not tell lies about me in the presence of the god.
It is indeed well that you should hear!

This final tribunal enabled the deceased to emerge victoriously from their trials and resurrection was promised as a reward for righteous living — living in accordance with the Heart. This ancient civilization was well aware of the importance of the Heart. To them, the Heart was the essential organ that made a human being divine and alive. They worshiped the Heart, unlike our technical computer age, which worships the brain, the mind, the intellect.

WE MUST RECOGNIZE THE IMPORTANCE
OF THE HEART
WE MUST LIVE IN ACCORDANCE WITH OUR HEART

BECAUSE THE HEART IS THE ESSENTIAL ORGAN
THAT MAKES A HUMAN BEING DIVINE AND ALIVE
OTHERWISE, WE ARE BETRAYING OUR HEART

The powerful myth of the ancient Egyptians demonstrates what we in our modern times have forgotten. We have betrayed our Heart. We keep serving the intellect, the wrong God.

Furthermore, the ancient Egyptians believed in reincarnation and life after death. Their efforts were toward preserving the essential organs for the afterlife. During the embalming rites where the organs were removed, the heart was left in the body while the essential organs of the liver, lungs, stomach, and intestines were preserved in the canopic burial jars. There was no jar for the brain — ever! This is a little food for thought.

Chapter 8

THE DYNAMIC PROCESS OF DISEASE AND THE PATH TOWARD WHOLENESS

"When you realize
HEART & EARTH
are spelled with the same letters,
it all starts to make sense."

The Heart Field

It is important to note here that we are not speaking of the heart as a mere substantial organ but the energetic Heart with its high virtues of unconditional love, wisdom, nurturing, caring and compassion, to name a few. What most of us do not realize is the fact that our energetic Heart is not only in the middle of our chest. The Heart is a field within our body's overall human auric field.

THE LOCATION OF OUR ENERGETIC HEART
IS NOT ONLY IN THE MIDDLE OF OUR CHEST
BUT MORE SO

OUR HEART IS A FIELD
WITHIN THE HUMAN AURIC FIELD

Chakras are energetic wheels that supply the body with life force. Without the Chakras and the corresponding energetic fields / layers, the human body would not be alive.

The aura of the human body consists of seven levels / fields that correspond to the seven chakras of the human energy field. The Heart field is the fourth level and corresponds to the Heart chakra. The Heart chakra is the bridge between the three lower chakras and the three higher chakras. The three lower chakras correspond to the human or animalistic part within us, whereas the three higher chakras correspond to the Divine part of our being.

The Heart chakra, the 4th level / field, is the bridge between being human and becoming Divine. It is a frequency higher than the mind field. The 3rd chakra / field, the Solar Plexus, corresponds to our thought processes and the mind and intellect. The 4th chakra / field corresponds to our higher feelings like unconditional love, compassion, and forgiveness.

OUR HEART FIELD IS THE BRIDGE BETWEEN BEING HUMAN AND BECOMING DIVINE

While in the so-called Third World countries where humans are battling mere survival, they might primarily be functioning in the first two levels of the human energy field. Societies of the developed world primarily function on the third level of the human energy field. To elevate our energy from the third level to the fourth level is no easy task. Hence, most people in our hemisphere reside in the 3rd level, the mind field.

The intellect is our home, power is our driving force, money is our love, and science is our God. The chief of a Samoan tribe in the South Pacific described our values to his fellow tribal members after his return from Europe in the late 1800s in his book *Tuiavii's Way: A South Sea Chief's Comments on Western Society*. He called white men "The Papalagi" and observed that:

"The Papalagi loves his mind and feeds it thoughts from his head. He never lets it go hungry and it does not distress him if the thoughts eat each other. He finds it difficult not to think and to live with his limbs as well. Often, he lives only in his head, and all his senses are in deep sleep, even when he walks upright, talks, eats, and laughs. The thinking and the fruits of his thinking — his thoughts — hold him captive as if he were intoxicated by his own thoughts. He is a human being, whose senses live as enemies within his Spirit — a human being split in two parts. We should ask ourselves, who is stupid, he who thinks not much; or he who thinks too much?

The many papers (newspaper) also tell the Papalagi what he should think about this and that. The many papers want to make all people into one head; they fight your own head and your own thinking. They demand that each human being use the head and thoughts of the many papers.

The Papalagi chases through his life without rest; more and more he forgets how we can walk and stroll and move happily toward a destination which we don't seek, but which comes our way.

The round metal and the heavy paper, what they call 'money,' that is the true God of the white man. Money is his love and money is his God. Almost everyone loses his health to it. They think of money daily, hourly, every moment, all of them, all of them! Even the children! All Europeans!

The Papalagi strives to be God. He would like to crush the Great Spirit and take his powers for himself. But God is still greater and more powerful than the greatest Papalagi and his machine, and he still decides who among us should die and when. For there is nothing that the white man has created which can come even close to the miracles of the Great Spirit."

According to Peter C. Cavelti, who translated the book from German to English, "Tuiavii's legacy for today's Western reader is that he makes us see things from his perspective and, by doing so, leaves us with a deep sadness. That he does without cursing our civilization, but instead merely describes us as victims of our own inventions. His wisdom comes from simplicity, which is from God and is not rooted in education or intellectual knowledge. Today, his words promise to cast a spell over a new generation of readers."

By looking at ourselves through Tuiavii's eyes we are saddened by the loss of simplicity and humanity in our society. Yet each page, filled with Tuiavii's insight, brings us a step closer to the truth and ultimately, to understanding ourselves. His words leave us with something to ponder:

"Your people thought you were bringing us light.
Instead, you want to draw us into your darkness."

Chief Seattle's letter to the great chief in Washington, President Franklin Pierce, stated much the same as Tuiavii's observations in regard to society[5]. The difference is that the Samoan chief visited Germany in the 1800s, whereas the European pioneers invaded the Indian territory of the Americas.

Let's elaborate on to what degree we have become conditioned to live according to certain behavioral codes passed down to us during many thousands of generations. It is the doctrine of power, control, and violence that is governing our patriarchal societies nowadays. For — as countless sources attest and modern archaeological findings prove — there was once a better time, a golden age when our forebears honored nature, the elements, and our planet as manifestations of the Creator Energy.

Modern archaeological findings attest to the fact that the Neolithic age (10,000BC − 4,500BC) — which culminated with the Minoan civilization on the island of Crete — formed the basis on which all later cultures and civilizations have been built.

I have always been deeply intrigued by the cultures representing the cradle of human civilization, the Neolithic age. Riane Eisler confirms in her book, *The Chalice and the Blade*, the following:

---

[5] Chief Seattle (c. 1786 – June 7, 1866) was a Suquamish and Duwamish chief. He pursued a path of accommodation to white settlers. The city of Seattle, Washington is named after him. A widely publicized speech arguing in favor of ecological responsibility and respect of Native Americans' land rights had been attributed to him.

"Archaeological evidence suggests that "God" was considered female for the first 200,000 years of human life on Earth."

~ Vice

Ancient cylinder seal of the Mother Goddess holding two rams by the horns with primordial waters at its base and the Tree of Life on both sides (Achaemenide Empire, 5th century, BC)

Backside of bronze mirror depicting a Mother Goddess giving birth, Chandrakhetugarh (eastern India, 2nd century BC)

Archaeological findings bear witness that during the Neolithic age civilizations all over the world were far from being primitive. They were living in matriarchal communities a life of harmony, peace, and joy. Women and men were viewed as equal and all worked together for the common good of their community. There was no centralized and hierarchic structure of religious and social order.

The people of the Neolithic age revered the Great Mother Goddess as the "creatora" of all life and celebrated her with altars, shrines, and offering places. The Great Mother Goddess was viewed as the origin and regenerating source of all forms of life. She was seen as the life-generating and nurturing powers of the universe as an all-giving mother from whose womb all life emerges and to which, like the cycles of vegetation, it returns after death to be again reborn.

During the Neolithic times, everyone lived their life deeply embedded in a spiritual atmosphere of harmony with nature, the cosmos, and each other.

Women played a central role as leaders and priestesses and the male principle equally played an important role. It was clear to those people that the divine male — her son/lover/consort in the form of a young man or male animal — reinforces the creative female. By complementing each other, their power multiplies and becomes complete. For thousands of years, the Sacred Marriage between these two forces was kept alive through rituals and myths.

None of the Neolithic excavations unearthed any fortresses and arms. Rather than to conquer, plunder and loot, these communities co-existed in peaceful harmony. There is no single evidence that points toward a function to extract obedience, punish, and destroy. Those civilizations had no need to defend against intruders. Their focus was on their life and art and cultivating the Earth for their needs and purposes.

Eisler stated:

> "And if the central religious image was a woman giving birth and not, as in our time, a man dying on a cross, it would not be unreasonable to infer that the life and the love of life — rather than death and the fear of death — were dominant in such a society, as well as art."

But we have long since left this Garden of Eden when the matriarchate and the matrilineal were slowly replaced by the patriarchate and the patrilineal during the late Bronze age when metallurgy was developed and the blade became idealized. As Marija Gimbutas[6] wrote:

---

[6] University of California archaeologist and author of Living Goddesses and other books.

"The lethal power of the blade — the power to take life rather than give life; that is the ultimate power to establish and enforce domination.

The Goddess with her nurturing and life-affirming attributes was replaced by the condemning Yahweh / Jehovah who glorified conquest and male supremacy, which marked the beginning of the male dominator civilizations and the ranking of one half of humanity over the other; as practiced in the 'higher' civilizations of Sumer, Mesopotamia, Egypt, Greece and the Roman Empire, which nowadays is the holy Roman Empire."

It is also revealing what Wild Woman Sisterhood wrote about the advent of patriarchy:

"During ancient times, the crones, hags, and witches were frequently sages, leaders, midwives, and healers in their communities and were revered for their wisdom and knowledge. As history evolved and a patriarchal society took hold, the definitions of the crone (the crowned one), the hag (the holy one), and the witch (the wise one) were distorted."

Whether the evolution from the matriarchate to the patriarchate was regress or progress is questionable. What remains evident is that we strayed from a unified consciousness.

For the past 2000 years, church institutions, governments, and now corporations dictate how we're to think, live, and act. Using our example of treating disease, it is a sad fact that the billion-dollar pharmaceutical industry is geared towards sickness rather than supporting our health since health doesn't support their industry. And the masses buy it. In this way, symptoms are treated with medicines that will produce evermore symptoms, that then again will be treated with more damage-causing side effects — a downward spiral. How could we allow this and even buy into it?

"If you want to understand any problem in America, you need to focus on who profits from that problem, not who suffers from the problem."

~ Dr. Amos Wilson

His Holiness The Dalai Lama, when asked what surprised him most about humanity, answered:

"Man! Because he sacrifices his health in order to make money. Then he sacrifices money to recuperate his health. And then he is so anxious about the future that he does not enjoy the present; the result being that he does not live in the present or the future; he lives as if he is never going to die, and then dies having never really lived.

"We have bigger houses but smaller families, more conveniences, but less time. We have more degrees, but less sense; more knowledge, but less judgment; more experts, but more problems; more medicines, but less healthiness.

"We've been all the way to the moon and back but have trouble crossing the street to meet the neighbor. We built more computers to hold more information to produce more copies than ever but have less communication. We have become long on quantity but short on quality. These are fast times of fast foods but slow digestion. Tall man but short character. Steep profits but shallow relationships. It is a time where there is much in the window but nothing in the room."

What happened in the course of distancing ourselves from our center — the Heart and Soul — is that we have given our individual, inherent power away to a degree where we think we decide for ourselves, while we have become merely puppets on a string governed and brainwashed by fear and control. COVID-19 is teaching us a big lesson in this.

We buy what the media reports rather than listening to the wisdom within ourselves. We have developed our intellect to such ever-higher degrees that we are at the same time afraid to feel for ourselves and to think with our right mind, much less act in our own right. We have forgotten to listen to the wisdom within.

WE HAVE FORGOTTEN TO LISTEN
TO THE WISDOM WITHIN
WE NO LONGER THINK WITH OUR RIGHT MIND
AND ACT IN OUR OWN RIGHT

As a consequence, we prefer to live according to certain rules and norms, to fit in and belong to the larger mass while we slowly die an inner death — by constantly betraying our Heart until we cannot hear its message anymore.

Section 2

The Matrix of Healing

"The most sacred temple
is the one within your Heart."

~ Life and Zen

Chapter 9

THE HEART AS OUR HEALER – FEELING VS. THINKING

As much as dis-ease creates pain and destroys the Self, healing is a very joyous path. We begin to understand how we ourselves created the big dramas of our life, that we are responsible for all its manifestations including disease, emotional pain, confusion, and other miseries. We heal by summoning the courage to take a closer look at ourselves. We also stop blaming others. Remember: When you forgive, you heal — and when you let go, you grow.

"You must take personal responsibility. You cannot change the circumstances, the seasons, or the wind, but you can change yourself. That is something you have charge of."

~ John Rohn

STOP BLAMING OTHERS
SUMMON THE COURAGE TO
TAKE A CLOSER LOOK AT YOURSELF

"When you forgive, you heal and
when you let go, you grow."

~ Anonymous

55

We relax and forgive ourselves, as well as the ones who did us wrong. We recognize every choice we make offers new possibilities.

"Whatever you're thinking about is literally like planning a future event. When you're worrying, you are planning. When you're appreciating, you are planning. What are you planning?"

~ Abraham-Hicks

We understand that our every thought, feeling, and action carries a creative force — constructive or destructive — and that it is on us to choose one over the other and take responsibility for it all.

We realize that no matter how good or bad the circumstances were when we came into this life, our Soul had chosen them. Our Soul chose them so we could overcome hindering conditions, learn and grow. We chose them so we could learn — and it is entirely up to us what we make out of it.

We change where change is needed. We no longer listen to others but do what feels right to us. Importantly, we become who we want to be, not what others want to see.

"Be who you want to be,
not what others want to see."

~ G. Avetis

We release the past and live in the present moment. We let go of conditions that do not serve our Heart. We let go of beliefs that had been passed down to us. We cut the cords that bind, imprison, and hinder us. We free our Heart.

We no longer believe in fear. We recognize our true nature, which is Love because we start to hear the simple message of our Heart. We listen to the truth of our Heart. We act according to it.

An old Cherokee is teaching his grandson about life. "A fight is going on inside me," he said to the boy.

"It is a terrible fight and its is between two wolves. One is evil — he is anger, envy, sorrow, regret, greed, arrogance, self-pity, guilt, resentment, inferiority, lies, false pride, superiority, and ego." He continued, "The other is good — he is joy, peace, love, hope, serenity, humility, kindness, benevolence, empathy, generosity, truth, compassion, and faith. The same fight is going on inside you — and inside every other person, too."

The grandson thought about it for a minute and then asked his grandfather, "Which wolf will win?"

The old Cherokee simply replied, "The one you feed."

By letting go of our lower self with its false ego pride, anger, greed and lies, we align ourself with our higher nature which is love, compassion, peace, and joy. We feel instead of think. We stop the complications and recognize how simple life can be. We feel the power of the Heart and surrender completely to its own intelligence and wisdom.

We experience that our open Heart is our best protection. We trust our Heart exclusively. With the Heart as our leader, we are re-aligned, we feel peaceful. There is peace in our Heart. We feel our true power rather than a fake demonstration of power. We have built a new foundation, built ourselves anew.

Exclusivity = trust at all times not sometimes, yes, and sometimes not

Mind you, what I am describing here sounds very simple. Yet it is most challenging indeed. Challenging because it is extremely hard to achieve. I daresay more than 95 percent of the human population lives almost exclusively in their mind.

For — in order to leave the realm of the intellect and with it the mind field, of which I have written about earlier — we need to be able to elevate our consciousness, we need to raise our frequency. And this takes a huge amount of awareness, courage, and discipline. Especially when triggered.

I always say, "The Heart and the mind are both powerful leaders in their own right. In the same way as you cannot serve two masters, you cannot live life from your Heart and your mind. You must decide and choose one — and stick with it."

A life lived from the mind is always a life lived in compromise. If you seek fulfillment and want to live your dream and aim for your destiny and true life purpose, you must live life from your Heart.

The Invaluable Wisdom of Your Heart

the Heart feels _____ the mind thinks

the Heart trusts _____ the mind fears

the Heart dreams _____ the mind compromises

the Heart fulfills _____ the mind restricts

the Heart liberates _____ the mind controls

the Heart expands _____ the mind contracts

the Heart forgives_____ the mind revenges

Still hooked on the mind?

57

Again, it is a complex and incredibly courageous task to devote our lives exclusively to our Hearts. In practical terms, it means to give up the substantial need for love, approval, and belonging. It means to no longer serve our ego personality but become a servant of our Hearts. We feel, think, act, and live according to our Hearts. If we live the truth of our Heart, we are living according to our Soul. Our Soul is alive in our Heart, but unless our mind lives in accordance with our Heart, there is no Soul-Heart-mind connection.

BECOME THE SERVANT OF YOUR HEART
LIVE THE TRUTH OF YOUR HEART
THEN YOU ARE LIVING ACCORDING TO YOUR SOUL

THE LIVING GODDESS = THE HEART ALIVE

The 11th century Sufi saint Khwaja Abdullah Ansari said about this task to his disciples:

"Can you walk on water?
You are no better than a straw.
Can you fly through the air?
You are no better than a gnat.
Develop your Heart.
Then you might become someone."

The door of the Sacred Heart leading into the Temple the Living Goddess

The view into the Temple of the Living Goddess

Chapter 10

ECSTASY & BLISS – LIFE AS A DANCE

"May the sun bring you new energy by day
May the moon softly restore you by night
May the rain wash away your worries
May the breeze blow new strength into your being
May you walk gently through the world and know its beauty
All the days of your life."

~ Apache Blessing

When we have reached the point of ecstasy and bliss, we fully realize how much the Universe favors us, supports us, protects us, and takes care of us. We feel cradled by the universe. We feel as if the Universe dances with us, that we are in a harmonious joyous dance with the Universe. When Albert Einstein was asked, "What is the most important question to ask in life?" He answered, *Is the Universe a friendly place or not?"*

We have come to know that we live in a human-friendly universe. We realize that challenges are opportunities for growth. We accept tests, trials, and tribulations as a chance rather than a curse. The Chinese language consists of 50,000 characters, yet apparently, the word for both "crisis" and "chance" are one and the same.

We realize that challenges are opportunities for growth.

Life becomes easy, a play. We have arrived home. We are free. We experience living in an effortless flow. We remain appreciative, no matter what, because we see the blessings. We practice gratitude. We celebrate life. We experience full glory. We live in dignity. We realize our dream. We live our passion, alive and vibrant. We commit to what we believe in and we engage ourselves fully, no compromises.

Our eyes are open, we see *what is*. The glory, perfection, and perfect order become apparent to us. We are immensely grateful to be alive, to be part of the great family called humans.

It deeply humbles us. We recognize the beauty and the perfection surrounding us. By living in truth, we naturally reach a state of grace. We have great compassion for others because we truly care. Peace surrounds us and the ones we touch.

By living in truth, we naturally reach a state of grace

We create exclusively in accordance with our Heart and Soul — we become the co-creators of the Universe and are in the flow of life. We know our power transforms the world. Our positive feelings, thoughts, and actions clear negativity and pollution.

WE CREATE EXCLUSIVELY IN ACCORDANCE WITH OUR HEART AND SOUL AND BY DOING SO BECOME THE CO-CREATORS OF THE UNIVERSE

Be aware that word is intent

We practice proper language hygiene; we speak in clear terms without word fillers instead of talking much while saying nothing. We do not curse and cuss. We recognize that word is intent.[7]

As soon as a word or sentence leaves our mouth, it starts to create its own reality. We take responsibility for what manifests because of our word.

> "Be mindful of your Self-Talk.
> It's a conversation with the universe."
>
> ~ Master Jonathan Field

We spread blessings rather than curses. Whether we have much or little, we live in humility and dignity. We envision Peace on Earth. We align ourselves with others with the same vision. We give birth to the future and create Heaven on Earth. We realize that our pure intentions reach much further than simply the Earth plane; we literally shift the Universe. Our efforts affect *ALL THERE IS*.

We continue to heal. With the great capacity of our open Heart, we have become successful human beings. We inspire others to find their way home as well. We find ways to ease their pain. We understand that on some interconnected and energetic level their pain is our pain. As long as they are in pain, we as a human family are hindered in our progress and leave pain behind for all. We can FEEL what others are dealing with, even if they live on another continent across the ocean. We realize fully that we are all tied together in a great invisible matrix of the life-giving force and web of life.

---

[7] Compare Part VIII, Section 2, Chapter 99: "On Curses and Blessings and the Creation of Entities."

WE ARE ALL CONNECTED
OTHERS' PAIN IS OUR PAIN
OTHERS' JOY IS OUR JOY

"In ancient China, the Daoists taught

that a constant inner smile, a smile to oneself,

insured health, happiness, and longevity. Why?

Smiling to yourself is like basking in love:

You become your own best friend.

Living with an inner smile

is to live in harmony with yourself."

~ Mantak Chia

When the Soul Calls: True Stories of Deep Healing and Transformation

Chapter 11

THE GREAT WEB OF LIFE

"If only our eyes saw Souls
instead of bodies.
How different our ideals of beauty would be."

~ Anonymous

With great humility, we surrender completely to our Soul / Spirit, yet feel strong. There is a light force surrounding us, a powerful field preventing evil from penetrating. We feel part of the Higher Order and it empowers us to exclusively and unconditionally trust. By "exclusively and unconditionally trust," I mean trusting regardless of any kind of fear wanting to set in. Exclusive and unconditional trust means we trust all the time. We do not move from trusting in some areas and then in other areas we fear. We decide to trust and we stay with trust.

DECIDE TO TRUST AND STAY WITH TRUST

We recognize the great stream of the Universe has taken over. We are flowing in the primordial creative ocean of life, which carries each and every single one of us towards wholeness.

We are committed to the Divine Plan as envisioned and transmitted by the Ascended Masters of Light. We understand the true purpose of our life: to manifest ourselves as an expression of pure Love. This does not mean we become pleasers, but rather serve the truthful expression of our Heart and Soul. It means we love others as we love ourself as taught by the Christ — to serve others as we serve ourselves.

The Ascended Masters of Light are former enlightened humans who are now in Spirit form and assisting humanity, which is their destiny.

WE LOVE AND SERVE OTHERS
AS WE LOVE AND SERVE OURSELVES

We feel the interconnectedness of all living beings — of all that is alive: humans, animals, plant life, the mineral world, all the elements down to the smallest particles of which all creation is made. We experience that *We Are All One* — all part of the great web called Life. We realize how insignificant we are and yet how immensely important. Hildegard von Bingen stated, "Everything that is in the Heavens, on the Earth, and under the Earth is penetrated by connectedness."

A matter of perspective: Compared to a galaxy, we are insignificant. But looking at the importance of our individual lives and the impact our lives can have on others, we are immensely important.

WE ARE INSIGNIFICANT AND AT THE SAME TIME IMMENSELY IMPORTANT

In his bestselling book, *The Web of Life*, the physicist Fritjof Capra looks at the shift from linear thinking to systems thinking in science, showing how recent advances in a wide range of fields, from evolutionary biology and chaos theory to quantum physics and computer science, signal an emergent paradigm that differs radically from the clockwork model of classical science. He compares this shift to the Copernican revolution suggesting that the new perception of reality has profound implications not only for science and philosophy but also for business, politics, health care, education, and everyday life. He writes:

> "The new paradigm may be called a holistic worldview seeing the world as an integrated whole rather than a dissociated collection of parts. It may also be called an ecological view, if the term 'ecological' is used in a much broader and deeper sense than usual. Deep ecological awareness recognizes the fundamental interdependence of all phenomena and the fact that, as individuals and societies, we are all embedded in (and ultimately dependent on) the cyclical processes of nature."

Capra begins with a discussion of the cultural context in which this scientific revolution is unfolding.

> "As a culture, we are discovering that we cannot understand the major problems of our time in isolation. They are systemic problems, they are by nature interconnected and interdependent. Population growth is tied to poverty, for example, and the extinction of plant and animal species is inextricably linked to third world debt. Ultimately, these problems must be seen as just different facets of one single crisis, which is largely a crisis of perception. It derives from the fact that most of us, and especially our large social institutions, subscribe to the concepts of an outdated worldview, a perception of reality inadequate for dealing with our overpopulated, globally interconnected world."

Against this backdrop, he traces the rise of systems thinking — the sort of thinking that emphasizes the whole rather than the parts. While classical science insists that the behavior of a complex system can be best analyzed in terms of the properties of the parts, systems thinking reverses the equation by showing that the properties of the parts are not intrinsic but can be understood only within the context of the larger whole. In this sense, systems thinking means thinking in context.

"There are no parts at all.
What we call a part is merely a pattern
in an inseparable web of relationships."

~ Fritjof Capra

Capra concludes his book with some reflections on "ecological literacy." From his perspective, the emerging paradigm in science has profound ecological consequences. An understanding of reality, based on the essential interdependence and interconnectedness at the heart of things, restores our human connection to the entire web of life.

"Man does not weave this web of life.
He is merely a strand of it.
Whatever he does to the web, he does to himself."

~ Chief Seattle

One of the two angels guarding the entrance into the
Temple of the Living Goddess

Chapter 12

OUR DIVINE GUIDES – ANGELS AND MASTERS OF LIGHT

"The second coming of Christ now appears
as unconditional love within our own Hearts
and the awakening of humanity into Christ consciousness."

~ Anonymous

All along, we know and experience how much we are supported and guided by the Divine Force. We are empty shells, Beings of Light are our driving force. We resonate with them who form the embodiment of the masters in pure Christ Consciousness and who dedicate themselves to the uplifting of our planet's condition.

WE GIVE BIRTH TO THEM ON EARTH —
AS WE WALK THEIR PATH,
SPEAK THEIR WORDS,
AND OUR ACTIONS BECOME THEIRS

OUR LIVES BECOME A PRAYER IN GRATITUDE
WE ARE IN A PARTNERSHIP OF
SACRED COLLABORATION
WE ARE IN HOLY COMMUNION

OUR LIFE'S MISSION IS BEING ACCOMPLISHED
AND WE ARE BEING FULFILLED
THE ANGELS AND MASTERS OF LIGHT
HAVE REACHED US

THROUGH US, THEIR PURPOSE IS BEING FULFILLED
THEIR MISSION IS ACCOMPLISHED.
WE HAVE SERVED ONE ANOTHER

WE HAVE FULFILLED "THE GREAT PLAN" —
TO BRING LIGHT TO EARTH, LIGHT IN THE UNIVERSE
GLORY HALLELUJAH!

According to the shaman Umai in Olga Kharitidi's book *Entering the Circle*, every human being has a Spirit Twin; a Guardian Angel / Spirit Helper / Inner Guardian / Shadow Watcher. [The Spirit Twin] is intimately connected with the ultimate purpose given to each person at birth. They are the holders of the primary essence of our natural being.

The seven types of Spirit Twins that exist for people are: Healer, Magus, Teacher, Messenger, Protector, Warrior, and Executor (one who makes things happen).

~ Olga Kharitidi
Entering the Circle

Angels are supernatural beings described in all religions and wisdom traditions who inhabit the heavenly realms of Light. They never incarnated in a physical body. They are benevolent, celestial intermediaries between God and humanity. Other roles include protectors and guides for humans and servants for God. They act as an attendant, agent, or messenger of God conventionally represented in human form with wings and a long white robe.

Angels exist in hierarchic order as:

- Four Seraphim: fiery serpents with four faces and six wings

- Cherubim: the keepers of celestial records, sphinx-like, winged creatures with faces

- Thrones: glowing wheels covered with many eyes, God's chariot; they dispense God's judgment in order to carry out Her / His desires for us

- Dominions: middle management, responsible for ensuring the Cosmos remains in order by sending down power to governments and other authority figures

- Virtues: shaped like sparks of light, they are in charge of maintaining the natural world

- Powers: brightly colored hazy fumes, border patrol agents between heaven and earth

- Principalities: shaped like rays of light, they oversee everything, they guide our entire world

- Archangels: they do not deal with personal matters, only matters involving all of humanity

- Angels: also known as personal guardian angels of people; messengers to humanity

What is meant by Christ Consciousness? Christ Consciousness is an awareness of the Higher Self as part of a universal order. Although it can be interpreted in a number of ways, a common understanding is that Christ Consciousness is the state of consciousness in which a person has found self-realization and unity with God or the Divine. It may also be used as a synonym for the yogic and Hindu concept of samadhi, or deep spiritual bliss.

Although Christ Consciousness is not intended to relate solely to the personality of Jesus Christ, its combination of Christian language with Eastern religious and philosophical concepts makes it a controversial term to some. Yet, this is a common concept among many different religious traditions, and is not unique to Christianity.

It was named after the spiritual elevation Jesus achieved during his mortal life, and is symbolic of the enlightenment attained by spiritual masters after a period of suffering. As such, Christ Consciousness is available to all those who seek awareness and spiritual awakening, regardless of their personal religious adherence.

"God is Consciousness . . . not a creator.
God is the source of creation itself.
It — not he or she — is not independent of you.
It is the totality of everything.
So when I call myself God, I am not talking about
my personal self.
I am talking about the expression of the God Self
that rests inside of me.
The ENERGY, the verb, not the noun.
Once you think God is a noun, a person, a place, a thing,
you separate yourself from it and immediately become
a limited being.
That is what separates the believers (religious)
from the knowers (spiritual)."

~ Minds Journal

Section 3

Healing and Healing Modalities

Chapter 13

THE HEALING PROCESS OF THE HEARTPATH RE-ALIGNMENT

"Before you heal someone,
ask him if he's willing to give up
the things that made him sick."

~ Hippocrates

The process of moving from forgetting and disease to remembering and healing, may well take up our whole life. In fact, it has taken us uncountable lifetime experiences to arrive where we are at now. We will reach enlightenment once we become fully conscious. We become fully conscious or fully awake when no part of ourself is in the dark anymore. It has been said that this happens when we can clearly see all our past experiences throughout all the ages. Then we shall be free to choose to come back or to remain One with the Creator Energy / God Source. And no doubt, we will eventually get there after countless reincarnations.

However, if we are able to speed up the process in order to understand sooner and advance faster, why not do so? When we choose to walk the healing path, we always journey back home — home to our Creator Source — to God / the Goddess within us. Getting to know ourselves intimately — the lighter parts as well as the shadow parts — always results in bringing us closer to ourselves. It is not without reason that the sages always encouraged to "Know Thyself."

We must find out for ourselves that inside us
is a god or goddess in embryo that wants to be born
so that we can express our divinity.

~ Deepak Chopra

It is not only beneficial but also extremely self-empowering to have a close look at the workings of our psyche and the underlying dynamics that govern our lives. This is where the HeartPath Re-Alignment provides valuable tools for the individual to undergo a deep process of delving into the sub-conscious and carefully exploring what lies at the base of our thoughts, feelings, and actions.

The mind cannot grasp the truth; it has to be seen by the eyes of the Soul. The Soul will tell its story, and its revelation will result in experiencing the deep wisdom and the profound truth within. Great transformation will result and the perspective of Self, as well as of life in general, will expand.

ONLY THE EYES OF THE SOUL CAN GRASP THE TRUTH

What lay hidden in darkness will come into the light. Thanks to this memory reconstruction, confusion will turn into clarity, as we will finally understand.

This is the meaning of enlightenment: to truly know the Self with all the journeys the Soul has chosen in order to grow and advance, to experience the full spectrum of using power creatively, as well as in destructive ways. It is to see ourselves in experiences and expressions fully immersed in the light and clarity of the Creator energy, as well as in the experiences gained by serving the dark powers of evil, disconnection from Source, and the betrayal of our true purpose. Then, and only then — and with the full knowledge and realization of all our experiences — can we develop the courage to forgive ourselves and re-assemble all the parts of the large puzzle of the Self to become truly Whole.

ENLIGHTENMENT = PROFOUND SELF-KNOWLEDGE OF POWER USED CREATIVELY AND POWER ABUSED IN DESTRUCTIVE WAYS

For this to happen, it is not possible to exclusively look at the positive parts of our spiritual makeup. We all enjoy looking at the full moon and admiring its beauty. But can we deny the presence of the moon on a black night when the moon has fully waned and we are unable to see it? In the same way as we acknowledge the moon in all its phases, so we must honor all of our parts, the sides of us we are proud of and love to show, as well as the deeply hidden taboo parts we are unaware of.

Even more so, to become fully integrated, we must especially focus on the deepest unconscious shadows revealed in the HeartPath Re-Alignment process, the parts we were so deeply denying that we didn't even know existed. That is where the greatest part of our power is buried. If we ignore doing so, we stay fragmented.

The greatest part of our power lies in the parts we deny and even were unaware they existed.

But — Glory Hallelujah — when we do, we have liberated those imprisoned parts by bringing them into the light as well. In this way, our creative power is no longer stifled by our sub-conscious, deep-rooted fear of misusing our power again.

As Marianne Williamson so eloquently stated:

"Our deepest fear is not that we are inadequate.
Our deepest fear is that we are powerful beyond measure.
It is our light, not our darkness that most frightens us.
We ask ourselves, 'Who am I to be brilliant, gorgeous,
talented, fabulous?'

"Actually, who are you not to be? You are a child of God.
Your playing small does not serve the world.
There is nothing enlightened about shrinking
so that other people won't feel insecure around you.

"We are all meant to shine, as children do.
We were born to make manifest the glory of God that is
within us.
It's not just in some of us; it's in everyone.
And as we let our own light shine,
we unconsciously give other people permission to do the
same.
As we are liberated from our own fear,
our presence automatically liberates others."

Chapter 14

THE SUB-CONSCIOUS – A HUGE DATA BANK IN OUR ENERGY FIELD

"Things are not getting worse.
They are getting uncovered.
We must hold each other tight
and continue to pull back the veil."

~ Anonymous

In the same way that the Akashic Records are an energetic field around our globe that bear witness to literally everything that's ever happened on planet Earth since the beginning of time, so does the human energy field store everything that has ever happened to us from this lifetime spanning to all our experiences throughout all time. And even more so, all the experiences, thoughts, feelings, and actions of our ancestors are contained in the human energy field as well. Tremendous, isn't it?!

Our sub-conscious is THE most reliable memory bank imaginable. Like a hugely complex bio-computer, everything is forever securely stored in our body and our auric field, nothing is ever lost. If we were to see what it contains, confusion would give place to clarity.

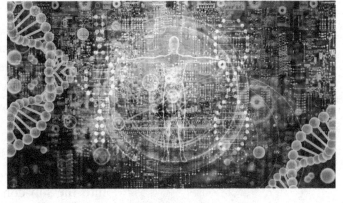

Yongue Minyur Rinpoche, Tibetan teacher and master of the Karma Kagyu and Nyingma lineages of Tibetan Buddhism in his remarkable book *In Love with the World*, states that "Enlightenment is the ability to directly see things as they are."

We would finally fully understand all aspects of our lives, as well as how the universe works. We would become enlightened, as all is being revealed in the Light and nothing is left in the dark.

"Enlightenment is the ability to directly see things as they are."

~ Yongue Minyur Rinpoche

Healing happens once the incidence of past trauma is being re-experienced. This process of healing happens on various levels: emotionally, mentally, and spiritually — by learning the truth. This can entail the truth of our Soul, or our life experiences, the larger picture of what actually occurred and what the full meaning is behind every experience.

It is extremely liberating to finally learn the truth.

But more so, healing happens on the "cellular memory level" in the body, healing what has ailed us. There is no doubt that this process of remembering what has been forgotten and denied by the psyche can be a painful one. However, it is also extremely liberating to finally learn the truth.

Modern science has come to recognize emotions as the link between body and mind. And not only that, research in the field of neurophysiology has proven that for the body's cells to unwind and relax from an experienced trauma — which froze the cellular memory of the body — it is necessary to re-experience all the emotions connected to the traumatic experience.

Only then will the hypothalamus react in a way that will result in true healing (the hypothalamus is said to control emotions). There is really no bypassing this, it is a prerequisite for peace on the cellular memory level. Only then can we return to a right relationship with the Self.

There seems to be much confusion about healing. Most people envision healing to be a relaxing and rejuvenating experience. A joyful massage, for example, or a light touch in a body therapy session, or simply a soak in a hot tub. Yet, true healing incorporates much, much more than simply pleasing the senses. As mentioned before, true healing is not for the feint of Heart. It demands courage and the determination to seek out Truth.

I liken our psyche to an iceberg. The tip of the iceberg, its smallest part, rises above the water. The tip refers to the conscious mind. With our conscious mind, we are aware of our thoughts, feelings, and actions. However, the main part of the iceberg lies invisible beneath the surface, which makes it very dangerous for approaching ships. The captain of the ship is never concerned about the visible part but focuses on the potential danger of the Invisible. Likewise, the invisible part of the iceberg is our sub-conscious.

The sub-conscious mind is the matrix for our conscious mind. All that we have ever experienced as too traumatic to remember drops into the sub-conscious. Not knowing what is in there makes the sub-conscious very dangerous. It has tremendous power to destroy our lives. Yet, just as our sub-conscious can destroy, it also has the power to heal us. And more so, our sub-conscious mind has limitless power.

The sub-conscious mind remembers everything. The Akashic Records are accessed via the sub-conscious mind. The conscious mind, however, remembers only a little of our current life and usually nothing of our past lives. Particularly, adults with their interfering minds, have forgotten their past lives, whereas young children might still remember some of their past related to their current life.

Again, all trauma too painful for our conscious mind to bear is being mercifully swallowed up by the sub-conscious. In comparison to the very limited capacity of our conscious mind, the sub-conscious mind is deep and as wide as the largest ocean. All experiences from this lifetime — too painful to remember — are securely stored in the sub-conscious and readily accessible once we tap into the sub-conscious. All feelings, all thoughts and all actions, including all our past-life experiences of every lifetime we've ever lived, are stored in our sub-conscious. Those are securely stored, as well as waiting to be accessed and released.

All feelings, all thoughts and all actions, including all our past-life experiences of every lifetime we've ever lived, are stored in our sub-conscious.

We must remember that our Soul chose all its experiences for its growth towards Enlightenment. Our very own and individual Akashic Record stores it in our human energy field. Hence, we do not need to run far and wide to find out about our past for it is right within us. This is why the HeartPath Re-Alignment is tremendously self-empowering. For we can find out by ourself the truth of all our experiences. We can know why our Soul experienced them, and for what reason of growth. This is the definition of "Enlightenment."

Enlightenment = what lies hidden in the sub-conscious comes into the awareness of the conscious mind.

All that lies hidden in the sub-conscious comes into the awareness of the conscious mind. Hence true knowledge of the Self. The sages of all wisdom traditions claim that true self-knowledge is the key to liberation from Samsara, the never-ending cycle of death and rebirth. That means once liberation is achieved, we can freely choose if we want to come back into the physical body or whether we prefer to remain in Spirit.

All to often, we are tempted to give our power to another authority: oracle readers, psychics, fortune tellers, and so forth for them to tell us who we are, and what happened when, where, and how. If they are genuine and without projecting their own lives and issues, it is our Akashic Record that they access.

Even so, no growth is in that because we are being told. We don't experience it. What someone else says might resonate with us or it might not. But nevertheless, we process the given information with the mind only. The body is not getting involved in remembering and releasing.

The reason why it is imperative we find out for ourselves rather than someone telling us is that all the ailments related to our traumatic experience are being naturally released and health can set in. All seemingly irrational phobias, panic attacks, mental dysfunctions and emotional issues, as well as deep conflicts with God, have their reason and their origin in experiences from the past. Hence, self-empowerment is possible once we see, understand, release, and integrate.

SELF-EMPOWERMENT HAPPENS ONCE WE SEE, UNDERSTAND, RELEASE, AND INTEGRATE

Chapter 15

THE VARIOUS HEALING MODALITIES OF THE HEARTPATH RE-ALIGNMENT

*"Your journey will be much lighter and easier
if you don't carry your past with you."*

~ Brigitte Nicole

The HeartPath Re-Alignment addresses the body, mind, and spirit as a whole. Thus, healing happens naturally and on all levels — emotionally, mentally, physically, and spiritually. This transforms the body and allows any discomfort, ailment, and disease the chance to heal and cure itself.

In my work, as mentioned before, I liken the physical body and its energetic field to an immensely complex bio computer, which contains all information about the individual: their biological structure, their emotional patterns, their mental thought processes, and the active programs governing their lives, as well as their relationship to planet Earth and Spirit. Just as a computer can only function according to its programing, likewise, we need to change our programing in order to heal our lives.

We need to change our programing in order to heal our lives.

Further, our auric field contains the history of our childhood to this present day, all our experiences from the past, past-life experiences, the whole history of our biological parents and ancestors, as well as their life plan chosen by their Soul. By looking at all this information, the cause of whatever ails the individual becomes apparent.

All healings are facilitated strictly under the guidance of the individual's Higher Power. At the base of this healing approach lies the axiom that the power and ability to heal oneself is found within oneself. The direct experience of being One with the Universe and having God as an ally, provides support to re-align with one's initial purpose of existence.

THE POWER AND THE ABILITY
TO HEAL ONESELF
LIES WITHIN

This leads to a fulfilled and peaceful life, thereby becoming a more successful, balanced, and healthy human being. Thus, the HeartPath Re-Alignment restores self-empowerment and guides the participant toward an enlightening and truly transformative experience. The result is reclaiming one's personal power and leadership of the Heart, as well as retrieving one's dream and true purpose in life.

RECLAIM YOUR PERSONAL POWER AND LEADERSHIP OF YOUR HEART

RETRIEVE YOUR DREAM AND TRUE PURPOSE FOR LIFE

The general healing room at the HeartPath Retreat Center

The story the Soul wants to tell needs to be heard and understood

At the start of each healing session, I align the individual with their Divine Source and guide them into a deep state of awareness and facilitate what is needed in order to get to the level of the Soul.

My role as a Soul counselor and facilitator is to hold the space so that the story the Soul wants to tell can unfold and is heard and understood. I have worked with adults of many different nationalities, belief systems and traditions, as well as atheists and I also use the same process with children. Each and every individual is unique, their life circumstances vary and their reactions to those circumstances are different. Therefore, it is necessary to adjust the healing approach to their specific needs.

In the case of trauma, the body has stored emotions resulting from it. Those emotions need to be addressed, re-experienced, and released. Or, if there is self-sabotage in one's life, it is because the subconscious intention is not in alignment with the conscious intention.

TENSU Body Injury Trauma Release

If the presenting complaint is a physical ailment, I will communicate directly with the body to get to the root cause beyond the physical symptoms. In the case of an accident followed by surgery, I work in the TENSU (Japanese for tension) Body Injury Trauma Release. (Compare Part V, Section 1, Chapter 44-46 on TENSU Healing.) TENSU Body Injury Trauma Release Healing accesses the trauma experienced during accidents and injuries and encourages the body to heal by restoring the natural energetic flow.

Wherever a body injury occurs, the body cells become frozen due to shock. An energy cyst is created in that region. No energy can flow in a healthy and natural way; everything is blocked. On an energetic level, that part of the body appears to be "dead." This is often experienced as numbness. Traditional physical therapy brings only slow and sometimes very limited results. By gently working with the injured body part, it's likely that the individual will experience the accident again.

They are "seeing" what happened while the accident occurred, even while they were unconscious. This initiates a very organic healing process. Like a computer that froze, the energy system gets rebooted.

The cells of the body remember the trauma and begin to release it. This experience is oftentimes accompanied by very strong emotional release. The benefit on the body is immediate.

Healings on the Level of the PowerLine

PowerLine healings serve to restore damages caused on the level of the PowerLine. The level of the PowerLine is a much simpler structure than the highly complex level of the auric field and its chakra system. A PowerLine healing is beneficial when a person wants to know and understand their Soul's deepest yearning, connect to their life task, anchor themselves deep within their existence, feel centered within themselves, live their essence and align their personal power, as well as resolve all issues associated with self-sabotage.

As we know, our physical dimension is the third dimension. Our auric field with its chakra system is in the 4th dimension. The PowerLine / Hara level is a deeper dimension and a higher frequency, in the fifth dimension. According to Barbara Ann Brennan's studies,

> "This dimension is the grid and matrix for the human energy field and its chakra system and, thus, for the human body to come into form. This is because the center of the Earth is a vibratory life source.
>
> Our body is a gelatinous form, held together by this one note, the sound the center of the Earth makes. It is this one note with which we have drawn our physical body from our mother, the Earth. It is this one note that holds our body in physical manifestation. Without this one note, we would not have a body. When we change this one note, we change our entire body."

"The one note the center of the Earth makes
holds our body in physical manifestation.
Without this one note,

we would have no body."

To better understand the concept of sound holding shape, it is helpful to look at the experiments in Cymatics[8]. You can Google it and observe the visuals. If one subjects sand particles on a metal plate to particular sound frequencies, the sand instantly aligns in order. Change the sound and the sand formation instantly adjusts to the new sound. Nicola Tesla said,

"If you want to find the secrets of the Universe, think in terms of Energy, Frequency, and Vibration."

The PowerLine level is a laser-like line (sound beam) in the center of our body called the Vertical Power Current, which energetically runs within the center of the spinal cord.

According to the studies of Barbara Ann Brennan, a healthy PowerLine, also called Hara Line or Line of Intention, is deeply anchored in the molten core of the Earth and runs in a straight line up to the physical power center located in the lower abdomen, called the Tan Tien (also called the Dantien), further up in a straight line to the Soul Seat in the center of the body on the level of the sternum (between the Heart Chakra and the Throat Chakra), and continues in a straight line up and clicks into the Point of Individuation, our direct connection to Spirit / Source.

When healthy, the PowerLine extends from about 3 1/2 feet above the head all the way down to the center and core of the Earth, Gaia, our true mother. In each and every way, the PowerLine is the umbilical cord to mother Earth. She welcomed us into this life on planet Earth. She nourishes us with Her food and She takes us back when our body disintegrates.

At its opposite end, 3 1/2 feet above the top of our head, the PowerLine ends as a small upside-down funnel — 1/3 of an inch in diameter — with its point upward and the larger end facing downward over the head. This is our God head, the Individuation Point (ID point). It is the connection to Source / Spirit / God / the Universe, our true father. The ID point contains our purpose for life, our life plan, our destiny.

To be specific, it will not say you are meant to be a in a particular position or choose a certain profession. It is a far grander purpose than simply an occupation. It has to do with your life task, what the Soul set out to learn. Our life plan is no simple undertaking. In fact, the Soul chooses to re-incarnate innumerable times until the set life task — the life task of our Soul, the purpose for our life, our life plan, our destiny — is fulfilled. From body to body, from lifetime to lifetime spanning over many thousands of years, we have evolved into who we presently are. Only after completion of the set life task does the Soul become free.

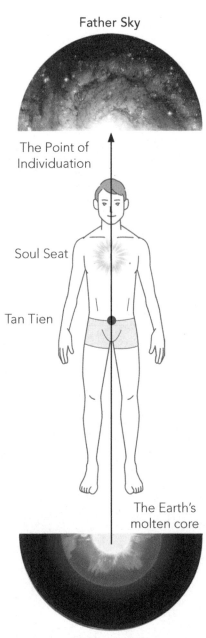

The PowerLine is the center for our spiritual and physical power.

Father Sky

The Point of Individuation

Soul Seat

Tan Tien

The Earth's molten core

Mother Earth

---

[8] Cymatics: The study of the visualizations of sounds. Cymatics analyzes sounds by applying basic principles of wave mechanics. Since sound is a type of wave, it can be displayed through visual media.

It is also possible that the healing might require work on the level in the 5th dimension, the PowerLine, known as the Hara Level or Hara dimension[9]. The Hara[10] refers to a specific area in the lower belly with its qualities of strength, energy, and focused power. It is an area of tremendous intentional power within the physical body that contains the Tan Tien.

The Tan Tien is a golf-size hollow sphere on the energetic level that gets activated with certain physical exercise, like for example, martial arts. It is referred to as the energy center within our body.

The PowerLine / Hara is also a center for spiritual power because it is the level of intentionality, our intention and purpose in life. Our intention is the root and foundation of all we do in the moment.

The book, *The Magus of Java, Teachings of an Authentic Taoist Immortal, the Story of John Chang*, shows an image of Master Chang's powerfully activated yin chi energy with which he is able to produce fire in his hands.

THE POWERLINE IS THE CENTER OF OUR SPIRITUAL AND PHYSICAL POWER

What the rare leaders who are serving the Light exclusively have in common are certain qualities they acquired in a constant purification process from lifetime to lifetime. Their souls have obtained those qualities on their journey in a continuous flow towards perfection. To become a powerful channel of Light requires purity in feeling, thought, and action. It also calls for deep compassion, serving truth regardless of consequences, and living according to the highest ethical principals — a life of virtue and discipline.

I perceive such individuals as having become invincible to destructive forces because their Vertical Power Current has widened beyond its natural size and they are literally standing in a protective, invisible shaft of light. Their PowerLine is naturally aligned, healthy, and balanced due to their pure focus and strength of intention.

The Vertical Power Current, which runs energetically within the center of the spinal cord and connects the various chakras with each other, is naturally aligned, healthy, and balanced due to their pure focus and strength of intention.

TO BECOME A POWERFUL CHANNEL OF LIGHT
REQUIRES PURITY IN FEELING, THOUGHT,
AND ACTION
IT ALSO CALLS FOR DEEP COMPASSION
SERVING TRUTH REGARDLESS
AND LIVING ACCORDING TO THE HIGHEST
ETHICAL PRINCIPLES
A LIFE OF VIRTUE AND DISCIPLINE

[9] All references on the Human Energy Field and the Hara Dimension are from Barbara Ann Brennan's books Hands of Light and Light Emerging.
[10] Hara: Japanese term in martial arts.

Once again, in order to better understand, I liken the path of the Soul to the film roll of a movie, where image after image develops into a whole movie. Every life lived is but one image.

Between these two opposites along the PowerLine there is also the "Seat of the Soul" in the middle of the chest located at the sternum. It's usually approximately 1-2 inches in diameter, but it can expand up to 15 feet during meditation. The Soul Seat carries our deepest longing for what we want to accomplish in our life, for us to find true fulfillment.

Approximately 2 1/2 inches below the navel is a hollow, rubber-like sphere with a membrane,1 1/2 inches in diameter, the Tan Tien, also referred to in martial arts as the area of the Hara. The Tan Tien can contain enormous power beyond the physical because it holds the one note with which we draw our physical body up into manifestation from the center of the Earth.

According to Barbara Brennan's extensive studies, most people's Hara Lines are seriously distorted:

> "Hara Lines of people of other cultures are different from those of Americans. People in different cultures distort their Hara Line in different ways. People within the same culture distort their Hara Line in similar ways. Therefore, people within the same culture suffer in similar ways."

An example of a typically defective PowerLine, which isn't grounded and can be dangling to the side rather than anchoring into the molten core of the Earth, thus unable to pull up the energy of the Earth into the Tan Tien. It can be interrupted between the Tan Tien and the Soul Seat, with the Soul Seat clouded / shrouded and is also not clicked into the Point of Individuation. The different combinations of distorted PowerLines varies according to the individual.

Barbara says this about the Hara Level, which I call the level of the PowerLine:

The Hara exists on a dimension deeper
than the Auric Field with its Chakra System.
It exists on the level of Intentionality.
It is an area of power within the physical body
that contains the Tan Tien.

It is the ONE NOTE with which you have
drawn up your physical body from your mother, the Earth.

It is this ONE NOTE that holds your body
in physical manifestation.
Without the ONE NOTE, you would not have a body.

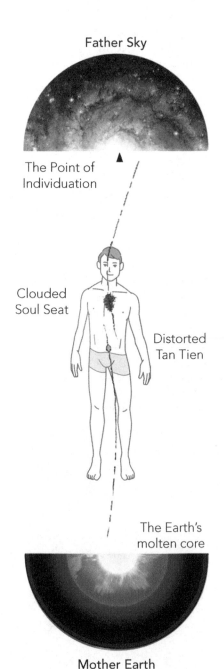

Father Sky

The Point of Individuation

Clouded Soul Seat

Distorted Tan Tien

The Earth's molten core

Mother Earth

When you change this ONE NOTE,
your entire body will change.
Your body is a gelatinous form held together
by this ONE NOTE.
This note is the sound the center of the Earth makes.

Damage on the level of the PowerLine can cause severe damage in our life. For example, individuals are oftentimes unaware that they are not grounded. They might feel like a boat floating in the ocean without an anchor; lacking the emotional connection to this planet and life on Earth. They might search for direction because they are unaware of the reason for their existence and they have zero clue about their purpose in life. They don't feel centered within their own energy. They might feel anger or fear and suffer from chronic depression. They are not in their own personal power.

Often, such individuals have developed a very strong intellect that houses their whole existence. They might be aware or unconscious of their lack of connection to source. Their rational mind explains everything. Life seems useless and ordinary, which causes deep spiritual pain. They might feel a deep yearning but are unable to identify as to what it is they yearn for, especially since they are unable to hear the voice of their Soul or to look at their life task from their Soul level. They

Antique Burmese painting depicting the importance of alignment in the PowerLine

might continually and habitually sabotage their life because their subconscious intention is not in alignment with their conscious intention.

PowerLine healings serve to restore damage caused on the level of the PowerLine. The level of the PowerLine is more simply structured than the highly complex level of the auric field and its chakra system. A PowerLine healing is beneficial when a person wants to know and understand their Soul's deepest yearning, connect to their life task, anchor themselves deep within their existence, feel centered within themselves, live their essence and align their personal power, as well as resolve all issues associated with self-sabotage.

The PowerLine Workout Fitness Program

"Exercise is a celebration of what you body can do.
Not a punishment for what you ate."

~ Women's Health, UK

The PowerLine workout:
The Swim move, done 10 times
in repetition

The PowerLine workout is a series of exercises done in sequences of a minimum of ten repetitions that focus on building core strength, mastering balance, maintaining breath awareness, achieving clarity of mind, improving flexibility, mastering the discipline of endurance and breath control, practicing constant connection to Spirit, and thus developing a healthy and aligned PowerLine. The entire workout takes one and a half to two hours to complete.

The PowerLine Workout was a gift from Spirit in 2007 as a brand new fitness program that pulls its strength from the focused mind and incorporates it into a disciplined body movement building core strength while mastering balance. I regard it as the PowerLine healing in physical form. It consists of two programs: the Basic Program and the Advanced Program.

These fitness programs are designed to create alignment of purpose and balance within oneself with the aim of achieving fitness in body, clarity of mind, and connection to Spirit. It is therefore a meditation-in-movement, a workout meditation, and perhaps THE Western answer to Eastern disciplines like Yoga and Tai Chi. It is the fusion of ancient wisdom and modern movement.

All the exercises of the Basic Program are done on a floor mat to train the body in the specific movements. Special attention is placed on precise, slow, repetitive moves in order to build body endurance. Focus is on breath awareness and muscle release during relaxation after each exercise sequence. Once all movements have been sufficiently mastered, one can progress to the exercises of the Advanced Program, which involves a core balancing device, the PowerLine disk.

The heart and core of the PowerLine Workout Program derives from the notion of an existing "PowerLine" (in Eastern cultures called the Hara Line) in the human body. It runs energetically along the spine and extends beyond. With focus and "high sensory perception," this PowerLine can be perceived as moving down to the center of the Earth and connecting up to One's Source, toward the Cosmos, the Divine.

It's a sad fact that most people's PowerLine is damaged in one way or another. Some are disconnected from the Source, some don't extend down into the earth, others are torn in-between, and some are distorted in other ways and not correctly aligned.

A damaged PowerLine always affects all areas of one's life from physical health to the emotional wellbeing, mental clarity, and spiritual consciousness of the individual. With awareness, focus and discipline, the PowerLine can be restored and re-aligned to its natural healthy state. The PowerLine Workout was designed with this intention.

My personal experience in working out at the local gym has shown me that my body responds badly to the use of fitness machines and weightlifting devices. I developed aches and pains, particularly in my shoulders, lower arms, and wrists.

Nevertheless, I was determined to find an ultimate workout for my body to get truly strong, toned and fit, using only my own body weight. At some point, I was introduced to a balancing board. As I started to work out on my own, a series of exercises came through ready to share with you.

You will feel it. With dedication to the PowerLine Workout, you will soon experience the core of your body strengthen and your muscles getting toned. You will notice a natural and dramatic increase of your overall body fitness and an enhanced clarity of mind, all resulting from setting your intention on your PowerLine.

As you are getting familiar with your exercises, you will transfer what you are learning in the exercise program into your daily life. You will get the feeling of standing in your own power and you will literally learn to balance your power with grace. As a result, your life will become more balanced and you will experience centeredness within yourself.

The Arrow move

PART IV

GENERAL CASE STUDIES

"Some people,
upon hearing your story
will contract.

Others, upon hearing your story,
will expand.

Nevertheless, this is how you will know."
~ Anonymous

The general case studies covered in this Part are divided into four categories:

- Physical Ailments

- Emotional Trauma

- Mental Conditions

- Spiritual Realizations

All the healing modalities applied were developed in my own healing practice in the course of thirty years as a result of my vast experience with my clientele. These are the HeartPath Re-Alignment healing approach and Maha Intensive, as well as healings on the level of the PowerLine and TENSU Body Injury Trauma Release healings.

My specialty and the primary focus of my work is a dialog process with the Sub-Conscious on the level of the Soul. My healing method is a synthesis of the various learned techniques which, over time and work experience, developed into my own healing modalities as mentioned above and described in detail in Part III, Section 3, Chapter 13: the HeartPath Re-Alignment with its Maha Intensive, the PowerLine Healing, and the TENSU Body Injury Trauma Release Healing).

It is important to point out that my training is not in psychotherapy, therefore, I don't follow the classic rules for therapists. I have worked with strangers, friends, and even family members and all the work I do with clients follows strict confidentiality rules.

After completing a basic training in psycho-spiritual session work at the Deva Foundation, NM, I went on to study Barbara Brennan's method of energy Chelation at the Barbara Brennan School of Healing in Long Island, NY. I also completed a 3-month training in Cranio-Sacral Therapy at the Osho Institute in Pune, India.

Because I do not run a therapy practice, my clients do not see me on a regular base as is the case in classic therapy sessions. A great number of my clients seek me out to "fix a problem," so to speak. Even though I always do follow ups and send a feedback questionnaire in order to let me know how they are doing following healings, I oftentimes do not hear back once the problem has been "fixed." Therefore, in some cases I am able to provide information as to how the work with me has affected their lives and healed their ailments, while in other cases, I am not able to provide such information.

The case studies presented are but a small sampling of the wide range of issues and situations clients come to me with. They do, however, provide insight into life challenges that many of us have faced, as well as describe ways in which I approach working with and resolving those challenges.

Chapter 16

ROBERT: THE 8-YEAR-OLD BOY WITH AN AGGRESSIVE BRAIN TUMOR

It is usually the case that young children who become sick — not children born sick — are subject to the emotional challenges of their parents. They are victims of the tension field between their father and mother.

Therefore, when Janine, the mother of an eight-year-old boy requested to schedule healing sessions for their son, my requirement was that I needed to work simultaneously with both parents as well. The boy, I shall call him Robert, was suffering from a very aggressive brain tumor the size of a fist located at the base of his skull just above his neck.

The first time the tumor was removed, it was followed by chemotherapy. Within six months, the malicious tumor had regrown to the same size. Again, Robert underwent surgery. This time, the treatment was radiation. Half a year later the tumor had grown back to its full size. The doctors were at a loss and declared that, unfortunately, there was no hope for a cure. Little Robert would have no chance to live.

The family drove more than six hours from Germany to my healing practice. They settled into a nearby hotel and then came to see me. Robert was bald, walked on crutches, and his eyes were crossed. I learned that Robert's mom, Janine, had insisted seeking out alternative treatments while the father, Fritz, remained extremely skeptical. I suggested that the first appointment every morning belonged to Robert.

After spending time listening to how Robert was experiencing his life and dealing with his ailment, we started to work. During the initial breathing meditation for relaxation, I observed that Robert's breathing pattern also needed attention. It was forced, abrupt, and very disharmonious. Thanks to this little boy, I learned that illness can be detected in the breathing pattern of a person.

Further on, I guided Robert to visualize entering his head and going to the location of the tumor. He was to explore and describe what was going on in there. He worked well and deep. He was able to hold his focus with a good amount of concentration. In the course of our healings together, he learned to mount an army of little light warriors to fight against the cancer cells. A great battle unfolded every day, but the light warriors were victorious.

The second daily healing session was with Janine. Over three days, she processed the suppressed memories of her childhood sexual abuse by her father. There was much emotional release. During our last session, I taught Janine how she could, when she was back home, help her boy by the "laying on of hands" as she was acquainted with basic Reiki skills.

Fritz, Robert's dad, initial attitude towards the work was arrogance. He had no inkling of his spiritual nature. He was a non-believer of all this "hocus-pocus" nonsense, as he called it. But for the love of his son, he was willing to remain open to allow whatever would happen. Spirit is merciful, indeed. Because if there was any help for little Robert, he very much needed the support of not only his mom but also his dad.

Contrary to Fritz's ignorance, he had a deep spiritual experience. The next day, Fritz reported that he had felt very hot from the inside out, like he was burning alive. For the entire night, he had to remain on the balcony outside their room, without closing an eye. It was the middle of winter in Switzerland, and Swiss winters are nasty.

The second and third healing sessions also resulted in very spiritual experiences. I noticed that Fritz had a great capacity for sustained mental focus. In the last healing session, I taught him how he could guide Robert every day with mental exercises to fight the cancer cells in his head.

Fritz was exhausted. The poor man had not slept for four days and nights as he spent every night outside on the balcony burning up with fire. I explained to him that he was having a Kundalini[11] experience, hence the uncontrollable heat.

After termination of the four-day healing session, Robert was walking without crutches, and for short amounts of time was able to look with his eyes uncrossed. Fourteen days later, Robert had a scheduled doctor's appointment at the hospital. The CT scan showed no trace of the tumor. His doctor couldn't believe it and suspected a technical failure with the machine.

The procedure was repeated. Again, the result showed no tumor. The brain specialist called in other doctors. They were all flabbergasted and decided to send Robert for yet another diagnosis to a different hospital. The parents declined, but they didn't share any information about the healing treatments they had undergone. They feared ridicule, skepticism, and non-belief. Their son was cured and nothing else mattered.

Yet, unfortunately, Robert's miraculous healing result took a sad turn. During my work with the three of them, Spirit gave me the message that after eight months all three of them must return for another healing

---

[11] A Kundalini awakening is a remarkably powerful spiritual experience, one that yogis and practitioners spend years preparing for. It is frequently reported to be a distinct feeling of an electric current running along the spine.

session cycle. I mentioned this during our final shared talk. They all agreed. Two months later, I saw father and son again as they participated in a weekend wilderness experience of rowing and rock climbing that I had organized for my child patients and their parents. Robert's hair had grown back, he ran and played and climbed and rowed. In short, he behaved in every way like a healthy boy his age.

Because of the radical healing results, the parents ignored their agreement to reschedule. Two years later, they called for an emergency session cycle. The tumor had returned. This time, Spirit told me it was too late — another 4-day session cycle would lead to no results. I learned then how imperative it is to listen to the messages of Spirit, and that when ignored, the prize will be bitter.

Only years later did I learn that Robert's father Fritz kept maintaining a long-term, extra-marital relationship, which he kept secret from his wife. Little Robert unconsciously tried to control the dynamics between his parents to keep them together, but failed.

Every part of our body possesses a certain quality and is responsible for a certain emotional response. The brain is our control center where we mentally process all that is going on in our lives. Ailments of the brain have to do with control. In general, the brain also has to do with wrong thinking. What type of wrong thinking remains to be discovered and released, in order for health to return.

What could possibly be the deeper underlying reasons for an eight-year-old child to manifest a severely aggressive brain tumor? Or any life-threatening disease for that matter? When a tragedy of this kind hits an innocent child, it is only natural that we get angry and argue with God because it seems so unfair. We blame God and hold Him responsible for such injustice. Or we try to negotiate, ask for more time, for this and that. It is immensely hard to be dealing with the challenge of a very ill child. Faith is often the very last hope to keep us sane when the doctors say there is no more they can do.

If we look at the situation from a higher perspective, we might begin to understand that all life is interconnected, an energetic wave affecting everything else. We might then see there is no God out there to punish or revenge. Rather, it can be explained by the law of cause and effect: Karma.

Here is an explanation about what I have observed in my healing practice over the course of my vast working experience. Children being born with birth defects most likely were battling the same challenge in their previous incarnation or an incarnation energetically linked to their present life. But children developing an illness later are most likely subject to the tension field in their parents' environment.

Chapter 17

INGRID: THE WOMAN WHO LOST HER SENSE OF TASTE AND SMELL

While working in Germany, Ingrid, a woman in her early sixties, signed up for healing work. Her presenting complaint was that she had undergone nose surgery more than twenty years ago due to nasal breathing difficulty. The procedure was performed with local anesthesia. As a result of the surgery, she had lost her taste and smell, which was bothering her greatly. She shared that whatever she ate, it all tasted like cardboard. Ingrid remembered the smell and taste of different foods but she couldn't smell or taste them anymore. She couldn't smell the scent of a flower or any less-attractive odors. She had lost it all. This made her deeply insecure to a degree where she felt alienated from life.

While in a deeply relaxed state, I guided her to the time before the nasal surgery. She once again experienced great difficulty in breathing through her nose. She commented that she was almost exclusively breathing through her mouth. At night, she snored loudly. Her siblings and classmates ridiculed her because her mouth was constantly open. She became an outsider.

But when I asked her if she could describe the scent of the forest after a rain, she vividly described it. The same when I asked her to describe the taste of spaghetti bolognese and the smell of a hot cup of coffee. She did so accurately. We then moved forward to the time of the surgery.

She described the surgeon injecting the anesthesia. She could smell it and she hated the smell. It was incredibly pungent to her to the degree where, inwardly, she forced her nose to close to stop smelling this horrible substance invading her body.

I suggested for her to keep her nose open, by focusing on the ugly smell entering her nose and body even though her system revolted. I encouraged her to continuously keep smelling the ugly smell and endure the obnoxious sensation. She hated it and all her cells rebelled against it. It was torture for her. But she kept her nose open during the entire procedure.

Coming out of the experience, she commented with, "Wow, what was all that about?!" I offered her water and a mint gum. Tasting the gum, she said, astounded, "How refreshing! I smell mint. I can taste it, it's peppermint. We sat a bit longer while she recovered from the shock of the instant cure of her taste buds returning.

Such is the miracle of our body intelligence and such is the power of our mind. We can will our body to do something and it obeys. I requested that she contact me in a week to report if her senses of taste and smell had fully returned and stayed. When she called me, she commented that she had a new life and was overjoyed with her newly regained experience of being able to taste and smell again.

Chapter 18

JUDY'S ALMOST MISCARRIAGE

I was called to the house of a student of mine who was in her fourth month of pregnancy. She had lost a baby prior to this pregnancy. Another potential miscarriage was unbearable to contemplate, yet she faced the same fate once more.

When I arrived, Judy stepped out the door with her cosmetic travel bag in hand and ready to rush to the hospital. I gently ushered her back inside and said, "Judy, let's work. There is a reason for this." Luckily, Judy trusted me and lay down on the couch. After a short period of guiding her deep within, I asked her guidance, the Holy Mother, to show her the reason for her distress that threatened the life of the unborn baby.

The Holy Mother took Judy's hand and led her into her marriage. Judy saw from a higher perspective the extremely disturbing relationship between Adam, her husband, and her. They had been high school sweethearts, and decided to marry against the will of her parents. Judy's father not only denied his blessing for the union, he also told Judy, that from then on, she was on her own and never to come home and bother him if there were any issues. Judy knew well that by marrying Adam she was going to be without any moral support from her parents.

Adam, a talented jazz musician with a promising career, and Judy, a professional singer, were deeply in love. At the time of their commitment, Judy was unaware that her husband was suffering from a very severe anxiety disorder. Adam's mother kept covering it up. Soon into the marriage, Adam suffered daily panic attacks. His mother kept protecting him and blamed Judy for his condition. In the eyes of Adam's family, Judy became the scapegoat for Adam's anxiety disorder. She was terribly wronged and she suffered much.

By now, Adam was in therapy and under heavy prescription medication for his mental illness. Adam also had developed a severe drinking disorder, which made his situation all the worse. Yet, in the eyes of Adam's family — and especially his mother — it was all Judy's fault. For many years, they blamed Judy as the cause for his mental illness.

Adam's family is fundamentalist Christian. As you might have guessed, Adam was his mother's favorite. She idealized her son and kept not only enabling his behavior but also kept encouraging him in his distorted world views. In their marriage, Adam turned into a screaming, abusive, and controlling tyrant. In his presence, Judy was forced to burn her books of healing and angels. When Judy got pregnant for the second time, their marriage was seriously in danger of falling apart.

During the healing, the Holy Mother showed Judy how the severe dysfunction of their marriage had led to her first miscarriage. I personally felt this was a blessing in disguise because it could have pointed Judy toward realizing the incompatibility of their relationship. And knowing Judy, she would never want to be a single mom.

But Judy was not ready for a divorce. Instead, they decided she should get pregnant again. When she did within the year, they were sure it was their baby giving it a second try. And this time, thanks to the healing and looking at the underlying reasons for her distress, Judy did not have another miscarriage. Judy gave birth to a healthy baby girl, Genevieve. In another chapter, I will describe what happened from then on, and Judy's long and arduous path towards healing her life.

Little Genevieve was one-and-a-half years old, when Judy and Adam finally separated. A week later, Judy's parents came to visit. After announcing to them she was getting a divorce, her father, that very same night, fell asleep in the arms of his wife and never woke up again. There had been no symptoms of any kind of discomfort or disease. Yet, the parallels between her father and her husband later became evident in losing both at the same time.

Now, thirteen years later, Judy wrote me, "It is such a great honor that you include this deep and personal story of mine in your book. It feels like full circle to have gone through such an experience and to now see my healthy baby girl become a prospective student of your work. Imagine if you had not done this very powerful session with me, and dear Genevieve might not have come through in this lifetime?! My next chapter in life is truly because of you, your amazing healing work, and the realignment process helping me to become who I am today — because without this healing, I might have never fully seen the dysfunction and stayed with him."

Chapter 19

GUDRUN: THE HEAVY CURSE OF FIFTY-SEVEN ABORTIONS

Gudrun, a German woman past menopause, came to see me. During the initial interview, she confided that she had aborted fifty-seven times. Though she would have wanted children, her husband refused to start a family. Apparently, Gudrun was extremely fertile. Every time she became pregnant, her husband demanded that she have an abortion. He did not allow her to take contraceptives. He was also not allowing her to have her uterus removed. He demanded daily sex but was unwilling to undergo sterilization himself.

What I heard was shocking. I remarked that her husband was a control freak of the highest order and inquired why in the world she stayed with him. She claimed they had gone through a lot together and that they only had each other, no family or friends.

I asked Gudrun if she had ever thought of the possibility that all the different times she got pregnant could have been one and the same Soul trying desperately to incarnate and be with her? Gudrun had never thought of that. She remarked that such a possibility would make it all the more terrible. I suspected deep Karma at the core of all the abortions, which she expressed as her presenting complaint. All these fetuses she had aborted were haunting her. Her sleep was regularly interrupted by intense nightmares. She intuited that she was victim to a curse.

In our work together, Gudrun saw herself in a past life. She was a female acquainted with herbs and other techniques. She had many women come to her seeking an abortion, women of different ages and life circumstances. They were in a panic for being pregnant. To them, abortion was the only solution, Gudrun their only hope.

Her conscience weighed heavily on her for killing all those lives when weighed against those women breaking down sobbing and giving her all kinds of reasons why, unfortunately, the baby could not live. Those were pregnancies out of wedlock, forbidden relationships of adultery, incest, rape, and the like.

When those women sought her out early into their pregnancy, she aborted with herbal tinctures. When the pregnancy was more advanced, she inserted a knitting needle through the vagina and up the cervix into the uterus. If the cervix was missed, the uterus wall got perforated, which resulted in complications like heavy bleeding, infection, and sometimes with death. The responsibility of having the death of those women on her conscience, weighed even heavier than the abortions of all those fetuses.

She didn't want to do this dirty work anymore. But there was no one else who would do it. And those women were desperate and begged her, "Please, please, please! This one more time," again and again. Gudrun, in that past life, saw herself getting older and older, unable to leave that vicious cycle. Upon dying, her last thought was, "Oh my God, forgive me. I have sinned. I will be cursed."

When I asked Gudrun's Higher Self why this past life was shown to her, Gudrun got the following answer: Because she had caused the death of all these lives, as a consequence, she herself did not deserve to have children in this life.

The curse was her self-imposed punishment to balance her wrongdoings. Gudrun sobbed deeply upon this realization. It all made sense to her. The life her Soul had chosen, the husband she had chosen, his controlling demeanor over her and her body, the pattern they had lived. With her husband as her mate, Gudrun's Soul had chosen the perfect match to prevent her desire so that Karma could do its work.

Then Gudrun asked her Higher Self if she would stay cursed into all eternity. The answer she received was: "As soon as she has paid for every single death she had caused, the Karma would be balanced and the curse would be lifted." Then she asked if the fifty-seven abortions in her present lifetime would also be punished. The answer again was that it was part of the curse from the previous life. In her current life, Ingrid was punishing herself for her wrongdoings from her past life. By not being able to bear children in this life, she had to get rid of them on her own by aborting them.

Gudrun kept sobbing silently. After a long while, her tears ceased a bit and she kept getting lost in her thoughts. I suggested she ask if her wish to become a mother would ever be fulfilled. The answer she got was that maybe in her next life she would be allowed to become a mother.

Now, Gudrun broke down sobbing uncontrollably. The prospect of becoming a mother, not this time but maybe the next time she incarnated, was overwhelmingly fulfilling to her. She spoke of the sacred experience of motherhood. How all life is sacred and should be honored. All the bitter tears she had kept within, of never having been allowed to fully carry one of her pregnancies and give birth to her child, started to release. She realized how deeply she wished to have a family. Gudrun was way past menopause. She realized that her Karma in this lifetime was to balance out her wrongdoings from her past life and the price she paid was to remain childless.

Chapter 20

RAMON'S PSYCHIC HIP SURGERY

I met Ramon and his life-partner in Buenos Aires, where I spent time to further my tango studies. Ramon became my principal dance instructor at a well-established tango school. Though only in his late twenties at the time, he was for nine years the dance partner of the owner of the school and was considered one of the world's most renowned dance performers. Ramon is also a fantastic teacher.

In 2019, Ramon and his life partner were on a trip around the world. They started off in Australia, then on to New Zealand and Hawaii. From Hawaii, they spent two months here at my HeartPath Retreat Center. Both of them had undergone healing sessions with me in Buenos Aires and they expressed interest in the PowerLine Healing & PowerLine Workout Training Certification Program. The morning program consists of the workout, an intense, 4-hour session each day.

Ramon described a block in his right hip that caused him quite a bit of discomfort. It impacted his mobility during the exercises and reduced his movements quite a bit. He shared that as a young boy of eight, his mom took him to get vaccinated. The doctor gave him the shot at his right hip. As a result, a black tumor the size of a fist developed on his hip. It needed to be surgically removed. From then on, Ramon always felt his right leg was shorter than his left leg. While dancing, it caused him a great deal of effort to move evenly and balance it out so that this handicap would stay unnoticed. With the PowerLine workout, this issue started to surface as the pain became intense.

I suggested a body healing session. Ramon regressed to the time of the vaccination and shortly after when the tumor started to grow. We moved forward to the time of the surgery when the tumor was cut out. He described the weird sensation of his right leg having shortened.

I could perceive a string on the energetic level that confirmed Ramon's sensation of his shortened right leg. This energetic string pulled the hip and leg together. Energetically, it looked like a shortened tendon.

I prepared Ramon for the upcoming surgery by telling him what I would do. I then took a light sword and energetically cut the string that kept pulling Ramon's leg higher and thus made him feel that it was shorter. It took a moment for Ramon to take a deep breath. Then he reported that he no longer felt the pull on his right leg. He sat up and then stood on his feet and walked several steps. He said both legs were now even and had the same length. For the remainder of the PowerLine workout, Ramon had no more pain in his right hip and his mobility was now evenly balanced between both legs.

Chapter 21

Gloria: When Shit is Finally Released

Gloria was one of the women whom I had met while I was on tour working in Monterey, Mexico. Professionally, she is an architect. She signed up for the Maha Intensive and we agreed on a date when she would travel here to the HeartPath Retreat Center.

During the initial interview, Gloria shared that she was taking a number of different prescription medications for fiebre de Malta (brucellosis), fiebre de dengue (dengue fever, breakbone fever), typhus, Proteus syndrome, and allergies. But she was dealing with more physical symptoms of chronic bronchitis, urinary tract infections, arteriosclerosis and lower back pain due to scoliosis.

Gloria spoke at length about her marriage of nineteen years as a very conflicted one. The relationship with her husband had mystified her during their whole time being married until just before her husband passed away.

They were both architects working together in their firm, co-living partners, and good friends. They rarely had sex, though he always treated her with kindness, respect, and affection. She always blamed herself for his lack of sexual interest and her image of self and her self-worth suffered greatly. When he became seriously ill, she took good care of him to the best of her capabilities.

On his death bed, he lifted the veil of confusion and confided that he was gay. She was in huge shock. For nineteen years, she had blamed herself, had tortured herself with self-doubt, had cried bitter tears because she could not find fulfillment as a woman. But she had never, ever thought about the possibility of him being homosexual.

In our work together, she processed all the unresolved feelings she had never allowed herself to feel. The first layer was anger for having been misled. The anger against her husband was released. The second layer brought forth a great deal of sadness for having lost her best years in a marriage that did not bring fulfillment. This brought forth sadness and compassion for her husband who secretly had lived his life undercover.

The next layer revealed love and gratitude for her husband who had always treated her kindly, who had never exposed his tendencies in society and their circle of friends. No one had ever known. Up to the moment of her healing work with me, Gloria had not shared her husband's secret with anyone, not even her best friend.

We were mid-way into the healing work when I knocked on Gloria's bedroom door here at the HeartPath Retreat Center. Gloria opened the door and burst out with, "Since yesterday night, I have pooped five times, every time the amount of a whole cow dung." For the remaining days, Gloria's bowel movements continued to happen several times a day, every time a huge amount. Gloria kept saying that she had no clue where all the shit was coming from, and how in the world her intestines had stored such a huge amount up to now.

She remarked that she must have lost more than twenty pounds. Gloria was a slender woman with zero body fat and small breasts. Three weeks upon returning home to Mexico, Gloria called and reported that all her physical conditions and accompanying symptoms had ceased and that her doctor had released her from all medications except malaria for when she suffered from a future malaria attack.

Chapter 22

THE REVENGE OF A CACTUS

The following true account I did not personally experience in my healing practice. It is the story coming from the practice of a friend of mine, a homeopath. She shared that Nadine came into her healing practice. Her leg was severely swollen. Her husband had driven her to the emergency room because within two days the swelling had not subsided but worsened.

The doctors checked Nadine's blood and did other analyses but were mystified by what could possibly be the cause of the severe swelling. She was in much pain and unable to walk. The doctors decided to amputate her leg in an attempt to save her life.

In a last hope to save her leg, Nadine's husband drove her to the practice of my friend. She did her own testing and asked questions but could not find out what could possibly be the reason of this serious condition. My friend kept on asking about their life, their life circumstances, their family and living situation, and their home. Nothing they said led to any possible clues.

My friend didn't give up asking questions. She asked about any important event during the days prior to the swelling of the leg. Nothing to report. They said they loved their home, they loved their children. Nadine reported that she particularly enjoyed taking care of her plants, at which point her husband remarked, "Yes, but you hated the cactus and trimmed it so much there was barely anything left."

My homeopath friend's ears started to ring. She asked Nadine to describe what she had done. Nadine said she had never liked that cactus. It had been given to her as a gift. Over the years, it had grown a lot and had always been a nuisance to her. Therefore, recently, she decided to almost completely cut it off. She remembered that when it fell down, a couple of spines stuck to her leg. She had removed them by pulling them out. Now the homeopath knew what to do and gave Nadine the remedy for it. The swelling subsided and Nadine's leg was saved.

This story teaches us that consciousness is in all living things and beings. All life is sacred and must be treated with reverence and respect. Even seemingly lower-level creatures like plants need to be loved and protected.[12]

---

[12] The book *Nature Spirits and What They Say: Messages from Elemental and Nature Beings* by Verena Stael von Holstein speaks about the knowledge and wisdom of nature spirits.

When the Soul Calls: True Stories of Deep Healing and Transformation

Chapter 23

ISABELLA: THE DEEPER REASON FOR HER SWEAT GLAND REMOVAL

One of Isabella's presenting complaints was that she had undergone surgery a few years ago to remove her sweat glands due to intense uncontrollable transpiration. As a result, she no longer sweat excessively but she was unable to lift her arms without them immediately turning numb. Therefore, a second surgery was performed yet it led to no results. It seemed she would never again be able to lift her arms without them instantly turning numb.

During her third healing session with me, Isabella saw herself as a young woman. The scenery was Europe in the Middle Age. From a distance she saw a large plaza with the populace all gathered awaiting a spectacle. She saw her mother sobbing and leaning on her father. She recognized other people from her community. In the middle of the plaza a tall pole had been erected. A number of young men were piling up wood for a large bonfire. They were overseen by some church clerks in dark robes. She described the scene in great detail and emotionally detached.

Upon asking her from where she was seeing this, she realized she was imprisoned in a dungeon. All of a sudden, she started screaming in realizing that the pile of wood was being prepared for her. They were going to come for her! She was terrified, petrified. She kept screaming and sobbing in panic. Her breathing became very heavy and forced. Men came and pulled her out and dragged her out of the dungeon and over to the pole where they tied her up. No amount of screaming and protesting helped.

Isabella was reliving this experience with her whole being as if it were happening right then. The pile of wood was set on fire. The heat was unbearable. Isabella started coughing uncontrollably. The smoke suffocated her as the fire quickly consumed the dry wood and tongues of fire crawled up to where she was tied to the pole to consume her body. She saw herself falling unconscious.

Her spirit left her body and all of a sudden there was tremendous peace. She started to see it all from above. She was no longer in her body. There was no pain, her body didn't suffer anymore. She looked at the crowd that had witnessed her being burnt alive. I regressed her further back so she could see what had led up to this unfortunate fate. She saw herself enjoying a peaceful and tranquil life, wandering in the forest and strolling the meadows to collect all kinds of herbs she prepared as teas, balms, and tinctures. The populace called her to tame high fevers and cure other maladies. She aided as a midwife as well.

The next day, Isabella arrived for the next healing session. We talked about her experience from the day before and she expressed her sentiments and gave her comments. She spoke about the pile of wood for the bonfire and how for the longest time, she had zero clue that they were going to burn her at the stake. She saw all those people gathered and had the feeling that it was for a spectacle but she was unaware that her burning alive was going to be the spectacle. She also spoke about how peaceful all of a sudden everything was and there was no more pain once she had crossed over to the other side.

The entire time Isabella explained this, she leaned comfortably into the couch in a very relaxed way opposite from where I sat. I kept observing her position for about half an hour. She had her arms all the way up and folded comfortably behind her head.

After a while, I asked how her arms were doing. Only now did she realize her position and become aware that there was no more numbness. She realized that her sweat glands had produced excessive sweat due to her past life when she was burnt alive at the stake. Her cells had released the memory during the previous day's experience when she re-lived her pain and released her terror. She regretted having undergone the two surgeries, which could have been avoided had she had only found her way to my healing practice earlier.

Chapter 24

PETS AS EMOTIONAL FILTERS OF THEIR OWNERS: THE HEALING OF COOKIE

The following is the account of my former student and assistant, whom I'll call Judy, and her recent experience with her dog Cookie. Judy is currently the lead accountant on a popular TV show and way too overloaded with her work obligations. I'm including her story in order to bring awareness to the fact that when we are choosing to become pet owners, be it a dog or a cat, we don't just get a companion. We are getting a creature with a Soul that becomes subject to how we deal with life — a being that will process and filter all our unresolved negative emotions and thoughts. Here is Judy's story as she told it to me in her own words:

> **June 15:** As Cookie lay on the bed, I centered myself and put my attention on my Heart. I began breathing deeply feeling the expansion of my breath and my energy field. As I tuned into my channel, I expanded my awareness and kept breathing into the flow of my channel. I felt blocked in my sacral, root, and crown chakras. I prayed and continued to breathe, asking my angels to bring their presence into the healing and please be with Cookie and me, so that I could see what needed to be shown.
>
> My heart was breaking, and I feared my very depleted and blocked system would not allow me to open as much as I needed to in order to do anything to help Cookie. I knew the significance of two enlarged lymph node tumors, most likely cancerous. I have never had a dog more than ten years old with cancer survive, and Cookie had just turned eleven. Also, my current life circumstances and sacrifices were preventing me from caring for Cookie. Andre was taking care of him.
>
> After my long days of work, even something as simple as walking Cookie 2-3 times a day felt like a chore, overwhelming, and adding to the daily pressures in my life. I missed having a house where he could run and be free. In my townhouse complex, he had to be walked on a leash.
>
> I felt much guilt having an animal I love so much, yet dependent on others to care for it. At times, Cookie's constant barking and neediness caused me to "snap" at the end of the day after hours and hours of being in a high-pressure environment, which caused me much anxiety. I often have to take CBD drops to calm my nerves.

As I tuned in to Cookie, the space above my crown chakra continued to expand, yet I felt how tired I was, how drained. I put both of my hands on each side of Cookie's neck where the bulging lymph nodes were remembering that the vet said the enlarged lymph node in his hind leg was also a concern. I breathed and continued tuning in allowing my breath to carry energy channeling through my hands. I began to move the energy and "sense" the tumors. They were huge black globs, thicker than mucus and sticky like tar. I knew right away it was all related to me and the festering anger I felt within.

I started sobbing and sobbing, coming to the realization that Cookie had been "filtering" so much of my inner turmoil that he had black masses in his body. I asked for the masses on his neck to speak to me and reveal what they needed me to understand, all the while breathing very deeply and bringing the energy down from the divine, praying to Jesus to please heal Cookie.

Truthfully, I did not want Cookie to leave the planet and knew he would sacrifice himself in order to relieve me of any pressure, overwhelm, and stress that he could. As I filled his energy field by "laying on my hands," he became extremely calm, "melting" into me. I felt a peacefulness come over his system, and I started having visions. The black masses showed me incidents of me enraged and exploding. The masses were toxic, like poison, and I saw what a "poisoned" person I had become filled with bitterness and rage.

I cried and cried with the realization that Cookie had taken this on so that I wouldn't have to. The tumors showed me a dark room, an empty chamber of dimmed crystals and black tourmaline. I asked the tumors what the message was that they carried. I heard, "I'm dead." I wasn't ready for Cookie or myself to die! The more I cried and brought energy through the channel, the more relaxed Cookie became. It was the closest I ever felt to him, as he had always been my daughter Genevieve's dog.

With the deep realization of how much I wanted to live, and how much I wanted Cookie to live, I saw the black sticky goo was becoming permeable and malleable. So, I picked up one of the black tourmalines in the chamber and with intention began visualizing the black tumor on his left side, drawing out the black goo from the lymph node.

It took a long time, probably an hour for both lymph nodes to drain and be cleaned out energetically, all the while transforming the goo into light as it was absorbed into the black tourmaline. Cookie was snoring and in a deep sleep.

I moved my hand positions to his spine and neck and asked for any remaining presence of the black goo to tell me what else it needed for healing.

As I cried, I told Cookie over and over again I wanted him to live, and I was going to change my life. I asked him to please stay until Genevieve finished high school and that our lives would not be the same without him.

About two hours later, fatigue began setting in. I didn't know if I had done enough, yet the realization of how much anger, bitterness, rage, and guilt I was carrying was in fact "killing" both of us. I was so angry my life had taken a turn far away from joy, fulfillment, and total alignment. My immune system and Cookie's were taking a beating.

I could no longer filter out the "bad," the "toxins," the "dark energy" in my life anymore, and had to come to terms with the fact that it was not going to get better unless from that moment forward I stopped the "yelling" internally and externally in my life, and started "loving" again. I had to open myself, allow the anger and rage to filter out of my life and fill my emptiness with healing and love.

I thanked Cookie, my angels, Jesus, and the tumors for their powerful message for my life — and asked that this healing bring healing to all that is.

June 16: After another long day of work, now filled with worry that Genevieve's dog was exiting and the impact that would have on her, I laid Cookie on the bed and begin breathing and moving my energy, expanding my field out into the universe, seeing myself as a ray of light, continuing to breathe deeper and deeper. I was so tired and emotionally drained from the day. I felt weak, yet told Cookie over and over that I truly wanted him to stay and how much I loved him.

Earlier during the day, each time I started to feel like I was in a pressure cooker or felt deep resentment and anger, I would breathe into my energetic channel and move the energy out, surrendering to Jesus and my angels. I started to become increasingly aware of how much negativity I was exuding.

Each time I felt stressed, I stayed present with it, and instead of bursting out or holding back and internalizing, I gently, calmly breathed it out and thanked Cookie for reminding me who I am, that I'm connected to the Divine, made of the Divine, the Divine lives in me and I don't need to endlessly suffer. I worked with Cookie's energy, tuned in, and again brought my awareness into my hands, placing them on his neck, cupping them over the huge tumors on each side, feeling his swollen glands, fearful, worried, and sad. I prayed that whatever needed to be shown, would be revealed.

As the energy flowed through the channel[13] into my hands, I filled his system with the higher vibrations moving through me, and asked for his tumors to show me what I needed to see. I felt the "black poison" of the previous day's healing was now cloudy and thin vs. thick and goopy. I thanked the black poison for the prior message and asked what was needed for healing.

I saw Cookie running in the grass without a leash, yet tied to a chain. I decided then and there that he was going to live his last days without a leash with plenty of time and freedom to run around and explore. I saw moving houses soon, and how stagnant I had become. The constant race against time, being buried by life, and the daily anguish of not feeling supported in my life nor having my needs met, the constant pressure of having to do it all by myself.

As I tuned into the tumors, more images came, certain instances of frustration and times I verbally attacked Andre. I allowed it all to come up and deeply felt each vision and the guilt associated with it. I saw the last two years of my marriage, and looked at the time before and after my move to Atlanta, how much I had taken on, when my "dream" of family was shattered.

I saw the disillusionment about family and work and the need to come back into who I really am, all that had been lying in wait in the shadows, putting myself last. Then, the realization finally came that mostly I'm angry at myself for allowing myself to be lost. The more I gave, the more unfulfilled I felt. My life purpose of servitude and motherhood wasn't filling me, it was draining me.

As I breathed and continued moving light and energy into Cookie's system, I saw myself in sync and flowing like the calm waters in a river. Flowing easily, quietly until I was still. Not stagnant, yet still. I saw I must seek peace within and stop all the yelling and "noise." My ability to run energy during this healing, was not near as strong and vibrant as the previous day.

Feeling the swelling of the tumors under my hands, I asked for a message, while continuously asking Jesus to heal Cookie, thanked him for taking into his body all the blackness and darkness of my life, and telling him he didn't need to do that for me anymore. It was time for me to take care of myself.

---

[13] The Vertical Power Current in the center of the spine.

Too exhausted to cry and too tired to "sense" any longer, I focused the last of my energy into my hands and thanked Cookie, Jesus, my angels, and Cookie's lymph system for it's strength to filter and protect me from my lack of self-love. I asked for forgiveness for myself and Cookie and felt compassion pour into my Heart — for myself. I felt my open Heart and complete love for Cookie fill up and transform my sad and angry Heart, until I lay down with him and fell asleep.

June 17: Cookie went under anesthesia to get scanned and more tests were run. To the surprise of the vet, the tumors are gone. There wasn't any swelling anywhere. The vet said that usually when one lymph node is enlarged it can be for a variety of reasons, yet when two or more are enlarged and especially the size of Cookie's, it usually points to cancer.

How I related the healings to the TENSU healing I received after my car wreck (Judy's car accident and her healing are described in the TENSU Healing section) is that the energetic cysts that formed in Cookie's lymph system from the shock and traumatic effects of my repeated rage, high levels of anxiety, overwhelm, and outbursts caused Cookie to develop the growths because he could no longer filter out the toxic energy I was radiating outwardly.

Seeing the goo-like thick substance, his tissues weren't completely frozen, yet definitely the blocked energy caused by the substance needed to be removed energetically like a body session combined with flowing and re-flowing his energy from the laying on of hands.

The second healing, although I wasn't doing very well and it was much shorter, served to remove more of the residue stuck in his system, yet mostly stuck in mine, which was also an amazing result from the healing. I needed to witness the rage, overwhelm, pressure and deep guilt, and the lowering of myself again and again to become fully aware that I could change it.

I saw that my own behavior and panicked reactions had boiled over from the subconscious and that I needed to change my life. This brought forth a healing process for both Cookie and me due to the insight and awareness that came through, the deep crying and grief, the emotional release, and the peace that came for both of us afterwards as we slept side-by-side.

Chapter 25

ETHAN, THE MIRACLE BOY: SURVIVING A FRACTURED SKULL AND A SEVERED SPINE

One time, when my dad and my uncle Guido were visiting from Switzerland, we were having breakfast when the phone rang. On the line was a familiar voice I well recognized. It was Dylan, who, during the time we were building the lodging facility, "La Hacienda" at the HeartPath Retreat Center, had plastered the floor and walls of the Native American room in the traditional mud plaster fashion. I had seen him limping and at the end of his workday, he requested a healing.

We sat down on a banco right there in the courtyard. He shared that he had been suffering from gout for fifteen years. I asked him to close his eyes and performed a very basic laying-on-of-hands healing while dialoguing. Dylan was receptive. He described in detail what I was doing to his body. I told him he didn't deserve to live in pain and that he deserved to be pain free. I did not hear from Dylan for a year. On my birthday, my husband bumped into him and Dylan told him that since the healing, he was pain free and could again participate in the Native American dances. It was the best birthday gift I had received.

Since that time, Dylan has called me his angel and every now and then has sought me out for a healing. One time, he arrived with such severe pain that he could barely walk on crutches and was deeply bent over. As soon as we entered the healing room, he declared, "I will walk out of here a healed man."

With a sinking feeling, I had to admit that his faith was bigger than mine. During the many years we had known each other, Dylan had developed a bond and deep trust in me and shared much that he said he had never told anyone else.

The day when Dylan called during breakfast, his voice was broken and in panic. "You must come to the hospital," he said with urgency. "My son is dying." I immediately got into my car and left to see him. Arriving at the emergency room of the hospital, many relatives were in the waiting area. Dylan was falling apart and told me his son had been in a car accident and was now in a coma. His most severe injuries were a fractured skull and a severed spine. The doctor's diagnosis was "zero hope for survival."

We went in to see him. I closed my eyes and immediately perceived Ethan's spirit floating above his body. Silently, I communicated with Ethan and asked him how he was feeling. He was feeling well and peaceful, he said, though confused. I asked him if he knew what had happened and why he was not in his body but floating above it.

Much later, I learned that he didn't want to return to his body because two of his cousins he had been close with had died and he wanted to be with them.

I opened my eyes and asked Dylan if Ethan's mom was in the waiting area. He confirmed she was. I asked him to bring her in. Dylan and his ex had been divorced for many years.

Ethan's mom was Native American as well. I looked at both of them and felt their excruciating pain and deep sorrow. I instructed them to each take one of Ethan's hands and take turns speaking to him, that they must speak to him from the very core of their Hearts and tell him of their love for him, share their feelings of despair in case he left them.

I told them that even though Ethan was in coma he could hear every single word they said, and feel every thought they had of him. His mom spoke first telling him about early childhood memories and why he was so very special to her. She shared all the reasons why she loved him so very deeply. She went on to say that if he left, she would be devastated and that her life would fall apart forever. She begged him to stay and listed all the things they could do together if he returned, the things they had done and that he loved, and things waiting to be explored.

Then it was Dylan's turn. He spoke of his deep love for Ethan and how proud he felt when Ethan was born. That he wanted to do so much more with Ethan and to PLEASE stay, that if he left, there would be a hole in his life and in his Heart that nothing could ever fill.

The desperation of both parents was deeply palpable and their feelings so earnest. We all cried as we sat with Ethan, just looking at him. Then, all of a sudden, Ethan opened his eyes. It was just for a moment, yet we all had seen it. It was a confirmation he had heard them. Ethan stayed in a coma for seventeen days and then slowly recovered. The doctors and hospital staff named him the "Miracle Boy."

For years after the accident, Ethan battled with drug addictions. Today, almost 20 years later, Ethan has a slight limp but is finally doing well.

Section 2

Emotional Trauma

Chapter 26

ESTEBAN'S SEVERE CHILDHOOD TRAUMA, HIS WIFE VERONICA, LITTLE ESTEBAN JUNIOR

Some years back, a Mexican family from Monterrey — Esteban and Veronica with their lovely three children Carola, Cruz, and Esteban junior — rented my lodge facility for their holiday ski vacation. Upon learning of my vocation and work, Veronica remarked that she had been suffering from severe, almost daily migraine attacks for ten years. No doctor had been able to prescribe anything that would bring her relief. She was curious if a healing session would bring any results.

What surfaced in the healing were some deep, unresolved issues with her dad. There was a good deal of emotional discharge as she processed her relationship with her father. During the next few days, I was busy with my own schedule, so I didn't see anyone. On the fifth day, Veronica reported that, surprisingly, there had been no more migraines since the healing work. To me, of course, it was no surprise.

As a result, her husband said he carried very deep childhood trauma and signed up for a healing session as well.

In a nutshell, Esteban shared with me his life story. He grew up as the second oldest in a family of four siblings. His father was an insecure, jealous man, an alcoholic who had many unjustified suspicions toward his wife. When Esteban was sixteen years old, his mother, after yet another ugly jealousy outbreak, gathered all her children and decided to leave her husband and find refuge at her parents' home not far away.

They had been walking for more than an hour, when his mother decided to give her husband one last chance. So they all turned around to walk back home. Everybody rejoiced in the reunion. Esteban decided to run to the store and buy a gift for his parents.

Upon his return the police were there. His mother was dead. His dad explained that he had tried to kill himself but his wife, unfortunately — trying to prevent him from shooting himself — was shot. The police handcuffed him regardless and took him away for further interrogation. After two months, his father was released and returned to the family.

The passing of their beloved mother was a huge shock to all and the family broke apart. Her death became a taboo subject, and even more so, the circumstances surrounding her death. Nothing was ever talked about again. Esteban carried a tremendous amount of guilt. He felt responsible for his mom's death. He was certain, had he been home, the incident would never have happened and his mom would still be alive.

Esteban requested to get relief from his burdened Heart. I guided him to return to the age of sixteen and re-live the nightmare once again. As he did, he described in detail the circumstances. The fight between his parents, his mom's decision to leave, the walk to his grandparents' home, the return home, the happy reunion, him running to the store for the gift, and running back home excitedly. And then the unspeakable, the shocking confrontation with the unbelievable truth — his mom had been shot dead. Everything was re-experienced in minute detail and there was much emotional release. Esteban felt terribly guilty for having left his mom, thus, losing her forever.

After a long pause of reflection and inner process, I asked Esteban if he would like to talk to his mom. "Of course," he responded, and soon enough, she was present. Esteban broke down completely as he felt his beloved mother by his side. They had a very heartfelt and loving energetic exchange. He was astounded to experience his mom in utter peace and wellbeing. I guided Esteban to ask her simple questions. What surfaced was that after the initial making up (which was when Esteban left), his father had another attack of jealousy. He took out the pistol from his desk and shot his wife. Esteban was in utter confusion. It absolutely resonated with him what his mom revealed.

How could it be that the police released his dad, the murderer of his mom, as not guilty and he went on living as a free man up to his death?! Esteban's head was turning upside down with a hundred different thoughts. His mother's presence had felt authentically real, Esteban entertained no doubts at all. Her message had been clear and short.

His next thoughts circled around the fact that "Oh my God, our father killed our mom and no one knows, except me. I must let my siblings know, so they know the truth as well." To contact his older brother was out of the question because his brother had always been in alignment with his father. He would ridicule Esteban's communication with their mom, a dead person, a spirit. But he decided he wanted to tell the truth to his sister and youngest brother.

As the vacation ended and the family left for home, Esteban was in deep process. During the course of it, he suggested introducing my work to various groups interested in healing work in his home town of Monterrey, Mexico. Esteban had invited his sister to attend, though he had not yet told her. He had only told her that he wanted to set up an important meeting with her and their youngest brother to share the painful truth he'd just learned about. He assumed that his sister, during her healing session with me, would find out on her own.

His sister came to the first introductory and signed up for a session with me. But, she said, not for a healing, only to talk. As she entered and sat down, she told me, their father, prior to passing away, had been ill for two years. He was very ill at the time and had asked her to take him in for the last part of his life. She took care of him until he passed away. On his death bed, he confessed to her what lay heavy on him.

He had killed his wife and disguised it as suicide. But, she said, she had known the truth for a long time. Her youngest brother — at the time of the tragedy only six years old — had witnessed the homicide through the window. Because the family had strayed from each other due to the tragedy, no one communicated. She commented that she was certain Esteban wanted to share with her something that she had not only known for many years because her younger brother told her, but that had been confirmed by their father prior to his death. She remarked, "Esteban thinks he wants to bring the family back together by uncovering the truth when in fact Esteban has been the one who did not know."

Upon leaving Monterrey, Esteban and Veronica signed up for the 12-day Maha Intensive with me and we decided on a date for them to return to New Mexico to do some additional healing work. Upon arrival, each separately shared with me that their marriage was in a serious crisis and that there was much tension between them. Furthermore, their youngest, Esteban junior, was having to undergo surgery upon their return home because the poor little boy was struggling daily with his bowel movement. No stool softener was bringing release. They consulted the three best pediatricians in Monterrey. All confirmed that the only solution was to shorten little Esteban's large intestine by cutting out a piece.

As Veronica and Esteban started the work, what surfaced in the course of the healing process was the repetition of a pattern they both knew from their parents' relationship dynamics.

Esteban realized that his relationship with Veronica was identical to the relationship dynamic his parents had had. Esteban was in the same position as his mom, defending himself constantly against wrong claims. Veronica was plagued by jealousy and hysterical outbreaks of accusations, just like his dad had done. Esteban also commented that Veronica's constant demands and complaints made him withdraw into himself and he no longer felt he loved her. He saw himself different than her and was starting to envision a new life for himself. As a result, their sex life was suffering, because he no longer felt any attraction for her. He realized his mom must have felt the same towards his father. He saw that she no longer was in love with her husband but stayed for the sake of their children and out of pity.

Veronica confessed that the main reason for her insecurities was that Esteban no longer desired her, no matter how much money she invested in sexy underwear in an attempt to seduce him with her behavior of seduction and charm. If that didn't work, after accusations and hysterical outbursts, she attempted to bring him back closer to her, which had the exact opposite effect.

She realized that she behaved much like her dad who used charm and seduction to win his wife back, yet her mom wasn't interested and had emotionally distanced herself from her dad. Veronica clearly saw the parallels and recognized Esteban's behavior as the same as her mom's.

Veronica and Esteban started an open dialogue to better communicate and came to the decision to give their relationship one last chance. Again, for the sake of their children.

Upon returning home, the profound inner work both had undergone had such an effect that little Esteban now was able to have daily bowel movements effortlessly and thus no longer needed surgery. As in the example of Robert, the boy with the brain tumor, little Esteban had been the victim of the tension field between his parents. Once that cleared, his ailment ceased permanently.

Chapter 27

EMMA: CHILD VICTIM OF TORTURE, RAPE, AND EXPERIMENTATION

Several years ago, Emma and her two male friends rented my casita. I developed a friendship with Emma and gained her trust. It took months before Emma confided that she was dealing with tremendous childhood trauma that scarred her for life mentally and emotionally to the degree where she was unable to work. She was dealing with nightmares and flashbacks that were extremely painful emotionally, debilitating, and confusing to her. In the beginning of our friendship, Emma was never able to look me in the eyes and was plagued by severe paranoia. She was physically weak and unhealthy. We did a series of healing sessions during the time she stayed here and then later over the phone.

Emma had grown up in New York. Her father had been high in the military and was stationed overseas prior to Emma's birth. When Emma's parents returned to the US, Emma was still a toddler. When she was four years old, her dad, with the consent of Emma's mother, started to take Emma 3-4 times a week to a science lab and left her there with his military colleagues who experimented on her. As a toddler, she endured sexual abuse in the lab with the scientists. Even more so, they infused her with substances and played hour-long tapes of *Alice in Wonderland* and movie scenes from Walt Disney, and constantly repeated sentences. They placed electrodes on her head that she said "messed with her head."

Emma shared that the worst was not all the sexual abuse and horrible stuff like electroshocks they did. The worst was that they messed with her head with their brainwashing experiments. Lucky for little Emma, she got dropped as an unsuccessful case when she was six years old because she didn't respond well enough to their experiments.

She vividly remembered the outlay of the lab and the scientists. She particularly feared the scientist with the glasses. During the sessions, she broke out in panic attacks, a cold sweat, stuttering, and uncontrollable shivering. It was extremely hard for her to remember those scenes, there was much resistance in talking about what had happened. Therefore, I suggested Emma mold in plastilina clay models of herself and the scientists working on her. This she did in minute detail.

By doing this, Emma was able to dissociate to a certain degree from the severe trauma and the alienation it had caused her. By speaking about the doctor conducting the experiments on the little girl, she was able to put sort of a safety belt around herself — the adult — and the little girl Emma who endured those experiments.

The healing work of remembering the horrors of her early years were so tormenting to Emma that she needed a break of 7-14 days between each healing session, in order to recuperate. She felt drained and weak for days, unable to get out of bed. She had some dark spots on her forehead and was convinced they had developed as a result of where the electrodes had been placed.

I suggested that Emma needed to work with a decoding specialist, someone familiar with brainwashing methods. I did some research and found some therapists familiar with the MK-Ultra method of torture[14]. I also suggested that she participate in a yearly conference of victims of MK-Ultra and Project Monarch (similar to MK-Ultra) to share her own experiences with other survivors. Apparently, the movie industry has quite a few celebrities who were themselves victims.

When Emma moved, she stayed in contact and we did a series of healing sessions over the phone. The next step in her healing process concerned the betrayal by her mother who had allowed all of this to happen. To process the far deeper trauma regarding her father was something that would have to occur sometime in the future. He had passed away years ago, but Emma's mother was still alive. Emma described her mother as mentally absent, physically functioning to a certain degree, emotionally withdrawn, not present, and in utter and complete denial about what happened to Emma.

Emma shared that she was doing communal service and attempting to have a life. We are still in contact. To this day, she suffers from flashbacks that cause her to have severe panic attacks. It is clear that much more long-term healing work is needed in order for her to further release her trauma.

> **Note:** Apparently, when WW II ended and the atrocities and war crimes of Nazi Germany were brought to light during the Nuremberg trials, a good number of former scientists from Nazi Germany fled to Great Britain and Canada. They were contacted by the CIA and invited to the US to continue their experiments and further their studies. The victims were usually orphans kept in government institutions, prisoners, and juvenile correction centers throughout the US and southeastern Canada. MK-Ultra involved more than eighty academic institutions, prisons, and organizations.

---

[14] MK-Ultra was a top-secret CIA project in which the agency conducted hundreds of clandestine experiments — sometimes on unwitting US citizens — to assess the potential use of LSD and other drugs for mind control, information gathering, and psychological torture.

Chapter 28

CLARISSA, THE MYSTERIOUS LIFE-LONG GUILT FOR BEING ALIVE

While I visited with my family in Brazil, a distant family member wanted to have a healing session with me. I agreed but asked Camila, my daughter in law, to stay present and translate for me because Clarissa only spoke Portuguese. Her presenting complaint was a problem with her Thyroid gland that worsened after a Laser treatment. But the healing went into a totally different and unexpected direction.

Clarissa was in her late sixties and a devout Catholic. She was still a virgin who had never in her life been in a relationship. She came from a wealthy family of landowners. Her assets accumulated in her bank account while she lived an extraordinarily modest, secluded and uneventful life.

Like always in my healings, I aligned Clarissa with the deity of her choice, which was in her case Jesus Christ. I asked her Thyroid for anything to report but that brought no results.

All of a sudden, Clarissa saw herself in uterus shortly before birth. She could not understand what was happening. I encouraged her to just witness and experience without questioning what she sees. She was in the womb with her twin sister. Her twin sister was with her head towards the birth canal and ready to be born. Not so Clarissa. She was turned around as if resisting birth. The birth of her twin sister was fast and easy. There had been no complications.

Now the doctor and midwife concentrated on Clarissa. Her birth was quite problematic as she needed to be turned around. But apparently it did not work. The doctor and nurse were unaware that while they concentrated on Clarissa and neglected her twin sister for the time being; her twin sister stopped breathing. When Clarissa finally was born her baby twin sister had unfortunately died.

Clarissa was beyond flabbergasted and deeply shocked. What she had just experienced shook her to the core. She had never known she had a twin sister. No one had ever told her that she was born with a twin sister who had died at birth. Clarissa's parents had never talked to her about her birth circumstances. How could all this possibly be true? Yet, Clarissa did not in the least doubt her experience. It had felt too real.

While still laying on the couch she processed her life up to now. She shared that it all made so much sense. All her life, from childhood on, she had always felt guilty. Guilty for being alive. Guilty for having a life. Guilty for having a good life. She always felt she did not deserve living though she could never explain her feelings. She stayed living by herself and never entered a relationship because she always felt undeserving of it. She could not logically explain why. But now she knew and now she understood.

After this experience, Clarissa stated to Camila that she wanted to learn English for the purpose of studying with me, though Camila reported that as time went by, the initial desire subsided.

Chapter 29

MIA: LAST JUDGMENT – WHAT HAPPENS AFTER DEATH

Mia, a woman in her mid-forties, with three adult children, was in a marriage crisis. Just recently, the children were no longer living in the house, so she and her husband decided to sell their home. Mia's husband was a passionate golfer and wanted their new home to be part of a golf club, an idea which Mia dreaded. The shallowness of the privileged society and their artificial lifestyle with no deeper meaning was what Mia longed to avoid.

Mia had found a fixer-upper she fancied in the Florida countryside and kept seeing herself living a very different life, spiritually-oriented, and more fulfilling to her. She also wanted to devote her life to healing and helping others. Their marriage was clearly at a crossroads.

During the initial interview, Mia shared that her mother had become pregnant with Mia when she was sixteen years old and had tried to kill herself with sleeping pills. Her biological father was twelve years old when he impregnated her mom during the only time they'd had sex. He joined the Navy when he was old enough and left Mia.

Mia's grandparents reluctantly took her in as a baby. Mia adored her grandma. Soon enough, her mom married and picked her up to live with them. Mia remembered Jack, her stepdad hitting her over and over because she wouldn't stop crying in her crib. Even as a toddler, Jack beat her up. He also started sexually molesting her when she was only a year old.

Mia loved her mom but she knew that her mother hated her and she never protected her from her stepdad. Jack was extremely physically abusive. He hated Mia, whom he considered a burden. They had a dog, Blacky, that Mia loved. One day, Blacky disappeared. Her parents told her he had run away. Mia didn't believe them. Blacky would never have run away. He loved Mia and was always with her.

Mia missed Blacky a lot. She suspected that her stepdad had done something to Blacky in order to cause her pain. Years later, Jack told her with contempt that he'd killed Blacky by shooting him. For her entire childhood, she was scared to death of him. One day, Mia heard her grandma say to her mom, "This beating must stop or one day he will kill Mia." So she knew her grandma was aware of how much Jack physically abused her throughout her childhood.

Another animal Mia deeply loved was her horse Rex. She took such good care of Rex and loved riding him. Rex was also very scared of Jack, who would beat Rex bloody while Mia kept crying, "Please, please, please, stop!!!"

Jack kept molesting Mia sexually and only stopped when Mia was eleven years old because she didn't allow it anymore. He kept punishing Mia for it by beating up her beloved horse.

When Mia was twelve years old, her parents made her get rid of Rex. They said they were moving to Kansas and the horse was not worth taking along.

Living in Kansas on a ninety-acre farm was Mia's worst period. Jack beat her all the time. He was angry because Mia wouldn't allow him to touch her anymore. He then started molesting her younger sister. Mia felt very ashamed for not having been able to protect first Blacky, then Rex, and now her sister from her stepdad. She ran away from home at age fourteen, never to return. She also helped a pregnant foster sister run away from home so that her baby wasn't taken away. Her mom always had up to six foster kids in their home.

Mia completed a series of two Maha Intensives, one immediately followed by the next. In the course of it, Mia discovered how deeply she dealt with betrayal issues in her life. Her whole childhood was marked by deepest betrayal, betrayal by her mom and grandma for not protecting her, betrayal by her biological father who was not interested in her, and the worst betrayal by Jack, her stepdad.

Mia shared that prior to her mom's death, she had forgiven her. As a sorry old man, Jack had asked for her forgiveness and she had forgiven him, though it had been extremely challenging for her. During the healing, she processed a lot of anger towards her biological father for having left her. She did meet him in person for the first time when she was thirty years old and he confirmed that she was the product of his and her mom's one time of having sex.

During one of the sessions when Mia was in deep process for all the injustice she had witnessed, Jesus took her to Heaven. He led her into a large audience hall. Assembled were her mom and stepdad Jack, her grandparents, her biological father, her sister Julie, Blacky, and Rex. A large screen appeared and every single scene of her childhood was projected on it for everyone to see. There were her mom and biological father and how they met. Her mom's suicide attempt was witnessed by everyone. Then there was Mia, newly born, a tiny, tiny baby. Her grandparents took baby Mia in. Now all could see her mom with Jack, him beating baby Mia while she cried in the crib. Beating her again and again over nothing when she was a toddler. Every time he lost his temper, Jack beat her. Everyone was watching this.

Scene after scene appeared, like a silent movie playing. Mia glanced over to Jack and her mom and saw her mom and grandparents wiping away tears. Jack was sobbing. Then there was the constant sexual molestation. As Mia grew from childhood into puberty all sexual molestation scenes were shown on the screen. Then there was Mia and her beloved dog Blacky, how they walked and played, the way she talked to him, as well as sharing times of utter despair for all the beatings and abuse. Then all could see Jack taking out his gun and shooting Blacky while smiling. Blacky had done nothing wrong.

Mia cried very bitter tears for her beloved Blacky. She looked over at Jack in the audience hall. He had his head deeply bent in shame while sobbing uncontrollably. Then there was Rex, her horse, the second animal Mia had bonded with. All the times of beating Rex were displayed, and Mia's heart broke for all Rex's beatings. Her heart broke when she was forced to leave Rex behind for a new life in Kansas until Mia could no longer take her miserable life and ran away. Everyone was crying deeply and lost in deep thought. Mia looked at all of them. Blacky and Rex were doing well now having done nothing wrong but bring her joy.

The screen went dark. Jesus guided Mia out of the hall and told her that in the Great Hall of Records every single life is recorded from beginning to end. This is the way for every single Soul on Earth. Every right act, as well as every wrong act, is later witnessed by all the players involved. He told her this is what is called "The Last Judgment." There is no God condemning, judging, and punishing. One's own conscious Soul is the judge. Everyone is accountable for their wrongdoings. Nothing ever escapes the Great Witness.

Mia felt extremely peaceful and calm after her experience. She shared that it was a good feeling to know that there is justice in the Universe. With her emotional release from the past and her new understandings integrated, Mia returned home to her husband and family to start her life anew.

Chapter 30

NAMASTE, THE DOG WITH HIGH AWARENESS AND A MISSION TO PREVENT A CHILD'S SUICIDE ATTEMPT

Prior to the start of the next story, I would like to say what a blessing a blessing it is that — finally — more and more people are realizing that animals do indeed have a consciousness and a Soul. The South African animal communicator, Anna Breytenbach, and her telepathic conversation with a black panther, who was originally called Diablo and later renamed Spirit, is a profound testimony of it.

In 2019, *Discover* magazine wrote an article titled "Dogs and Their Owners Share Similar Personality Traits." To me, cats do also, as well as parrots. All pets usually do. I have no doubt that animals do have souls. When a pet is bonding with its owner, the pet willingly sacrifices its life to save their owner's life. This is how their Soul progresses. In my healing practice, I have witnessed many times that when a pet dies not a natural death but from an accident or a life-threatening disease; and the owner came in to work with me, it was the very body part or disease that ailed them. But now to the story …

Sophia shared with me the following story of Namaste, her dog. At only four years old, Namaste was dying. Sophia and her husband Luther were in disagreement as to whether to release Namaste from his suffering or let him pass on his own. Therefore, they consulted a recommended animal communicator to find out what Namaste wanted. The woman responded that Namaste wanted to stay as long as possible, unless he was in a lot of pain or suffering from seizures.

But then the animal communicator said, "There is much more that Namaste would like to share." Other than the information on Namaste, the animal communicator had no information about Sophia and Luther or their life together.

She proceeded to say that Namaste was talking to her about their daughter. She continued with, "Namaste has been in the car many times with your daughter and her boyfriend. They are too engaged with themselves and are not paying attention while driving. They must be more careful when driving." Then she said, "Namaste is also showing a boy, around sixteen years of age in a room full of Star Wars' pictures. Namaste says that this boy should always stay away from drugs, even just smoking, or he will face serious consequences."

Sophia and Luther were listening with fascination. Namaste's consciousness was amazing! Everything was correct. The animal communicator continued. "Now there is something I don't quite understand. Namaste speaks of a fall, and says that his whole purpose for incarnating was to prevent the fall. Do you have another daughter?" she asked.

Yes, they did, one about twelve years old. Sophia and Luther knew precisely what the woman was talking about. Their daughter had almost died when she rode her bicycle down a slope and smashed into an oncoming car. As a result, she has since suffered from paralysis on the right side of her body and can't use her hand anymore.

The animal communicator continued by addressing the husband. "Namaste says that in a recent past life, that you were a soldier during the US Civil War. You had a horse and you loved that horse so much that when the weather conditions were nasty, you took the horse into the tent to sleep with you. That horse has reborn and it wants to be with you again. Please look for it."

Sophia and Luther were in utter amazement. Luther had the house decorated with soldier and cowboy memorabilia that directly related to what Namaste was saying. But he didn't currently have a horse. He decided to start looking and after some intense searching found the horse and they were reunited.

Namaste, this wise dog, knew much and it was to everyone's benefit that he was able to share his knowledge, thanks to the animal communicator. He died of cancer shortly after he had saved the youngest daughter, Tania, from "the fall." Tania grew up and was partially paralyzed from the accident before she underwent hand surgery, which improved her condition.

Some years back, the girl involved with the fall, Tania, now a woman in her twenties, found her way into my healing practice. Tania shared that she was born in California. At about twelve years of age, her parents decided to move to Santa Fe, NM. Tania so dreaded the move and hated having to give up her old and familiar life. She didn't enjoy moving to a new and unknown place and resisted the change.

During the healing session, I regressed Tania to the time of the accident. She saw the circumstances leading up to it. She had been suffering from depression from being forced to move and carried much resentment for having to start a new life in a new place. It got so bad that she didn't want to live anymore.

Tania saw herself on the bike. She was riding far too fast down a slope towards a road. She lost control of her bicycle and saw the oncoming car approaching, witnessing the event in slow motion. She was at full speed heading towards the oncoming car.

The crash would have been at full speed, but then there was Namaste who ignored her panicked screams of "Namaste, Namaste, no, no, no!! Namaste, get out of the way!" Namaste paid no attention to her frantic yells. Reaching her, he violently slammed into her from the side and thus was able to partially reduce the speed and her impact with the car.

Lying on the massage table, processing what she'd relived and digesting it, Tania realized that driving down the slope into the car had clearly been a suicide attempt. This was not surprising to her because she still recalled how much she dreaded leaving California and moving to Santa Fe. For her, the accident had been an attempt to escape from her life and out of her body.

Chapter 31

GEORGE: ANOTHER EXAMPLE OF ATTEMPTED SUICIDE DURING CHILDHOOD / ADOLESCENCE

In the course of my healing practice, I have worked with countless individuals who were processing their buried childhood memories. I was astounded to learn how many accidents that happened during childhood were in fact covered up suicide attempts. Children swallowing pills and harmful chemical substances contained in cleaning products or glue, children nearly drowning, children falling from cliffs or walking into cars or falling off a horse, or suffocating themselves with a plastic bag, etc. The list is endless.

Suicide in children is unfortunately quite common. This leaves much to ponder, such as why do these Souls who only just recently incarnated want to leave so quickly again? Do they subconsciously regret having come into a body again? Are they not happy with the circumstances they find themselves in? Are the expectations set on them too high and cause too much stress for their little system to process?

Apparently, Japan has one of the highest suicide rates, even with very young children, due to the pressures to succeed in school. The number gets much higher when considered under the light of fatal accidents that were in fact successful suicides, as described below in George's story.

George grew up by a lake. In winter, he loved to ice skate on the frozen lake and during the summer, his favorite activity was swimming in it. From a very young age, season after season was spent in this rhythm of play and fun activities whenever time allowed. He was in puberty when problems at home began to occur.

His father had expectations that George couldn't fulfill. His dad, a simple farmer, wanted George to take over the farm once he was old enough. But George dreaded the simple life of working the land. He felt that all too often his childhood was spent in helping his parents work the land and tend to their cows and sheep. He had witnessed his parents struggling with bad crops, livestock diseases, and more. From 5 am until nighttime. It seemed his parents did nothing but work. He wanted a different life for himself than working the land with his hands and straining his body with heavy physical work he didn't enjoy.

George liked school and wanted to take the academic route. He also loved sports and fancied possibly studying at a sports academy. Since George was the only son, his father was deeply hurt. George loved his dad and hated to see his father disillusioned and falling into a depression.

It was during this period of his life that George challenged himself to swim further and further from the shore. The physical activity of swimming helped him forget about the guilt he felt for being unwilling to follow the path his dad had chosen for him, especially since he was their only son.

He told me that during one time when he was quite far from shore, he experienced a life-threatening situation. Perhaps it got triggered because he had exhausted himself swimming to his very limits. All of sudden, he had a very painful muscle cramp in his right calf. The contraction hurt so much that he was unable to continue swimming.

George struggled to keep his head above water. He was all alone out on the lake, so no cries for help would be heard. He realized that this might be his moment to die. At first, he panicked. Then he experienced an altered state of consciousness where utter clarity set in. He looked at his life as if from above and saw the whole situation clearly. He realized he had provoked the situation by swimming too far out, because subconsciously, he wanted to die and be done with the conflict with his dad.

In that moment, he realized that he didn't want to die, he wanted to live. He started to breathe slowly and focus. He said that he even started to pray, asking for help. With only one leg to swim with and his two arms to help, he slowly made his way back to shore.

He shared with me how this experience had changed his life. As he stumbled home and entered the house, his parents immediately noticed something was wrong. He was shaking and stuttering, unable to speak. They sat him down while his mother went to the kitchen to prepare some hot tea and a hot water bottle. Recovering from the shock, he broke out in tears and told his parents his whole experience. Both parents began crying, too. His mom told him she could not bear losing him. His dad expressed that George should do with his life what he wished to do. He apologized to George for the burden he had caused and gave him his blessing to pursue his own dreams.

George described that he felt so relieved. He vowed to make his life worthwhile now that he had been gifted with a new life. His dad became very proud of him. None of the old expectations ever got mentioned again.

During the healing, George processed his childhood. He saw himself at four years of age playing with his twin brother Gabriel in the living room. He was five when Gabriel passed away from meningitis.

The tragedy not only hit his parents hard, it also caused a deep crisis for little George. George cried as he re-experienced the death of his twin brother. Gabriel had been his buddy and playmate and George felt utterly alone and abandoned when his brother no longer was alive and part of his world. Little George kept trying to imagine where his Gabriel had gone and fantasized about being there with him.

When I asked George to move a bit further to an important incident in his life, George saw himself entering the room of the live-in maid and grabbing a bottle on her bedside table. He opened the bottle and took one swallow. It tasted sweet. Little George was delighted to have grabbed a bottle of liquid candy and he swallowed the entire contents.

When the maid found her bedroom door open and she saw little George laying unconscious on the floor, she let out a loud scream, which alerted George's mom who was working in the kitchen. They immediately carried him to the truck and drove him to the hospital. Unconscious, George saw himself happily united with his twin brother. But a rough awakening came when his stomach was pumped.

Processing this childhood experience, George realized this had been his first suicide attempt. The fact that he subconsciously tried two times to exit his life provoked many different thoughts in George. He had been totally unaware of his suicide attempts, not even remembering the incident at five years old, much less realizing that both were not mere accidents, but actually suicide attempts.

When the Soul Calls: True Stories of Deep Healing and Transformation

Chapter 32

AVA: A 4-YEAR-OLD GIRL – WITNESS TO MURDER

I met Ava during one of my stays in Buenos Aires. As soon as she sat down in my practice, she burst into tears. She shared that she had been living a beautiful and easy life. She wasn't facing any challenges of any sort but ever since she was a child and for as long as she could remember, she could never fully enjoy happiness. She didn't understand why she felt constantly depressed because she had parents who loved her and had always provided for her and whom she loved and siblings she loved. Her father was a general in the military and her mom was a housewife. Ava worked as a tango instructor and shared that she enjoyed her work and was in a relationship with someone she liked.

Upon starting the healing session, I aligned her with her higher guidance and requested to be taken to the core of what ailed Ava. She immediately saw herself as a 4-year-old girl inside their house by the entrance. The whole family was present. Her father was opening the door and two of his friends whom Ava recognized were entering. They brought with them a very simply dressed young woman who was very pregnant. All of them went down to the cellar and the young woman gave birth to a little baby boy.

I asked Ava if one of the men was the father of the baby. Ava responds with "No" and that the father of the baby was afraid to come. His friends promised to take care of it for him. As soon as the little baby boy was born, Ava's father put him in a plastic bag and suffocated the baby to death. Everyone then went upstairs and the two men with the young mother left.

Ava wiped away her tears, feeling very sad. She was in shock over what she had just witnessed. Her father had killed a little innocent baby. Ava loved her dad and knew he was a good man. How could he do such a thing?! How could everyone witness first the birth of the little baby and then his death?! Even how the mother of the baby was sent away as soon as she had given birth and the baby was killed. Ava couldn't understand it. It felt so cruel and heartless to her, even how the mother of the baby was released as soon as she had given birth and the baby was killed.

I asked Ava to find out why the young mother was not allowed to keep her baby. Ava got the answer: The father was married with a family of his own and had a position of respect. The young woman he'd slept with was a simple country girl, much beneath his status.

Ava felt so very sorry for the baby. "The little baby boy didn't even have a chance to live. He was robbed of his life just like that. How very, very sad. How can anyone do that?! How come everyone behaved as if that were okay?!"

I asked Ava if she would like to give recognition to the little baby boy by honoring him. Ava confirmed she'd like that. "Why don't we build him an altar and lay him on the altar and pray for him?" Ava agreed and visualized setting up a beautiful altar with a nice piece of white cloth and laid the baby boy carefully on it. She arranged candles around it and placed flowers there as well. She put a little stuffed dog in his arms and sat there by his side.

Suddenly, the little baby sat up as if nothing had happened and he played happily with the little dog who was alive, too.

I saw a past life where the boy was in a male body, a shepherd tending to sheep. He had a very close bond with his dog. The little boy was saying that he wanted to become a shepherd again, wandering through the countryside with his flock of sheep and sleep again under the night sky with his dog. Ava was crying that this could not be for the boy.

She also felt very sorry for the young mother whose baby had been taken away and killed. The young mother had entered the altar area in shaggy, old, and dirty clothes. Ava felt such pain for her and couldn't understand why the young mother had been shamed for giving birth instead of honored.

I asked Ava if she would like to take the young mother and help her bathe in the nearby flowing waters, and handed her some clean fresh clothes. Ava did just that. Now the young woman, refreshed and cleanly dressed, sat down with us and watched her baby boy playing on the altar with the little dog. Soon, Ava's mother joined them at the altar, as well as Ava's sister. They also felt very sorry for what had happened.

By now, a line was beginning to form with other mothers who had been shamed in the same way as the young mother. They all requested to be taken to the water as well and given a refreshing bath and fresh clothes, to be honored in their position of sacred motherhood. The line became longer and longer but Ava didn't mind helping each mother to bathe and handing them fresh clothes. Everyone was sitting down forming a circle around the altar, silently honoring life. The little boy was happily oblivious to it all and fully engaged in playing with his puppy.

Ava's father neared the area together with his two friends. He felt ashamed for what he had done and sat down by his wife who felt sorry for his actions, too. Everyone was very moved and all were crying.

At last, the father of the little baby, entered and looked at his baby. He, too, was crying and asked the young woman whose baby he'd fathered for forgiveness. Now everyone present stood up and went to the altar to honor the little baby boy. Then they sat down again. With this, the healing circle was now complete.

I asked Ava if she felt there was anything else that still needed to be done. Ava said that she was now calm and at peace. She was glad she had come for the healing and now understood what had ailed her throughout her life. She wanted to talk to her parents and family about it and was willing to forgive her father.

Section 3

Mental Conditions

Chapter 33

PHOBIAS AND PANIC ATTACKS IN GENERAL

"F-E-A-R has two meanings:
Forget Everything and Run
Or
Face Everything and Rise.

The Choice is Yours."

~ Bright vibes

Phobias such as fear of heights, fear of flying, elevators, drowning, agoraphobia / xenophobia, claustrophobia, and so forth are classified as anxiety disorders that can cause a huge amount of stress not only for the person experiencing it but for their family members and friends. Individuals who are victims of phobias are restricted in their freedom of choice and action.

Therapy remains unsuccessful for such people because phobias cannot be explained by the rational mind. Most often, individuals suffering from phobias do not seek out situations that would cause them to confront their ailments. Rather, situations that could provoke an anxiety attack are strictly avoided.

It's important to note that phobias are not irrational at all. Such fears have a well-based reason and a perfect explanation. Oftentimes, a deep-rooted trauma is being experienced in one's current life that has its roots in a past life, one's current life being a repetition of sorts of a traumatic past-life experience. In this way, phobias might have childhood trauma as a symptom, though the core of phobias is usually related to a traumatic past-life experience in which the individual lost their life.

THE ROOT CAUSE OF ANY PHOBIA AND PANIC ATTACK IS A TRAUMATIC PAST-LIFE EXPERIENCE

For example, when Anton came to my healing practice for the Maha Intensive, he spoke of a traumatic experience from childhood. He remembered that as a 8-year-old boy, he almost drowned in icy water when he was ice skating with his friends on a frozen lake. This incident produced quite a scare for he and his parents.

From then on, he avoided water altogether and never learned to swim. He said he enjoyed exotic vacations in tropical paradises like Thailand and the Maldives, but would just dip his body in the water in order to refresh himself. He avoided open water as much as possible. He also admitted that even just taking a soak in the bathtub would bring up images of drowning.

During one of Anton's sessions, a past life came up. He saw a ship sinking in the ocean and he and his parents and siblings asleep in their cabin. He vividly described the panicked situation, people screaming and crying for help — and then the violent flood of water pulling the ship down in a huge swirl. It all happened quite rapidly and there were no survivors. Everyone drowned, including him.

Releasing this deep-rooted and unconscious trauma of a violent death in a past life seemed to free Anton from his phobia. Half a year later, Anton sent me a postcard from a vacation in Tunisia reporting that he was taking swimming lessons and quite enjoying it.

A panic attack is described as a sudden episode of intense fear or anxiety. It is based on a perceived threat rather than actual eminent danger. Often, there is no point in trying to rationally explain to individuals suffering from a panic attack that what they experience is based on a perceived subjective reality, rather than an objective real danger. For them, the attack is very real and grounded in a reality that only they can perceive.

During a panic attack, there is a heightened vigilance for danger, accompanied by anxious and irrational thinking. It's usually accompanied by strong feelings of dread, danger, or foreboding.

144

Yongey Mingyur Rinpoche, the Tibetan teacher and master of the Karma Kagyu and Nyingma lineages of Tibetan Buddhism, describes in his book, *In Love with the World: What a Monk Can Teach You about Living from Nearly Dying*, his sudden onsets of panic attacks. They began in his childhood and despite his vigorous mental trainings as a monk and meditation master, still continue to haunt him as an adult whenever triggered.

For example, when he secretly decided to leave the safety of his monastery. For the first time in his life, he found himself without company and protection. While at the main train station in Varanasi, he experienced an intense panic attack that he was unable to control despite his efforts using mental exercises. I could clearly perceive that his panic attack was triggered by severe alienation, and I felt great compassion for him.

One of the physical symptoms at the onset of a panic attack is the outbreak of a cold sweat with tingling sensations and chills, mostly in the hands and arms. The individual might experience a feeling of intense heat and an ice-cold sensation. There is also a feeling of light headedness and nausea. There is trembling, shortness of breath (sometimes accompanied by a choking sensation), chest pain, numbness, and a racing heart. It's clear the energy system of the individual suffering a panic attack is experiencing what they perceive as a death threat. They might suffer from fear of going mad, losing control, and even dying.

Light headedness and nausea = lack of grounding because of energetically exiting the body.

During one of my strolls through the Santa Fe flea market, a dealer whom I knew asked me to help his life partner who was having an asthma attack. He said they were ready to leave for the emergency at the hospital. She didn't have her asthma inhaler with her. As I entered their camper, Joana was choking and in panic. I had her recline on the bed and asked her to close her eyes. Then I guided her in slow and concentrated breathing. I also instructed her how to relax her muscles. Her energy system soon started to relax. It took some time but Joana recovered and there was no need to go to the emergency room.

The deeper cause of asthma is shock. What happens at the onset of shock is that the person is breathing forcefully in and holding their breath. We can easily observe this with animals. When they perceive danger, their energy system stops to operate. They hold their breath, listen intensely, and all focus is concentrated on the possible danger. It's a survival mechanism. Once the danger has passed, they relax and breathe regularly.

For a person suffering from an asthma attack, which then triggers the panic attack, their energy system freezes. The recognized remedy is their inhaler, which releases their spasm. But what if there is no inhaler and the emergency room is far away? Plus, when the symptom is always covered over by the intake of medication, the root cause can never reveal itself.

And there is always a root cause. The same goes for allergies. Nowadays, more and more people are suffering from allergies of all kinds. The more common ones are food and animal allergies. People's physical systems feel threatened and react with severe symptoms. The underlying reason can only be found in very early childhood trauma and past-life experiences.

Chapter 34

Susan's Terror of Parenthood and Her Daughter Jenni: A Different View of Autism

Susan, a very devoted and loving mother of six children sought me out. She carried a huge amount of fear and insecurities. She was also plagued by guilt. During our work, she confessed to a very deep secret she had never told anyone. Her oldest daughter, Jenni, twelve years old, suffered from autism. Susan said that when baby Jenni was only a few months old, Susan had a panic attack about becoming a parent and she suffocated her baby with a pillow in an attempt to eliminate her. Thank God, she came to her senses and the baby survived.

The natural and strongest bond a baby has is with their mother. The baby's auric field has not yet developed and it is the mother's auric field enveloping both. Therefore, the danger of being eliminated by The One who is the only protection produces an extreme existential threat. This could well be the cause for Jenni developing autism.

After Susan finished her 4-Day session cycle, she signed up Jenni for the work as well. Arriving at my practice, Jenni was hiding behind her mom. She clutched the teddy bear in her arm and avoided all eye contact. She kept staring at the floor. When she talked, she yelled. But she was willing to work under the condition that her mom stay in the doorway of the room.

Because it was impossible for Jenni to work directly with me, I laid her teddy bear on the massage table. Jenni sat down in a chair with her back to me. As I asked the bear questions, Jenni would answer.

Jenni was very hesitant at first but with every day became more fluent and calmer. She saw her current childhood environment embedded in family life. She recognized how she forcibly separated herself from her parents and siblings. She attended a school for special needs and never spoke even though she possessed a bright mind and easily followed the school curriculum. She was very lonely living by herself in a fantasy world. She saw past life after past life where she had separated herself from everyone and had lived a solitary existence. She concluded that she wished to change and become an active part of her environment.

Her parents later reported great changes in her behavior. Nine years later — during a workshop I gave in Europe — Jenni came to visit with her parents. Her wish was to study with me and become a facilitator but, unfortunately, the challenge was that dialoguing with others was still difficult for her. But even so, Jenni had made remarkable progress and felt very drawn to healing work. Because she is very intuitive and sensitive, I suggested she finish school and then start with Reiki and other energetic healing approaches that do not necessarily involve the extent of dialogue my healing approach does, such as Cranio-Sacral Therapy.

Chapter 35

ALEXA AND HER FEAR OF HEIGHTS

Alexa was a student of mine, a married woman with adult children. During her final training class, I took her entire group for a week-long wilderness trip to the Havasupai Indian Reservation, the south rim of the Grand Canyon.

We arrived at the hilltop parking lot at 4 am. Since it was still dark, we prepared our backpacks and camping gear for our three-night stay down at the falls. As dawn approached, we prepared breakfast so we could witness the sunrise at the edge overlooking the spectacular Grand Canyon. And there it was — what a miraculous view presented itself in front of our eyes.

Alexa stared down into the canyon and declared that she would not join us and instead stay up at the parking lot for the three days. It was only then that I learned of her tremendous fear of heights. This came as a surprise, for she lived in Austria and her husband's passion was hiking trips into the Alps, which he had to do without his wife because she always refused to join him.

Everyone ate breakfast, except Alexa. She had lost her appetite and was shaking with fear. I suggested we work and get to the bottom of her phobia. She lay down and closed her eyes as I guided her deep within herself.

She instantly saw herself as a Native American, a young woman wearing moccasins and traditional Native garments of animal hides. She was standing at the edge of a very high cliff, blindfolded, her hands tied with rope. There were a group of people present, part of her tribe. They pushed her over the edge and she fell into the abyss.

Falling, she didn't understand the reason for her death sentence. There was no crime she had committed nor had she dishonored her tribe. Quite possibly, it was a sacrificial death for her tribe.

Alexa slowly opened her eyes. She looked down at the deep descent with its narrow trail zigzagging down towards the bottom of the canyon. "Okay," she declared, "I'm joining you under the condition that you, Silvana, hold my hand."

She clung to my hand, as we started hiking down. At every bend of the trail, we changed positions so that at all times she walked by the mountain and not the cliff. I kept reminding her to breathe deeply, to enjoy the beauty of the magnificent hike, to deeply rejoice in the experience.

As we stopped at every turn to change positions, I invited her to look at God's creation surrounding us. Slowly, Alexa began to relax and her natural breathing pattern wasn't forced anymore. An hour into our descent, she declared that she was hungry and we took a break.

The rest of our trip was uneventful. Alexa had overcome her greatest fear. For her, it was truly liberating. It was her first experience in the mountains and she loved it. Her husband was very grateful, too. When we met, he pulled me into his arms and swung me high into the air.

Chapter 36

MENTAL ILLNESS: HERCULES, SUFFERING FROM GRANDIOSE DELUSIONS

Not all sessions end in healing. The following was a very rare case.

Hercules, an individual in his early fifties and very tall, had signed up for the 4-day session with me. He was a referral from the homeopath. He arrived in a taxi straight from a psychiatric clinic two hours away. He was one and a half hours late for his appointment, which created a problem because it would interfere with my schedule for the rest of the day.

Diagnosed as bipolar, I suspected he might be suffering from schizophrenia as well. He kept speaking without answering my questions. At one point, this extremely tall man got up and towered over me holding a ring with long spikes in front of my face. He said with a threatening voice, "You are aware I could destroy your beautiful face with this ring?"

Inside, I was terrified but responded calmly with, "I know" while looking him straight in the eyes. This startled him and he withdrew the ring and said, "You are not afraid. That is impressive. I have never experienced that." I ended the session at that point. Nothing had been accomplished.

The second day, he again arrived far too late and heavily loaded down with three large boxes filled with books of occult secret knowledge, his library of the Rosicrucian and Knights Templar, he said. I ignored it all. He also brought two paintings of high value he wanted to gift me with. Needless to say, I refused everything.

This day, he had a walking stick that apparently contained a secret dagger. Before I knew it, he was holding the dagger up against my chest, again probing my reaction. My apartment was located on the top floor of a three-story building. It had two floors and my healing room was upstairs under the roof. I was acutely aware of his insanity. Yet strangely, I felt very protected.

This sick individual proceeded to propose to me, promising me great fame and fortune. I announced that we had to end the session and that this would be our final meeting as the work was bringing no results. I went down to the living room and called a taxi, then grabbed his belongings to carry them downstairs and escort him out of the house while he loudly cursed at me. Three of my neighbors were alerted to the commotion so at least I had witnesses.

As the taxi arrived, the woman took one look at Hercules and told me she wasn't going give him a ride and was calling a male replacement.

I refused payment for my services stating that the work had brought zero results. Insulted, Hercules threw the whole bunch of bills at a plasterer, who was repairing some damage on the outdoor wall. I collected the money and handed it to the arriving cab driver. Hercules got into the cab and the driver handed him the bills. I saw them driving off and this was it for Hercules.

Section 4

Spiritual Realization

Chapter 37

ANNA IN THE REALM OF THE NATURE SPIRITS

Anna was one of the most renowned practitioners of homeopathy while I lived in Switzerland. I met her because I was curious to learn more about Kirlian photography and the photographic equipment she used. Anna promptly signed up for my intensive healing session cycle.

In the course of our work together, Anna entered the domain of the Nature Spirits. At first, she saw herself as a minor Nature Spirit tending to a cluster of flowering plants. She helped the plants grow from seed to flowering by keeping their etheric field clean. She was aiding soil conditions, the absorption of water, and she was also governing the light into every particle of each plant.

Anna experienced much joy in her role as a minor Nature Spirit. As the life cycle of the plants ended and they started to wither and decay, other Nature Spirits were in line to take care of the decaying matter. But Anna, the Nature Spirit, refused to let go and insisted on staying with the dying plants.

Her Nature Spirit guide instructed her to move on and accept a new task that was awaiting her in a slightly higher position. Yet Anna stubbornly refused. She was unable to let go and accept her new task that would allow a new experience. In her resistance, she got slowly pushed to the side by the other Nature Spirits as she witnessed them busy in their task of taking care of the decomposing matter.

With no task left for her, she watched the cycle of perfect order taking place. She no longer was part of it. While she had previously been a link in the chain of perfect order and harmony, she now witnessed that she had dropped away. She saw how all other Nature Spirits moved on once their particular task was completed.

Great sadness filled her and Anna cried bitter tears. She had dearly wanted to remain in her old position because she had loved her task so very much. She didn't want to let it go. But because Anna, the Nature Spirit refused to let go, she saw herself falling out of the great cycle of life and slowly dying herself. She could not go back and correct her wrong, it was too late. She was not part of the big plan anymore.

Anna's metaphorical experience as a Nature Spirit caused a great crisis for her, the professional homeopath. She came down with a high fever and strep throat and lay sick in bed for more than three weeks.

Yet, as a result of her deep work into the realm of the Nature Spirits, Anna realized that in her life as a practitioner she had for too long ignored the pleas of her patients to study with her.

It was imperative that she no longer refuse to pass on her knowledge. She began to understand clearly that her next step was teaching — she must teach and pass on what she had learned. This was her new task. Only by following through could she stay in the flow of her work, and by doing so, her life, as well as her work, would continue to expand.

Chapter 38

CLARA: HEALING THE RELATIONSHIP WITH HER FATHER

Clara and her life partner have undergone the Maha Intensive several times. During one of those healing cycles, Clara's intention was to clear her childhood, specifically the nonexistent relationship with her dad. She sent me the following email after our work.

"For all my life, what I can remember is that my father and I never got along. The longest conversation we have ever had was five minutes. When I traveled to see him this time, he was a different man — or maybe it was I who was different. Many things that irritated me about his mental condition didn't bother me this time. As a matter of fact, I was curious why he was saying what he was saying, so I simply asked him. He responded with some nonsense, but I simply went along with him and asked more. Finally, he just started laughing, which made me laugh, too. I'm not sure if he realized that what he said didn't push my buttons anymore. We had such a good time, and he cried when I left. I had never seen my father cry and needless to say, I cried, too.

But the most special moment came, when we said good-bye on the last day of my trip. I was heading toward the car, my husband was already sitting behind the steering wheel, and my father was standing with my mother and sister at the curb. As I was getting into the car, I had this strong feeling to turn back. I went toward him again, crying uncontrollably, when all of a sudden, my mother and my sister were stepping aside and two giant angels appeared between them and my father and me. It was as if my father and I were 'transported' into a different place. I no longer saw my mother nor my sister, I only saw my father.

We embraced and hugged and cried. I distinctly remember the atmosphere around us. It was as if we were not even standing on the ground. It was very bright all around us, but a different light than just plain sunlight. It was more of a greenish / bluish light rather than yellow. Those two angels were at least seven feet tall, dressed in white gowns. What I remember the most is that they looked so peaceful, not happy, not sad, not laughing or even noticeably smiling, just peaceful and blissful. I kept thinking to myself, "Is this the last time I would see my father?" The only 'answer' I felt was not to ask any questions but to simply enjoy my connection with him, like it didn't matter if this was the last time, the first time, or a time in between.

The only thing that mattered was the new love we felt for each other. When I got back into the car, my husband was crying. He told me later that he was so moved by what he had felt. He was very aware that something very special and different was going on with me and my father. He didn't see the angels, but when I told him where they were standing, he said that made perfect sense because it seemed to him that my mother and sister were 'being pushed out of the way' by some invisible force.

"Well, I cried for the next twelve hours, all the way home from Munich to San Francisco. The stewardesses couldn't calm me — even the captain came out to see if I was OK. I kept telling them that these were tears of joy, and that I was fine."

Chapter 39

Max: The Wise Young Boy

Max was Isabella's oldest son, 8 years old, a bright boy full of light. He requested his mom sign him up for the 4-day session cycle.

It is always rewarding to become witness to the wisdom of a child. In one of his sessions, Max had three experiences. In the first one, he was a boy walking on a path. He saw a sick cat walking towards him but before the cat reached him, he witnessed the poor cat crumble into dust.

In the second experience, he entered a restaurant and saw how someone was in great distress because he had lost a ring. Max bent down to help look for it, but the person sent him out of the room in fear that he would find the ring and not give it to the owner.

In his third experience, Max was walking on the street and saw how an elderly man lost his wallet. Max ran after him and handed the wallet to the man. The man was so grateful, he reached into the wallet and handed Max a silver coin.

Max saw three simple healer ethics in these experiences:

1. You cannot help everyone.

2. Even though you are able to help, your help might be refused.

3. When you are able to help, you are allowed to accept compensation.

His mom reported how after his healing sessions she saw Max standing in their living room surrounded by his two brothers and friends. He was explaining to them the meaning of "self-responsibility." She heard him say it the following way: "When you are small and you go on a hike, your father carries your backpack. But as you grow older, you each have to carry your own backpack and everything you put in is your own responsibility."

Chapter 40

ELLA: AN UNEXPECTED MESSAGE FROM SPIRIT

Friends of mine contacted me because their older daughter, Ella, was in crisis. They asked if Ella, in her early twenties, could visit and spend some time here at the HeartPath Retreat Center. Ella was from Holland and her parents were dear friends from when we were living in Afghanistan. Ella's best girlfriend had just recently committed suicide and Ella was struggling to understand why she had done so.

In one of Ella's healings, she wanted to contact her girlfriend and ask her for the deeper reasons of her suicide. Ella wanted to understand her and why anyone would choose to commit suicide. All of a sudden, Ella cupped her ears with her hands and kept turning her head from side to side. I asked her what was going on and Ella responded: "So much noise. All these voices, there are all these voices talking at once."

I encouraged Ella to attempt to cut out all voices except one and just listen to that one voice. This proved to be challenging at first because apparently all the voices were speaking at once, a whole cacophony of spirit voices.

"Listen to your girlfriend's voice, she wants to talk with you," I said. There was silence as Ella tried her hardest to cut out all voices and tune in to her girlfriend's voice.

After some time, she said, "You are very loved."

I responded with, "You see, Ella, your girlfriend is telling you that you are very loved. How wonderful. Ask her how she is doing."

Ella concentrated some more and then responded, "No, you, Silvana, are very loved."

"What do you mean I am very loved? Who is telling you that?"

Apparently, it wasn't her girlfriend speaking to Ella. Ella listened hard and then said: "Roberto. Roberto loves you very much."

Roberto and I had been lovers a long time ago. He had been my greatest love. But I chose motherhood over marrying him because my son was very jealous, and I at the time felt I was a mother first and then a lover. It had caused both of us deep pain. Had I married Roberto, I would have found fulfillment as a woman. But I would not have lived my destiny as a healer.

I had goose bumps all over. There was no way Ella could have known the name of the man I used to love. Even though my friends from Afghanistan and I stayed in loose contact, they went on to live in other countries while I with my family had lived our own lives far away from them. I had never talked about it to them, so I was utterly perplexed with what was happening. Roberto must have died, I assumed, and decided to contact my friends in Ecuador and ask them once Ella's healing session was over.

For the remainder of the healing session, Ella's desire to communicate with her girlfriend remained effortless. When she came out of the session, we talked for some time about suicide in general, her girlfriend, and what her possible reason of choosing to end her life could have been.

Back in my house, I called up my friends in Ecuador and inquired about Roberto. As far as they knew, he is alive and well, but they would find out and call me right back. A little while later the same day, I got a phone call with the confirmation that they had just talked to Roberto and that he was very much alive and well.

This experience stayed a mystery to me. I never found out who in the spirit world passed on this message to Ella. Had it been Roberto telling me from the other side it would have been more logical. But I was glad he was well. I chose not to call him myself because he was married and I wanted to avoid any conflict or upset.

Chapter 41

OLIVIA AND HER GRANDFATHER'S MESSAGE

Upon purchasing the empty piece of land here in the green valley of Pojoaque (Tewa for "Water Gathering Place") to build the HeartPath Retreat Center, I knew immediately where I needed to erect a stone circle. I always have had an affinity for megaliths and visited the ones in Carnac, France[15] and the island of Corsica in the Mediterranean. But I was not familiar with famous Stonehenge in Britain.

The purpose of a stone changes when it gets erected. They become transmitters of cosmic energy grounding it into the Earth. One of my stones I call Clara. This is how it came to be named Clara.

Clara used to be the center stone in the original, quite smaller stone circle I built. During that time, I once approached that particular stone and stood in front of it with my eyes closed. Suddenly, I heard a soft voice saying, "I am Clara."

I opened my eyes. It was the spirit of the stone that had spoken. Strange, I mused to myself, I would never call a stone "Clara." I closed my eyes again and instantly felt a strong purge from head to toe in my center line. Wow, now I understood Clara's purpose: clearing, to clear.

Upon erecting my new stone circle with much larger stones, Clara was placed in the power position standing right behind the natural stone slab that is the altar. Since then, I call Clara the teacher stone because Clara is the one who has given me the knowledge and insight of the standing stones.

Olivia was a student of mine. During one week of our trainings with a group of students, we worked with the huge boulders at the stone circle that I call "The Council of the Wise Elders." Standing by the altar, everyone was picking a boulder they felt called to work with. Having chosen, they slowly approached their elder. All were wearing eye masks as they started to tune in.

Everyone was in deep process when Olivia started coughing and gagging violently. I went to her and asked what was happening. She was sobbing and responded that her grandfather was pushing soil down her

---

[15] Carnac is a commune on the Gulf of Morbihan on the south coast of Brittany in north-western France.

throat and was telling her that he needed to tell her something painful to hear.

In Europe, we have a practice that when a child falls and cuts their knee open, soil is rubbed on it. It is supposedly healing. So it was clear to both of us why her deceased grandfather pushed soil down her throat.

I encouraged Olivia to listen to what her grandfather was eager to tell her. He wanted Olivia to pass on a message to his wife, Olivia's grandmother, who was still alive. Her grandfather told Olivia it was a secret that he took with him to his grave. The secret lay heavy on him and didn't allow him any peace. It was impossible to him to find peace, he confided. He had never dared tell anyone.

He shared that during WWII, he was released from active service in the German army because he was slightly impaired. Therefore, he was assigned to civil service. Every evening, he invented stories for his wife telling her in which parts of the city he had been with other crew members to clean up the remains of buildings that had been bombed.

But in truth, they were driven every day to the Auschwitz concentration camp to work. They had to dig mass graves for thousands of murdered victims and carry out the dead bodies from the gas chambers. This weighed heavily on him.

The next morning, Olivia called her grandmother and told her. Her grandmother couldn't have cared less. She was oblivious to it all. But that didn't matter. What mattered was that her grandfather had found a listening ear in Olivia and could release the secret that had burdened him so.

Chapter 42

CHARLES: COLOR DRUNK

Charles' wife, who worked extensively with me, sent her husband to undergo the session cycle because she wanted him to experience what had caused her tremendous transformation. He was a successful banker in a leading advisory position to the count of Lichtenstein. He reported that he was doing great in his job, his relationship with his wife and children was very loving, and that he was happy with himself. In short, his life was perfect, all was perfect.

It was the first time I encountered someone in my healing practice whose life was perfect. I felt a bit at a loss because there were no presenting complaints. All Charles brought to the table was curiosity as to what could or would happen.

Regardless, we proceeded with the given framework of the session cycle. During his third session, he saw himself in a middle-aged male body sitting at a piano playing for a large audience in a concert hall. Charles was stunned. He played piano in his current life, but it was only for family gatherings, never in public. He loved playing the piano, but only privately.

Charles' couldn't grasp what he was seeing. He had never believed in past lives. He was confused and questioned what was happening. I suggested he surrender to the experience and simply witness without judgment.

There were long pauses as bit by bit was revealed and he immersed himself more deeply into the experience. He kept seeing himself in large concert halls with ever-increasing numbers of listeners. He traveled throughout Europe from one concert engagement to another. There were long pauses as he kept listening to his various compositions.

Suddenly, Charles reported that he could not hear the music anymore. Instead, he saw the colors related to the respective sound frequencies. This was bliss, ecstasy. He couldn't grasp what he was experiencing as he was utterly immersed in an ocean of vibrant colors. He stayed in silence for a long, long time.

Charles remarked that he'd become completely unaware of his audience, oblivious of his hands playing the piano and the melodies they produced. The colors, the colors, the colors — an entire ocean filled with color. A different, unexplored universe presented itself to Charles. He was floating in an ocean of vibrant and moving colors. What a blissful experience.

As the concert pianist, this was how he died that lifetime, performing a concert and floating towards eternity in bliss, utterly and completely color drunk.

I left Charles for a bit so that he could gather his thoughts and process what he had just experienced. Getting up, he was thoroughly amazed and speechless. He said he would do some research to find out which renowned pianist had passed away while performing during a concert. Charles was changed forever, his mind expanded allowing the possibility of this new experience to heighten his consciousness.

Chapter 43

DAVID: THE YOUNG HEARTBROKEN WARLORD

I met David and his mom at a luncheon some friends were giving and the three of us started chatting. They were visiting from Israel and on a vacation in the US. David was eleven years old, not yet in puberty, a delightful and bright young boy. When he heard what my profession was, he asked his mom to sign him up for a healing session.

In sharing, David told me he felt great sadness and guilt but didn't know the reason for his feelings. He felt that he didn't deserve to feel lighthearted and happy in his life. He shared that ever since he was a small boy he had felt depressed even though his parents loved him, his relationship with his brother was excellent, and he received all the love and care he could want — he should be happy.

I guided David into a meditative state of awareness and aligned him with his higher guidance. We asked what he needed to see in order to understand his grief and guilt. David at once started sobbing uncontrollably. He saw a previous life as a war leader on a battlefield. His army was immense and counted many thousands of soldiers. But they were losing. He witnessed his men dying. There was no hope, not even for a single survivor. He knew he would die with them. I guided David to the time prior to the battle.

David was preparing his army for battle against another army. He felt great responsibility to lead his men, victoriously win the battle with minimal loss on his side. He designed the plan for attack and calculated the right timing for it. But they were surprised when the opposing army ambushed them with more men than anticipated. David had not taken into account that possibility and was devastated because he already knew they were at a severe disadvantage.

He watched his men fighting with great bravery at his side, but it was a lost battle from the start. It became a massacre. He died a miserable death with his men. While he defended an attacker from the front, another killed him from behind by spearing his heart.

David cried bitter tears as he faced all his feelings of responsibility and duty — and his failure. He was burdened by tremendous remorse. So many men had trusted him and lost their lives. So many wives became widows and children fatherless.

I left the room for a moment for David to reflect on his experience. When I returned, David sat up, wiping away more tears. He said he felt very calm and peaceful inside. His Heart felt at peace. By seeing his past, he finally understood the pain he'd carried for so long.

He felt how the burden of his position as a conqueror — and thus the risk of abusing his power — had laid heavy on him. He said that in his current life he constantly shied away from any situation that required responsibility and leadership skills. It had become clear to him that he is afraid of his power because his earlier lifetime had ended horribly. He now understood the reason for it all. It all made such sense to him as if a puzzle was finally solved.

David affirmed that he was naturally inclined to be a leader, that he differed from his classmates. He said he constantly thought ahead of situations and looked at all the sides for possible outcomes prior to the situation becoming a reality. He always thought of his pack and saw himself in the position of leading them through experiences. He concluded that by understanding what had happened in the past life that he would no longer avoid positions of leadership but live his natural talent by stepping up and into his power.

PART V

SPECIFIC THEMES & CASE STUDIES

When the Soul Calls: True Stories of Deep Healing and Transformation

Chapter 44

TENSU BODY INJURY TRAUMA RELEASE HEALING

"When it comes to making a big change in your life,
you have to want it more than you fear it."
~ Anonymous

The TENSU healing approach was a gift from Spirit when some years back a dear friend of mine was in a car crash that severely shattered her arm and hand. I combined very gentle intuitive touch with dialoguing. In a dream the following night, I continued working with her and woke up to the word TENSU. I Googled it. It is Japanese for tense, neurotic, agitated, rigid, taut, strained. Hence, the TENSU Body Injury Trauma Release Healing came into being.

Wherever an injury occurs, an energy cyst is created, an energetic block that physically impairs a person. It can result in various symptoms such as numbness, lack of mobility, a physical block or pain, and more. What generally happens is that in order to avoid causing pain and stress on the injured body part, the individual begins to compensate by overusing another body part.

As I described in PART III, Section 3, Chapter 15, "The Various Healing Modalities of the HeartPath Re-Alignment," when an injury occurs, the cells in that area become frozen due to shock. This creates an "energy cyst." No energy can flow in that area in a healthy way because it's blocked. On an energetic level, that part of the body appears to be "dead." This might often be experienced as numbness. Unfortunately, traditional physical therapy tends to bring slow and sometimes very limited success.

In the TENSU healing approach, the healer very gently works with the body part where the injury had the strongest impact. By doing so, it is likely that the individual will experience the accident again. They will be "seeing" what happened when the accident occurred, possibly while they were unconscious. This initiates a natural, organic healing process. Like a computer that's frozen, the energy system gets rebooted. The cells of the body remember the trauma and begin to release it.

This experience is usually accompanied by a strong emotional release. The benefit for the body is immediate. During the first session, the practitioner connects with the frozen tissue and by doing so begins to move it. The second session further moves and fine tunes the re-flowing of energy. The third session removes any last residual residue of trauma and the energy cyst.

If the presenting complaint is a physical ailment, I will communicate directly with the body to get to the root cause beyond the physical symptoms.

In the case of an accident followed by surgery, it is best to come for TENSU healings as soon as possible, even within the week and prior to starting with physical therapy. The process of the work is extremely gentle and the same as described above. The frozen energy around the area of the surgery will start to flow again and recovery time will be minimized.

Chapter 45

JUDY'S CAR ACCIDENT

You might remember Judy and her almost miscarriage from a previous chapter. She was adopted soon after birth by a childless family. She never learned who her biological mother was. Her parents knew the identity of her biological mom, but her mother told her that letters and pictures they sent remained unanswered. Judy received loving care but she always felt like an outsider. A few years after being adopted, her adoptive mother twice became pregnant and Judy grew up with two younger brothers.

Judy and I share the same birth date, which puts us both on the cusp of Libra / Scorpio. After her training in the HeartPath Re-Alignment, Judy became my assistant for several years prior to pursuing accounting in the movie industry. Because she'd been adopted, there was the possibility that Judy felt deeply embedded shame in regard to her identity. For her, letting go is extremely difficult.

An example involves Adam, her former husband from whom she was separated but who kept pursuing for more than eight years after they'd separated — and only was able to let go when he re-married. Her heart and soul kept clinging to this man who had abused her, continually used her financially to support not only his life but the life of his new family, which grew into four members. He kept controlling her via their daughter Genevieve for whom he never had been able to pay child support. For some reason, Judy always felt that he, as the father of their daughter, should be forgiven for his behavior. Because she never spoke up, Judy kept enduring ongoing emotional stress and pain until not long ago.

Baby Genevieve grew up under very dysfunctional circumstances. Judy did her best but, unfortunately, the courts didn't give her sole custody. Genevieve was very sick with fevers and throat infections throughout her childhood whenever she spent the week at her father's. Returning home to her mom, it generally took a week for Genevieve to recover. After a week with her mom, she was sent straight back to her dad's where she would get sick again.

This cycle was repeated into Genevieve's teens. The breaks from Genevieve gave Judy a chance to concentrate on work as she provided the only source of income since Adam only made $50 a week with his gigs. The financial stress of raising Genevieve rested solely on Judy and she worked hard with three and four different jobs at a time while taking care of her daughter. This only improved when Judy landed a job doing accounting at Sony and later at MGM.

Judy moved to Los Angeles and then New York. On her travels, she met her second husband and they were married a couple of years later.

Genevieve was now fifteen years old and felt responsible for playing the role of "rescuer" of her mentally ill dad. Adam had put her in the role of being the sole comforter in his life, and Genevieve learned that she alone understood him and could calm him whenever he suffered an anxiety attack, his condition worsening by the day.

Adam's mother had a complete break with her son and after many years of blaming Judy, can fully see the mental illness of her son. Not long ago, she almost passed away due to a brain aneurysm, and now, ironically, her son is taking care of her and in deep depression. Adam's second marriage is in severe crisis, their dysfunctional marriage falling apart and the children suffering. Genevieve takes care of her siblings whenever they are back in New Mexico.

Three years ago, Judy left her job with Sony to be closer to Genevieve's father and while driving, a drunk, hit-and-run driver totaled her brand-new Mercedes. The accident shattered her left arm in many pieces causing her hand to become lame. The accident was such a shock to her system that Judy completely retreated and even forbade her fiancé to see her.

The surgery of her arm was traumatic and resulted in fifty-one metal staples covering her lower left arm. Plus, the bad news from the surgeon was that Judy would unfortunately never be able to use her left hand again because there was wide-spread nerve damage. On top of all of this, Judy also got laid off from her new job and had no more income.

When Judy came to my house for dinner with Genevieve, she had already been through two full months of physical therapy with zero results. Her hand was numb and her arm was limp and useless. Judy called it a chicken wing.

As we sat by the fireplace while Genevieve was in the kitchen playing with my dogs and cats, I performed a TENSU healing on Judy. I closed my eyes and "saw" what her arm wanted to do and in which position it wanted to be moved ever so gently. There was absolutely no force or pressure. Nevertheless, Judy screamed and wailed in pain. She saw images of the accident and re-witnessed her terror.

For the entire time, there was a huge amount of uncontrolled emotional release. Afterwards, Judy experienced an ever-so-slight ability to move her arm and hand. Then, days after the healing, she was able to slightly move not only her hand but her fingers. She was also having a bit more mobility in her arm and shoulder.

During her second TENSU healing a week later, there was again the same intensity of emotional release and physical pain. But, very importantly, Judy realized the reason for her accident. She was on her way to an event to see her daughter with Adam waiting for her. She was totally upset and frustrated with having returned to New Mexico but now seeing with different eyes the painful past she wanted to fully leave behind. Yet, here she was having to revisit Adam and his new wife's loathing for her with all the same dysfunctions as before. That was when a driver without control of his vehicle smashed into her car from the left.

During the TENSU healing, Judy was able to experience the accident all over again. There were witnesses but no-one had been able to read the license plate of the hit-and-run driver. Soon after the accident, an orthopedic surgeon reconstructed the broken bones in her arm with plates and screws. Judy experienced it all again.

Following the second TENSU healing, much more of Judy's hand flexibility had returned. Only a few weeks afterwards, miraculously, Judy was able to return to work. Her recovery time was less than a month and she was able to type on the computer again. Within a year, her hand has fully recovered and there is no difference detected between her left and her right hands. She also made the difficult choice to cut all communications with Adam and start traveling again, taking Genevieve with her, in search of a new beginning.

Judy recently wrote: "Thank you for the TENSU healing you gifted me with, as without it not only would I have lost the use of my hand and arm and the future I am living now, but I wouldn't have been able to draw upon my memory of it to help our dog Cookie with his two lymphoid tumors."

Chapter 46

JACKIE: A DANGEROUS FALL FROM A HORSE RESULTS IN SPLEEN SURGERY

Not long ago, I used the TENSU healing approach of my practice on a woman who fourteen days earlier had been released from a 4-day stay at the hospital where she had undergone surgery on her spleen due to a fall from a horse. She had started immediately with physical therapy several times a week but reported no progress.

In order to gift herself with some precious mother-daughter bonding time with her eleven-year-old daughter, Jackie had booked an hour-long horse-riding experience with a supposedly professional company offering such services. Unfortunately, the owner of the company reeked heavily of alcohol and had zero clue about how to handle a fall from a horse and perform first aid though he was supposedly certified in it.

He did all the wrong things and simply dropped Jackie and her daughter off at the emergency room of the hospital and then took off. This was during COVID-19 with all its many restrictions and regulations. Jackie's daughter was refused entry because of the COVID restrictions and her age, but Jackie had no one arranged to pick her daughter up. Not exactly the issues one should have to deal with after a violent accident. Five days after her spleen surgery, the hospital released her knowing that at home she was the sole caretaker and provider of two toddlers and her eleven-year-old daughter.

Jackie arrived at my retreat moaning in pain. She reported a great deal of soreness on the entire left side of her body. The area around her spleen felt numb, but also hurt. She couldn't lift her left arm and every movement in every position caused pain. She was unable to find comfort even in sleep.

I helped Jackie onto the massage table and into a relatively comfortable position. As she lay there, I stood by her feet and induced a still point.[16] After a few minutes, I closed my eyes and connected with her body. I saw the different contorted positions her body had been forced into during the fall. Then I informed Jackie of my intention and encouraged her to share any and all upcoming sensations she might be feeling.

---

[16] Still point is a term in Cranio-Sacral Therapy. A still point is induced by stopping the spinal fluid from running up and down the spine. It shuts down the stress cycle by allowing the body and its nervous system to restore and rebalance itself.

I gently took her hand in mine while talking to her and started to ever-so-slowly and carefully move her arm. Jackie was to report every single time she felt pain. Soon enough, she began to continuously moan and wail in pain. Her breath became short and forced. At times, she stopped breathing and I had to keep reminding her to breathe deeply.

I guided Jackie through the pain and to a place where pictures and images of the accident came to her. She re-lived the trauma of the violent fall and her tremendous fear of dying. She saw herself lying on the ground momentarily unconscious. Next, she felt again the inexpertly grabbing hands of the guy who kept clapping his hand on her back, which was extremely painful to her. All the while, she kept screaming, "Stop, stop! You're hurting me! You reek of alcohol!"

Jackie re-experienced every second of the accident in minute detail with all her emotions and fear of death attached to it. She constantly kept returning to her thoughts of *"Thank God it was me, thank God it was not my daughter on that horse."* The very thought of her daughter in danger of dying was unbearable for Jackie.

The healing session exhausted Jackie. I helped her off the table and she went to the bathroom. She came back and stood in front of me and said: "Oh my, I can't believe it! I just pulled up my jeans with both hands. I was unable to do that before. Look, I can even lift my arm. I can't believe it! After ONE healing!" Jackie was overjoyed. She was also very sore, which I assured her would remain for the next few days. We booked the next healing session for a week later.

Jackie reported that she indeed had remained very sore for the next two days after the healing. I explained to her that the soreness was natural, that her tissues were starting to release the numbness from the shock and trauma of the accident and, therefore, she was experiencing soreness. This made sense to her.

During the next healing session, I started to work with more of Jackie's different body parts. I included the other side of her body as well and had her turn around on the table. I extensively worked on Jackie's head and neck, as well as directly on the area of the impact of the fall: her belly and spleen, rib cage, and hips. Her flexibility had increased a great deal in comparison to the previous time.

Again, Jackie dropped into a very deep process of much emotional release accompanied by constant moaning, wailing, and sobbing. She saw many different images of the accident and connected with all the emotions she had felt when it happened. This time, she realized how much fear of death she experienced and how deeply the trauma had anchored in her system.

It was imperative to do this work extremely gently and with zero force or pressure. I had to intuit what the body needed to do in order to return to the time of the trauma and the contortions it wanted to experience so it could unwind the trauma and then release it. A couple of days later, Jackie again reported more improvement and was looking forward to the third TENSU healing.

By the third healing session, she had regained almost all the movement capability in her arm and she had begun working again. With each additional TENSU healing, we continued fine tuning and kept releasing more of the cellular memory of the trauma. Jackie started to see past lives related to the impacted body parts and she experienced other important realizations.

In all, we completed two sets of three TENSU healings. Within a little over a month, Jackie felt almost fully recovered. She even participated in the PowerLine Workout, a challenging fitness program in and of itself.

Section 2

Depression

Chapter 47

THE UNDERLYING REASON FOR DEPRESSION & THE COLORATION IN THE ENERGETIC FIELD

We can choose to view depression not as a mental illness but
as a state of Deep Rest, a spiritual exhaustion that we enter
into when we are de-pressed (pressed down) by the weight
of the false self, the mask,
the mind-made story of 'me.'

We long to stop pretending, and express our raw truth!
To give voice to our secret loneliness, our shame, our broken
hearts, boredom, and brilliant rage.
Depression's call to truth needs to be listened to and
understood, not analyzed or medicated away.

There is no shame in your exhaustion. We are all exhausted,
my love. Slow down today. Allow yourself to rest, deeply.
And weep. And breathe. And being again. Now.
I say, our depression is holy. It contains the seeds of new life."

~ Jeff Foster

The major reason for depression is repressed anger. Instead of anger being expressed appropriately when the emotion is felt, it is being suppressed and thus internalized. This results in a loss of personal power when one's truth — instead of being expressed verbally — is being withheld and thus internalized. This often happens during one's childhood years and then continues as a pattern into later life.

Suppressed and repressed feelings of anger lead to resentment. During this phase, the person is often still very much in contact with their feelings. Utter frustration, rage, and rebellion can be felt during that stage. Usually they are not fully expressed but again suppressed.

In the later stage, resentment leads to resignation. This is the stage where, internally, the individual has given up the hope for any change. Viewed energetically, resignation is a standstill position where feelings are not allowed in anymore, nor are they being released. It is a stage of utter stagnation. All hope for change has been given up.

Resignation leads to the last stage: depression. Depression is a place beyond hopelessness. Severe depression feels like death. Energetically, all life has died and has given room to an emotional numbness. One might feel as if a large glass bell filled with cotton balls is surrounding one's head. This is what it felt like to me once. Outside of it, life goes on, but within in it there is death.

Coming from the notion that our body, our immensely complex bio computer stores anything and everything, there is good reason why our psyche signals a red light of warning when depression is starting to settle into our system. Those signs need to be read and understood, which most often is not the case. Unfortunately, our mind-based and success-oriented society immediately turns to the remedy of Prozac or other antidepressants whenever grief, injustice, deep frustration, etc., is felt or to treat any mental dysfunction, such as anxiety disorders, which can also lead to the symptoms of depression.

Sadly, the underlying reasons for a depression keep being ignored or not dealt with. This is never healthy. Nowadays, to a very large degree, we have distanced ourselves from a natural and healthy lifestyle. And what we call "normal" is the norm, meaning the majority of the population is dealing with it even though the norm or the majority of the population is sick to one degree or another.

OUR SOCIETY CALLS "NORMAL"
WHAT IS THE ACCEPTED NORM

YET THE NORM AND NORMAL
IS A FAR CRY FROM HEALTHY

Fresh anger is a natural outburst of emotion as a reaction to an intolerable situation. It lasts no longer than 10-15 seconds. I am referring to the original emotion of anger and not built-up anger from past situations projected onto current situations. On the energetic level, fresh anger looks bright red, like fresh blood, in the human auric field.

Anger that has not been expressed keeps building up. Suppressed anger looks dark red, like a wound left untreated.

Anger in the stage of resentment is very old stored-up anger that has never been released. There are strong feelings of bitterness and resentment associated with it. Resentment looks yellowish / green, like puss.

Anger in the stage of resignation has turned dark maroon / brown, like an old wound that has never been treated.

Depression on the energetic level looks like a cloud of dark gray to blackish energy.

"I sat with my anger long enough,
until she told me her real name was grief.

~ The Minds Journal

Fresh Anger	➡	bright red
⬇		
Suppressed Anger	➡	dark red
⬇		
Resentment	➡	yellowish / green
⬇		
Resignation	➡	dark maroon / brown
⬇		
Depression	➡	dark grey / blackish

Chapter 48

ELENA: AN UNDERSTANDING OF THE ORIGIN OF HER DEPRESSION

Elena, a woman in her thirties, came to see me because for three years she'd suffered from deep depression that put her life at risk. She admitted that she often played with the thought of exiting and bringing an end to her misery.

Elena's only son, Justin, had tragically passed away from leukemia at only five years of age. Life had been extremely hard for Elena ever since. Adding to it all, her husband Ethan recently told Elena that he was seeking a divorce because he could no longer watch her suffering and being unable to help. He stated that if he stayed, they would both die.

Elena shared that, for Ethan, the death of their son had also been deeply disturbing but she said he had been able to pick himself up after a year-long period of deep mourning, whereas for her this had proven to be impossible. She had lost her boy and nothing and no one would ever be able to make amends for this. She had lost what she called was the essence of her life.

The pregnancy with Justin had been challenging because Elena suffered from heart disease and her doctor had strictly advised to restrain from another pregnancy after Justin. As a result, Elena underwent a hysterectomy.

When little Justin passed away, Elena refused antidepressants because she wanted to feel the full measure of her grief. But as the year passed, she understood that without antidepressants she was unable to get out of bed and live a somewhat normal life. But she also felt the medications numbed her authentic feelings, adding to other negative side effects, and she wished to be able to wean off them.

During her healing process, Elena relived her life circumstances prior to the birth of Justin. She realized that she had never been truly happy in her life, not even when she fell in love with Ethan. She understood that even prior to her son's passing, she had suffered from a life-long lingering depression, which she had covered up with false behavior, a mask. In doing so, she had learned to deny her true feelings and kept pretending to the world that she was fine and all was well.

Looking at her early childhood, Elena saw herself as a girl of eight years old. Her mom had dealt with chronic depression. Elena's subconscious showed her how her mother rejected her life because she had given in to a marriage with a man she had never loved. The man she did love had left her for a girlfriend of hers, and in order to cover up her heart's pain, she had given in to the pursuits of Elena's dad. They married and had Elena.

Her mom felt her life was wasted. Because of her suppressed feelings of anger, she neglected her duties as a mother and emotionally never bonded with Elena. Elena's dad felt his wife's rejection. Their sex life was nonexistent, which turned Elena's dad into a frustrated workaholic. He was extremely strict with Elena and oftentimes punished her without any obvious reason. Elena, as a child, had swallowed all his pent-up feelings of anger, which were in truth directed at her mom.

As all this came to full consciousness for Elena, she started to process all the anger she had felt as a child towards her parents. During one healing session, she expressed her suppressed anger and as a result started to feel compassion for the life circumstances into which she had been born. While dialoguing first with her mom and then her dad, she was able to forgive both her parents. Her Heart started to open and love started to flow again.

Elena also realized that a good amount of the depression she had been dealing with was in fact passed on from her mother to her. She had taken it all on. She prepared a big package with all her mother's suppressed feelings and returned it to her mother. Her mother, in turn, received the package, kept what was hers and passed on the remainder to her father, Elena's grandfather. Elena's grandfather had been dealing with unresolved feelings of anger and as a result turned bitter because he had lost his leg in a useless war (WWI).

While Elena was returning to the time when Justin had turned ill, she looked at all the resentment and anger she had felt towards God. Her son had not even started his life yet. How in the world was such injustice possible?! She had been a devout Christian before, but when Justin died, she felt deceived by God and as a result turned away and no longer prayed.

Suppressed anger towards God is another underlying reason for depression. This is oftentimes so covered up that only very deep healing work can uncover it.

Elena reported that upon arriving home, her husband and she began to dialogue and share deeply what had been happening to Elena and her life circumstances leading to her deep depression. They were able to rekindle their original feelings for each other and decided to leave for a month-long vacation to Italy, France, and Spain. Returning back home, Elena decided to write down her life experience of losing a child in the hope her story might help and possibly inspire other parents with the same fate.

Section 3

The Vicious Cycle of Victim / Victimizer and Rescuer

Chapter 49

WHY THE ROLE OF THE RESCUER IS NEVER OF BENEFIT

"When you stop blaming others
For your own suffering
And take responsibility
For your own happiness
You shift from a place of victimhood
To a place of power."

~ The Voice from the Wild

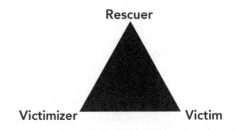

For almost anyone, life circumstances present us with moments where someone requires help beyond a kind word and a smile or answering a general question. We might be present when someone falls or has an accident or we might witness something that requires our interference and interaction. We do this willingly because life is a constant interplay between humans. And offering help is what good, generous, caring, and supportive humans beings do.

Sadly, it's a natural instinct that in our times is often neglected because many humans have become numb. Someone might get killed in front of witnesses but bystanders will freeze or turn away out of fear or helplessness in order to protect themselves. Others will simply exhibit pure apathy, such as in the case of a woman who was raped and killed in a courtyard surrounded by high apartment buildings at night when most people were at home. The onlookers watched from their windows but were too lazy to go downstairs and act and prevent someone suffering and losing their life.

How about all the professional journalists and amateurs in search of a great shot they can sell for a high price that will make them famous overnight who, instead of offering help, would rather take a video and photograph? Or the ones who document animal torture and experimentation who don't step in to prevent but silently watch and video?

Where is the involved and embracing Heart capable of empathy and compassion and feeling the victim's pain as if it were its own?! Apparently, people don't realize that those images, though bought for a high price, was the selling of their Soul and that the scenes they witnessed will haunt them for the rest of their lives and beyond.

The animal kingdom presents us with countless examples of animals helping their fellow animals and even other species. For example, the leopard who killed a mother monkey but then had mercy on the baby and tried to take care of it when its motherly instincts kicked in. Or the National Geographic photographer who was certain his last moment had arrived when his head and camera were swallowed by a large sea lion who then instead let go of him, turned compassionate, and during several days tried to feed him by offering him squid and other food.

We only need to open our eyes to spot victims needing help. In our circle of friends and close family members there are always victims to be found. And this is where it gets tricky. How much help do we offer, to whom, and under what circumstances? We are required to learn to decipher if the one in need of help is trapped in a situation that keeps repeating itself, in which case they need to climb out by themselves in order to leave their victim role behind and change their life situation. Or it could be that we intuitively feel that our help and involvement will change and transform their life.

In such a situation much is at stake. By helping or rescuing, do we indeed offer aid when most needed? It could well be. And by doing so, will the victim be able to transform their life on their own? The good intentions of the rescuer might get tapped again and again and the rescuer could end up exhausting their resources and good intentions.

Indeed, there is such a fine and challenging line between becoming the rescuer and offering aid. I learned this in my youth. The younger brother of my first boyfriend was consuming hashish, which during those times, was illegal in Switzerland. When his father found out, he reported his own son to the police. Perry learned his lesson, cleaned up his act, and turned his life around.

Whereas with my younger brother Franco, who was a friend of Perry, it became a whole different story. In puberty, Franco started to experiment with drugs just like Perry, but my dad felt sorry for Franco and also ashamed that his son would do such a thing. At age sixteen, Franco got caught by the police and by court order had to spend a few months at a youth detention center. When Franco married and had two children, my dad ended up financially supporting Franco for the rest of his life.

As a teen, hearing that Perry got turned in to the police by his own dad felt heartless to me. Yet I came to understand that what Perry's dad did was for his son's own benefit. In the long run, the role of the rescuer never serves the victim. The rescuer ends up becoming a victim themselves while the victim remains enabled to keep living their lifestyle.

This is the fine line I was talking about. We need to be able to distinguish between when our compassionate Heart is needed in giving aid and when our compassionate Heart needs to be strict, responsible, and resolute.

Section 4

Possessions and Entity Attachments

Chapter 50

EARTH-BOUND ENTITY ATTACHMENTS & POSSESSIONS

Upon dying, the spirit ideally chooses to leave the earth plane and moves on into the Light. However, there are some common reasons why a spirit chooses to stay earth-bound. One such reason is addictions. If a person who died suffered from addictions during their lifetime, they are taking their addiction with them even after passing on. Those addictions keep haunting them and demand to be satisfied. Since the person isn't in their body anymore and thus able to continue with their addictive habits, they attach themselves to someone who is alive and in a body with that same addiction. In this way, they stay earth-bound.

For example, in the case of heroin addiction, every time the addict satisfies their addictive need, the spirit gets their shot as well. I have perceived as many as four spirit entities attached to such addicts.

The same goes for any other addiction. As we all know, alcohol addiction is extremely common. So is cannabis addiction. Most regular cannabis consumers argue that cannabis is not addictive. And like with all addictions, the line between enjoying and consumption is very thin. There is a huge difference between need and not need. When something starts to control us rather than we controlling it, we can be certain that we need it.

Therefore, it would be much healthier to explore and find out why that substance is so direly needed. It can be to numb anxiety and stress, build confidence and self-esteem, to release any kind of pain, or for whatever reason. But all of those reasons have a deeper cause at their root. With an addiction, the person is always dependent and never free. And when we are not free, we are bound. Hence the word "earth-bound" for spirits that stay attached to the material plane after death.

It is never healthy to become host to an earth-bound entity, not even if the spirit is your grandma who died and means well and wants to protect you. This is because we're meant to be by ourselves. Our body is not designed to become host to an earth-bound entity wanting to accompany us. It's not our purpose to carry the weight of others. When you are traveling or hiking, you are carrying your own baggage, rather than the baggage of two, three, or four people.

One evening, I took a series of five pictures of a former relationship of mine while he was sitting at a table — stoned — and waiting for dinner. Upon scrolling through the images I had just taken, the second-to-last picture overlay the last picture. It shows quite visibly, an entity possessing my friend. It's the face of a man with deeply sunken eyes, three times larger than life, while my friend is pushed way down and to the side in the picture. I saw it at once and burst out with "Oh my, you're not by yourself!" But he didn't see the possession until fourteen days later, when he looked at the images again because a friend of his made the same comment I had made, "You're not by yourself."

Yet, earth-bound entity attachments are very common. In my practice I have often witnessed that the reason for a disease is an earth-bound entity attachment. For example, when a person who died suffered from a disease, let's say diabetes, and then stays earth-bound and attaches itself to someone close to them who is still alive, the disease might take over and the body of the live person will begin to suffer from that disease.

I often hear people say that a loved one is protecting them, that their father or whoever has become their angel. I keep advising clients to not seek such protection because by doing so, a pact is made that keeps the spirit from pursuing its own path after death. In other words, while we are here on Earth and in the body, we have certain tasks to accomplish and fulfill. This is our purpose while in our bodies. The same is the case when we leave our bodies behind. Our soul then moves on and has new tasks that it must fulfill.

An earthbound entity captured in a picture is extremely rare.

Keeping someone earth-bound due to love hinders their ability to pursue their own path. An earth-bound entity is not an angel. And, likewise, angels have never had a body. In a different chapter, I write about the hierarchy of angels. There are angels assigned with certain duties for humankind. For example, your guardian angel is assigned to guide and protect you. Your guardian angel does this better than any earth-bound entity ever could because it is the angel's purpose and assignment from Source.

The best and easiest way for anyone to detect whether they are dealing with an angel or an earth-bound entity is to feel where the energy is coming from. An entity is always either to the side of the person or to the side and up. An angel is always straight up, in a straight line about three feet or more above the person's head.

Another common reason for an entity to stay earth-bound is trauma. If a person suffered a serious physical trauma, they might not realize they're not in their body anymore. They stay frozen in the experience and it will take a long time to leave that state and be able to move on. I write about this in Chapter 52, which describes the Antelope Canyon Tragedy where a group of hikers were caught by a flash flood while in the slot canyon.

Another possibility is that a spirit loves the earth plane to such a degree that they never want to be anywhere else but on Earth. For them, life continues just as before even after they left their body, such as in the example in the next chapter "Olivia and the Drowned Spirits of Lake Powell." Archaeologists are well aware that ancient sites are still alive. The spirits of the past continue to live there. It's a good thing that in nearby Tsanqawi, excavation was halted to allow the spirits to rest in peace.

When an injustice happened like murder or severe abuse, the spirit of the victim might stay around and haunt the place. Houses and castles all over the world are well known for being spooky and haunted. While in Europe, I gave a workshop at a castle. Several of the group members were very sensitive, particularly to the dungeon. In the middle of the night, I got called to the room of one participant who was awakened by a male spirit wearing a black hat in her room.

Fear of God and fear of the Light is another common reason why a spirit stays earth-bound. While in their physical body, a person might have done something they feel very guilty about. Therefore, after death, they feel unworthy of the Light and fear God might punish them. Or the person practiced blasphemy, cursed, and ridiculed God and once they've passed on, feel guilt for it.

An easy way to detect an entity attachment is when you find yourself doing things you know are unhealthy for you or doing things you don't really want to do but you do it nevertheless. Usually, it's an entity attachment or entity possession talking you into doing it. It doesn't have to be something major like the man who murdered John Lennon, who kept hearing exact instructions in his ears of what to do and when to kill. The persuasion can be subtle and for seemingly small things. Yet,

191

I suggest you examine yourself carefully whenever you experience conflict between what you in your highest want to do and what you end up doing. It is then that you can find an entity attached to your field.

Chapter 51

OLIVIA AND THE DROWNED SPIRITS OF LAKE POWELL

During one of our wilderness experiences, I took one of my classes to impressive Lake Powell. We came driving from Canyonlands National Park where we had spent several days hiking in the wilderness and searching the canyons for remains of petroglyphs and pictographs of the ancient Anasazi. Arriving at the vastness of Lake Powell, we stopped to take in the breathtaking sight. Surrounded by sparse desert land, the deeply clear blue waters of the lake are overwhelming in its beauty.

Driving down to its shore, everyone was eager to get into the lake and refresh themselves from the heat of the day. I was not yet in the water when one of the group members panicked and cried for help. "No, no, stop pulling on me! I don't want to drown!" I ran towards Olivia as she stumbled out of the water. She was crying uncontrollably, her right arm covering her eyes. I had her lie down on her towel and asked her to keep her eyes closed while taking ten very deep breaths. Then I asked her to tell me what had been happening.

Olivia recounted that as soon as she got into the water, there were all these hands pulling on her and pulling her down. She panicked, so many countless hands. I asked her to find out to whom these hands belonged and how many there were. Olivia answered, "Countless hands. They belong to the ones that drowned."

We all formed a circle around Olivia and went into meditation. I guided the group back into a time when the area of Lake Powell was a very large region of many different canyons. The canyon with its countless arms reached far and wide[17]. The valleys were rich with wildlife and provided abundant food. The water of the large river and the various smaller rivers and creeks made it an ideal place for the Anasazi to live and settle down for countless generations. It was a very idyllic life they lived during those times.

Whoever passed on to the afterlife continued to live in the canyons as spirits. The Navajos, for hundreds of years, continued to live in the lands of their forefathers with its rich farming and grazing lands. They lived in harmony with the spirits of the region and became spirits as well when they passed on. There were tens of thousands of spirits still living their harmonious lives in the canyons of this region.

---

[17] Ninety-six canyons create a total of more than 2,000 miles of coastline, more than the west coast of the US.

When the waters came and started to fill the many arms of Glen Canyon, those spirits were all drowned (see the sidebar note). The countless hands grabbing for Olivia were those of some of the drowned spirits.

As our group witnessed those drowned spirits, the first step was to communicate to them that they had drowned. They were trapped in the water because they didn't understand what had happened to them. No one had communicated to them what would befall them.

The next step was to show them the way out. As we sat there on the shore of Lake Powell, we all lifted our arms and signaled the drowned spirits to follow in the direction of our hands up and into the Light. Not a single spirit hesitated. They grabbed their belongings in a bundle, threw them over their shoulders, and started the walk up the meandering trials and out of the canyons. They had their sheep and goats with them. We witnessed spirits of all ages from infants and adolescents to adults and the elderly, male and female. All walked steadily and peacefully up from the canyon valleys and towards the Light. It was a procession of tens of thousands of spirits.

The agreement stated that the National Park Service would help the Navajo but it turned out the exact opposite of what had been promised in writing. We learned this from the Navajo guardian Lower Antelope Canyon in an interview I did with him, which was recorded by one of our group members. In 1963 the two diversions at Glen Canyon Dam were closed to allow Lake Powell to begin filling. In 1980 Lake Powell reached "full pool," taking seventeen years to fill.

Coming out of our meditation, I acknowledged Olivia for her experience of the drowned spirits of Lake Powell. It was thanks to her sensitivity that those earth-bound spirits were recognized and thus were able to rescue themselves from the water and into the Light.

In the 1958 legislation, the US federal government tricked the Navajo Nation into handing over the large canyon area of Glen Canyon in order to build the Glen Canyon Dam and fill up the canyon with water to create Lake Powell. It was supposed to help the tribe benefit not only from its water sources, but also tourism at Lake Powell. It resulted in the tribe being the only ones not able to benefit from the retained water. It actually prevented the tribe from developing the shore because the park service has jurisdiction over the buffer zone surrounding the lake.

Chapter 52

The Tragedy at Lower Antelope Canyon

Throughout the nineties, I organized a series of spiritually oriented camping trips with Europeans in my training classes and visitors of the 3-week-long summer camp. The Four Corners area with its natural beauty of dramatic landscapes and its rich Native American cultural heritage and history was always the focal point.

Our group usually started off with visiting Chaco Canyon, then went on to Canyon de Chelly, up to Mesa Verde, further on to Monument Valley, then on to Canyonlands and the Lake Powell region. Nearby Upper and Lower Antelope Canyon near Page, Arizona was always an absolute must-visit on our trips: the dramatic swirling sandstone walls that have to be seen and experienced in person.

For this particular trip, we arrived the fourth week of August 1997. We first drove to Upper Antelope Canyon, which is easily accessible. As directed, we parked our cars at a designated parking area, paid the fees, and boarded the shuttle operated by a Navajo who drove us to the site.

Both Antelope Canyons are very sacred sites to the Navajo with deep spiritual significance. Entering Upper Antelope Canyon is akin to entering a naturally formed cathedral. Both canyons are a favorite destination for tourists from all over the world, as well as famous photographers. The canyons are close to each other and both are more than worth a visit to pay homage to the Earth with its natural wonders.

Upper Antelope Canyon is 4,000 feet above sea level with 120-foot-high walls, which were formed over hundreds of years by water running through sandstone. It is 660 feet long and an easy walk. We marveled at the beauty of the dramatic light and shadows the sun cast on the canyon walls and the spectacular sun beams on the canyon floor.

Then we drove off to visit Lower Antelope Canyon. To our disappointment, the shed where the entrance fee was collected, had the "Closed" sign up. Our group stood close to the entrance ladder, which led down into the slot canyon. It was barricaded off. The Navajo guide guarding the canyon informed us that fourteen days earlier, on August 12, a terrible tragedy occurred due to a violent flash flood that claimed the lives of eleven Europeans, most of them French.

The views in Lower Antelope Canyon change constantly as the sun moves across the sky, filtering light softly across the stone walls. These ever-moving sun angles bounce light back and forth across the narrow canyon walls, creating a dazzling display of color, light, and shadow. The Navajo name for Lower Antelope Canyon is "Tsé bighánílíní" or "Spiral Rock." Apparently, many years ago, herds of Pronghorn Antelope roamed freely in and around the canyon, which explains the English name.

This incredible canyon was created over a long period of time by the relentless forces of water and wind slowly carving and sculpting the sandstone into the forms, textures, and shapes we observe today. Lower Antelope Canyon is about 1335 feet long and takes 1 – 1 1/2 hours to hike. It is 150 feet high and varies in width from two to thirty feet wide. It is much narrower and more dramatic. Someone suffering from claustrophobia would probably not much enjoy it.

The process of cleaning the canyon and searching for the bodies was still in full progress, hence, the slot canyon was closed to hikers. I knew the guide, a kind and calm man whom I had interviewed once.

He shared that on that particular day, the weather had been nice and sunny when all of a sudden, the Earth started roaring and shaking. He was familiar with those signs and quickly went to the ladder leading down into the canyon to call on the hikers and warn them to immediately get out. But no one made it up. Within minutes, the flushing water from a nearby storm filled the entire area. The Navajo escaped in his truck to a higher area unaffected by the violent wall of water.

We stood there in shock. A very eerie feeling was in the air. We all felt very heavy. We found a place in the shade and sat down in a circle and prayed for the victims. Then we left, driving the short distance to the shore of Lake Powell.

There, we sat up camp and refreshed ourselves from the road trip by taking a swim in the lake and preparing a light meal. After some rest and towards the evening, we formed a circle and went into silent meditation in an attempt to connect with the poor victims of the tragedy. What I saw was a violent, crushing wall of water thrashing through the surrounding land and down into and through the canyon towards Lake Powell. The noise was deafening and the hikers were in utter panic. Everyone was trying to cling to the walls but within seconds were pulled off and swept away by the force of the water.

A month later, during the course of another camping trip with a group of mine, we again visited Upper Antelope Canyon, also referred to as "The Crack," and Lower Antelope Canyon, "The Corkscrew." Lower Antelope Canyon was open this time. We climbed down the wooden ladder and stepped onto the very narrow canyon floor. There was still much debris on the floor and the walls from the recent flood. I could only imagine how bad it had looked prior to the cleanup.

We walked for a bit and as soon as we found a spot where our small group of six could comfortably sit, we went into meditation in an attempt to contact the traumatized spirits of the dramatically deceased people who'd died in the flash flood and hopefully be able to assist them. Whereas the first time I had perceived the tragic events of the violent forces of water, this time, I was tuned in to the spirits of the deceased. As if time had stood still, all of the victims were still hugging the canyon walls, trapped as if glued to them. This must have been the moment when they realized there was no escape and they would die.

Though the water was no longer in the canyon, the spirits of the deceased stayed trapped as if frozen in time the moment when the water had swooped down on them and everyone panicked. Much like the victims of the volcanic eruption that buried ancient Pompeii, the spirits were frozen in the time-space of the experience.

It is usually quite easy for me to talk to spirits, have a conversation with them and guide them out of the traumatic experience and into the Light. But the spirits of the eleven victims of Lower Antelope Canyon were unapproachable. They didn't notice I was speaking to them. They were stuck in a moment of panic and kept saying, "What happened, what happened?" over and over again. I gathered that the tragedy of the event was still too fresh and it would take much more time until they would be able to respond. Unfortunately, this was the last time I visited the region of Antelope Canyon.

As in any traumatic event that causes a shock, the individual who experienced the trauma gets shocked. Shock is a frozen state of being. Shock is also a critical condition brought on by the sudden drop of blood flow through the body. Shock may result from trauma, heat stroke, blood loss, severe infection, poisoning, an allergic reaction, severe burns, or other causes. To describe it in visual terms, if you cut yourself superficially, you immediately start bleeding. But if you cut yourself deeply with a puncture wound, you will not immediately bleed as much due to the shock to the flesh.

Section 5

The Dark Powers of Evil

Chapter 53

A LOOK AT THE DARK POWERS OF EVIL

Exorcism is definitely not my field of expertise. In the course of my healing practice, there have been a few cases where I suspected evil spirit possession. I did not feel I could do much except pray with those individuals. And teach them how to pray to the Source of Light. Since they were all from the Christian tradition, I advised them to call on Jesus Christ to protect them.

One such person, Rex, presented me with a well-known image of Jesus. He told me he was praying every day to this image. I was familiar with the image except his version had shifted drastically and didn't look like the original picture anymore. I strongly advised him to no longer pray to that image. So, he gave it to me and in return, I gave him an Open-Heart image of Jesus.

During the few times I've been asked to work with someone suffering from schizophrenia, I was helpless in regard to being able to assist and bring relief. The person was in too much mental delusion and it felt like my attempts were interfering with a karmic fate that needed to be lived out.

As a child living in Switzerland, every Christmas season a movie was played called *The Frozen Heart*. In it, the main character sells his Soul to the Devil for instant earthly gratification. As a consequence, the man loses his Heart and Soul for three lifetimes, each life condemned to living with a mental disorder.

This movie impressed me and its message made a lot of sense to me. It still does because it is not an easy task to switch sides once there is an

According to the shaman Umai in Olga Kharitidi's book, *Entering the Circle*, there are two reasons for [mental illness / schizophrenia]:

- their Soul has been lost … either because it was stolen from them or unconsciously they gave their Soul away, perhaps in exchange for something else they want.

- The second reason why people can become crazy is because they are occupied by a foreign power [earth-bound entity attachment].

alignment with Evil. Evil does everything to keep Souls in its grip once they have been recruited. And the price is high like, for example, deep mental confusion.

In the beginning, when I started to train individuals in my work, I decided to include the much-ignored theme of the Dark Powers of Evil. In all the trainings I had taken, this theme had never been addressed. Everything was always just about the Light. Especially with the New Age community that is often in full denial of any powers of the dark type.

Yet, I happen to believe that Evil gets much easier entry by being ignored rather than by taking a close look. We need to fully understand its various workings in order to know how to deal with it. It's helpful in case it does come up, and in these days and times, it does come up far too often. People need to make a personal choice. Do they want to serve the Forces of Light or are the Dark Powers their masters? For example, how many are aware that fear is the gray zone for Evil and its easiest entry into the human energy system?

YOU NEED TO MAKE A CHOICE
OF WHO IS
YOUR MASTER

DO YOU WANT
TO SERVE THE FORCES OF LIGHT
OR
ARE THE DARK POWERS YOUR MASTERS

Nowadays, with all the confusion, it is not so clear anymore whether the majority of people are aiming to serve the Light and shy away from worshiping satan. But even if people insist on wanting to align with the Light Forces, if such individuals' lives are consumed by fears and worries, they serve the dark powers nonetheless.

THE LEVEL OF FEAR VERSUS TRUST
DETERMINES
WHOM YOU ARE SERVING

Such individuals provide an entry for the dark spirits of Evil that feed on fears of all kinds. On a national basis, we saw this with 9/11.

Human history has witnessed countless examples where terrorist attacks, invasion, wars and conflict in general have shown how fear, distrust, greed, lust for power, etc. have had such a huge negative effect on humanity. Our global family has been traumatized for generations because of people, groups, and nations doing horrible things to each other. That trauma is deeply embedded in our psyche.

A perfect strategy to manipulate the population into fear is by creating chaos. Society at large and our communities everywhere are split into two categories. No one knows what's true and what's false anymore. Some say the media and government are lying and spreading incorrect information. Others insist those are all conspiracies. Billions of people all over the globe are being consumed by fears of all kinds. The suicide rate has risen drastically.

The American Psychological Association wrote in a report that "Suicide rates have increased substantially over the past two decades." According to research completed by Johns Hopkins Medicine, the suicide rates since COVID have increased slightly in many states across the country.

This research also states that certain demographics of people — such as the elderly, unemployed, and those with pre-existing mental health conditions — were at a higher risk for experiencing suicidal thoughts or attempting suicide. The study lists that there are several key factors that increase the risk of suicide during COVID, including:

- Social isolation

- Financial strain

- Lack of access to mental health treatment

- Long-lasting COVID symptoms

All of these elements can lead to severe mental health distress. And looking at history of past pandemics only confirms these risks. Some experts say that an increase in suicide rates during COVID is inevitable. Other experts state that suicide during COVID might become as detrimental and deadly as the virus itself.

That being said, there are some warning signs to watch for. They include:

- Persistent feelings of sadness or hopelessness

- Constant worrying

- Feeling on edge

- Turning to drugs or alcohol to cope

- Finding daily tasks difficult

- Changes in sleeping patterns

- Thoughts of harming oneself or others

- Suicide attempts

The World Health Organization (WHO) published a statistic on June 17, 2021 listing the following key facts:

- More than 700,000 people die due to suicide every year.

- For every suicide, there are many more people who attempt suicide. A prior suicide attempt is the single most important risk factor for suicide in the general population.

- Suicide is the fourth leading cause of death among 15-19 year olds.

- 77% of global suicides occur in low- and middle-income countries.

- Globally, ingestion of pesticide, hanging, and firearms are among the most common methods of suicide.

THE POPULATION IS BEING MANIPULATED INTO FEAR BY CREATING CHAOS AND SPLITTING SOCIETY UP

It's all extremely confusing. All of this is part of the chaos we're experiencing — and that includes racism, conflicts, religious fanaticism, economic disparities, fame at any cost, addictions, deliberate misinformation, corporations with more rights than individuals, politics, consumerism, competition, lawsuits over the silliest of things, disconnection because of technology, extremely violent movies, misogynist song lyrics, a drugged society (both pharmaceutically and recreationally), global warming, white supremacy, insurrectionists, etc. We are living in extremely chaotic times. Yet, a universal law states "Out of chaos a new order is created."

OUT OF CHAOS A NEW ORDER IS CREATED

I don't watch the news, so I'm not well-versed in the daily political affairs of the world. But I can clearly see that the big world-wide division of Humanity is a matter of consciousness. When will the population at large wake up and listen to their own inner Self rather than blindly believing what they are told? How much worse does it have to get before the larger part of our global population realizes that a handful of people and organizations control the masses? Humanity is currently at a critical stage. Global warming and its effect on Nature was the primary theme before the mass hysteria regarding COVID took over.

THE BIG WORLD-WIDE DIVISION OF HUMANITY IS A MATTER OF CONSCIOUSNESS

The level of consciousness between individuals is the great gap that divides humanity. Sadly, this has always been the case. And with the level of consciousness, the choice of alignment is, in short, with either the dark powers of evil or the Light Forces of Source. The Light Forces of Source always strive to free and liberate, whereas the dark powers of evil aim to dictate, control, and turn humanity into a race of slaves bereft of the ability to think, feel, and act according to our own free choice that comes from deep within and is in alignment with our Heart and Soul

MAKE YOUR CHOICE: WHOM DO YOU ALIGN WITH THE LIGHT FORCES OF SOURCE OR THE DARK POWERS OF EVIL

"I believe humanity has grown along two different paths. In the West we have taken the yang approach, turning outward. We modify and catalog our environment to suit our desires. Our science is a yang science, our lives are yang lives.

In the East you have taken a yin approach, turning inward. You modify and train the human being, in both mind and body, to become potent and complete in the environment that nature has already created for you, to reach your full potential while altering nothing. It is time for humanity to develop Yin-Yang Ku [God / One]."

~ Kosta Danaos
The Magus of Java

It has been stated before: "Who has eyes to see will see. Who has ears to hear will hear." Yet, our inner eyes and inner ears need to open in order for us to see and hear. With all due respect, it's high time for us to wake up from our "sleeping beauty" state and look reality in the eye. Too many people are living their lives in a comfortable state of drowsy awareness, ignoring the warning signs history has presented us time and again, which some of the older generation still remember only too vividly.

Many references to this are found in the Bible and the quote doesn't refer to one's physical eyes and ears, but to one's spiritual eyes and ears.

WHO HAS EYES TO SEE, SHALL SEE WHO HAS EARS TO HEAR, SHALL HEAR

The first night after focusing in class on the workings of evil, I went to bed exhausted and quickly fell asleep. I was already in deep sleep when I woke up to a disturbing image. A huge, black tarantula was sitting by the right side beside my head trying to get to my right temple to insert its poison. At the same time, I was told to leave the subject of the workings of the evil powers alone and never bring it up again.

I turned the light on, sat up in bed, and started praying. For two hours I prayed nonstop while the tarantula was fully present. I do admit I was terrified. After two hours, I lay down again. I turned my head so that I had my right temple protected by laying on my right side. The tarantula stayed in its threatening position but I was now able to fall asleep.

I intuitively knew that the tarantula would only aim for my right temple but not attack my left temple. I assumed this must be because the right part of our head from the ears up is the creative and intuitive part, whereas the left side is our logical / analytical part. Since my primary mode of operation is the right side of the brain, the tarantula aimed to destroy that part.

Just recently, almost thirty years later, I read the book *Nature Spirits and What They Say: Messages from Elemental and Nature Beings* by Verena Stael von Holstein. On page 217, it states that Rudolf Steiner described the Ahrimanic beings[18] as spiders. "A kind of network of spiders. These will be automaton-like spiders, existing on a level between the mineral kingdom and the plant kingdom, but vastly intelligent. These spiders will be dreadfully evil, they'll span the whole earth with their webs and those humans who haven't created for themselves the possibility of raising themselves to the Spirit will become entangled in these spider's webs."

Ever since then, this theme of the dark powers of evil is included in my trainings. It is such an important subject and should not be neglected. The threat was never repeated and the tarantula has never returned. The lesson was to not give in to fear and act regardless of the threat.

When the movie *Rosemary's Baby* with Mia Farrow came into the movie theaters, I was in my teens. I read in the tabloids of the tragic murder of pregnant Sharon Tate, the wife of Roman Polanski who directed the movie. It has always been obvious to me that the price Roman Polanski paid for exposing Evil was the sacrifice of his own baby and beloved wife.

Again, getting out of the clutches of Evil is never an easy task. Do not underestimate its power. One is playing with fire when doing so. Oftentimes, an entry for Evil is gained by sessions of spiritualism or a fascination with occultism, such as by being attracted to playing with a

---

[18] A term for evil beings in *Anthroposophy* by Rudolf Steiner.

Ouija board[19]. This is partly described in PART V, Section 9, Chapter 62: "Jackie's Aid to Her Mother." During the course of clearing hidden childhood trauma, Jackie encountered the archetypal battle between good and evil within the very intimate context of her biological family.

But other factors can also contribute. For example, by being lost and seeking God and stumbling into a trap. In the book *Three Nights with the Devil: A True Story of Deliverance from Evil*, British author Peter Hockley recounts his own experience. In his book, he describes how he found in a bookstore a copy of a book by an American author who claimed that he is talking with God. Hockley read the book and was fascinated by the conversations with God and the questions the author posed, which were being instantly answered. He decided to have conversations with God as well and was unaware that he was walking into a dangerous trap. Thanks to a friend, he found deliverance from evil.

GOD'S DOMAIN IS WITH SOURCE

STAY AWARE
THAT THE MUNDANE WORLD
IS SATAN'S TERRITORY

Evil is strong and powerful. Leave evil alone because the chances are huge that it will destroy your life, which is the goal of evil. Sadly, I have seen again and again individuals suffer from tremendous physical pain and even die a very painful death as a result of tampering with evil.

"The enemy is fear. We think it is hate, but it is fear."

~ Gandhi

It is clear that the person becoming a victim of Evil possession must take self-responsibility because there is always a factor that called Evil in. It is also necessary to choose the Light and only the Light. When you align yourself with the Light and stay focused on your Heart, rather than the mind where fear resides, you instantly find peace, trust, and confidence.

---

[19] A board printed with letters, numbers, and other signs to which a planchette or movable indicator points, supposedly in answer to questions from people attending a séance.

THE MIND IS
THE RESIDENCE OF FEAR

THE HEART IS
WHERE TRUST, CONFIDENCE, AND PEACE RESIDE

No switching sides allowed when it comes to Evil and the Light. We must become fully aware that the mundane world is satan's territory. Unless we consciously align ourselves with the forces of Light, we can easily slip into the grip of the dark powers of Evil.

I never knew that fear has a smell, a taste. Fear smells / tastes like a cold metal rod in your mouth. It was ever present everywhere in the air when I traveled to Rangoon, Burma in 1998 to visit Aung San Suu Kyi, the Democratic leader under house arrest by the current tyrannic military regime, the SLORC. Spies occupied every corner and building of the city. They were in hotels, restaurants, shops, and marketplaces. People whispered. They didn't dare talk for fear of getting themselves and their families eliminated.

ALIGN YOURSELF WITH
THE FORCES OF LIGHT
OR
YOU CAN EASILY SLIP
INTO THE GRIP
OF THE DARK POWERS OF EVIL

NO SWITCHING SIDES ALLOWED
WHEN IT COMES TO EVIL AND THE LIGHT

CHOOSE THE LIGHT AND STAY WITH IT

Fear is THE number one ingredient upon which the dark powers of evil feeds. The more fear, the more the dark powers can invade a human energetic system and have you in their grip. Getting initiated into the dark path is the worst and most extreme because it then becomes a chosen path of free choice. But lack of faith, hatred, dark thoughts, ego and vanity, greed, arrogance, the lust for power, and ingrained materialism also contribute.

FEAR IS
THE NUMBER ONE INGREDIENT
UPON WHICH
THE DARK POWER FEEDS

Though I fully recognize the nature of our individuality, it is my experience that people in general can be divided into two categories: the Warrior and the Worrier. The primary mode of the warrior is trust and faith, whereas the primary mode of the worrier is fear and anxiety.

It is easy for you to determine to which category you belong. Simply ask yourself how your first reaction to a situation is, any given situation. Answer honestly and you will know the answer. Most people tend towards fear. Someone in fear is always easily controlled and manipulated.

Fear is an emotion tied to the past and projected into the future. Fear is never in the present. Let's say you worry about getting sick. Your level of fear of getting sick is tied to what you know about the illness, for instance cancer or HIV or the big one of our current time, COVID-19. The knowledge of the illness is related to the past, what you have been told or read. Even if your grandmother just died of an illness fourteen days earlier, it is still the past. Your worry is then projected into the future of what could happen to you if you get the illness — and you could die as well.

FEAR IS AN EMOTION
TIED TO THE PAST
AND PROJECTED INTO THE FUTURE

FEAR IS NEVER
IN THE PRESENT

If you were able to remain fully present in the moment, of the "Here and Now," fear would drop away. Throughout all the ages, sages have said that the only sacred moment is the present moment. Be in the present moment and you are with God / Source of Light.

The creative and living life force of the Universe, God, doesn't live in the past nor in the future. The present moment is the moment of God. God resides in your Heart. Be in the present moment and you are with God. Leave the present moment and your Heart and you have left the divine territory of God's presence.

"Breathe. Let go. And remind yourself that this very moment is the only one you know you have for sure."
~ Oprah Winfrey

THE ONLY SACRED MOMENT
IS THE PRESENT MOMENT
BE IN THE PRESENT MOMENT
AND YOU ARE WITH GOD
GOD RESIDES IN YOUR HEART

GOD, YOUR HEART, AND SOUL ARE ONE

Chapter 54

URSULA: POSSESSED BY THE DARK POWERS OF EVIL

Ursula, a woman in her mid-twenties, was driven by friends to my healing practice from two hours away in Germany. She was fully bent over towards her right side and holding her belly area tightly as if she were in great pain. I helped her upstairs into the healing room and sat her down.

Ursula told me that the first time she'd felt pain in her belly was a couple of years ago in her early twenties. At first, she ignored it but as the pain persisted and worsened, she went to various doctors to have it checked. She tried holistic approaches, which brought no improvement, and went on to allopathic medicine with traditional doctors. No one was able to find the cause of her ailment. Some of them suggested her condition was psychosomatic or even imagined.

Ursula used to live by herself but as her condition worsened and she became unable to take care of herself, her father took her in.

She reported that she experienced daily encounters with evil spirits molesting her. The lights would turn on or off by themselves, pans would fall from the shelf with a loud noise, and she kept hearing other sounds whenever she was by herself in a room, such as the crackling of a fire. I asked her if she believed in the forces of the Light, Jesus, and the angels. She said she did, but she had not been praying at all. Because of her answer, I taught her how to pray and we began every healing session with prayer.

At the time, I was in training with Barbara Brennan, so I decided to do a series of hour-long healing sessions by laying on of hands combined with dialogue. I started at Ursula's feet and noticed that she was lacking connection to the Earth, she was utterly ungrounded. I focused on charging her field with energy and connecting her to the ground. I only slightly succeeded. I asked Ursula if she felt she was inhabiting her body. No, she responded, someone else was inhabiting her — she had no idea who it could be.

I soon determined that whoever was inhabiting her was not an earth-bound entity, but rather a dark spirit possession. Ursula came for a series of ten healings which I gifted to her since I considered myself in training with the chelation approach (Barbara Brennan's body of work).

At times, I was working in silence and at other times we dialogued, especially when Ursula commented that someone had just stabbed my own heart with a dagger or cut off my hand, etc., which happened quite a few times in the beginning.

Ursula could never tell who it was but just kept saying they were evil. Sometimes, she saw herself laying naked on an altar in a dimly lit coved crypt with black candles arranged around her. She noticed figures dressed in black robes with hoods, their faces covered. She said she was being sacrificed in a black mass for satan.

Ursula urgently needed to leave the territory of evil. By instructing her in prayer and aligning her with the forces of Light, her pain started to cease. She learned to command evil to exit her body and leave her in peace whenever she heard noises or became subject to other paranormal activity. She was able to walk upright more and more. The tension in her solar plexus had ceased and the pain in her belly was fully released. There was a natural spring nearby where Ursula lived with an altar to the Holy Mother. Ursula walked there daily to fill up a 1-liter bottle and kept drinking it while praying.

It took Ursula more than two years and an immense amount of pain and suffering until she was able to free herself from the clutches of evil. She definitely learned a very important lesson, which is: to never, ever play with evil.

Section 6

Projections & Transferences

Chapter 55

GENERAL PROJECTIONS AND TRANSFERENCES

One of the most unpleasant challenges in my work concerns the projections and transferences therapists and facilitators are subjected to. This can happen in the course of the healing process but also comes up during trainings. I have also observed many times the intense projections placed on gurus and spiritual teachers in spiritual centers and ashrams. But projections and transferences also happen easily in all kinds of relationships and with authority figures.

In order to explain what a projection is, I need to refer to the subtle energy field that surrounds the human body and its chakra system (See Part III, Section 1, Chapter 6, "The Forsaken.") The chakras are energy wheels that provide the human body with energy consciousness and information from the Universal Energy field. Without the human energy field, also called the human aura, we would not be alive, our bodies dead shells. Hence, the aura — the energy field surrounding the human body — is the matrix upon which the physical body can grow.

The former NASA scientist, Barbara Brennan, did extensive studies on the human energy field and its chakra system. According to Barbara, most people have three or four chakras spinning counterclockwise at any one time.

In Chapter 6, I described the seven chakras and the seven layers of the human energy field. In a healthy energy system, the Universal Energy flows into an open chakra and provides the subtle and the physical bodies with energy. A healthy chakra is open and spins clockwise. It is placed in

For further information, I highly recommend Barbara Brennan's books *Hands of Light, Light Emerging*, and *Core Healing*. Though I do recommend that *Hands of Light* is read first for a fully comprehensive understanding. The other two books build on the knowledge of her first book.

According to Barbara, most people have three or four chakras spinning counterclockwise at any one time.

the center of the body, is fully developed, and not displaced to the left or right of the center, or tilted forward or backward.

When the energy from the Universe can flow without hindrance into a chakra, the greater and objective truth of the Universe becomes the reality of the individual. The individual is seeing Truth objectively through all the chakras that are open. Again, this is because the chakras are spinning clockwise and bring the energy from without into the system.

When, on the other hand, a chakra is spinning counterclockwise, the chakra is not able to bring in the energy from the Universal Energy field and thus puts out energy rather than taking it in. Hence, the subjective truth of the individual is projected as the perceived truth. This is called "projection" — a projected reality is placed onto the subject and perceived as truth when in fact it is a distorted viewpoint that has nothing to do with Truth.

Projection

Open Chakra	Closed Chakra
Clockwise Spinning Chakra	Counterclockwise Spinning Chakra
Universal Truth becomes personal truth and reality	The personal perception of truth is being projected out into the world as truth and reality
Objective Reality	**Subjective Reality**

Objective reality expressed

Subjective reality expressed

IN A HEALTHY ENERGY SYSTEM THE UNIVERSAL ENERGY FLOWS INTO AN OPEN CHAKRA AND PROVIDES THE INDIVIDUAL WITH THE GREATER AND OBJECTIVE TRUTH OF THE UNIVERSE

IN A PROJECTION THE SUBJECTED TRUTH OF THE INDIVIDUAL IS PROJECTED AS THE PERCEIVED TRUTH

IT IS A DISTORTED VIEWPOINT THAT HAS NOTHING TO DO WITH TRUTH

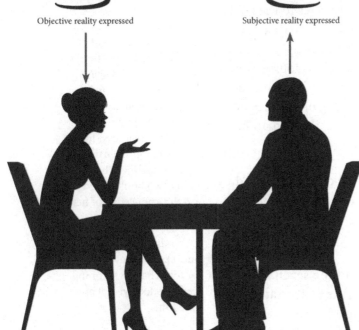

Transference is the unconscious redirection of emotions that were felt in childhood towards a parent or a substitute. The transference can be based on something from childhood, but doesn't occur until the individual is an adult. This happens for many therapists and facilitators — and sometimes happens vice versa.

Transference occurs when a person redirects some of their feelings or desires for another person or situation to an entirely different person. For example, transference in therapy happens when a patient attaches anger, hostility, love, adoration, or other feelings onto their therapist.

Many times during the healing process, the individual undergoing the process transfers or projects onto facilitators and therapists what they never had. For example: the unconditional love of a parent and the understanding, nurturing, and other qualities they had been missing since childhood. We become their stable anchor and safe life support, their "good mother," and oftentimes, the goddess guiding them into a new Universe providing new life. They view us as the supportive "good mother" whom they praise to heaven.

With these projections, we are walking on thin ice because the next moment we might be cast into hell and become the "bad mother / father" simply because of something that was said or required and was not to the liking of the person. Or, when in the course of their healing process, something in the present triggers subconscious emotions that were felt in the past during their childhood years. In my case, this happens particularly in trainings where, naturally, all woundings come up and are ready to be transformed.

Particularly, the so-called positive projections and transferences might sound flattering. But they are not, it's a trap to be avoided as it is their own perceived reality, and their reality might change from one moment to the other. When this occurs, I always aim for them to realize that what they see in me is already in them. Still dormant maybe, but nevertheless waiting to be recognized. I also explain what projection and transference are.

Furthermore, I provide clients with the meditation exercise of the Number Eight Circles. The numeral "8" has two circles. I invite the individual to see themselves in one of the circles and the other person — me or an important relationship they are co-dependent[20] with — in the other circle. Any and every relationship should always be viewed as an individual standing by oneself in the circle, never two people standing together in the same circle.

Co-dependency in relationships and in the context of healing sessions happens all too easily and must be brought to awareness because co-dependency is never healthy. In my opinion, the only healthy interdependent relationship is with the Divine Source, our personal Divine Deity, and/or our Guardian Angel.

THE ONLY HEALTHY INTERDEPENDENT RELATIONSHIP IS WITH THE DIVINE SOURCE OUR PERSONAL DIVINE DEITY AND/OR OUR GUARDIAN ANGEL

Inner Child[21] journaling[22] work is very beneficial, as well, because the individual learns to dialogue with their Inner Child, be present for their Inner Child, support it, and protect it.

Furthermore, I teach my clientele to cultivate the Inner Witness[23], the part of the Soul that sees and observes without any judgment. Then, of course, most importantly, the alignment to their God Source and Higher Power to guide them through life. With the aid of these various tools, the individual learns to empower and stay within themselves rather than hand their power over to someone else.

---

[20] Co-dependence is characterized by excessive emotional or psychological reliance on another person.
[21] Inner Child work is a beneficial approach in my healing practice for overcoming childhood trauma.
[22] Simple dialogue during daily contact in meditation with the Inner Child by asking how it feels and what it needs.
[23] Working with our observant self that is witnessing from a higher perspective.

Chapter 56

EXPERIENCES OF PROJECTIONS & TRANSFERENCES IN MY HEALING PRACTICE

Becoming part of deepest transformation often leads to profound projections and transferences that take place without the conscious awareness of the participant. When projections occur during the healing process, it is necessary to explain to the client what is happening and what a projection and transference are.

> The most dangerous psychological mistake
> is the projection of the shadow on to others;
> this is the root of almost all conflicts.
> ~ Carl Jung

A good place to recognize the depth of the distortion is when, for example, feelings of love and affection are felt and expressed, and then all of a sudden, those feelings turn into their exact opposite. The circumstances play only a small role in this. Falling from love into the extreme opposite always points to the viewpoint of a child in its wound rather than an adult with an objective point of view. The way an adult in their dignity handles such situations is by seeing what happened, take proper action, and let that person and/or situation leave their life.

I remember Barbara Brennan standing in a circle surrounded by us students, and leading us through a Core Energetic exercise. Some students completely dropped into their adolescent years, danced around with their hands to their heads making "stupid cow" remarks, pointing their "F" finger at Barbara, and sticking their tongue out at her. I never had this particular experience in my trainings but I felt utterly sorry for Barbara being subjected to such behavior.

One time, while in Austria teaching a healing course, the heaven-praising projections of my workshop participants were so intense that while eating in a restaurant with the participants, I decided to order French fries and Coca-Cola so that in the eyes of the health freaks present I could drop down to Earth instead of being constantly glorified. Upon seeing what I ate and drank, I heard one of them say to another, "Look how transformed she is. It doesn't affect her in the least." Ha, I thought, what else can I do when even my grossest example is not affecting them in the least. So, I talked to them.

＊ ＊ ＊ ＊ ＊

While at the ashram of Baghwan Shree Rajneesh / Osho, in Pune, India for training in Cranio-Sacral Therapy, I observed many projections and transferences placed on him, even though he was deceased. During breakfast and lunch, his discourses were broadcast over loudspeakers and everyone was forced to listen to his teachings

Osho would say things that completely resonated with me so that I comfortably sunk into my Heart and listened with full attention. Then, the next statement would utterly contradict what he had just said, so my mind came into action to question and doubt what was being said. When I, in utter disbelief, turned to others and said, "Look what's happening. A moment ago, he just stated the exact opposite. This doesn't make any sense," they would respond with, "Yes, isn't he wonderful?!"

I often wondered into what gaga land I had stumbled. I understood that a lot of his teachings might not have been with the intention of bringing clarity but rather to purposely confuse. Even though this was possibly to get people to use their critical thinking skills, I doubt it. His followers were so deeply attached to him and brainwashed, anything he said was just seen as words from their "spiritual master" and therefore sacrosanct. They made him untouchable, a saint to be revered and not questioned, just followed. They literally became sheep or lemmings. It was one large playground of emotions and confusion. When I later worked with a handful of Sannyasins, Osho's disciples, this was confirmed.

Why a guru would purposely contradict himself to his followers left me questioning his intentions, as well as his sanity. In the Pune ashram it is a known fact that Bhaghwan/ Osho was addicted to laughing gas that he apparently consumed in high quantities while seated in his dental chair (which was on exhibition in a smaller meditation hall). He was regularly drugged.

Many of his followers mirrored Osho's behavior of addictions. I met quite a few who changed their sexual partners every day. Taking into consideration that any sexual partner's energy stays in our energy field for nine months, we can easily determine how many energies get intermingled in the course of one month — and the confusion and harm this causes a person. As an example, staying at the ashram for thirty days and having daily sex with a different partner who on their part is also practicing daily sex with different partners adds up to 900 people energetically occupying one's energy field for nine months!

＊ ＊ ＊ ＊ ＊

There have been other side effects of my process work with my clientele. In my healing practice, men have attempted to seduce me during the healing process. Women have, too. This was because when people began to connect to themselves, they projected onto me their subconscious emotional attachments and desires for intimacy.

Because I work from the level of Soul, it is effortless to ignore the hidden sexual intentions when clients sign up to work. I concentrate on them as a person, rather than pay attention to their sexual identity. I keep in mind that they signed up for healing work, to heal, not to get tangled up in more confusion.

I remember the case of a man who came to work with me. While I went to the bathroom to wash my hands, he undressed and got underneath the sheets. Upon returning, he had the top sheet pulled down to the very edge of his pubic hair. I admit it was very pleasing to the eye, but I ignored it completely. I handled it very naturally, which taught him a lesson. In the next session, he still undressed but covered his body appropriately.

At the completion of the session cycle, he presented me with a love letter. I read it out loud in front of him. The words were moving. I honored the outpouring of his Heart and reminded him that contrary to his belief, he had not fallen in love with me, but rather with himself. I suggested that he share his freshly open Heart with his beautiful wife with whom I had also worked. After this, I received a heartfelt letter written by both of them. I have no knowledge if the husband ever shared with his wife the feelings he had projected onto me. Nor was it of importance to know. The fact was that their relationship with each other had been transformed.

* * * * *

A young man I met during a Transpersonal Conference in Prague, Czechoslovakia, befriended me. When he signed up for the healing process, he asked if he could stay at my home to avoid the hotel costs, which are extremely high in Switzerland. He arrived from Hamburg by train in the late afternoon and we ate at a nearby restaurant.

Upon returning home, I presented him with the session work schedule for the next day and then went to bed. I was almost asleep when I heard my bedroom door open. The guy entered, stark naked, with a full erection sticking out in front of him. Utterly startled, I sat up in bed and said in a very strict voice, "You leave my bedroom at once and get dressed. I will meet you in the kitchen."

I got dressed and went to the kitchen. There, I asked him what his intention had been when he signed up for the work. He responded with, "To do healing work."

I made it very clear to him that if he were going to stay at my home for the duration of the work, he had to get any amorous thoughts completely out of his mind. He understood and completed his healing cycle with a very transformative and deep process — without any further disturbance.

Section 7

Conscious vs. Sub-conscious Intention

"Self-sabotage is like a mental tug-of-war.
It is the conscious mind versus the sub-conscious mind
where the sub-conscious mind always eventually wins."

~ Bo Bennet

Chapter 57

SABOTAGE & SELF-SABOTAGE

We know that sabotage is the deliberate attempt to damage, destroy, obstruct, or hinder a cause or activity. It's an action aimed at weakening an effort through subversion, obstruction, disruption, or distraction. One who engages in sabotage is a saboteur. To deliberately stop someone from achieving something is an intentional obstruction leading to failing to achieve a desired outcome. In politics, we often hear of the intentional destruction of proof of evidence. Then there is also information sabotage by the media, the web, and other sources spreading highly suspicious information.

The acts of sabotage become self-sabotage when we become the saboteurs and the act of destruction is aimed at ourselves. Sadly, it is very common that we become the saboteurs of our own lives. For example, one can be unconsciously sabotaging one's financial savings attempts. Or we might have all the reasons to be happy with our life but then in a moment of utter thoughtlessness and confusion we destroy it all. Or we might be dreaming of a new life in a different state and town and are planning towards it only it will never come true because we stay stuck in our old lives while finding reasons and excuses for why it cannot be as we had planned.

"Self-doubt does more to sabotage individual potential than all external limitations put together."

~ Brian Tracy

Let's look at the deeper reasons at the core of self-sabotage. Self-sabotage occurs when our conscious intention is not in alignment with our sub-conscious intention. In the example of above, our conscious intention could be to save money for a new car, a more favorable home, or being able to move to another town where we would like to live and possibly study, etc. We sabotage this conscious intention by taking actions so that our plans fail. For example:

Conscious Intention

- I want to save money.
- I want to move out of state.

Sub-conscious Intention

- I don't deserve a better life. I'm unworthy of it.
- I'm afraid of change. Change is scary.

Our sub-conscious intention is to work against our sub-conscious desires. We stay stuck in the situation we're in. The core cause for self-sabotage is unworthiness and self-hatred. The following chapter is an example of the workings of self-sabotage.

"People with low self-esteem
are more likely to sabotage themselves
when something good happens to them,
because they don't feel deserving."

~ Anonymous

Chapter 58

THE STORY OF RICK AND JULIE

Rick studied law at Yale University and once finished, he was hired by one of the most prestigious law firms in New York City. He had dated various women but on the occasion of going home for Thanksgiving, he bumped into his high school sweetheart and sparks were reignited. At the time, Julie was a schoolteacher in his hometown.

They started dating, at first long distance until Julie agreed to move in with Rick in his Manhattan apartment. She soon got hired by a highly respected private school in the district. They shared many interests, like the arts and especially their love for nature and animals. They were very happy with their life together and were planning to start a family. Both of them were also saving to buy a house in the suburbs to raise their children.

Rick loved his job and had no idea that his boss, Dan, had other intentions for him. Upon getting promoted to become the assistant to Dan, who was the founding director and owner of the firm, Dan implied that he fancied him as his son-in-law for his second daughter, Lea, who was studying law at Harvard and was soon going to be finished. Rick had always been private about his personal life and was struggling to tell Dan that he was planning to marry Julie, the woman he was living with.

But Rick was also flattered with the proposed prospects. He was in a dilemma but decided to put it aside since there was no urgency. A year later, Dan sent Rick to Boston for a week-long appointment with one of the firm's clients. Dan arranged for his daughter Lea to assist Rick in the meetings. It was the first time Lea and Rick met. She was a very attractive and sexy young woman. She was also used to having her way. Under the pretense of talking over their client's business case, they went out to dinner almost every night and on the fourth night had sex.

Arriving back home from his business trip, Julie felt something was off with Rick and confronted him. Rick felt awful but insisted that all was fine, just that he had a load of work. He couldn't bear to tell Julie the truth and felt horrible for having betrayed her. He knew in his Heart that he only loved Julie but Lea's seductiveness had been irresistible to him. His inner turmoil brought about by his dishonesty caused emotional distance and separation between he and Julie.

Because Rick carried such unbearable guilt that he wasn't dealing with, it became a habit for him to have a few drinks at some bars with colleagues before going home. Sometimes, he came home drunk, which had never happened before. Julie was puzzled by Rick's change in behavior. Their sex life had also become very infrequent.

When Lea joined her father's law firm, she immediately became second assistant to her dad. Rick was now officially her boss. Lea wanted their relationship to continue and Rick was too weak to resist. Within the deepest part of his Heart, Rick knew he and Julie were meant for each other, but he felt unworthy of her love and affection because he had betrayed her. He hated himself for having turned weak because of Lea.

Because Rick kept denying anything was wrong, Julie decided to hire a detective who within fourteen days presented Julie with evidence that Rick was having an affair with the daughter of his boss. Rick could no longer deny the facts. Julie wisely decided to end their relationship and moved out of the apartment. But she also spoke to Rick about their connection and love and told him she was going to give him a year to think over what he wanted for his life. If he agreed, they could meet after a year and share their thoughts and experiences.

After Rick's breakup with Julie, Lea proposed for she and Rick to live together in an elegant Manhattan townhouse her dad had bought for her. Within half a year, Lea's parents started wedding plans. Upon their engagement, Dan announced that he was going to retire within five years and planned to leave the law firm to his daughter Lea and his future son-in-law, Rick. It looked like a bright future for the young couple.

The only problem was that apart from their professional interests and sex, there wasn't any compatibility between the two of them. Rick and Lea were very different individuals in their outlook on life. They fought often and Rick started to drink more and more. He got a DUI, which became a wake-up call for him. He felt he'd hit rock bottom and needed to change his life.

In a moment of utter clarity, Rick decided to look for another job in another city. He broke up with Lea and gave his resignation to Dan. Dan was very disappointed but confessed that it didn't come as a surprise, since he was familiar with his daughter's short temper. Greenpeace International's legal unit hired Rick with the offer of a top position in Denver, Colorado. While in college, Rick had visited the Four Corners area for rock climbing, rafting, and mountain bike activities and had since then felt drawn to the Southwest. Meanwhile, the year of separation Julie had proposed was coming to a close. What a roller coaster year it had been for Rick.

Rick contacted Julie and asked her out on a date. They had not seen each other for an entire year. When they met for dinner, Julie looked as lovely as always and behaved in her natural and lighthearted ways. Rick was so happy to see Julie and again felt very drawn to her. There was not a hint of blame or shame on Julie's part and Rick was able to open up completely and share the whole truth of his downfall.

Julie confessed that she had waited for this meeting but after that was planning to leave the city for a healthier life somewhere else. She had no definite plans yet but simply expressed that she dreaded New York and was looking to move. She had saved a bit of money and was intending to continue her studies in environmental science. They both laughed at the odds that he just got hired to work for Greenpeace while she intended to further her studies in the same field.

Right on the spot and very spontaneously, Rick invited Julie for a holiday to Hawaii prior to starting his new job in Denver. Julie accepted. They spent a month together and then invited their family and closest friends to join their wedding celebration. They were married in traditional Hawaiian wedding attire by the beach on the island of Maui. It was a very happy and joyous celebration.

They moved to the outskirts of Denver. Julie pursued her studies as planned and got pregnant with their first baby while working on getting her master's degree. She then was hired by Greenpeace as well. Within five years, their marriage was blessed with three children, a very happy family.

Both their lives could have taken very different turns had Julie reacted differently and not been able to stay in her Higher Self and wisdom when it mattered most. Had Rick not realized his self-sabotage and the false direction his life had taken, which culminated with the DUI, he might not have been able to turn his back on temptation and make the decision to turn his life around.

Changing one's life for the better takes courage and perseverance. It also takes love and respect for yourself and a good amount of clarity in your intention for the true meaning and higher values in your life to arise and be sustained through life's roller coaster ride.

"Never underestimate the power you have
to take your life in a new direction."

~ Germany Kent

Section 8

Healing in the Fifth Dimension

Chapter 59

HEALINGS ON THE LEVEL OF THE POWERLINE

In Part III, Section 3, Chapter 15 "The Various Healing Modalities of the HeartPath Re-Alignment," I give an in-depth description of the fifth dimension, what in Japanese is referred to as the Hara dimension and healings on the level of the PowerLine.

Again, our physical dimension is the third dimension and is related to the material world. Our auric field with its chakra system is in the fourth dimension and contains all our emotions, thoughts and feelings[24]. The PowerLine / Hara level is a dimension deeper and a frequency higher, in the fifth dimension. It is also called the "level of intention" because it is directly connected to the task of our Soul and therefore related to our life task.

I do believe that living life from the Heart, not the mind, is essential for personal happiness. While the lower three chakras deal with the human being in the physical dimension, the upper three chakras are connected with the divine dimension. The Heart chakra (4th chakra) is the bridge between the lower and the higher dimensions, between being human and being divine. By bridging these two aspects of

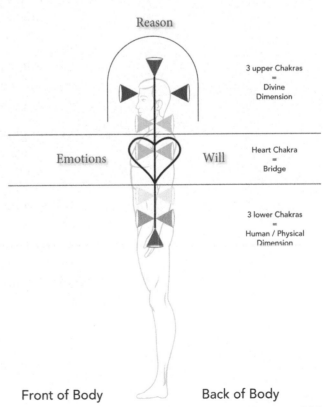

Reason

3 upper Chakras
=
Divine
Dimension

Emotions   Will

Heart Chakra
=
Bridge

3 lower Chakras
=
Human / Physical
Dimension

Front of Body   Back of Body

---

[24] There is a difference between emotions and feelings. Emotions are experienced in the second layer of the human aura, whereas feelings refer to the fourth layer of the human aura, the layer / level of the Heart.

our human experience together via the Heart and re-aligning them, individuals have been able to voice the truth of their Heart, to see their life from the level of the Soul, and to heal pain and disease caused on all levels.

Thus, we carry the purpose of our Soul and its life task from lifetime to lifetime, numerous lifetimes, until our life task is completed and we have fulfilled our destiny (See Book 2, Section 1, Chapter 97: "Good and Evil / Destiny and Fate.")

3rd DIMENSION → MATERIAL REALITY

4th DIMENSION → ENERGETIC REALITY

5th DIMENSION → LIFE TASK OF THE SOUL

Damage on the level of the PowerLine can cause severe damage in our lives. For example, such individuals oftentimes:

- are not grounded and might feel like a boat floating in the ocean without an anchor; lacking the emotional connection to this planet and life on Earth. Life here might feel threatening.

- might be aware of their lack of connection to Source and are confused as to the purpose of their existence. Life seems useless and ordinary. They might feel a deep yearning but are unable to identify what it is that they yearn for, especially since they are unable to hear the voice of their Soul or to look at their life task from their Soul level.

- might continually and habitually sabotage their life because their subconscious intention is not in alignment with their conscious intention.

- might continuously find themselves in the role of the victim and powerless to get a grip on their life and leave the victim role behind. Might be dealing with power issues.

PowerLine healings serve to restore damages caused on the level of the PowerLine. The level of the PowerLine is much more simply structured than the highly complex level of the auric field and its chakra system. Therefore, healings on this level are usually shorter than regular healings.

Chapter 60

HEALING IN THE FIFTH DIMENSION: JUDY IN HER POWERLINE

Here is Judy's experience of the healing in her own words:

I began my training with Silvana back in 2003, when I took courses in the HeartPath Realignment Process. It's a rigorous 2-year program and took me two additional years to complete all my case studies. By early 2008, I was able to open my own healing practice. I have always been drawn to spirituality and spiritual disciplines, yet never could have imagined the thrilling road ahead sharing Silvana's work and the profound healing results it provided for my clientele.

When Silvana began training students in a new modality called the "PowerLine" providing intense physical workouts and a 2-session healing process of balance and alignment, I was excited to discover the evolution of her work for myself. From my training nearly twenty years ago, what used to take four sessions to complete could now be achieved on the deepest and highest levels of the energetic field in a simpler version of her healing work using basic principles of how our physical body connects to the power of the earth and how divine power connects with our Soul and Life Task.

In 2020, I signed up for the PowerLine Training, Workouts and PowerLine Healings. My experiences were so inspired that I am writing about it because coming into my own PowerLine and the PowerLine Healing truly changed my life. In addition, the PowerLine workouts were an enormous benefit to increasing my strength and vitality, giving me more mental clarity and focus, and becoming healthier overall in my everyday life.

The PowerLine Healing began with an interview and discussion about my present life situation. I shared with Silvana that my life was in crisis. I was struggling, feeling abandoned by my husband, who had not been holding up his financial and family responsibilities. Ultimately, I was not living my full potential and was disconnected from meaning in my life. Through the PowerLine Training

Program, I learned that I could live from the level of my PowerLine, so that my life purpose and soul's desires could be more fully connected to my heart, giving me more fulfillment, sense of wellness, and joy.

The first PowerLine Healing session broke down the posture or stance one needs to take in order to perceive their PowerLine. After some time and practicing the correct position in Silvana's classes, I was able to direct my attention to the center of my body where I recognized this centeredness extending upwards towards the heavens and downwards into the molten core of the earth. I perceived a faint "line" of light that ran along my spine and visualized a small narrow tunnel where the earth and sky melded together within me, connecting my physical body into an illuminated, yet ethereal, thin channel similar to a laser beam or pin light.

In the pose or posture of the PowerLine, my legs were sore trying to hold the position, and I felt a burning sensation from the movement of powerful energy in my feet. With my back straight and leaning against a wall for support, I began thinking about my life and my future and questioned myself, *"Why am I living a life separate from myself, fragmented, feeling so unsupported in life?"* I kept opening my knees wider, while sinking my trunk down as far as I could. I could feel a wave of energy flow, and something opened in me that had been dormant for a long time.

Session #2 of the PowerLine Healing was vivid and completely unexpected. It began with deep breathing and a visualization for relaxation and quieting my mind. I went into an almost dreamlike state, nearly asleep, and with my inner eye I tuned into the four points on my PowerLine and felt a major problem in my Tan Tien. The purpose of the healing was to realign my PowerLine. So, as I went deeper into the imagery, I saw it was not a straight line along my spine as seen before in Session #1, but this time it was coming out of me on a diagonal, piercing through my belly button and area of my Tan Tien.

It was a spear. A spear was piercing me, a Roman spear. I was in agony. Led by Silvana through the PowerLine Healing, I looked at my feet and saw myself as a Roman guard in a large temple complex. There were festivities all around, and it was summer. After some time, it dawned on me that we were celebrating the Summer Solstice.

I was myself moving quickly and silently with intense purpose through the temple halls, walking past high priests through the royal courtyard. Barefoot and wearing a white tunic, I was a male, 18-19 years old. Then, I came upon a gruesome sight: slaughtered animals, too many to count. The wretched smell of flesh penetrated my nose. They had been beheaded, gutted, and left to bleed all over the white marble floor in the name of sacrifice.

I was horrified at the spectacle. With even more determination and anger boiling inside me, I walked faster, further down into the temple chambers, where I met up with 3-4 other temple guards. There was an exhilarated silence in the air as rage welled up inside me. Then, I saw it ... shrouded and covered with a cloak. Yet, even underneath the heavy fabric, I could see its golden, luminous glow making shadows on the stone walls. It took all five of us to lift and carry the golden orb, down the long corridors through an exit in the bowels of the massive complex.

Once outside, we came to a burial plot nearby and immediately started to hide it in the sand. As we rushed to move the earth, hatred and fear coursed through my blood. I didn't understand the images I observed coming through, what was happening or why. I felt, though, the golden sphere contained an evil presence, and the sacrifices done in its name were an atrocity to all Romans.

By burying it, I hoped to crush its power. Yet, the other guards caught up with us, and we were taken away. I saw myself being put to death. My own brother, a young temple guard like me, kept taunting, bullying, and brutalizing me for what I had done. Stealing the golden relic of worship was cause for imminent death. Then, my brother threw a spear at me, severing my gut. My Tan Tien was ripped open, and the message that came to me was, *"As I stand in my power for what I believe in, I die ...."*

The last words spoken to my brother through grimaced teeth were "Do it." My brother was clearly opposed to my deepest values. He believed with the masses, and not what I believed ... that the large golden disc contained an unspoken evil, not something to be worshiped. As I was dragged away and lay dying, my last thought was, "Let Go." Then, I was tossed into a burial hole, my face covered with sand, and I felt the spear going deeper into my gut through my spine, before it all went black.

As I came to, out of the disturbing imagery, my heartbeat was noticeably racing, and I felt a pulsating sensation in my Tan Tien. I perceived an enormous glowing energy within me. Silvana asked me to tune into my PowerLine, and this time I was suspended directly in the middle of it, surrounded by purple flowing energy. It was a healing, because the Roman guard's noble actions, even though it caused him a painful death and abandonment by his own brother, it released buried trauma in me from that past life.

Then, suddenly, I heard a deafening sound — a loud, slow rumbling on the lowest frequency level audible, then another loud sound of fire crackling, splitting my ears open, like the sound of lava bursting out — the first Sound of the Universe. Soon, the sound of my Soul followed, a loud glorious "AHHH" penetrated my being, with one single, l-o-o-ong note reverberating through me. And I started sobbing, while a song from my childhood poured from my heart, "He's Got the Whole World in His Hands."

As the healing continued, I saw myself carrying my baby girl, standing in my power as a Mother. It was a revelation that I hadn't been in my power for more than 1800+ years, since Roman times. In fact, I was the baby girl, coming into my power. Then, I saw my Soul Seat surrounded in vibrant white, violet-colored light in the shape of a funnel radiating out into five points of a star. A deep release came over me, and I realized it was also time for my daughter to come into her own power.

After the PowerLine Healing, the purpose of my life became clear: *"Be In My Power."* I have to be the inspiration of my own life and trust myself. I am noble, like the Roman guard, and need to believe in my highest interests, and express them in my life. Staying fully anchored to the earth, allowing energy to flow from God and the Source above is how life is truly meant to be lived.

Afterwards, in my reflections with Silvana, I understood that if something is feeling disconnected in my life, or if I can't visualize my own PowerLine, now that I've learned how to do it, then something is disconnected within me. I can begin a daily healing conversation with myself of what the disconnection could be or represent.

And, after further discussions, I began to understand the abandonment and emptiness, like "death," I was experiencing in my marriage. I understood the connection of my Roman brother who threw the spear at me in the past life was in fact my husband in this lifetime. Negative thought patterns needing transformation were, *"I have to suffer for love,"* *"He abandons me in a hole,"* *"He doesn't believe as I do,"* *"I spill my guts to you, and you rip me apart,"* and *"I am buried alive."*

When I went back to my room after experiencing the intensity of the PowerLine Healing, I looked up Roman temple worship and discovered the Sun God "Sol" in Roman mythology (an image called "Sol Invictus" can be found on Wikipedia).

Section 9

Communications with the Ones Beyond the Veil

Chapter 61

THE HEALING POWER OF COMMUNICATING WITH DECEASED LOVED ONES

"Death is nothing at all. It does not count.
I have only slipped away into the next room.
Nothing has happened. Everything remains exactly as it was.
I am I and you are you and the old life
We lived so fondly together is untouched, unchanged.
Whatever we were to each other
That we are still.
Call me by the old familiar name.
Speak of me in the easy way which you always used.
Put no difference into your tone.
Wear no forced air of solemnity or sorrow.
Laugh as we always laughed at the little jokes we enjoyed together.
Play, smile, think of me, pray for me.
Let my name be ever the household word it always was.
Let it be spoken without an effort, without the ghost of a shadow upon it.
Life means all that it ever meant.
It is the same as it ever was.
There is absolute and unbroken continuity.

What is this death but a negligible accident?
Why should I be out of mind because I am out of sight?
I am but waiting for you, for an interval,
Somewhere very near, just around the corner.
All is well."

~ Anonymous

Losing loved ones is one of the most painful experiences most of us have to face at some point in our lives. Oftentimes, the pain is so intense it can lead to depression. We loose the presence of someone important and our world falls apart. The death of a beloved pet can be equally traumatizing. All kinds of emotions might accompany the occasion from deepest agony to guilt, shame, despair, and hopelessness. The sudden absence of a loved one leaves a hole in our life that can never be refilled.

At age twenty-two, my baby daughter died at birth from anencephaly. Less than ten years later, my mom lost her battle with lymphoma. Three decades after, my younger brother Franco died. Two years later, my only child Marc passed away suddenly in 2014 from a heart attack. A year later, my dad passed away, and last year my older brother Carlo died which made me the only surviving member of my immediate family. It seems loss is a constant reminder of the impermanence of life, a reminder that we are only temporary visitors here.

When we lose someone close to us, the pain is often so intense that we cannot imagine how life could possibly continue without their presence. We might debate with God as to the injustice of their passing and feel that we should have left instead of them, especially if our loved one was a child whose life had only just begun.

Losing my son Marc came as such a shock that I only slept a total of eight hours during a seven-day period. I cried rivers nonstop. I was having a nervous breakdown. A friend of mine, a doctor of family medicine and also a psychiatrist, strongly recommended that I take antidepressants temporarily. I refused. I knew feeling the pain to its full extent was only natural and eventually, in due time, the flow of the river of tears would cease. And so it did.

Pain of this extent is certainly experienced as a death from deep within oneself. Our old self must die in order for rebirth to occur and our new life to integrate the agonizing experience of loss. It helps to change the living situation or the home that was shared and continues to carry all memories. Oftentimes, the individual left behind gets visits while awake or in dreams from their loved one, especially if there was a strong love bond, which was the case with my daughter-in-law Camila and my son Marc. This then makes it challenging to move on with life and hopefully find new love.

Especially if a loved one left suddenly, important conversations might have never taken place and things may have been left unspoken. And if the deceased one takes a deep secret with them, it will burden them and us beyond death until that truth is revealed. We saw this in the case described in PART IV, Section 4, Chapter 41, "Olivia and Her Grandfather's Message," where Olivia, in the course of a healing exercise by the stone circle "the Council of the Wise Elders," was contacted by her deceased grandfather who needed to pass on a message to his still-living wife. Olivia's grandfather only found peace once he had passed on a deep secret he didn't dare to tell his wife while alive.

Many people are not even aware that communication with their loved one is a possibility once they have crossed over. Given the choice to do so, some are afraid to even give it a try. Yet, of all the many individuals I have assisted in my healing practice to connect with a loved one, no one has ever regretted the experience of having done so. At all times, the encounter was enlightening and enriching and the contact was authentic, tangible, and released deep emotions.

In general, individuals feel that being able to once more see their loved one in their minds' eye and hold them in their Heart brings closure to a painful chapter in their life. Being granted the opportunity to communicate any worries, express guilt long held, any feelings of conflict or doubt, clear misunderstandings, or simply to express their love for one another and to hear that their loved one is well, content and at peace, brings great relief and comfort.

Very challenging is a sudden and unexpected death such as in the case of an accident with instant death or a heart attack or something that doesn't allow the opportunity to say goodbye, or in the case where the loved one drops into a coma and later passes over. Those who are left behind are filled with lingering questions, preoccupations, and worries that remain unresolved.

Usually, devout religious individuals find comfort in their faith and accept the death as God's will while deep within questioning the value of God's choice while going on with their lives as best they can. Yet, losing a loved one shakes our fundamental belief systems to the core going beyond where pure faith and religion can go. What is needed is a direct inner channel to the Divine, a spirituality lived from deep within oneself in order to be able to accept the choice of the other Soul having parted.

What often occurs when communicating with a loved one is that it brings about a chain reaction of ancestral clearing and healing that releases the individual from a heavy burden they never knew they were carrying, as well as behavior patterns passed down from generation to generation. If people only had a clue that loved ones who have crossed over take with them a load of unresolved issues that cannot be resolved

If people only had a clue that loved ones who have crossed over take with them a load of unresolved issues that cannot be resolved while they reside in the spirit world but that can be healed when the person left behind connects with them.

Crossing over is much like walking through a curtain. The seeming separation from a loved one is an illusion.

There is no judging God or entity out there waiting to condemn.

while they reside in the spirit world but that can be healed when the person left behind connects with them.

Furthermore, secrets can come to light as we saw for example in Part IV, Chapter 26, "Esteban's Severe Childhood Trauma," where the homicide on his mother by his dad was covered up as suicide, and Chapter 32, "Ava: A 4-year-old Girl Witness to Murder," where Ava as an adult suffered from lingering unexplainable depression due to her severe early childhood trauma. Misunderstandings have the opportunity to be cleared. If the death circumstances is surrounded by mystery, violence or an injustice, such as a covered up homicide, the injustice might deeply plague the deceased and cause them to stay lingering in the astral realm as an earth-bound entity rather than seeking to move toward the eternal light of Source.

We need to consider that crossing over is much like walking through a curtain. The seeming separation is an illusion because all life is interconnected and continues whether we live energetically in Spirit or in the body.

It is no surprise that children, with their lack of the interfering mind, oftentimes display profound wisdom. When my son Marc died, my grandson Philip was only seven years old and Lucas was five years old. When Lucas was sad, Philip said to him, "Of course he is still with us. The only difference is that now we can't see him."

Religions like Hinduism and Buddhism, rooted in a belief of reincarnation, also tend to have an easier connection to the beyond than atheists and followers of religions that deny or ignore such a possibility.

Communication with a loved one can also assist in losing one's fear of death. By learning that Life after death is a reality and how it is on the other side, and by hearing of the true values of life, inspires to engage in what really matters. For individuals who have stifling concerns about what others may think if they act the way they really would like to but have always been afraid to do so, it is very healing to learn that there is no judging God or entity out there waiting to condemn. Being in contact with a loved one can also help in clearing spiritual conflicts, which is quite common among Catholics. They can, of course, plague others as well.

Last but not least, communication with a loved one helps the person left behind to let them go and release any binding attachment. The realization that the loving bond of the Heart will never cease supports and suggests the necessity to live life fully while in the body. Love is never lost.

Yet, whoever leaves the physical plane did so by the choice of their Soul. It was their Soul's choice for whatever reason, and more than likely it will be revealed through communication. The task at hand for the one left behind is to learn to live life without the loved one. In this sense, death and departure of a loved one can become a powerful teacher, especially if their relationship was one marked by co-dependency and the deceased carried the life for the two of them.

It does take time to be willing to leave the old life behind and make adjustments. Years ago, I worked with a widow who was in much conflict concerning the letting go of her very large ranch and her herd of a hundred Buffalo, even though she couldn't afford the upkeep anymore. It was a process for her to realize she wasn't failing her deceased husband by changing her life. Another person I know took years until she was ready to sell her property because she had buried her husband on the land and felt she would be betraying him if she sold it.

There is order in the Universe. On the level of the highest plane — the Source of light — all is in perfect order. What happens needs to happen and there is always a perfect explanation for it. Once we start to fully understand this, realizations fall into place like the pieces of a mosaic. What puzzled us before, becomes suddenly clear. We begin to fully understand.

And we accept the fact that our loved one has departed because their personal life task and capacity for personal growth in their current incarnation here on Earth had reached its limit for the time being. When leaving the earthly realm of matter and returning to Source / Spirit, a new task is waiting for them to fulfill. For this very reason, it's necessary for them to be able to remain in peace so they can focus and do what they need to do. When the right time arrives, there will be a reunion, the loving bond will be celebrated, and new plans for new life together will be made.

A new life *together*, though, is very often not the case. Each Soul has its own spiritual journey to accomplish, and the next incarnation may be with other Souls in order to accomplish other tasks and lessons.

While we can see how communication with a deceased loved one is of much benefit for both parties involved, the following account of Jackie addresses the deep healing possible for a loved one who has crossed over and those left behind.

When the Soul Calls: True Stories of Deep Healing and Transformation

Chapter 62

JACKIE'S AID TO HER DECEASED MOTHER

Jackie said that she draws a blank when it comes to childhood memories. Upon regressing her, weird images appeared. She saw herself as a four-year-old girl with a man she didn't recognize. Apparently, it was her biological dad, John. He kept intentionally burning her on her back with the car's cigarette lighter while he was drunk. He was often drunk. He also dripped hot wax on her. All little Jackie wanted was to be left alone. When she was alone, at least there was no pain.

Her mom, Carol, closed herself up in her room all the time. She was sick and constantly in bed. Carol bled a lot. Jackie remembers always seeing a lot of blood in the toilet. Carol was suffering from Crohn's disease. She didn't take care of Crohn's disease is a chronic (long-term) disease that causes inflammation in the digestive tract. It belongs to a larger group of illnesses called inflammatory bowel disease (IBD). her three kids. Jackie, from an early age, took care of her little sister and mom, preparing food and doing all the chores.

Crohn's disease is a chronic (long-term) disease that causes inflammation in the digestive tract. It belongs to a larger group of illnesses called inflammatory bowel disease (IBD).

Soon after her mom kicked out Jackie's dad out by changing the front door lock, Dick became her step dad. He was very abusive verbally. Jackie could do nothing right in his eyes. Throughout her childhood, Jackie was very afraid of Dick. He never had a friendly word for her and treated her very badly.

Following her healing session, Jackie requested stomping in a water-filled bathtub to release the anger she felt towards Dick. Afterwards, she felt tremendously relieved.

When Jackie was twelve years old, her mom disappeared and couldn't be found for days. Finally, Dick found her in their family cabin far off in a remote area of the New Mexico mountains. She had committed suicide overdosing on prescription pills.

I suggested that Jackie learn more about her mom's upbringing by dialoguing with her mother and asking questions. I asked for Carol to show an image of herself as a baby. Instead of seeing her mom as a little girl, Jackie saw her grandma, Luise, as a young woman. Jackie learned from Luise that she had been forced to marry a cowboy so that her father could benefit from gaining pastureland. But Luise detested the cowboy, never feeling attracted to him. She already had four children when she finally met someone she liked. He was Native American. They giggled a lot.

At a drive-in movie, they had sex once and Luise became pregnant. When baby Carol was born, Jackie saw that a yellow blanket was held up so Luise would not see the baby and get attached to it, which she was forced to give up for adoption. But Luise heard her baby cry and it broke her Heart. Jackie sobbed witnessing this. A few years later, Luise committed suicide.

The couple who adopted baby Carol were Hispanic and devout Catholics. Her adopted mom, Josephine, had a big heart and loved Carol very much. But Carol was not a happy child. She was part Native American and felt different and out of place. She couldn't accept the fact that her biological mom had given her away. Carol developed an arrogant attitude towards everyone around her and towards life in general.

Jackie was appalled dialoguing with her mom. Carol's indifference to her life and everyone around her was a shock for Jackie. At one point, Jackie broke down sobbing because she realized that after dying, her mom didn't go into the Light but attached herself to Jackie's younger sister, Susan. Growing up, Jackie and Susan had been very close. A few years ago, Susan flipped completely. She was in utter denial that her life partner was sexually molesting her own daughter and while she kept living with that man.

When Jackie's niece, Mariah, confided in her and described the different occasions of sexual abuse, Jackie offered emotional support to Mariah and in Susan's eyes, Jackie became the villain. She threatened Jackie by offering Jackie's children to demons. Jackie was forced to get a restraining order against her own sister to protect herself and her little children.

On working with Jackie, she mentioned that her mom had a fascination with the Ouija board. Jackie's brother, Ralph, mentioned that both he and their mom have an "M" in the lines of the palms of their hands and that his mom had always been proud and told her son it meant "magic."

Sadly, Ralph had always been verbally abusive to Jackie and kept threatening her. Jackie was forced to cut family ties with him as well. With her sister and her brother out of her life, her only family was her children and grandma Josephine.

When Jackie recently became pregnant, she panicked. Taking care of yet a fourth child as a single mom would definitely ruin her life. But she was also conflicted because accepting what life presented was what "good" people did. She contacted the spirit of the baby to apologize and explain why this was not a possibility. She had the strong impression it was a girl. When Jackie received the birth date, she was shocked to learn it was the exact birth date of her mom Carol.

This infuriated Jackie for she intuited that her mom wanted to get back into a body. Jackie underwent an abortion but for months, she kept contacting the spirit of the baby, speaking of her deep love for her, explaining why she had made the right decision, and that it was to protect the baby and keep it away from harm. Jackie always felt she was destined for motherhood and it didn't bother her to raise her children on her own. She feels very protective of children and is an excellent mom. Her little family represents her world.

During the following healing sessions, Jackie kept dialoguing with her mom, who kept staying in the astral realms of evil. This was a huge shock for Jackie. She felt deeply disappointed and confused because everything Jackie had known as a child about her mom had been a lie.

Recently, Carol's best childhood friend contacted Jackie via Facebook not knowing of Carol's death twenty years earlier. In a series of emails, this childhood friend confirmed Carol's intense sudden mood swings (just like her sister Susan and her brother Ralph) and also her interest since middle school in magic and the Ouija board. She confided to Jackie that the mood swings were the reason why she had a falling out with Carol when they were young adults and they never contacted each other again.

In working with Jackie dialoguing with her mom, Carol kept speaking of the fire she was in. At the beginning of that particular healing session, Jackie kept seeing water and a person tumbling into the water. I asked Carol if water was stronger than fire. She confirmed it was. So I asked Carol if water had healing properties. Carol confirmed it did. I then suggested Jackie take her mom down to the ocean.

As Jackie attempted to take her mom by the hand, Carol pulled away, which caused Jackie deep pain. She sobbed uncontrollably while she witnessed her mom running towards the water and jumping in. Jackie observed her laying on her back with her arms spread open as if she were enjoying herself. Jackie was moved and was lost in a long silence as she watched her mom. She decided to leave Carol to the healing properties of the ocean.

The experience of her mom refusing Jackie's helping hand left Jackie feeling devastated, confused and angry, yet still willing to keep dealing with her pain in order to help Carol and guide her towards the Light and the healing she needed.

About two weeks later, Jackie reported that she kept having a feeling that there was a lot of turbulence and commotion in the water where her mom was. This was followed by an intuition and inner knowing that Jackie needed to leave her mom in the healing ocean.

In a dream that Jackie had shortly after, she saw Carol lying motionless but not in water. Jackie went and lay beside her. She then saw herself walking in a forest and kicking some rocks and by doing so discovered a huge room full of white and purple crystals. Looking up,

241

she saw me, Silvana, in her dream and said, "Look at all these crystals." When Jackie shared that dream with me, I suggested that the crystals were for clarity, the color white represented purity, and the color purple referred to spirituality.

For a couple of months, Jackie processed her feelings before she was ready to continue working with me. For her next healing session, Jesus Christ took Jackie on a ride in a blue convertible through the Northern New Mexico countryside to the very church where Carol's adoptive parents had been married and her mom, Carol, had been buried right between Jackie's great-grandparents.

Witnessing the love of that community, Jackie got the message that "authentic love is eternal." She understood that Carol had been embedded in love. Jackie then perceived that her mom was tired and had been questioning a lot about life. Carol then appeared to her as a three year old, and Jackie witnessed a dark evil beak picking at little Carol. Jackie learned that was the time when little Carol's mental instability began.

I suggested Jackie ask Jesus from what past life Carol knew the energy of evil. Jackie saw a male figure, in a khaki-colored cloak with a hood, writing hastily at a desk who then quickly left and disappeared. He had seen something he wasn't supposed to see: a crypt underneath a church that served as a torture room, a place from where he previously had heard screams.

The monk was in deep shock and disbelief about what he'd witnessed: the abbot of the church in the presence of others involved in the ritual sacrifice of a darker skinned baby with dark curly hair. Her mom's Crohn's disease came up for Jackie while she was in deep shock and sobbing uncontrollably. She realized that she was the monk who had witnessed the ritual and why her entire life she had never ever wanted to get involved with evil. She also felt tremendously grateful for the protection she'd received all her life and understood why she felt so protective of her three children. She also understood why she denied the little Soul to be born for it would have contaminated their life. Jackie was heartbroken for the little baby's Soul and she sobbed deeply.

Jackie understood that she has been casting those dark spirits of evil away for lifetimes whereas her mom had given in and absorbed them from a very early age on. She then understood her mom's disconnection with Jackie and life as a whole and her entanglement with evil: she knew nothing else. Jackie now understood why from childhood on she had wanted to be left alone and not be touched because she felt unworthy of love.

Jackie then saw her mom as a fetus floating in water and Jesus Christ opening his arms and taking her into his Heart where from now on Carol would stay and fully heal.

Jackie's deep insights into the archetypal battle of good and evil within her biological family circle caused a desire within to completely shift course with all the wrongdoing.

At the beginning of her final healing session, Jackie perceived that her mom as doing better in the healing presence of Jesus Christ. Carol felt deeply embarrassed for having been so naive and fallen into the trap of evil and pulling everyone else in, especially her daughter Susan. Jackie has forgiven her mom because Carol came across as sincere and authentic.

Jackie then expressed her desire to help her sister Susan find deliverance from evil and in the process understood that Susan needed to get out on her own because it was her chosen journey and her own process. Jackie sobbed for her little sister whom she loves so very much but saw the gap between them growing bigger as her sister walked away in the opposite direction. For Jackie, it was a sad "goodbye" as she mourned her sister's Soul.

When I asked Jackie to tune into her brother Ralph, she perceived his anger and rage and said he was, in his arrogance, unconscious, whereas Susan was conscious of her chosen path. Jackie concluded that Ralph being unconscious of his battle between good and evil was more dangerous because of his ignorance. Jackie also saw her brother plagued by loneliness because everyone turned away from him, appalled by his arrogant attitude.

As Jackie looked into Ralph's future, she saw him in the wilderness by himself waiting out his time, still full of arrogance in his assumption that he never harmed anyone, ignoring his countless wrongdoings, and all the hurt he'd caused. Moving even further into the future, Jackie perceived Ralph with regret of not having known his daughter, Bonnie, while feeling sorry for himself.

When Jackie tuned into Bonnie, she perceived her as a smart hawk who enjoyed stealing, not out of need but for pleasure and to get attention. She misses and idolizes her dad because she doesn't know who he is.

I asked Jackie to unite the two of them. They faked happiness upon their encounter. Bonnie was acting while Ralph did his best to impress his daughter. Together, they turned Bonnie's mom into the villain.

Jackie then received the message from Jesus Christ that *"Through the good and the bad, the truth has to be available because the lies keep piling up."* She understands the importance of authenticity and transparency and how the Souls of biological family members can have utterly opposite paths. Jackie concluded that hatred has the deepest roots. Like a destructive weed, it keeps poisoning the soil of goodness. It can live on so very little but ignoring it doesn't make it go away.

Jackie then got a painful look at her own hatred triggered by her judgment caused by the injustice to children, like the little baby victim of the satanic ritual she saw in the previous healing session. As a result, it dawned on Jackie that forgiveness doesn't mean to justify or pardon evil behavior.

Rather, when one forgives, it eliminates the seeds of hatred within oneself. She saw herself pulling all the weeds of judgmental hatred out of her system, becoming a big pile beside her, which she then threw into the fire to be completely purified and disintegrated into smoke and tiny particles, and reconstructed differently, becoming fertilizer for goodness.

Jackie understood her next step was to see the blessing and be grateful for all the incidences of hatred that continue to give her a chance for transformation. She very much feels on the right path remembering what she already knows deep within. The task for Jackie is to not only see fully with her human eyes but to develop her capacity to see with divine eyes.

When Jackie decided to look at her hidden and buried childhood memories, she had not anticipated the Pandora's box about to open up. Much Soul growth has since occurred as her process continues unfolding.

Section 10

The Direct Experience of Union & Galactic Experiences

Chapter 63

GOD EXPERIENCES DURING HEALINGS

Again, it takes much courage and self-discipline to stay honest in front of ourselves and acknowledge our deeply wounded parts. When individuals are truly committed to their healing and willing to leave the pride of their ego-self behind and face what needs healing, those fragmented and forgotten parts can come together and fully flow again as a whole.

I remember working with an individual, a high authority figure in the church. When anger came up for him, he bypassed his chance of healing it. Instead of facing the anger and give it healthy expression, he chose to ignore it and controlled it by deep breathing. He afterwards realized he had missed his chance to heal and was sorry for his lack of authenticity.

The sad part is that suppressed anger will resurface and find an expression, most definitely when it's not appropriate. While in a healing in the healing room, we can box and kick and scream and yell "I kill you." We cannot do this in our regular life. Accessing deeply rooted anger needs to be faced in the healing practice where it can be transformed and integrated.

Individuals willing to do the deep work required, face such an array of their crooked selves that it is very much a journey into the underworld, which has fascinated all cultures during man's entire time on Earth. Seldom is it a literal descent but more so a metaphorical voyage into the darkest corners of our psyche. We can find it described in the world

The deep work required to face our shadow is a journey into the darkest corners of our psyche.

literature of Greek mythology, the tales of knights fighting dragons, and many more.

I always remind my clientele that the deeper we are willing to dig into our wounding, analyze it in order to better understand and face our shadow parts, the higher we will rise like a phoenix rising from the ashes. To delve into our most painful self, to face our most fragmented parts, is never an easy task. Yet only in doing so can we become whole again.

Oftentimes, in the course of the Maha Intensive, individuals have faced so much of their crooked self that they are not only ready to go home, they are ready to leave the planet. By having completed the deep work, though, their reward is waiting. And during their next and final healing session, they experience proof of it.

Very often, during the last healing of the 12-day Maha Session cycle, the individual has what I call a God experience. This can have very different expressions and is utterly dependent on the individual. In general, a feeling of unity and profound peace is experienced, accompanied by deep trust and confidence in the guidance of the Divine. The perfect order of the universe is fully recognized. And the lessons learned become a blessing.

During a God experience, the individual accesses a much higher frequency than they usually operate in, and they awaken to their innate nature of holiness. Heat might be felt as in the case of a Kundalini experience. They float in an ocean of bliss and ecstasy and often sob with deep feelings of gratitude. They might feel called to enter into service and devote their life to being a facilitator / healer. And much more.

A God experience can never be invoked, it must be authentically felt. It is not that we look for a God experience, rather it is that the God experience finds us.

Chapter 64

GALACTIC EXPERIENCES AND ENCOUNTERS

In Europe, generally, people experience more past lives related to Earth and in this sense are more earth-bound. Here in the US, extraterrestrial encounters during regressions are quite common. During the nineties, a study was conducted revealing that 89 percent of the American population accepts the possibility of life outside planet Earth, while at the same time, 89 percent of Europeans did not believe that this could be the case.

This might have to do with the genetic code and genetic material of the citizens of the European countries. If we take American history into account, it becomes evident why Americans have a different viewpoint on the subject. The fact is that the US, as we know it now, was built in a little over two hundred years by a population with a pioneer mindset.

Europe on the other hand, continues to trend towards tradition, and traditional values and morals are exercised and fully in practice. Europe draws upon its past. America looks towards the future. There is no judgment on what has more value, it is simply an observation that has been mirrored in my work in Europe and the US.

It is also reflected in the fact that the US already has its first spaceport in place and is exploring Mars in order to look for microbial life, test new technologies, and lay the groundwork for human exploration down the road — while, sadly, millions of people around the world are battling war, famine, and natural disasters.

Furthermore, the amount of money spent on the War on Drugs since its inception (it's estimated that $1 trillion has been spent) seems ridiculous in the face that it has done nothing to stem the spread of drug use in our society. Whereas in Europe, Holland instigated an approach to deal with drug addicts, modeled after other European countries, and are having positive results.

While working with individuals in their galactic experiences, I have observed that people with the First Wounding, the Schizoid Wound (see Chapters 78 – 79) oftentimes feel very drawn to mentally escape this planet and its seemingly grave conditions. Life on other planets is favored and idealized and perceived as harmonious and peaceful — and certainly much more conscious than here on Earth. Food intake is light and plant-based and the Souls living there are spiritually more advanced. They possess supernatural powers and communicate telepathically, which might very well be the case.

This has been attested to by individuals who experienced life in the Pleiades, and the stars Sirius and Arcturus. But galactic encounters are not always pleasant. Some of the environments have been described as lacking light and warmth from a sun and with zero vegetation and animal life. There might be a lack of conception via sex but instead, an experience of cold and artificial fertilization in a lab of beings lacking emotions and feelings of love.

The inhabitants of the binary star system Zeta Reticuli, better known as the aliens "The Greys," became well known through the Roswell incident and the accounts of Bob Lazare who worked for a number of years at Area 51. During the mid-nineties, I participated at a transpersonal conference in San Francisco and met Harvard professor John Mack who lectured about his countless recordings of world-wide abductions, implants, and mutilations performed by inhabitants of Zeta Reticuli.

While participating in a workshop in Sedona during the nineties, I witnessed the entire group of falling into a kind of mass hysteria about having had experiences regarding abductions by extraterrestrials. I personally do not recount any such experience nor have I ever worked with victims of abductions. The subject of extraterrestrial life is not a specialty in my healing practice. Anyone interested might want to look into the work of John E. Mack and his book *Abduction: Human Encounters with Aliens*.

But since each and every one of us who possesses a body has clearly incarnated here on Earth for particular reasons and purposes, I tend to focus more on the lessons that need to be learned while here, rather than encourage people to mentally escape this Earth plane to spend time imagining being out on other worlds. When individuals tell me this is their first incarnation on planet Earth, I do admit that I don't agree for the following reasons.

- First and foremost, all life is evolutionary, all lifeforms are evolving. An incarnation is possible in many different shapes and forms. As examples, I have worked with individuals who inhabited a rock, a wooden sculpture, and many other more primitive lifeforms. For many here on Earth, incarnating into their current body has not been an easy task.

Whenever working with individuals longing for their place of origin, I guide them to return to where they came from. This is always a very soothing experience that brings much comfort. Usually, they return to the stage prior to their birth and experience themselves in spirit form. Everything is pleasant there, it's calm, peaceful, and harmonious. I let them be in that place for however long they wish to remain.

After a period of utter bliss, enjoyment and rejuvenation, they realize what is missing in the spirit world. There is no friction, no growth, no advancement on the Soul level. In order for the Soul to advance, there needs to be experience. But experience can only happen here. Planet Earth is the playground for experience where growth can happen and the Soul can advance. This realization encourages gratitude for one's chosen incarnation here on Earth.

Imagine you are traveling to a foreign place with barbarians with weird habits that are utterly appalling to you. This is an extreme description, yet some individuals do feel severely alienated by the conditions here. Having come here to Earth, one would face such challenges that, in order to be able to adapt, we first incarnate in simpler lifeforms and only then do we eventually incarnate to the peak of consciousness on this planet: the human being.

- Another equally important reason is the fact that all life is sacred. It is a sacred privilege to have come into a human body here. It points to the fact that we as Souls had the courage to incarnate during a time when the planet is in utter turmoil and chaos. Change is called for and the fact that we chose to partake in that change points to the courage we have as Souls.

Planet Earth is the playground for experience where growth can happen and the Soul can advance.

Chapter 65

AMBER IN THE COSMIC SPACE OF UNITY

The following is not an authentic account of a healing session but rather a parallel reality and a combination of various individuals. Amber is a woman who all her life felt different than anyone else. She shared that for the greater part of her life she has not been able to identify with anyone. Her memories go way back into her early childhood and she shared that as a girl, while her kindergarten companions played with dolls and trains, she painted.

Amber mainly painted the sun and the moon and other planets. She painted the beings living on those planets and described how they were living. Much of what she said was beyond the comprehension of her parents who thought Amber was living in a fantasy world that appeared very real to her.

But what Amber revealed also had profound wisdom. Her parents had no clue where this wisdom came from. From the time she was a toddler, she asked countless questions about the source of food and refused all meat and fish products. When her mother would go to look for her, she would find Amber talking to the wind, or a tree. Little Amber insisted that they whispered to her and she had dialogs with the elements. She behaved as if she were living in a parallel reality.

As a small girl, Amber had many visions of peace on Earth. She was extremely sensitive to disharmony and, for the sake of Amber, her parents had to learn to communicate any conflicts calmly and in creative manners rather than just vent their feelings.

When her brother fell severely ill, she was only six years old. Her parents were in huge distress over it, yet Amber remained calm and in complete silence seemingly communicating with her brother who told her that he might be leaving and not coming back. Amber passed on this information to her parents with a calm and understanding voice. Soon after, her brother passed on, but not before Amber had delivered his message that they should not grieve for him because he was fine and his leaving was what he wanted.

Amber's role with her parents was reversed. It was as if Amber were the parent and teacher to her parents and her environment. Having incarnated with those gifts, it was easy for Amber to deeply listen. She was able to tune into animals, plant life, the elements, and human beings and telepathically communicate with all of them. She explained that when she does, she simply focuses and then merges with the subject of her attention until there is no separation. Once she is in the stage of having merged with them, they share themselves with her.

Her parents enrolled Amber in the Waldorf school because they didn't want to subject her to a regular school system with its many rules, regulations, and restrictions. Amber shared that she liked school but even though she felt supported and recognized, she also felt that once she was done with schooling she wanted to travel to find solitude somewhere in the wilderness and far away from civilization in order to deepen her communication with all living beings and the cosmos. She did this and left when she was twenty-one years old. Her parents knew better than to hold her back and gave their blessings for her journey.

Amber traveled to the Siberian Taiga and spent two years living in the wilderness. She met simple people with profound wisdom and hermits who shared their knowledge with her. For the first time in her life, she had met her kin. An old wise woman who lived a solitary life took her under her wing and instructed her further in the wisdom of the Earth, medicinal herbs, and the right season and time to harvest. She gathered wild berries, beets, and mushrooms to nurture her body. She drank the fresh, life-providing water of the springs, and swam in the rivers and lakes. Oftentimes, she didn't meet anyone for days and would walk barefoot to communicate with the Earth. The soil of the Earth gathered the information of her body and kept healing her.

Amber felt strangely at home in the solitude and the company of wild animals who did no harm to her, as if they felt her benign intentions. Every day, she spent in deep reverence for life in all its shapes and forms. Life in itself became a constant and never-ending prayer. She received profound teachings and had powerful visions. Everything and all felt magical and filled with pure life essence.

During the warmer months, she slept underneath the stars and observed the cycle of the night sky and the phases of the moon. The beings of the Cosmos spoke to her of her origins and gifted her with visions of her galactic heritage. She visited the Pleiades, which she knew from before her current life and particularly Sirius, her spiritual origin and home.

Sirius was her grand teacher, the spirit flowing through our physical sun, the same sun she had drawn over and again as a child. Now she understood. The star Sirius was the original source of everything, that keeps our physical world alive, the home of humanity's great teachers. It all started to come together for Amber and she understood her childhood gifts and her present incarnation.

At some point, Amber felt she had learned what she had come to learn and it was time for her to leave the wilderness and return to humanity.

PART VI

VARIOUS CASE STUDIES OF CHILDHOOD SEXUAL ABUSE

First of all, these healing stories are exactly the way they occurred as with all case studies, with the exception of Casandra, where I didn't disclose the full information of her healing process. Secondly, I never put words in the mouths of my clients but only repeat to them what they have said. This is very important. They must speak from their own experience. By doing so, it becomes their truth and also their reality.

I am only the witness. This is my role, to witness what they say and experience. During the Maha Intensive, everything is documented in writing by me so clients can process their work as many times as need be by reading and copying my notes, as well as the additional notes taken during the follow-up interpretation with me the next day.

During individual healing sessions, I always suggest that the session be taped, otherwise much of what happens is forgotten. With the exception of Oliver who found it unbearable to face the truth and interrupted his healing cycle after two sessions with me (see Chapter 73, "Little Oliver and His Brothers: When Belonging is the Priority"), there has never been anyone in the 30+ years of my healing practice who claimed that what they saw and related in the work was a production of my own imagination.

In one case, while working in Europe, a client saw a battlefield when I regressed her to her childhood. She was so shocked that she opened her eyes, got up, and declared she couldn't go on because it was too painful for her to see.

Clients intuitively understand that the intrinsic intelligence of the Soul knows that only in looking at what occurred in the past that what caused the pain and trauma can then be healed. I also always point out that the worst is over — it happened already, they survived it, and are now here in my practice to heal. The repeated assurance that the worst is over seems to remedy their distress while facing their trauma.

We all hold the key to our own healing within ourselves.

I also teach that we all hold the key to our own healing within ourselves. Years ago, when I burnt myself completely out through an overload of work and was facing severe vitamin deficiencies, I kept hearing the message from my body that I needed oxygen in order to cure my condition. By lucky circumstances, a Swiss entrepreneur rented one of my rooms at the lodging facility and spoke to me of his experience in walking the Camino to Santiago de Compostela in Spain. Upon hearing his account, I instantly knew I had to do the walk to bring the oxygen into my system. I flew to Spain, walked the 500+ miles, and returned home free of the vitamin deficiencies.

Our body and energetic system always know what is needed for healing.

Our body and energetic system always know what is needed for healing. Usually, when repressed anger due to inflicted abuse comes up, I suggest working through the anger by using a punching bag. But recently, a client requested she needed to stamp her feet through water.

255

This was a first. I filled the bathtub adjoining the healing room with six inches of water and she stepped in, stamped about, and was able to access her anger and fully release it.

The healing motto for my clients is always that whatever their guidance says needs to happen for healing to occur should be done. The only rules are not hurting oneself, not hurting someone else, and not destroying property. Many individual's guidance request involves screaming or punching pillows. Sometimes, it's singing to themselves. For some, I suggested they paint their story or to sculpt it in plasticine clay.

What needs to be done for healing to occur is very individual. Practically all of my clients felt the need to confront their perpetrator, and especially if the abuser was a parent or sibling.

In my healing practice, I have often observed how clients, when faced with such intense information, have a wide range of reactions. When the subject of abuse initially comes up, at first, most are in denial that any such thing could possibly have happened. Such a painful truth is too shocking to them. They have difficulty trusting the images they saw in the healing session, question its validity, and their own sanity.

Phases of Healing

Denial

Questioning and Doubt

Anger

Grief

Acceptance

They need time and space to digest the experience and go through an array of emotions. Generally, they first experience a denial phase, then question and doubt, and even anger comes up before they arrive at a place where they accept and admit transgressions. All this requires deep healing work over a period of time and a series of Maha Intensives before the healing of their past can take place. It is an extensive process and a deeply individual journey toward healing. It's important to note that there are some relationships that are never mended and/or situations that remain unresolved.

While anyone who delves deep into their sub-conscious is able to access their personal history and the abuse inflicted on them, it doesn't suffice to merely see the circumstances and the truth of what happened. Having the images held in one's mind is only the first step to healing. I must emphasize that for true healing and curing to happen, it is necessary to not only see the painful images but to feel them as if they were happening now. This is a complex and painful step-by-step process that takes time and much healing work.

Furthermore, the facilitator cannot check out mentally when images trigger their own experiences and emotions but rather must be able to stay with the victim regardless. They must see with their compassionate Heart as if they were feeling it, too, yet at the same time must stay neutral and unaffected.

Only the fully developed loving Heart is capable of holding this space of true witnessing that provides the space for release and healing to happen for the individual.

Section 1

The Tragic Theft of Innocence

Chapter 66

CHILDHOOD SEXUAL ABUSE AND CHILDHOOD RITUAL SEXUAL ABUSE

"I know this transformation is painful.
But you are not falling apart.
You are just falling into something different
With a new capacity to be beautiful."

~ William C. Hannan

I have had the fortune of working with whole family clans, meaning the mother and the father plus their adult children have found their way into my healing practice. Accompanying each individual separately and hearing their own experience from their perspective has given me deep insights and understanding of not only how and why destructive family structures get formed but also some of the underlying reasons for childhood sexual abuse.

According to my thirty-one years of healing practice experience, every second woman and every third man with whom I've worked has been sexually abused in their childhood. Sadly, we are living in a sick world and childhood sexual abuse is very common. Often, it happens as early as when the baby is only a few months old. Of course, only very deep work with the sub-conscious can bring those traumas up into the conscious. Countless times, victims get images of their father putting his penis into the mouth of the little infant for the baby to suck.

There is no way an adult would consciously remember experiences as far back as earliest childhood. Deep sexual trauma is usually never consciously remembered by the individual and only very deep work with the sub-conscious can uncover it.

The healing work requires much patience and expertise. Usually, the sub-conscious releases the images willingly, but mentally, it is very challenging for the victim to accept. There can be denial that the abuse ever occurred, and it might take several healing sessions and time to accept the painful truth.

Furthermore, during the healing session, the individual might become frozen as if the past event were happening right then — which is the same reaction the child had when the abuse originally happened to them — and they see the images but have difficulty expressing what they're seeing. There are long periods of silence, and when asked, only bits and pieces of information come forward. It feels much like digging for something that has fallen into molasses. Sometimes, and this is rare, the entire abuse scenario is released in a seemingly effortless flow. Every person is different and the way they handle it is unique.

I witnessed as a very young mother how my boyfriend, I'll call him Paul, wanted to playfully put his penis in my little baby Marc's mouth while I was changing his diapers. I was shocked and immediately ordered him to never, ever do that again, that it was deeply wrong!! Ours was a very active and fulfilling sex life so there was absolutely no reason for him to look for another outlet for his sexual frustration. I figured there must be another, far deeper reason for Paul's weird behavior.

Paul's father suffered from polio as a child and as a result, his body was crippled and he remained physically impaired the rest of his life. I suspected that his father had done the same to Paul when he was a baby.

Another time, Paul put his tongue in Marc's mouth and two-month-old baby Marc vomited in Paul's mouth. That taught Paul a lesson! Again, I scolded Paul and forbade him to do such things! I intuitively knew that to perform such weird, absurd, and perverted acts to a little baby was definitely not natural. I had the feeling Paul was repeating an experience from his own past, an experience he wasn't conscious of. And by repeating the experience, he was unconsciously trying to bring it into his conscious mind.

For the perpetrator, the trauma they experienced as a child and that has been embedded in their subconscious, wants to be repeated consciously even though they are completely unaware of what they're enacting.

The underlying reason for this kind of behavior is that what was experienced as a child wants to be repeated. In the deepest sense, it is an act towards healing because for any healing to occur, everything concerning the abuse needs to come up and out into the light. It needs to be looked at — and it needs to be recognized as unnatural and psychologically disturbed.

I did what any healthy mother in their right mind would do: I interceded and prevented. But unfortunately, I have come to learn that childhood sexual abuse has often been a green light for the father because the mother looks the other way. Often, the reason is that she was herself sexually abused as a child but isn't conscious of it, and therefore has blinders on due to deep denial, fear, shame, or trauma. Because she was sexually abused as a child — oftentimes, but not always — she despises and abhors sex and avoids it as often as possible, which leads to sexual frustration for her partner.

The healthy thing for any couple is to have sex. The man craves it, but if the woman denies him the pleasure, his sexual frustration will lead him to search for an outlet. Many times, he will turn to his beloved child. The mother, relieved and unaware of what her husband is doing, is spared.

Surprisingly, women have often told me they endure sex for the sake of keeping the peace in the household — and while having sex, will occupy their minds with something more pleasant. They have also told me how much they hate fellatio, that "going down on a man" disgusts them and they won't do it. Upon me explaining that it is a natural act between a woman and a man in love, they've told me that they can endure sex if they must, but that they will never perform fellatio.

It would become a completely different process for mothers to fully understand that while natural sex is a healthy act between two adults, it causes deep and almost always life-long damage for an adult if adult sexual acts were performed on them as a child.

What I have also learned is that any child who was subjected to sexual abuse intuitively knew that what was happening to them was wrong and forbidden. Even the smallest baby is already aware and knows a deeply wrong thing is being done to her or him. It is the same case with animals. When pets and livestock are sexually abused, they know that something unnatural and wrong is happening to them. It humiliates and shames them. I have worked with men who turned to their pets for sexual activity.

Any child intuitively senses when an act with sexual undertones is being performed. The most damaging part is that a child loses their innocence and purity. From then on, it's what I call a "spoiled child." Childhood is gone, the child robbed of their innocence. They've been introduced to the adult world. They experience shame because they know something forbidden occurred.

If a child could turn to their mother, which children often do as a natural impulse, share what happened, be heard and believed by the mother, the damage would not be so intense. But a mother — especially one who was abused herself — will not listen to the words of her child, she doesn't side with the child and defend them, then the child ends up left alone to cope with her or his experience, an internalized process that is very deleterious psychologically.

"Animal sexual abuse ... has increasingly been the subject of veterinary science as well as criminology. Animal sexual abuse can involve a distressingly wide range of animals and can result in a wide spectrum of injury including death."

~ Animal Rescue League of Boston

Many individuals who find their way into my healing practice seek me out due to a disease, such as cancer, chronic depression, or a mental condition. They are unaware that deep, unresolved childhood sexual abuse might be the cause of the disease. This is, of course, not to say that childhood sexual abuse is the root of many diseases. But it is the cause of some diseases. It is simply to emphasize that most individuals are unaware that sexual abuse ever occurred in their childhood.

<h1 style="text-align:center">Chapter 67</h1>

A DIFFERENT PERSPECTIVE ON THE POSSIBLE UNDERLYING REASONS

> "Perhaps our eyes need to be washed
> by our tears once in a while
> So that we can see life
> with a clearer view again."
>
> ~ Anonymous

I worked with a number of women who processed deep sexual childhood trauma and whose mothers also found their way into my healing practice. Because their daughters shared the trauma of the sexual abuse with their mother, I was allowed to address it during their own healing process.

A comment I've heard over and over from mothers whose daughters were sexually abused by their fathers is, "At least he didn't go to a prostitute or someone outside of the family — it stayed in the family." This is shocking. The fact that a mother would rather sacrifice her innocent child to adult sexual play and incest, while avoiding potential social scandal is deeply disturbing.

If adults only knew the deep and damaging impact to a child's life. Depending on the extent of the sexual abuse, the child might not feel pain but become aroused. For example, a child who is sexually caressed, not necessarily the genitals but somewhere else on their body with sex being the underlying intention of the victimizer, that child will experience very different sensations than a child who gets penetrated by a finger or even the penis.

The forbidden sex also becomes a taboo subject. The perpetrator says to the child, "This is our secret ... no one should know, just you and me." The child may then get emotionally favored by the perpetrator, treated specially, and rewarded for this special position. Or, the child may be scorned, berated, and even ostracized by the perpetrator but the perpetrator will continue sexually abusing the child. This adds another layer to the child's trauma.

I need to make it clear that I am talking about insecure, sexually, deeply wounded men. I am not talking about sexually virile men, the wolves who have sex with many women, perhaps including men. And for having done all of it, got bored and in the course of their predations sought to conquer ever-younger women until they expanded their hunt to explore the taboo: sex with a child. Clearly, I am talking about a different kind of man.

In my experience, a man turning to abuse his child — or any child — for sexual satisfaction has a very fragile self-image. It may be that his sexual needs have been rebuffed many times by his partner and he feels very sensitive about it. Or he might not even be in a relationship, is unable to get women to date him, or can only attain sex by buying it. He may even have been abused himself as a child and therefore has a warped understanding about sex, relationships, and appropriate sexual partners. Whatever the situation, he has developed a very unhealthy and repressed view of his sexuality.

His relationship towards himself and his body is not healthy. He may carry shame for his sexual impulses and desires, feel undeserving, not masculine, or strong and virile. He doesn't dare approach another woman for fear of possible rejection. So, he turns to a child. A child is by far inferior to him in size, strength, and intellect, someone he can have control over, especially emotionally.

With a woman, he might have no control. She could be ridiculing, rejecting, demeaning, and dismissive of him about his appearance, looks, masculinity, intellect, or male prowess — all of which wear a man down to the point where he feels gutted, emasculated, powerless, ineffectual, and undesirable. Eventually, to meet his needs both emotionally and sexually, his low self-esteem drives him to do the unthinkable.

Any healthy baby has sensation in all parts of their body, so they're curious, enjoying the sensations and pleasures of exploring and touching every body part. To be able to touch and explore freely is necessary for healthy development. How often do we see babies grab their feet and make gurgling sounds of laughter. In this same sense, it is only natural and healthy for a baby to touch its genitals. It will do so every time they are naked. It's a healthy impulse to know one's body. After all, we can't deny our body is our own.

However, if a parent smiles when the baby grabs its feet but pulls its hands away and says "no" or "bad" whenever the baby touches its genitals, the baby learns that there is something wrong with that body part, that to touch its genitals is not approved of and even forbidden. Hence, it develops shame for that body part or, conversely, an unhealthy fixation on it. The healthy and natural development of the child gets stifled because there is one body part that is taboo and cannot be touched.

Life force = Sexual force

If the sexual force gets stifled through shame, the life force is diminished as a result.

Such babies grow into children whose innate sexuality is denied — but sexuality is our life force. Our sexual force and life force are one and the same. They are not separated and can never be separated. And they should never be denied.

Every child has curiosity about their sexuality and wants to explore it in healthy, innocent, and pure ways. In America's sexually repressed society, it is easy for things to turn crooked. It is regarded as less damaging for a child to watch horror movies and movies with scenes with graphic violence rather than for a child to watch sexual love scenes in a movie. But even though healthy sex is natural, sex scenes in movies are considered pornographic.

Based on my work experience, vaginal penetration usually doesn't happen when a child is very small. Unless an erect penis is only the size of a small finger, penetration would be literally impossible without inflicting serious ripping damage, which would not remain unnoticed. Penetration or not, it is nevertheless still sexual abuse and the damage is permanent until the trauma is re-experienced and released.

In general, the damage is more serious when the perpetrator was the parent, grandparent, or another family member than when the abuse was inflicted by someone outside the family. This is because a family member is perceived by the child as a familiar person who is trusted and the child has confidence in. Therefore, severe betrayal issues will inevitably be inflicted upon the victim.

Childhood sexual abuse becomes "childhood ritual sexual abuse" when the child knows that every time a certain act is performed, it will be followed by sexual abuse. These can be simple acts or full-fledged habits. For example, a father comes home from work, puts on his slippers, waits for the mother to go to work, and then goes into the child's room to sexually abuse her or him. In this case, the child knows that when the father exchanges his street shoes for slippers, he won't go out anymore but will wait for the mother to leave the house — then the abuse will happen.

As we shall see in one of the following chapters in this Part, Heather and her sister knew that every time her father and grandfather got drunk, they would drag the two girls down into the cellar and sexually abuse them. Or in the case of little Oliver, described in an upcoming chapter, he might have had a feeling that when mama was at work and his brothers brought home friends, those boys would come into his room and sexually abuse him.

Some of the cases described are extreme, shocking, and very out of the ordinary childhood sexual abuse that I usually experience in my healing practice. I include them here so that readers understand to what extremes childhood sexual abuse can go.

Section 2

Case Studies

Chapter 68

CASANDRA: FROM THE WOUNDED TO THE HEALER

Casandra, a woman in her thirties, was plagued by many fears, obsessions, anxieties, and existential worries. She was initially timid but brave, with a remarkable drive for healing her past. Casandra said she was loved by both parents but that it was a very lopsided love. Upon sharing some of her childhood memories, Casandra remembered that as a child her mother was always sad and depressed.

Little Casandra felt responsible for her mother's happiness, so as soon as she could write, she wrote her mom a love letter every day. Then the day came when her mother ridiculed her little girl for expressing her love to her. Little Casandra felt very sad and stopped writing the love letters.

Casandra and her life partner became students of mine in the 2-year Training Certification Program. Her life started to quickly transform. Casandra was gifted with profound qualities of wisdom and insight. Her deepest struggle was fear. She is a typical example of the "wounded healer."

As Casandra regressed into her early infant stage, her sub-conscious started to release weird unimaginable images of her father torturing her as a baby. She saw him holding burning matches to her genitals that inflicted burns on her labia, which he then tended to by putting ice cubes into her diapers. She also saw something that was unbelievable to her: He would prepare her milk bottle, mix his semen in it, and give it to her.

The wounded healer is a term created by Carl Jung. The idea states that an analyst is compelled to treat patients because he himself is wounded. In healing, this doesn't apply. All of my students were wounded healers. But their reason was not to analyze themselves but rather to help release others from their suffering that they themselves knew only too well.

Casandra was extremely confused as to why her father would do something so perverse and unimaginable as forcing his semen in a milk bottle on her and torturing her by burning her labia.

For months, Casandra was unable to accept these weird images coming up. It seemed far too cruel and extremely unreal. Why in the world would her father have done such a thing?! It confused Casandra tremendously. She could not wrap her mind around those images. At the same time, she doubted if she could come up with such craziness.

Casandra had two sisters, but for years the family had been estranged from each other, everyone living their own life. It was a surprise when all of a sudden, her older sister Alegra got in contact with Casandra and upon hearing that she was undergoing healing work and training, spontaneously signed up to work with me as well. Casandra hadn't shared any information about her session experiences with Alegra. When Alegra came to see me, she explained that she was on dialysis and other organs of her body had also given up their functioning. She was facing several serious health issues.

When Alegra was describing her childhood to me, she stated that her sister Casandra was born when Alegra was six years old. She recalled a great love for her sister and how every day she would beg her mother to wait when changing Casandra's diapers because she feared her mother was so absent minded that baby Casandra could roll off the changing table and get hurt. That was a great preoccupation for Alegra. She made it her task to take care of her baby sister. Alegra also mentioned that she discovered strange redness and blisters on her sister's genitals as if she had been burnt. As a six year old, it puzzled and greatly worried her.

When I shared this information with Casandra during her next healing session, she no longer doubted what she had seen in her previous sessions. We talked about that fact that I was certain her father had subconsciously re-enacted what had happened to him as a baby. Casandra expressed her desire to fully release her childhood sexual trauma and accept it as fact.

During the next healing when I asked her Higher Self what was needed for healing, Casandra received the answer that the acts of violence needed to be repeated in order to have it released and for healing to happen.

For the following healing session, Casandra understood that she not only had to see the images and accept them as fact, but that she needed to re-experience the pain and abuse inflicted on her. She was able to drop into her feelings of terror and panic as she began to feel the heat burning her. She (the baby) kept turning her head in disgust and refusal while her father lovingly but desperately forced her to drink the bottle of milk mixed with semen.

This experience brought healing. It is one of many testaments to the fact that each and every one of us holds the key to healing within us. Our Soul will always tell us what is needed for healing and curing — all we need to do is get our mind out of the way and listen.

Casandra was able to release her trauma on a cellular level. In the months following the healing, she went to her parents' home and confronted her father. She told him what she had experienced, what he had done to her during her infant years. She shared that he then went into the bathroom but in his shock, he left the door open. There, she saw him looking at himself in the mirror and saying over and over to himself, "I never did such a thing to her. It's not possible that I would have ever done such a thing. Could it be that I have done this? I don't remember ever having done this."

For more than a year, though, Casandra insisted that no one could ever possibly have experienced something as terrible as her. Ever! I responded: "Casandra, the day will come when in your own healing practice that a woman will come in, you will witness her story of sexual childhood abuse. Your whole Heart will be with her. Not one moment will you descend into your own story of abuse and what happened to you. Your whole Heart will be with that person. It might take some time but when this time comes, you will know that you have healed and your story belongs to the past."

And so it came about. On the occasion of a walk in the countryside of Bavaria in Southern Germany two years later, Casandra shared with me in detail the stories of two different clients of hers and their shocking stories of childhood sexual abuse. I listened with full attention, then I asked her what she had felt while she was accompanying them on their healing journey. She responded that she felt so sorry and that her whole Heart was there in the moment with them.

I inquired whether her own childhood abuse popped up and distracted her. "Not at all," she responded. I hugged her with affection. Casandra had released her past childhood sexual abuse. She had fully healed and was now very capable in accompanying others on their journeys toward healing.

Something else that plagued Casandra as an adult was a voice in her head that constantly repeated that she would die from cancer. There was no chance of survival for her — it was her fate. I suggested that she needed to develop the inner discipline to disregard the voice, to not listen to its message, to counteract it by immediately concentrating on her Heart and feeling her own innate love, trust, and confidence.

She needed to assert that: "This is not true! I will not die of cancer! I am healthy and happy. Leave me in peace!" Within a month, the voice she heard had disappeared.

When you hear destructive voices in your head, you need to develop the discipline to drop into your Heart and disregard the voices.

267

On a different occasion, Casandra called me from Europe and asked for advice. She had been dealing with pain in her abdominal area for over fourteen days. It was turning chronic. She had consulted a doctor who determined it was her pancreas but he was unable to find the actual cause of the pain.

I went into meditation to look at her body using remote viewing. The message I got was that Casandra should go on a fast. For fourteen days, she was to only live on liquids: juices, soups, and water. Casandra followed the advice. The pain completely subsided and didn't return. As a side effect, Casandra reported that she'd also became free of all fears and obsessions.

Remote viewing is clairvoyant viewing from a distance without the object or person present.

Chapter 69

JUNE: DEEP SEXUAL TRAUMA RE-SWALLOWED BY THE SUB-CONSCIOUS

June is a long-time family friend. I was in my early teens when I first met her. She came to my healing practice because she was curious about my work. As we went deeper into the process, we looked into her childhood. She saw herself as a twelve-year-old girl. At some point, June started gagging as if to vomit. The feeling persisted, her body reaction very strong.

She saw herself as a child, her father forcing her to have oral sex. She felt so disgusted. She gagged to an extent that I brought a bucket for her to vomit in. The images arising were utterly confusing to her. She was just past her first period when she "saw" her father having sexual intercourse with her. He impregnated his own daughter. Her mother arranged for an abortion. June was thirteen years old at the time.

June left my practice in disbelief and shock. I handed her the handwritten notes of the healing session as witness to what occurred during the healing. I did not hear from her for some time.

My healing practice was flooded and I was very busy. At times, June and I talked over the phone but she never mentioned the healing work she had done with me. Two years after her session experiences, she contacted me and wanted to meet for an important sharing. She told me she had joined a self-exploratory healing group of women. "Can you imagine," she shared with me, "I just found out that my father sexually abused me and even impregnated me when I was only thirteen years old. And my mother knew it and arranged for an abortion."

I looked at her stunned. "What do you mean, you just found out," I asked. "You saw it all and experienced it on a cellular level when you came for the 4-Day Session cycle with me. I handed you the written documentation. You have it all in writing, in black and white."

June didn't remember. She had completely blanked it out. Certainly, because she never wrote the content of the healing session, which is my primary homework requirement. Had she done so, her childhood sexual abuse would not have been blocked out. As it was, and due to the depth of the trauma and the taboo subject, her sub-conscious re-swallowed what came up during her healing work with me, and it only re-emerged two years later.

This is not uncommon. Due to the severeness of the trauma, the psyche and conscious mind of the person denies that it ever happened.

The sub-conscious might re-swallow what was too painful to see due to the denial of the conscious mind.

Therefore, it drops back into the sub-conscious, as we shall see in the story about Oliver in Chapter 73.

Another example to the sub-conscious swallowing a trauma as an adult is the following experience of an old friend of mine, Raja, whom I had met a long time ago, while living in Afghanistan. Her husband served his country as a diplomat. In regular intervals of four years, they were stationed in various countries all over the world. Raja was very used to living abroad. At the time, they had been stationed in Jakarta, Indonesia.

Her husband received his new assignment in Bonn, Germany. The packing was completed and the next day they were to fly to Germany. But on their very last night in Jakarta, Raja and her husband were awakened by two burglars. It was pitch dark in the room. Raja told me that both had knives being held to their throats. Their individual reactions to the situation were very different. Her husband fought with one burglar and ended up with numerous cuts on his face that required reconstructive surgery.

Raja, on the other hand, screamed and the burglar took off at once. To Raja's utter frustration, she remembers the entire incident while her husband's memory is blank. He doesn't remember a single thing of the dramatic night. They were both in their forties when this occurred.

This example proves the mercy of the sub-conscious. It swallows anything too traumatic for the conscious mind to handle, independent of a person's age.

Chapter 70

DONNA: FIVE BURST CYSTS IN HER UTERUS

I had met Donna and her family on several occasions. She was married to a Black man. They had no children, which was a surprise because Donna grew up with six siblings and maintained extremely close family ties. She shared that a week earlier, she was driven to the emergency room. The surgeon removed five burst cysts from her uterus. Cysts are artificial children. They grow when the woman has a desire to have a child and for some reason, she isn't able to get pregnant.

Cysts = artificial children

Regressing Donna to her childhood and the trauma related to the cysts, she saw herself as a four-year-old girl. Her best friend was Cynthia, a Black girl her age, who lived right down the block. Usually, Cynthia would come to Donna's home to play.

One day, Cynthia took Donna to her home to play. As they entered the kitchen, little Donna met Cynthia's mom and older sister, who both looked at her very strangely. For some reason, they seemed worried. But Cynthia didn't pay any attention and took Donna upstairs to her room to play. Soon after, Cynthia's father entered the room. He was drunk and very angry at little Cynthia for having brought a White girl into their home. He scolded his daughter while showering a litany of curses about White people on little Donna. He blamed the miseries of his life on White people and Donna became the victim of the full impact of his curses.

Then, he roughly grabbed the two little girls, pulled them out of the room, and up a flight of stairs into the attic. There he sat each of them on a chair, back-to-back, took a rope and tied them to their chairs, all the while cursing. Then he blindfolded both girls.

Donna, the adult, described the scene vividly in a childlike voice from the perspective of little Donna, the child. Then, Donna started to gag and cough and kept turning her head forcefully from side to side. I asked her what was happening. She responded with, "He's feeding me a soup. I don't like that soup. No, no! I tastes ugly. I don't want any soup!" she screamed and whined.

But all resistance was useless. The soup was forced down her throat. Little Donna, in her innocence, didn't know that Cynthia's dad was masturbating into her tiny mouth. She heard the voices of her mom and sister calling her home from out on the street. Shortly after, Cynthia's dad untied the rope and took off their blindfolds. Donna jumped from her chair, ran down the flight of stairs, and out of the house. Arriving home, she didn't tell her mom or anyone else what had happened.

Donna came out of the session feeling very thoughtful. She had not remembered anything of what she had just experienced. She expressed that in her former relationships with men and now with her husband, she always made sure she gave a very good blow job.

Cynthia's dad's curses remained active for all of Donna's life. Prior to her marriage, she exclusively dated Black men. She never felt any attraction for White men. Donna also felt deep shame for her skin color. When I asked Donna if she liked children, she responded that she and her husband loved children. I inquired, "Why haven't you started a family if you both love children?"

"Oh no, who would want to have children with me, a White woman," she responded. We spoke for a long time about the curse Cynthia's dad had placed on her and the effect it had on her life and her choice to never have children. This was the only time I worked with Donna.

Chapter 71

ANNABELLE: THE LITTLE GIRL WHO DIED IN CHILDHOOD

Annabelle, a woman in her late forties, came for the Maha Intensive. When I asked her Inner Child to appear, Annabelle saw a white coffin. I encouraged her to open the coffin and look at who or what was in there. As she did, a little girl of five years of age was laying lifeless in it. Her name was little Annabelle. We asked little Annabelle to tell us how she had come to die.

Little Annabelle took adult Annabelle by the hand and led her down a wide, stone slab, spiral staircase by which they arrived in the cellar. The cellar was large and dark and smelled musty. They were now standing in a long corridor that had many different compartments, all with lattice doors, locks, and lattice walls. A little light came in through small window slits. I recognized it was the cellar of a large apartment building. Little Annabelle went straight towards one of the compartments.

There was a man standing in front of a table with his back to the door. He was with little Annabelle, who had her panties removed and was sitting on the table in front of him. We were told that little Annabelle was five years old. The man moved his hands along her tiny legs and she felt ticklish when he kissed her thighs. Then he moved his fingers closer to her "mushi"[25] while talking to her in a childlike voice. "Aye-aye-aye, look at that little mushi."

Little Annabelle didn't feel comfortable at all. She knew the man, but could not see his face. She knew this was wrong and her little body tensed up. As Annabelle the adult was describing the images appearing, she tensed up and stopped breathing. I instructed her to take deep breaths, relax her body, and look at everything little Annabelle was showing her.

Little Annabelle was now afraid. "Don't be afraid, don't be afraid," the man with the familiar voice said. "Look, I'll show you something. It's our little secret, just for you and me. I will show you." Now a snake appeared and the man encouraged little Annabelle to touch it. "Don't be afraid, don't be afraid." But little Annabelle was afraid and refused to touch the snake. She also felt ashamed. She intuitively knew this was wrong.

The man kept touching his snake. Then the snake started to attack little Annabelle's thighs. She could feel the snake moving while the man

---

[25] "Mushi" is a polite German slang word for the female private parts.

was holding her thighs so tight together that it hurt. After some time, she felt wet and started to cry. The man pulled her close to him and kept saying, "It's alright," while rubbing her back. He wiped off the liquid and put on her panties and Annabelle ran away.

I gave Annabelle some time in silence so she could digest what she'd seen and experienced, and encouraged her to take very deep breaths. Then I instructed her to return to the scene little Annabelle had shown her. I asked her to have the man turn around for her to look at his face. It was her father.

Adult Annabelle was in shock but little Annabelle had known it. I asked Annabelle to move further in time to see what happened afterward. She saw little Annabelle running to her mama, crying. She told her mother of the snake papa had shown her down in the cellar. That he had touched her down at her mushi and that she was afraid. Her mother didn't believe her and declared it a fantasy. She scolded little Annabelle for lying and called her a bad little girl. That was when little Annabelle died.

The subject never came up again until the healing session. Little Annabelle grew up without ever again remembering the abuse. It dropped completely into the sub-conscious. It never happened, so to speak, because her mother denied the fact and dismissed it as a fantasy.

Chapter 72

URSULA AND "MA GANGA"

A young woman, Ursula, came to see me due to severe acne on her buttocks that resisted all treatment. She was devastated because if caused a problem in her relationship. As we looked at the cause of it, she dropped into a past life where she saw herself as a young female bathing in a river. People were crowded around for a ritual bath. She was wearing a long, wraparound robe like all the other females. Everyone was gathered in a big crowd, all bathing in an enormous river. Ursula said it was a religious bath for ritual purposes and she kept repeating the words "Ma Ganga."

All of a sudden, she felt someone behind her. The person began to rub against her body. She felt greatly ashamed and did not dare to move or turn around. Then she realized it was a male body because she felt his erection. He was masturbating against her body. When he let go of her, she waited for a moment and then turned around. She saw a young male who had turned to walk away. She felt deep shame and hoped that no one had noticed.

As she was processing what she had just experienced, she saw herself as a little girl in her bed. Her father was spooning her from behind, his erect penis between her legs. She was five years old but this continued until she got older. Advancing in time to when Ursula was eight years old, her father would still regularly come into her bed. She saw the scene where she had been sleeping and awakened when her father got under the covers with her.

Sometimes, her mother would walk in on them. To her, her husband was just cuddling with his daughter from behind. Ursula endured his sexual assaults until she was eleven years old. She felt deeply ashamed and always pretended she was asleep. She never dared to speak to her mother about it nor did she tell anyone else. It stopped when Ursula was twelve and she started to lock her room.

Her conscious mind had not remembered any of this. What she did remember was that her father moved out when she was sixteen. Her parents divorced a year later. She kept resisting visiting her dad. Her mother never understood why. To her, it had to do with the rebellion of a sixteen year old.

Ursula didn't want to be alone with her father anymore and requested supervised visiting times. She couldn't explain why at that time, since she'd blocked out the memories, except that she had a weird feeling when thinking of her dad.

As we talked about her experiences from the previous day's session, I learned that Ursula knew next to nothing about India. She didn't know what a Sari was and she had never heard of the sacred river Ganges in India. It was all new to her. I explained to her that the Hindus call their river "Mother Ganges," hence, "Ma Ganga," and that to them it represented the life force of India.

Again, Ursula had no recollection of the childhood sexual abuse of her father. She felt very ashamed for her father, that he would use her to sexually stimulate himself. She also suffered from tremendous unworthiness, which tied in with her shame in regard to the abuse.

A month after Ursula underwent the healing session cycle, she called and reported that the acne on her buttocks had ceased completely but left some ugly marks that hopefully would disappear over time.

Chapter 73

LITTLE OLIVER AND HIS BROTHERS: WHEN BELONGING IS THE PRIORITY

Oliver had been diagnosed with severe PTSD and was in treatment at the VA, but that it hadn't helped him in the least. He shared that he was still suffering from nightmares.

Oliver arrived here from Florida after an extremely painful breakup with his former relationship of eight years. His girlfriend had gotten pregnant with twins. They took a trip to Colorado and upon their return, her mother had made arrangements for an abortion, which his girlfriend was going to go through with. For Oliver, this was murder — and he had already begun bonding with the fetuses during the ultrasound exam and wanted to become a dad. Recovering from the shock of his girlfriend's decision, he could no longer be with her and thus terminated the relationship.

When I met Oliver, his mom had passed away two years earlier from cancer. He said he had been very close to his mother, and so took care of her until her passing. I had the impression they shared an overall mutual refinement. His two older brothers, though, took after their father, much cruder in their behavior and character.

His mom was originally from the Azores, one of two autonomous regions of Portugal. Oliver shared that his mother had been a nurse and worked the night shift at the hospital. His dad was in the military.

When Oliver was ten years old, the family moved to the US military base in Berlin, Germany, the year when the Berlin Wall came down. Life was extremely challenging for Oliver. He shared that he often ran away, felt alone and not understood. He was under psychiatric care during that time. I don't know why, but assume it was because he felt miserable and kept running away from home.

When Oliver was eleven years old, his father flew with him to Arkansas and then on to El Paso, Texas where he submitted him to the William Beaumont Army Medical facility. Upon arrival, he dropped Oliver off and left.

This was Oliver's first hospitalization. He described his experience there as horrendous. He was treated for schizophrenia, subjected to sleep deprivation, heavily sedated with drugs, was shot with medications after he refused to take them orally, and had to watch *Lawrence of Arabia* over and over.

He had to be restrained while suffering from disturbing hallucinations like being burned alive. One time, he looked in the mirror, saw a fire, and thought he was on fire. Though not real, he experienced a severe panic attack. After twelve days at that facility, he was driven by ambulance to a private facility near Albuquerque.

As an adult, Oliver first joined the army, completed sniper training, and then went on to the navy. He was stationed overseas but was never sent into combat. Arriving back in the US, Oliver realized he wasn't suited in the least to be a soldier. It didn't agree with his principle of preserving life rather than killing. He chose to study massage therapy. As he described in an email to me, "... from a license to kill to a license to heal."

When I regressed Oliver to his childhood, he saw himself as a little four-year-old boy. It quickly became extremely challenging for Oliver to look at the images emerging. He kept stating that all he saw was poop-smeared paper towels. Lots of them. His mom was not around. His brothers were bringing home their friends. He kept seeing images of his brothers with their friends together with him in the bedroom and lots of poop-smeared paper towels.

All of these images were extremely confusing for Oliver. I kept asking about his dad. That part was to remain unclear because Oliver couldn't bear to look any further. He interrupted the healing process. What Oliver saw was too shocking for him and he dropped into deep denial of it all.

Until the day of the healing session, Oliver had no conscious memory of anything of the sort ever happening. If there had been any childhood sexual abuse, it was too severe of a trauma for Oliver to look at. I recorded the two healing sessions on my phone and handed it to him to play it back and listen to it all. Unfortunately, he erased the recording that had the four-year-old childhood memory on it.

To this day, Oliver regards his experience with the army and navy as the cause of his severe PTSD. He strictly refuses to believe that in his childhood he could have been subjected to sexual abuse. He recently stated that he had questioned his brothers and his father who all said they didn't remember anything of that sort ever happening. "How could I not believe them and cut myself off from them. My dad is my blood. I can't separate myself from him."

Oliver mentioned several times that his dad was a fundamentalist Christian who went to church religiously. He also said that what came up during the healing session was in my own mind and I had projected the disturbing images onto him.

I remain firm in my opinion that the origin of Oliver's trauma is early childhood sexual abuse. I believe that until Oliver is willing to dig deep into his sub-conscious and bring up what happened, his symptoms will not cease. I told him that in order to heal and be able to begin living a healthier life, the origin of his trauma needed to be addressed. I also suspect Oliver might have been another victim of the MK-Ultra experiments.

Chapter 74

RUDI: ENDURING RAPE BY HIS MOTHER FROM AGE 8-14

I met Rudi during an introductory film course I participated in at the Esalen Institute in Big Sur, California. When Rudi learned of my profession, he took me aside and said he wanted to share with me his trauma of sexual childhood abuse. We agreed on a time to meet later that day.

Rudi shared that starting at age eight, his mother would come to his bedroom 3-4 times a week and, via anal penetration, would rape him with a dildo. After that, she would prepare an enema by injecting water up his rectum to clean out any residue so that he wouldn't, as she explained to him, get pregnant. Rudi endured his mother's sexual abuse until it suddenly stopped when he was fourteen years old.

He shared that as an adult, he had been in therapy for many years and had been happily married to his wonderful wife for many years. Rudi also said that because his healing path from trauma to recovery had been so extensive, he now devoted his life to health and healing and had built a large health care institute in a big city in the mid-west with seven hundred employees.

As ridiculously unreal at this story sounds, Rudi didn't make it up. It is very possible that his mother was sexually abused by her father from exactly the same age on until, for some reason, it stopped when she was fourteen[26]. Obviously, his mother hadn't resolved her trauma of sexual abuse and re-enacted it via the sub-conscious and, like with in a split personality disorder, projected it onto poor Rudi with his mother playing out the role of her own father. The regular sexual penetration of her father, followed by an enema to prevent pregnancy, must have been what she had experienced as a child.

---

[26] Unresolved childhood sexual trauma might be re-enacted as described in Chapter 66, "Childhood Sexual Abuse and Childhood Ritual Sexual Abuse."

When the Soul Calls: True Stories of Deep Healing and Transformation

Chapter 75

SALLY: HOMOSEXUALITY AS A RESULT OF CHILDHOOD SEXUAL ABUSE

Sally was a young woman in her twenties; very intellectual and rational in her ways. She had almost finished her studies and was in her finals. After her initial Maha Intensive, she decided to study healing and became a student in the 2-year Principal Training Certification Program of the HeartPath Re-Alignment.

Sally shared that all her relationships had always been homosexual and she was currently again in a lesbian relationship. Her two older sisters were also lesbians. She had a short, boyish haircut, always dressed very masculine, and behaved very mannish.

Regressing Sally to her childhood, she discovered her childhood sexual abuse by her dad and that he had also sexually abused her sisters. Her sisters were her role models and she started to mold herself after them.

After the first training in Austria, the group arrived here at the HeartPath Retreat Center for the next training. The first week into the training, Sally shared that my dress code was interfering with her ability to concentrate on the class curriculum. She stated that my décolleté was distracting her and asked me to change my dress style. My wardrobe consisted of long, flowing skirts and tight tops. I always dressed decently and very feminine. The group listened to Sally's request.

I honored Sally for bringing up the matter and told her that I wouldn't change my style of dress, but instead encouraged her to stay in touch with her feelings in regard to the matter and that every day during sharing time to bring up the subject and her process with it.

During the three weeks of training, Sally brought it up every day. It took courage for her to express her sentiments on such a seemingly trivial matter when all the other members were sharing their process about much deeper concerns.

Five months later at the next training here at the HeartPath Retreat Center, I was surprised to see Sally wearing a long, flowing dress. Her hair had grown down to her shoulders. She wasn't wearing a bra and her breasts were swaying freely as she walked.

During the morning sharing time, I asked Sally how she felt in her body. "Fine," she replied. I asked her to share every day with the group how she felt living in a female body, wearing feminine, long flowing

There are various and very individual reasons why a Soul might choose homosexuality in their upcoming life. For example, it could be that in a previous life, they were holding judgment and were even prosecuting homosexuals and their Soul might now feel inclined to atone for the pain they had caused. Or they might have never had the experience of homosexual love and want to incorporate the experience. Or they enjoyed their homosexuality in previous lives. The possible reasons are endless. Each chosen Soul path is deeply individual and it's impossible for me to state the countless reasons for choosing homosexuality in a Soul's current life.

skirts. She had left her masculine attire at home and for the whole time presented herself in the feminine attire. It was obvious to all that Sally was undergoing a profound transformation in regard to her identity as a woman. She shared with the group that she had ended her relationship with her lover.

Sally remained single for more than a year. Her next relationship was with a man. Two years later, she married. The couple started a family and have two adorable children.

Sally's story is an example of homosexuality as a result of sexual childhood wounding. But of course, homosexuality as a natural and organic life path can also be chosen by the Soul prior to incarnation. Whatever the individual case, if the Soul chose the experience of homosexuality, it's not related to childhood wounding and childhood sexual abuse.

"In Egypt,
two male royal manicurists named
Niankhkhnum and Khnumhotep
were found buried together in a shared tomb
similar to the way married couples were often buried.
Their epigraph reads: 'Joined in life and joined in death.'
Having lived in 2400 BC,
they are believed to be history's
oldest recorded gay couple."

~ Greg Reeder, Egyptologist

284

Chapter 76

CHILDHOOD RITUAL SEXUAL ABUSE: THE STORY OF HEATHER AND HER SISTER

During my trainings in Europe, students often requested I work with them after class. Heather, a woman in her late thirties, was raising her son on her own. Unlike many who are not aware of their sexual abuse in earlier childhood, Heather remembered every detail. Her father was one of the judges at the district court in Heather's hometown in Austria, a highly respected man of the community.

Heather and her older sister knew that whenever their father and grandfather got drunk, they would drag the two girls down into the cellar and sexually abuse and rape them. During one of those times when her grandfather forced his penis into the 6-year-old mouth, Heather bit his penis. She laughed with great satisfaction as she remembered this incident. Even though she was badly beaten up for it, she didn't care because the satisfaction of her revenge was all too sweet.

Heather also processed the day when she brought her girlfriend home to play. Her girlfriend was dragged down into the cellar as well and raped. After that, her girlfriend mysteriously disappeared. Heather kept missing her in class. For days, her girlfriend didn't come to school and Heather was in great distress.

Maybe a week later, her mother showed her an article in the newspaper that said her girlfriend had gone missing and the police were looking for her. Heather remembered her mother reading the article aloud. About a month later, the body of her girlfriend was found, dead from a head wound. The circumstances remain a mystery.

All these memories coming alive were hard on Heather. She was in a trance as she processed what she was releasing, only barely aware of the training class. This ritual sexual abuse had started when she was six years old and continued into puberty. When I asked Heather where her mother was, she was either not at home during those incidences or she turned a blind eye on it all. Heather and her sister never spoke to their mother about it. As is so often the case, their mother might well have been sexually abused as well as a girl.

In the course of releasing the trauma of the sexual abuse, Heather's cells released the stench of alcohol. For an entire week, the dormitory where the participants were staying reeked like a liquor store. The stench was suffocating. This was the first time I witnessed the release of alcohol on a cellular level. It is truly remarkable what our energy system holds and expels on the physical level whenever accessed, ready to be released and integrated — even after decades or even lifetimes.

In the midst of one of Heather's healing sessions, she suddenly saw a long metal pole and knew with certainty this was the murder weapon with which her girlfriend had been killed by her father and grandfather! This was quite a shock for her. Never before had she connected the dots.

During the whole fourteen days of training, Heather was in a deep process with all the traumatic images coming up during her evening healing sessions with me. Heather stayed physically present in class. We had brought in a mattress for her to lay on as she was too weakened by her process.

One morning at class, Heather suddenly jumped up and started sobbing and screaming. She had just realized that the same fate might happen to her six-year-old son because she had left him in her parents' care. Heather at once drove home to get her son and arranged for her girlfriend to take him in while she completed her training.

At the time of the training, Heather's grandfather had passed away. But she confronted both her parents. To my knowledge, both her parents remained in denial. I don't know if her sister also confronted them.

Oftentimes, when severe trauma is inflicted, siblings separate from each other. They fall out of contact, don't communicate, and live separate lives. They handle the trauma that had occurred differently.

PART VII

CASE STUDIES OF
SPECIFIC CHILDHOOD WOUNDING

When the Soul Calls: True Stories of Deep Healing and Transformation

Section 1

Childhood Wounding

Chapter 77

THE DEVELOPMENT OF CHILDHOOD WOUNDING

Childhood Wounding refers to trauma inflicted by the parents or primary care takers, the environment, life circumstances, and more. A wound inflicted never has its origin in this lifetime. Rather, the origin can be found in past-life circumstances, which reinforces the current life trauma. How so? A wound is always only a symptom. In order to heal, we need to look at the core of what ails us. Then we need to have the courage to face and analyze it in order to learn from it and heal. This is our very own individual and personal life task.

A wound is always only a symptom. In order to heal, we need to look at the core of what ails us.

Emotional wounds are inflicted during the various childhood developments.

- The first wound, Schizoid Wound, happens prior to birth, during birth, or shortly after birth.

- The second wound, the Oral Wound, occurs during the breastfeeding phase of the infant.

- The third wound, termed the Psychopathic Wound, is inflicted during the early childhood years.

- The fourth wound is called the Masochistic wound and happens during the autonomy phase of the child.

- The fifth wound, the Rigid Wound, occurs during adolescence.

Each and every one of us is meant to be whole and complete rather than crooked and distorted. Remember: We are all goddesses and gods who have forgotten who we really are. Barbara Brennan's spiritual guide, Heyoan, said the following about this.

"We have already died, in forgetting who we are.
Those parts of us that have been forgotten are walled off from Reality.
We have come into incarnation to retrieve them.

So, although we fear death, we have already died, and in the incarnation process of re-integrating with our greater being,
we actually find more life."

~ Heyoan

"Your journey begins with a choice to get up, step out, and live fully."

~ Oprah Winfrey

A wound inflicted by trauma creates the distortion of who we truly are. It shows where we need to pay attention and heal in order for our lives to become whole and complete. What we have learned, we can cross off our list, so to speak. A lesson learned doesn't have to be repeated. It is very much like being in school. We learn and then progress to the next level.

Depending on the age we were as children when the strongest wounding was inflicted, we speak of first or primary wounding, second or secondary wounding, and so forth. Oftentimes, the primary wound is covered by or merged with a secondary wound.

By "covered up," I mean that there have been many times I have worked with individuals who at first only displayed the primary wound. After a series of healing sessions, the secondary wound appeared and might in fact be much more strongly developed than the primary wound.

I remember one individual who, during the Maha Intensive, in his first healing was working on just the primary wound. As he cleared the primary wound, the secondary wound appeared and there were no longer any signs anymore of his primary wound. After the secondary wound was cleared, the third wound appeared and the secondary wound was completely released. When the third wound was cleared and healed, the fourth wound appeared and was subsequently cleared.

Or the different wounds can be merged and appear all at once. Everyone is uniquely individual and the emotional / energetic makeup and how individuals deal with their life and present themselves to the world is very individual as well.

More than likely, everyone has not just one wound but a combination of wounds. As a healer working with my clientele, I always focus first on the primary wound. Once cleared, later and all by itself and during the healing work, the secondary wound appears. Such was the case with Mary, as you shall see in Chapter 79, where the Schizoid Wound was very predominant at first and later the Oral Wound became dominant.

Wounds are mostly repeated, meaning, for example, a mother with the Schizoid Wound, who hasn't transformed her wound will automatically raise a child with the same wounding. The same applies for the other wounds. Children learn what parents teach them and by their parents' examples. Because, as children, we learn by inspiration from our parents, we become encoded with the same programing as our parents have.

Growing up, our parents mirror to us certain relationship dynamics in their relationship with each other. As children, we become subjected to these dynamics absorbing them without being consciously aware of them.

Once we become adults, we recreate those same dynamics. All of this happens subconsciously and without our awareness. There is really no exit from this unless we transform the actual wounding.

Subconsciously, we also mirror the characteristics and behaviors of our parents. As adults, when we attract a partner and enter into a relationship, we either mirror the characteristics and behaviors of our mother or our father. Without realizing it, we choose THE perfect partner for us to become aware of previously unconscious behavior patterns that were handed down from our parents to us.

For example, if we choose a partner who mirrors the unresolved behavior patterns of our dad, we automatically and without our conscious awareness slip into the role our mother played in her relationship with her husband. This occurs so that the relationship dynamics of our parents are re-activated. We re-activate the dynamics because it's what we know and are familiar with or we don't know any better. Our parents were our first role models and teachers. In this way, we're deeply connected to them.

Such is the power of programming. We are the carriers of ancestral behavior patterns passed down to us. Once we start to work deeper, we become aware that those dynamics didn't emerge with our parents. They were passed down to them by their parents, usually, for generations. The healing becomes a clearing of ancestral memory data that we no longer wish to carry with us. In the process, we become aware that all wounding is not a curse but a blessing because our Soul wants to heal and become whole.

For those interested in a more in-depth study of the developmental stages of childhood wounds, I highly recommend Barbara Ann Brennan's books *Hands of Light* and *Light Emerging*. She not only explains in detail

"Your life does not get better by chance. It gets better by change."

~ Jim Rohn

the psychological attributes but also elaborates on the energy distribution in the auric field, the brain, and the various body parts. Furthermore, her book, *Light Emerging*, has excellent illustrations that show the human interaction of the different Wounds and their defense mechanisms.

Once we start to become aware of our wounding and begin the process of healing by addressing the physical, emotional, mental and spiritual aspects of our wounds, our lives begin to drastically change.

We let go of our painful, self-created reality of life and repetition of destructive situations and destructive behavioral patterns resulting from self-sabotaging our lives. We release distorted negative belief structures that keep us from attaining our full potential and, as a result, gain control of our lives. Life then becomes more fulfilling, balanced, lighter, richer, and vibrant.

LIFE BECOMES MUCH LIGHTER
WHEN YOU DON'T CARRY
THE BAGGAGE OF YOUR PAST WITH YOU

Section 2

First Wounding

Chapter 78

THE SCHIZOID WOUND

Souls incarnating with this wound resist coming into the body. They have had many experiences of existential threat in previous incarnations, were sometimes tortured and killed, often for being different and for their beliefs that were not in accordance with the norms of the time, and the society in which they were living. For them, life on Earth was dangerous and insecure.

Their programming is "Life on Earth is dangerous. Humans are brutal. I don't want to be here. I am not from here. I am from a better place than Earth." Incarnating into their current body, there might have been threatening circumstances during pregnancy, at birth, or shortly after birth. Thus, the wound inflicted in previous incarnations finds a mirror image in their present life situation.

Such individuals might have been born with their umbilical cord wrapped around their neck, their first suicide attempt. Or the unborn child refuses to turn around, headfirst, down toward the birth canal. Such babies are afraid before they have even arrived. Their traumatic experience took place before birth (for example the child was not wanted), during birth (for example a very complicated birth), or shortly after birth (for example a perceived hostility from a parent).

Once incarnated, they might be hypersensitive to their environment. They feel highly vulnerable, they might be shy and afraid. Whether there is an obvious reason or not isn't relevant because to them it's very real. Their current experience is overshadowed by circumstances that happened in previous lives. Growing up, they constantly try to escape their body whenever they feel threatened. To literally do this is difficult, so they learn to do it energetically, which ultimately results in scoliosis.

- Such individuals feel they don't belong here

- They experience life as existential threat

- They feel afraid and operate in constant fear mode

- They have difficulty changing a set schedule

- Planning ahead and sticking with a schedule helps them feel safer

- They talk in absolutes

- They cannot feel their own individualized essence

- A raising of the voice, an intense look, an unexpected situation, or something unpleasant can provoke it.

- Even if something is said that's kind but critical, such individuals might say," Oh my gosh! He just completely exploded on me," which is how they perceived it.

- Just standing too close can easily provoke fear. Intimacy can as well.

- They feel they have no right to live

- They carry a lot of self-hatred and have no clue what self-love is

For example, I once worked with a married couple where the woman had to learn to feel comfortable looking into her husband's eyes and find love and affection in his eyes.

In general, individuals with the Schizoid Wound have very weak boundaries. Their auric field doesn't provide protection. They can be easily penetrated and they lack emotional boundaries. Because they lack protection, they can easily be penetrated. Deep within, they are afraid of people and avoid human contact as much as possible. Because humans are perceived as brutal, untrustworthy and dangerous, such individuals sometimes develop deep love and care for animals and the planet, which is a true blessing for them, for the planet and for humanity, as in the case of Greta Thunberg.

Every time a person with the Schizoid Wound feels threatened, they leave their body energetically. Their body becomes vacant, so to speak. Their eyes become empty, their head is usually tilted to one side. When they flee, they withdraw into a space beyond physical reality into the spiritual world, yet not to Source. Because they are not connecting but fleeing, being in that spiritual space only provides temporary relief from the perceived danger. In that space, they create a fantasy world that feels safer, which is what they did in previous incarnations when they were being tortured.

Such individuals are extremely spiritual by nature, though they have not yet learned to connect to their God Source. Instead of connecting up in a straight line, they flee in a spiral somewhere up and to the side. Because this is done habitually, such individuals have not learned to ground into the Earth. I often witness how individuals closer to Spirit than to life on Earth have not yet fully incarnated into their body. They are energetically floating above the ground. I've observed this countless times. The thought of inhabiting their body is alien to them. This makes existence on Earth feel even more insecure, dangerous, and threatening. Such individuals do not feel integrated within themselves, they feel split in their intent for having incarnated and the challenges life presents.

While it is easy for such people to feel the unified essence in that "We are all One" and interconnected with one another, individuals with the Schizoid Wound lack the experience of their individualized essence. They have not yet been able to feel their own individualized essence. On the energetic level of the aura and the chakra system, most of their chakras are distorted, sending energy out instead of taking it in. This indicates their distorted projection of life in the physical body that differs vastly with that of the greater truth of the universe. Their first chakra has not connected downwardly to grow roots into the Earth. (For the Human Energy System and the Chakra System, refer to Part VIII, Chart 1, which shows the seven layers of the Auric field and the corresponding seven chakras.)

Their body is usually elongated with an imbalance between the left and the right side. They are uncoordinated and the different limbs seem disconnected and separate like a puppet hanging on a string. Their joints are thin and weak because energy leaks out in those places. Their hands and feet are constantly cold. They usually suffer from back pain, a result of scoliosis, which, in turn, is the physical consequence for habitually exiting their body in this lifetime.

Though they are hyperactive, a person with a pronounced Schizoid Wound is usually not seeking physical activity. They are ungrounded and can appear flaky and chaotic because everyday reality and simple tasks, like staying committed to a schedule or a set plan, might be challenging for them. During sex, they feel the life force.

Such individuals live primarily in their mental structures. They process through reason, the intellect, and rationality. They love to intellectualize as it's the territory they feel safe in. They communicate in depersonalized expressions and talk in absolutes. They don't mind spending hours, weeks, months and years on end at their desk, computer, or in the lab while real life is happening outside in nature. Yet the wonder of nature with its animal kingdom, the plant world, and all its elements would be the best remedy for connecting with the miracle of life. And for connecting to themselves.

Body

A person's body is usually elongated and asymmetrical with an imbalance between the left and right side, with one side either higher or lower than the other (eyes, eyebrows, lips, shoulders, or legs not level with one another.)

Energy Distribution

The person is uncoordinated with energy leaks from the wrists and ankles and cold hands and feet. They're not grounded to the earth. Their energy moves diagonally up and out of the body with the head tilting to one side.

295

*Planet Earth is
a school for Soul.*

So then why do individuals with the Schizoid Wound keep incarnating? Because in order to learn and grow, the Soul chooses to incarnate. Planet Earth is a school for Soul. Here, we learn about ourselves, learn to love ourselves, learn about human interactions.

A characteristic of individuals who incarnate with this wound is self-hatred. They feel profoundly unworthy — and they feel undeserving. They might be successful at presenting themselves to the world or in their profession and life, yet deep down they feel undeserving of their accomplishments and possessions.

Because the individual with the Schizoid Wound has such weak boundaries, people constantly violate their boundaries. Therefore, they need to learn what their boundaries and limits are. They need to become aware of their comfort zone in interactions with others. Having their boundaries respected is essential for them in order to feel safe and secure. They have to learn to say "no" if inconvenient and feel comfortable with stating their truth. By doing so, they have their boundaries identified and strengthened.

They also need to have their spirituality confirmed. Individuals with the Schizoid Wound are highly spiritual, though they might still be unaware of it. Paying attention to their spiritual nature can lead to developing higher sensory perception by paying attention to their feelings and emotions and trusting their intuition. Becoming in tune with their intuitive feelings affirms their identity in their physical body and in this life and helps in their taking a firm stand in life. Their connection to planet Earth needs to develop so that they can fully land here on this planet and integrate themselves to life on Earth.

For all of us humans, the task at hand is to learn to love Life, to appreciate one's life as a miracle, appreciate our body, view our body as a temple in which our Soul dwells, to fully love ourselves.

When I hear people say this is their last life on Earth and that they will definitely choose to never come back again, my red flags go up. Those statements do not come from a place of love, but rather from a judgmental perspective and a desire to escape. What we need to understand is that in order to leave something, we first have to love it. If we want to leave this planet, we first have to love it with all our Heart. We can only leave it behind and become free of it after we fully love it.

IF WE WANT TO LEAVE THIS PLANET
WE FIRST HAVE TO LEARN TO
LOVE IT WITH ALL OUR HEART

I have heard countless times "I'm not from here. I'm from a planet more evolved than Earth. I'd rather be there than here on Earth." I have worked with priests, clerics, and spiritual leaders of different religious belief systems who have made this comment, among others.

This raises some very deep questions, like: Why did we incarnate on planet Earth? Why are we here now rather than somewhere else?

We need to understand that our Soul chose to incarnate on Earth. There is no authority "out there" commanding us where we have to go and be. Being here on Earth is not a condemnation. It is meant to be a sacred experience. We have to make it one. Being HERE NOW is the choice of our Soul.

Our Soul, in its everlasting wisdom, knows exactly which experiences we need to have in order to grow. And the more we grow, the more we learn to appreciate and love Life — in all its shapes and forms. We are meant to make the best of our experience here and the most of our lives. We are meant to live our full potential.

BEING HERE NOW IS THE CHOICE OF OUR SOUL

A former mentor of mine, the motivational speaker Les Brown, often spoke about the cemetery as the richest place on Earth. He would say, "So many dreams not lived, so much talent wasted, so many gifts buried. That's why it is important to live fully and to die empty."

'Live fully and die empty."

~ Les Brown

When the Soul Calls: True Stories of Deep Healing and Transformation

Chapter 79

MARY: A STORY OF DEEPEST TRANSFORMATION

Mary found her way into my healing practice many times. Over the course of ten years, she underwent more than fifty 4-day healing session cycles. Her main theme was existential threat. Mary's life was dominated by fears. She felt more at home in the Spirit world than here on Earth. This resulted in an aversion to being in the body and to accepting the conditions of life on Earth. Mary also dealt with a huge amount of self-hatred. She had zero clue what loving oneself meant.

Many of Mary's past-life experiences showed torture, gruesome experimentation on her body, and usually a very violent death. At one point, she asked her Higher Self to show her the reason for why her Soul had chosen such violent experiences in Germany's concentration camps. As a result, her guidance took her into a previous life as a male where she had been the owner of large opium plantations in the Golden Triangle (the area of Thailand, Laos, and Myanmar in Southeast Asia). Much wealth was accumulated by distributing it to countless addicts whose lives became hopelessly dependent on the drug. She came to understand that due to the suffering she had caused in all those addicts' wasted lives, she chose a life in the concentration camp to consciously experience pain.

In the very early stages of her exploration of the Self, Mary arrived one day for another cycle of healing sessions. She had lost a huge amount of weight, looked thin as a stick, and was nervous and shaky. What concerned me the most was the expression in her eyes. They were restless and flickering as if a fire was burning her alive and she was turning insane. I was alarmed and asked her if there had been any changes in her life. She shared that she had begun taking Kriya Yoga and described the meditation exercises. She complained about feeling a huge amount of heat, like from a fire burning her up from the inside out.

Chakras fulfill various functions, such as supplying the physical body with cosmic energy, and psychological functions to metabolize feelings. Blocked feelings result in blocking the energy intake of the particular chakra, which eventually results in disfigured chakras resulting in disease. Chakras are also responsible for spiritual growth / development. Chakras open naturally, depending on the level of consciousness of the individual. Since the first chakra has the lowest vibration and the seventh chakra has the highest vibration, much harm can happen when higher chakras are forcibly opened.

For individuals who undergo spiritual exercises that stimulate the opening of their chakras before they open naturally, the process can be quite dangerous. This is the reason why help and guidance is needed, otherwise, the person can burn up from the inside out. Instead of a natural Kundalini experience, it becomes a forced and premature kundalini awakening. (Refer to Gopi Krishna's book, *Kundalini*.)

Mary needed grounding. I strongly recommended she stop with the meditation exercises at once. I advised her to choose something she enjoyed that also grounded her, suggesting gardening, ceramics, or painting — something to connect her with the Earth, to work with her hands.

She choose ceramics, so I suggested she model her experiences in clay. When she arrived for her next session cycle, she presented me with figurines she had made. They expressed suffering, were disfigured, distorted, and immensely raw — an extension of her. They were beautiful, amazing even. She, though, hated them, thought them ugly. I instructed her that the next step was to photograph each one and write down their story.

She did. From then on, she formed all her healing experiences in Earth-colored clay. She despised them and didn't want to have anything to do with them. She insisted on leaving them with me. She also gifted me with a representation of me, a steatopygous Mother Goddess with a snake up her back, looking over her head. In one arm, the figurine was holding Mary's own Inner Child. In the other, the figurine was cradling Mary's head with Mary standing headless in front of the figure, me. In the course of our work, Mary produced three large binders containing pictures of the figurines and their stories. She gifted them to me.

Profoundly developed thighs, buttocks, and hips.

It was in her thirty-second healing session cycle, that Mary was ready to clear her mother, Denise. In general, clearing the connection with one's parents is essential for the healing process because all primary experiences and resulting emotions are tied to them. For this reason, the mother and father are usually cleared within the first few session cycles. But Mary had resisted doing so. She hadn't felt ready before.

Mary described Denise as having done her duty as a mother in that she had fed and clothed her, yet all with a lack of emotional and heartfelt nurturance. Mary as a child had felt deeply neglected by Denise.

From what Mary described, her mother was a woman with a passive-aggressive behavior pattern. She had been living by herself in a big house after Mary's father passed away and was now at the age where she could no longer safely live alone.

Mary, her husband, and their three children all had an extremely close relationship with Mary's two sisters and their families. They spent all their holidays together, but always excluded their mother because they found her behavior unbearable. When the three couples got together to discuss the future of their mother, none of the sisters was willing to take their mom in to live with them. It was Mary's husband who suggested she could live in the downstairs apartment of their home.

So the mother moved in and again was left very much to herself. Even the kids avoided her. During the healing work on clearing her mother, I gave Mary the homework assignment of writing a daily letter to Denise without ever sending it. In her letters, she should fully allow herself to express all her feelings and not hold back any sentiments.

As a result of those letters, Mary regressed to the age of an infant. She bought herself a baby bottle and started to feed herself daily with it. Mary reported that the process of letter writing and the bottle feeding lasted a full month.

Without a clue of the deep internal process her daughter was undergoing, Mary's mother strangely underwent a transformation. Everyone noticed it and the children started to seek out the company of their grandma. All of a sudden, her mother became fully integrated into the whole family clan and everyone enjoyed each other's company. She was included in all the family gatherings.

It became very obvious to Mary that as she underwent deep transformation by healing her early childhood wound during the nurturing phase, her mother — without any conscious awareness of it — followed suit, because we are all energetically interconnected. Because of her deep work on her Oral Wound, Mary experienced the healing of herself and her mother. She became aware of the tremendous love between Souls by agreeing prior to incarnating to play the role of the villain in a beloved's life so that healing and transformation can occur.

SOULS AGREE TO PLAY THE ROLE OF THE VILLAIN IN A BELOVED'S LIFE SO THAT HEALING AND TRANSFORMATION CAN HAPPEN

Mary, in her deep process of healing and transforming first her primary wound, the Schizoid Wound, had then been able to heal and transform her secondary wound, the Oral Wound. Her life became lighter and more vibrant. Mary continued forming her life story in clay. Years later, she started to paint her new clay figurines in bright colors.

Ever since Mary presented me with her first clay figurines, I told her she needed to express her healing process in a book and have her clay figurines exhibited in a gallery. The stories accompanying the clay figurines are exquisite and full of deep wisdom. I hope one day Mary finds the strength and courage to do just that because it would deeply touch and inspire others in their own healing and transformation.

Section 3

The Second Wounding

Chapter 80

THE ORAL WOUND

This wound is inflicted at a very early age, during an infant's nurturing phase. Breastfeeding time is the most sacred sharing time between a mother and her baby. An everlasting bond is created between the two wherein the baby experiences the merging with its mother as the source of nutrition, warmth, security, and loving care.

The wound develops because the baby feels abandoned. The most dramatic is if the mother died, or there might be a big family to take care of and the mother is overworked and sleep deprived. Burdened with many duties, she only does what's necessary like feeding, bathing, and dressing. But for the most part, the infant is left by itself a lot. Oftentimes, the mother refuses to breast feed for reasons such as lack of time, fear of sagging breasts, the lack of milk, or a breast infection. Sometimes, the mother becomes ill or a family member or friend falls ill or dies. It could be for many other reasons.

But even if the baby is breastfed in such circumstances, that is not the experience a baby should have. Breastfeeding should be a sacred sharing time between mother and baby. That doesn't happen if the mother is feeding her baby like an automaton. In such a case, the mother views feeding time as a duty rather than a joy. It's her responsibility to feed the baby, therefore, she does it. But it doesn't fulfill her as deeply as it should. Rather, she is doing it with an absent mind and heart. Her attention is on the time she is losing by feeding her baby, as well as her other responsibilities. The result is that the baby will constantly feel abandoned and neglected.

Such infants compensate their lack of attention by walking very early. From early on, they want to become independent. Yet, the not-well-enough-cared-for child tends to become dependent. It clings and grabs for attention. If this remains denied, a decreased aggressiveness might well surface where the child behaves in ways that will get attention.

A NOT-WELL-ENOUGH-CARED-FOR CHILD TENDS TO BECOME DEPENDENT

Girls growing up with the Oral Wound will become mothers inflicting the same wound on their babies. They never learned from their mother the blissful experience of becoming a mother and the joy of breastfeeding. Such mothers lack the experience of having been loved themselves as infants.

For boys, it's much the same. If they were neglected and abandoned as children, they grow up to become adults who neglect and abandon their children or their partner. Most of all and with either gender, such individuals neglect themselves and their own needs. They are unable to take care of their own needs. The Oral Wound is turned against them.

In previous lives, these individuals often experienced famine and death by starvation. They might have had to flee their home due to catastrophic weather conditions or war, leaving their possessions behind and starting a new existence from scratch in a completely different environment.

Where they arrived, they were viewed as outsiders and outcasts. They had to work hard in order to survive. Life was hard on them. They became the victims of life. They were not in control of life, life controlled them. The programming of people with Oral Wounding is, "There is not enough of anything. I never get what I want. I am too weak and cannot do it on my own. I need someone to take care of me. No one ever loves me." Hence, such individuals keep facing many disappointments in their life.

As a child, they never learned from their parents to ground to the Earth. They don't know how to grow roots. They never had the experience to stand on their own two feet, never developed natural boundaries and healthy cord connections.

Rather, their first chakra[27] is crippled and underdeveloped. Instead of being connected down to Earth, it stays contracted and thus underdeveloped because of the lack of grounding down into the Earth.

Healthy energetic cord connections are established between the corresponding chakras of parent and child. For example, from solar plexus to solar plexus, from Heart to Heart, etc. and that continues between adults in their important relationships.

---

[27] Root Chakra; for more information on the Chakras refer to PART III, Chapter 6.

As adults, instead of growing energetic roots that would anchor them into this Earth existence and thus strengthen them, their energetic cord connection is hooked into someone close to them. This can be one of the parents, or someone else they become dependent on. In their adult life, it will be transferred to the person closest to them: their spouse, life partner, best friend, etc. They'll become dependent on that person and demand mothering from them. They will want that person to become their life rescuer. They cannot stand on their own two feet and are utterly dependent on that one person.

Energetically, Oral Wounded people are still children who haven't yet come into their auto-nom phase. In healthy childhood development, the auto-nom phase is the stage where children start to view themselves as individuals apart from their parents. Their identity is not closely tied to the identity of their parents anymore. They might be criticizing the shortcomings of their parents and become rebellious towards them. Hence, individuals with a strongly developed Oral Wound have never gone through that auto-nom phase. They have never grown up, and subconsciously, they seek a caretaker.

Such individuals feel extremely dependent on others

- They exhibit profound neediness

- They refuse to take self-responsibility

- Their behavior is passive-aggressive

- They suck energy from others by talking in a low voice and constantly asking questions to keep them engaged in boring conversations

- They also suck energy with their pleading eyes

- They feel a victim of life

- They feel unable to do things on their own

- They feel there is never enough for them

- Their life force is weak

- More than sex, they want cuddling

- They need a lot of nurturing and hugging

Ashrams, cults, and sects are filled with individuals with this wound. In communication with others, they ask a lot of questions to keep the other person engaged, but they don't allow time to let the answer sink in. Instead, they're already asking their next question to keep the attention of the other person engaged.

Unfortunately, and as a result of not connecting the first chakra down into the Earth, such individuals are not aware that they are sucking energy from others. Imagine for a moment that you are living your life in a room that never gets fresh air. You're constantly inhaling pre-digested air — for your entire life — never new and fresh air. Such is the energy field of a person with the Oral Wound. Because they unconsciously suck energy from others, people tend to stay away from them. This only reinforces the ever-painful Oral Wounded person's experience of abandonment, which in turn leads to deep pain on the Soul level.

The body of a person with Oral Wounding is usually long, thin, and underdeveloped with a lack of muscle development throughout the body. Their chest is collapsed and their shoulders bent forward. Such individuals are hypoactive with low energy. Their eyes are pleading "Please help me, I'm lost, I don't have anything." Think of a poor beggar in India and you get the picture.

As adults, they easily collapse under stress and as a result become spiteful and passive. When they speak, they complain in a low and whiny voice. Their perception and belief is that they are victims. To them life is not fair. The person with an Oral Wound generally feels deprived, and complains about a lack of energy and emptiness. They are extremely attached to regular eating times as if their life depended on it.

Such individuals refuse to take responsibility. While I was absent from home working in Europe, my former husband, Andy, who had a profound Oral Wound, refused to lock the main doors of the house prior to traveling to Thailand. This might sound very weird since all one needs to do to lock a door is to turn a key. Yet, a person with the primary wound of the Oral Wound refuses to take responsibility for such trivial matters. They comply with what is convenient for them, but they aggressively refuse to do their duty. Andy also refused to lock the shed's gate, which I was unable to lock because it was stuck. During the night, my donkey, Sara, was attacked by a pack of dogs, which resulted in her getting twelve stitches.

Individuals with the Oral Wound have learned to expect very little of life. Usually, they just get by. They also give very little of themselves. They are generally never generous but instead are very stingy. There is much passivity in their behavior patterns and they don't dream big dreams. A small insignificant life is enough to them.

Their energetic field is depleted, calm, and quiet. In relationships, they express a neediness and dependency that quickly becomes next to unbearable for their partner. Oftentimes, such individuals prefer to cuddle than to have sex (though, with my husband Andy, this wasn't the case. We had daily sex twice for the entire time we were together.). Because their life is full of many disappointments and rejections, they might become demanding and even bitter. And they definitely always behave passive-aggressively. Oftentimes, their underlying aggression turns into greed.

Body

The person's body is usually long, thin, and underdeveloped with a lack of muscle development throughout the body. Their chest and shoulders droop forward.

Energy Distribution

Hypoactive with low energy. They have pleading eyes and are not grounded.

How can someone in the Oral Wound change their life around for the better? The first step is to become aware of their tendency to depend on others and to grasp and suck their energy. When I work with individuals in their Oral Wound, I use the word "Energetic Vampire." It's never pleasing to hear painful truth spoken. It's bitter medicine to swallow. Yet it is also serving their highest by naming the issue for what it is without beautifying or clouding it.

When these individuals become fully aware of how much energy they've been sucking from others, the desire to leave the vicious cycle of victimhood behind follows as a consequence. This process progresses into becoming aware of the energy deficiencies in their own energetic field. They will be eager and more than willing to heal it.

I recommend spending time alone in nature while practicing deep breathing and concentrating on physical activity, which will bring oxygen into their system and present them with the simple everyday adventures that nature offers. It also helps them overcome their fear of abandonment and being left alone because it's their choice to spend time alone. Simple tasks like this require courage, strength and effort in the beginning, yet the rewards are waiting to be harvested.

When they charge their field by taking in energy directly from Source and Earth rather than sucking energy from others, they will learn to trust the abundance of the Universe, which in turn lessens their tendency to grasp. As they practice opening themselves to a larger life experience than the small life they are used to living, they're also starting to expand their experience of the abundance of life. With this, they begin to fully embrace life and all the adventures it offers. As they learn to leave the role of victimhood behind once and forever, they declare themselves capable of running and controlling their own life. This in turn counteracts abandonment by fully reclaiming their life.

Chapter 81

EDITH: THE EVER VICTIM / THE EXPERIENCE OF ABANDONMENT & HER TRANSFORMATION

During one of our trainings, the group was learning about the Oral Wound. One of the group members, a woman in her thirties, whom I shall call Edith, displayed very strong signs of the Oral Wound. Because it was her primary wound, it dominated her entire life.

Upon my initial interaction with Edith, it was very apparent what plagued her most — the painful abandonment she constantly and repeatedly felt. In the company of others, she unconsciously sucked energy from them by engaging them in meaningless conversation.

People in the presence of someone with the Oral Wound feel as though they are being sucked dry by an energy vampire without being able to pinpoint what actually is happening to them. The draining happens through the pleading of the Orally Wounded's eyes and their non-stop talking in a low voice, which forces people to "elongate their ears in order to hear," so to speak.

Additionally, there is also an energetic sucking through the solar plexus. To avoid this, people unconsciously move further away from such a person because they don't feel comfortable being in front of them. They might even instinctively turn their body to the side, so that their Solar Plexus cannot be sucked from. Again, it all remains instinctive and with only a vague feeling of discomfort.

Edith was devastated because she didn't understand why everyone all of a sudden would get up from the table the moment she attempted to sit down, or leave the room all together when she entered. It seemed everyone turned away from her and left her to herself. (When this occurs to a person on a regular basis, it's very painful for the person caught in the pattern.)

Edith's presenting complaint was that no matter what, she always ended up alone. She felt the victim of life and of any situation. When talking of those experiences, she was complaining in a whiney, low voice, difficult to hear. Unconsciously she did this so that the listener would be forced to move in closer to her.

Edith also felt she never got enough of anything, not enough love, not enough attention, not enough nurturance, not enough affection, not enough understanding. This had brought her to the sub-conscious conclusion that she wasn't enough. As a result, she demanded very little from life. She merely just wanted to get by, survive the struggles rather than claiming her life and gaining full control of it.

Since her childhood, Edith had felt abandoned and neglected. Her experience was that she was not valuable, so she learned to not demand her place in the family structure but rather remain quiet. She was part of a large family of immigrants from Yugoslavia to Austria and had a number of siblings. Her mother must have had her hands full with so many children. Edith felt life controlled her mother rather than her mother controlling her own life. The same was the case with Edith. Her life was an endless stream of painful, repeated experiences of neglect.

During her initial healing sessions, Edith started to understand her behavior patterns and the deeper cause of them. She was in the process of accepting her wounding, and was starting to see the underlying reasons for her painful day-to-day life experiences, as well as the role she played by invoking them.

She was in the middle of her session cycle with me when her training class with the group started. Typical of her Oral Wound behavior, she complained in class using her whiney, low voice. She kept sucking energy from others by demanding their attention, which resulted in the group members turning away and ignoring her. The trainees were just learning about this particular wounding, so Edith's behavior would lead to an authentic life demonstration rather than the Oral Wound explained only in theory.

Due to Edith's daily complaining in her low, whiney voice, another student, Julie, got provoked and started to verbally attack Edith. This resulted in Edith feeling even more sorry for herself and complaining more. I suggested the two work it out on the boxing bag. While each of them took their position opposite one another with the boxing bag in between, I invited Edith to state what ailed her in one sentence and give it a physical expression by punching the boxing bag. She stated her complaint, "I feel the victim in my life." I suggested she envision the boxing bag as her life and give it a hefty punch. Her punch was hesitant and without any power.

Her next sentence was, "My life sucks." Because she dropped into her whining mode again, Julie felt triggered. She gave the boxing bag a powerful punch and yelled: "Stop whining, stop your constant whining! You are such a whiner! What a loser you are! I can't stand your constant self-pity!"

That in turn triggered Edith to feel even more sorry for herself. She broke down in tears. I encouraged Edith to instead of dropping into victim mode, that she should pause and listen to Julie's message, to fully take in Julie's statement. Then I instructed Edith to take the warrior stance and stand strongly on her two feet, take five very deep breaths, and ground her feet into the Earth.

By doing so, Edith became more present within herself, as if a tiny bit of her inherent power arose within her.

"Now, Edith, respond to what Julie said. She called you a whiner. Are you a whiner? She called you a loser. Are you a loser? Take two more deep breaths and respond," I instructed.

Edith took two deep breaths and then gave the bag a powerful punch. "I am not a whiner! I am not a whiner! I am not a loser! I am not a loser!" she declared and didn't stop punching the bag.

"Now, approach the bag as if it were your life and talk to it while punching," I said.

Edith yelled, "My life doesn't suck! I am not a victim of life!" The whole group kept watching in amazement, as with every strong declaration, Edith came more and more into her power.

Julie started to join in by punching the bag from the other side stating, "Yes, you are not a victim of life! Your life doesn't suck! You are a winner and not a loser! You aren't a victim of life! You're on top of your life!"

It became a deeply heart-moving, beautiful, and very energetic dance between the two of them. All witnessed Edith gaining power and Julie encouraging and supporting her in stepping fully into her power. And the more Edith reclaimed her power, the more Julie liked her and encouraged her. In the end, Edith broke down sweating and panting and rubbing her hands to soothe the pain from all the punching. Julie hugged her tightly and congratulated her.

From then on, Edith's life and her experience of life changed drastically. Not only did she finish her training in the HeartPath Re-Alignment, which in and of itself is extremely demanding with all the homework assignments. She also got her certificate as a yoga instructor and started teaching yoga classes.

Chapter 82

THE ENERGY-SUCKING RENATA

While I was in training at the Barbara Brennan School of Healing on Long Island, I experienced the following. The class curriculum consisted of the teaching materials for a class of 100 trainees and 20 facilitators, and small groups of ten for sharing time, led by two facilitators.

For the entire freshman year, my then boyfriend and another dear male friend and I kept joking as we observed one group member, Renata, clearly in her Oral Wound. When all group members sat in a sharing circle, Renata would grab everyone's attention with a remark or a question and in doing so, co-opt the entire sharing time for herself, never leaving any time for other group members to share. I wasn't eager to share myself, but I felt sorry for the group members who desperately hoped to be able to share. It was a mystery that both facilitators never remarked on or did anything about this.

When sophomore year arrived, I remarked to my boyfriend and friend that I desperately hoped to be released from the same sharing circle with Renata. When we received the announcement of the small group participants, my heart sunk. I was going to be together with her again. I was devastated. I so resisted spending another entire year in the presence of this person and listening to her nonsense.

Right at the beginning of the small group sharing circle, I announced that I needed to share something. I stated that it was very challenging for me but I had to state my truth. Renata was sitting exactly opposite me. I started by looking at every member in the group, including her. I shared my observations of the past year and admitted that my only wish for this new school cycle had been to be spared another whole year in the presence of that particular person. With that spoken, I looked straight at Renata.

She now realized that she was who I was talking about. A second passed and then she let go with a long, ear-shattering scream. This took place in the large ballroom of the Hilton hotel. Everyone, including Barbara Brennan, stared at us as Renata got up and took a few steps towards me. She sobbed loudly and broke down, accusing me of causing her this pain.

The two alarmed facilitators ran to her rescue, took her into their arms, and kept saying, "Yes, why did you do this? Why?" I felt sorry for them in their ignorance. I also felt that I needed to speak my feelings and thoughts because if I failed to do so, I harmed myself.

Fourteen days after returning home from that class, I received a very long, handwritten letter from Renata. She explained that she was truly grateful for the incident and stated that she is now processing my statement and working with her therapist in healing her wound. She thanked me abundantly for having brought it up and bringing it to the forefront of her awareness.

At the next class meeting, I witnessed her remarkable change. Renata became a group member like everyone else and no longer sucked up everyone's attention. She shared with the group her process in healing the Oral Wound by having become conscious of her behavior patterns of sucking energy from others. She again expressed her appreciation to me and suggested to the group that we meet in the disco of the hotel to celebrate her new life. Happily, we all joined her.

Chapter 83

THE WORRIER & THE WARRIOR, FEAR VS. TRUST

Barbara Brennan wrote:

> "Fear is the emotion that is associated
> with being disconnected from reality.
> Fear is the emotion of separation.
> Fear is the opposite of love,
> which is being connected to the unity of all things."

Within two months of moving from Switzerland to Santa Fe, I met Andy, a painter. He was a former hippie who years before had lived a simple life on a homestead without water and electricity. For food, he went hunting. A favorite quote of his was "Who has much, gives much; who has little, gives little."

We started dating and fell in love while he persistently proposed (thirty-seven times) before I gave in. Married, we lived together for two years before I asked for a divorce. Andy was living with me on the property when Mike, the builder, and I drew up all the plans for my center.

When the building process began, Andy was constantly interfering in that he was always telling me what I should do. One day, I sat him down and asked him how his paintings were coming along. He responded that he was loaded with work and preparing for two shows in different cities. I explained that each of us had our own work to do and that one should not interfere with the other. From then on, I was able to work on my own.

Andy was extremely stubborn, dependent, and controlling due to neediness and worries. I recognized a very developed Oral Wound in him, which burdened the relationship, especially because Andy chose to stay ignorant of his Oral Wound.

He claimed that we needed to do everything together: go to town together, visit friends together, shop for groceries together, go to the movies together. I dreaded the weekly art show openings he attended that I generally found boring. If I was somewhere by myself, I knew that within a little time he would call and share with me a worry he had.

Daily, Andy would drop into several mental / emotional holes for issues as small as the UPS driver not arriving on time or a client's appointment getting canceled. Very soon in our relationship, I figured out that Andy was being plagued by fears and worries. Since my mode of operation is quite the opposite, we joked between the two of us that we were the "Worrier and the Warrior."

When Andy dropped into his daily holes, he expected me to drop into the hole with him, which I refused. I sat him down and explained that when he dropped into holes that he needed to figure out how to get out again by himself. I explained that I would be there with my loving presence but not down in the hole with him. Our relationship was burdened by it and I felt I was carrying the both of us.

Andy was also very possessive about the food I prepared. He wouldn't let me share it with the building crew. He wanted it all for himself, though I prepared large quantities. Rather than sharing, he watched it go rotten until food ended up in the garbage bin.

When my training group arrived from Europe, the students were learning about the childhood wounding of the Schizoid Wound and the Oral Wound. I didn't bring up the fact that Andy's Oral Wound was very developed. One day during class, the students brought up the subject by asking me if it was possible that Andy was constantly in his wound.

Andy volunteered for the healings and received a healing from almost everyone in class. The healings were simple exercises for the trainees to get acquainted with energy distribution. Because the person with the Oral Wound lacks grounding, whoever was performing the healing encouraged Andy to feel the strength of his legs and encouraged him to stand on his own two feet. Andy always responded with, "Yes, of course, I have very strong legs and I always keep telling Silvana that I am standing strongly on my own two feet."

Andy was also very stingy with finances. Individuals with the Oral Wound are used to living very small. Since they can barely take care of themselves, they refuse to share what little they have, so to speak. This alienated me because I am by nature a very generous person. Though we were married, when we traveled to Thailand and stayed on Ko Pi Pi Island right by the beach in a very modest guest house for $15 a night, Andy split the lodging bill into two and we each paid $7.50 daily.

We were in love when we met but the feeling of Love is oftentimes not enough in a relationship. It is not healthy for one to carry the other.

It seems ironic — and yet also so perfect and divinely orchestrated — that ever since I started my own healing path and entered my healership, I've attracted wounded men. This had never happened before. All my significant relationships prior had been healthy, functional, and fulfilling. It was as if Spirit wanted to present me with firsthand personal experiences and study cases.

> "Do not commit
> to someone based on their potential.
> They may not have a desire to reach it."
> ~ Anonymous

While at the Barbara Brennan School of Healing, I dated John who had a profound Schizoid Wound. Moving to Santa Fe, I met Andy who presented me with the Oral Wound. This was followed by Renato with a profound Psychopathic-Masochistic Wound. Then Tony came into my life with his Rigid Wound. Indeed, we learn much while in relationships.

Julia Roberts said about this:

> "Women, you are not rehabilitation centers
> for badly raised men …
> It's not your job to fix him, change him, parent him,
> or raise him.
> You want a partner, not a project.

When the Soul Calls: True Stories of Deep Healing and Transformation

Section 4

The Third Wounding

Chapter 84

THE PSYCHOPATHIC WOUND

Children developing the Psychopathic Wound from an early age were caught in a conflicting position between their parents. They didn't get enough support from the parent of the same sex The parent of the opposite sex wanted something from the child that their spouse could not give. In this dynamic, little girls become papa's little princess, and likewise, the boy becomes mama's prince. Overtly or covertly, it was communicated to the child that they are better and more special than the spouse. There was an underlying sexual seductiveness at play, though it usually never involved sexual abuse.

I have often observed that the child was put in the position or role of the same sex parent, becoming the energetic and sometimes emotional partner of the parent of the opposite sex. In this dynamic, the child sides with the parent of the opposite sex because they don't feel supported by the parent of the same sex.

Thrown into this mix is the child's needs. When the child realized they couldn't get what they needed, the feeling of betrayal set in. Betrayal then becomes a very painful pattern in their life. Because the needs of the child were not met, the child sets out to manipulate their parent and they quickly learn to do whatever they need to control that parent in order to have their needs met.

People with the Psychopathic Wound carry deep fear of failure, which they desperately try to hide by energetically blowing up their upper body to appear bigger and more impressive than they feel. The lower part of their body is depleted and weak because they are not grounded, which makes them feel even more unsafe. They are in constant alert mode for

Body

The person's upper body is often more developed because such individuals lack grounding and pull all their energy into their upper body to appear bigger and to impress others. Muscles in the upper body might be very developed.

Energy Distribution

They pull their energy from the Will centers (the back side of the body) up and over their head to intimidate others.

any possible danger or attack and they fear being betrayed even by their close friends.

Individuals suffering from the Psychopathic Wound often lie and cheat and they generally lack scruples in their actions. They find excuses for their behavior and are time and again forgiven by others. They view themselves as being above the law and believe that the rules others abide by don't apply to them. They may be unaware of their control issues but they always know what they want and they need to dominate. They use extreme manipulation to get what they want, and they can display strong narcissistic tendencies, be sociopathic, and/or are megalomaniacs. Former US president Trump is an extreme example of this wounding.

- Such individuals love power. They need power to feel strong. To have power shows that they are better than others and they use that power not to serve but to exploit.

- They also need to control others, which they do by bullying, overpowering, or by undermining through seduction.

- Their sexual expression is often hostile and belittling rather than honoring and loving. They are unable to unite their heart with their genitals, so they use sex for pleasure rather than a true expression of a love connection.

- They have difficulties trusting others because deep down they are fully aware of all of their nasty and ugly behavior and thus cannot trust themselves. It's like a boomerang coming back at them. What they instigate with their arrogant attitude shoots back at them. They fear betrayal by others, which in turn is what they practice on others.

- In their mind, they've created an image of their perfect mate, which occupies their fantasy world.

- They display an inflated ego with a predominant attitude of superiority and contempt.

- They idealize themselves, their beliefs and their actions. Like a cock-of-the-walk, they present their chest high up and their energy over the top of their heads. This is what is evident from the auric level and highly recognizable in their interaction with others. With this, they aim to intimidate. It expresses "I am powerful, my will be done."

Not long ago, I was at the plumbing store while waiting for my contact person, Carl, to order some plumbing parts. Carl was busy with another customer, obviously a plumber, who kept praising his plumbing expertise so loud everyone was forced to listen.

At one point, he turned to me and offered to give me his card, saying, "In case you need the best plumber in town."

I responded, "No thanks, your mouth is so big and loud I cannot even see your face."

That shut him up and he left silently like a dog with his tail between his legs, while Carl chuckled.

Such individuals need to control others and situations in order to feel that they have a right to live because deep down they feel small, inferior, and powerless. In my work, I have often seen how hidden underneath the warrior's armor is a little child in fear. These individuals demand others' submission, declaring what they can do and can't. They do so in a bossy and dictatorial voice, and with blunt manipulation. They make big promises they don't keep and all the time use the phrase "Trust me'"when in fact they are the least to be trusted.

They consider themselves superior to others because the person with the Psychopathic Wound needs to rule and be on top. They usually find a "perfect match" with a person suffering from the Masochistic Wound, a partner who is intimidated by their temper and keeps their mouth shut when the person with the Psychopathic Wound starts to scream and yell.

Obviously, to constantly give in and keep one's mouth shut is not a healthy situation, as you will see with the example of Jane & John in Chapter 86 where Jane, with her Psychopathic Wound, drove John almost to suicide.

Often, when interacting with individuals in their Psychopathic Wound, one instantly experiences opposition. You are either on their side and agree with their viewpoint, and if you don't, you are perceived as against them, which puts you into the position of being their enemy — and an enemy has to be fought and killed, so to speak. They are again on a battlefield fighting a war. Only now, it's with words of disrespect and belittling.

A battle can easily unfold in the form of a heavy debate. Such individuals love debating. It's a fight in another form. What they fear most is failure and defeat. They need to win because if they don't win, it means that they are bad. And they need to be good in order to have a right to live. Its hard for them to understand that in life there can be a win-win situation. They are not used to surrendering and accepting defeat or compromise.

In healing work with these individuals, past lives came up where they were warriors, army leaders and fighters, often fighting for a noble cause and higher good. They sacrificed much on the personal level to win high goals and defend their country with their life. This made them "right / good" and the others "wrong / bad." But in the end, they were defeated or betrayed, often by the ones they had fought for or the ones they most loved. As warriors, they died an honorable death on the battlefield, usually by a deadly wound inflicted to their heart.

In their current life, they still feel at war and that they must win their fight, only the war is now happening on a different level. Because of their betrayal issues — either they betray or they get betrayed — from their past lives, once again, their heart is getting wounded. Such individuals usually suffer from diseases of the heart. Their programming is, "Submit. I am stronger than you. I am controlling you. I dictate what you have to do. I will fight you and I can eliminate you. My will wins. I am right, you are wrong. I am good, you are bad."

As with all wounding, in order to heal, one initially has to recognize that something is wrong. People with the Psychopathic Wound will not easily find their way into a healing practice or therapy because they fear to admit that something could be wrong with them and their behavior. They are hypersensitive to criticism because if something is indeed wrong with them, they are not only "bad," they also don't have a right to live. Another thing that can happen is that they offer to work with me or a therapist so I or the therapist can exercise our craft.

The first step for individuals with the Psychopathic Wound is to start looking at their distorted view of life. It has to "click" for them that they are not at war anymore and that others are not out to get them and hurt them. They need to let go of the constant alert mode and relax into their existence. Life can be beautiful and effortless without the individual's will forced on situations.

It takes discipline for them to counteract their instinctive reaction of exploding every time they feel triggered. A good exercise for them is to take a few deep breaths and envision themselves grounding into the Earth and growing deep roots. This simple exercise immediately connects them to their core and moves their attention away from their mind. A further step is to then consciously connect with their heart region and look at the situation with the wisdom of their Heart.

This will initiate the process of de-programming their distorted view of their ego personality that will ultimately lead to surrender to the greater reality of life, their deeper self, their sexual feelings, and love. They do this by grounding themselves in reality and understanding that they don't need to control others, that others are perfectly capable of running their own lives. Individuals with the Psychopathic Wound must open up to collaboration and teamwork rather than controlling others.

Individuals in the Psychopathic Wound must also make the conscious decision to be honest and put all their efforts into being kind, compassionate, and acting with integrity. In essence, they must learn to live Life from their Heart rather than their will.

Once they start to surrender their life to honesty and integrity, their quality of life and their life experience will deeply transform. They have the ability to build on their past-life experiences as leaders and co-operate with others towards the common good.

Again, let's remember that most of us have not grown up in ideal situations. In addition, we all incarnate with a variety of traumatic experiences from past lives. We arrive with heavy baggage, so to speak. We incarnate again and again to heal and become whole. Our primary wounding is the indicator where we need to focus strongest in order to heal and find fulfillment for our life. Whether we identify with certain wounds to the extreme or to a lesser degree is deeply individual.

Healing work with individuals with a profound Psychopathic Wound can be extremely tiresome and challenging for the facilitator. One feels as if they are walking on a sword's edge. Every look, every word, every gesture is constantly under high surveillance. People with the primary wounding of the Psychopathic Wound feel so extremely vulnerable once they start to open up and trust that even the slightest move suggesting that they might have acted incorrectly can have devastating results.

I remember working with a woman, Jenny, who attacked me with energetic arrows from six feet away that hurt all over my body. I decided to bring this to her attention by verbalizing it matter of factly. She had been unaware of it and her behavior softened as a result. She realized that she often did this and had no conscious awareness of it. But what I described resonated with her. Barbara Brennan in her book Hands of Light has images of the various forms of defense mechanisms used by individuals in their wounds. By showing Jenny the visual image of what she was doing, she became fully aware and understood.

A student of mine, Annetta, had the Psychopathic Wound as her primary wound. She did every possible thing to constantly please and accommodate me with the expectation of me aligning with her. But I could only do that so long as our alignments were in sync.

During the training classes and the individual healing sessions, it was near to impossible to make her become aware of her destructive behavior patterns, such as her constant need to be right and making other group members wrong, and her actions that were self-destructive. One time, she fled the class and I found her upstairs banging her head violently onto the wood floor.

When, during one session, I was finally able to help her break through and recognize her wounding, I afterwards silently cried with exhaustion and gratitude that it had finally "clicked" for her.

When the Soul Calls: True Stories of Deep Healing and Transformation

Chapter 85

Xavier's Control Mechanism

Xavier was a man about forty years old when he came to see me. His wife had recently left him taking their six children with her, the oldest one thirteen years of age, the youngest one two years old. His wife's leaving came as a blow and totally out of the blue. He had not been prepared at all. He shared with me the day he came home from work and clothes and furniture and all were gone. The memory still hurt and he sobbed. He could not grasp the injustice that had befallen him. After all, he had been financially responsible for his family, he had provided a suitable income, and was always under the impression that all was well.

I asked Xavier if there had been any signs of his marriage being in crisis. I felt that a mother with five school-aged children and a toddler would think well before making the decision to leave the marriage. Xavier continued crying and said that for him all had been well. I let him sit quietly with his thoughts for a bit when he came up with, "Okay, maybe I lost my nerve sometimes, but that is only normal. After working hard all day in the office and coming home, I need peace and quiet. I can't deal with the kids and all their screaming."

I asked Xavier if they had a caretaker or a cleaning lady. He responded with: "Why should we? My wife stays at home and takes care of it all. She has no job, that's all she does."

I started to get a pretty good idea of what his wife's daily plan looked like with the chores of cleaning the house, washing the laundry for eight people and cooking their meals, plus taking care of their six children. I asked Xavier if he participated in the family chores. He did not quite understand the question. He remarked that the kitchen and house were his wife's domain. After all, he wasn't asking his wife to help him at his place of work.

Except when Xavier cried, his attitude carried an underlying arrogance and aggressive undertone. I could feel that he felt energetically attacked by the questions I asked. He was getting slightly defensive and I had to explain that I was asking him to describe his family life so that I could get a better idea of what was going on. There was no judgment on my part. After that, he relaxed and said that his family life was divided into his wife taking care of the children and the house, and him being the breadwinner.

Because Xavier's Psychopathic Wound was so strongly developed, his behavior in general was extremely defensive. Healing work with him proved challenging in that he constantly reacted as if attacked. I paid close attention to my own inner feelings toward his behavior and made certain that nothing I felt or verbalized had the slightest hint of judgement about his arrogant behavior. I also, during the entire time, neutralized my energy field by grounding deeply into the core of the Earth, which energetically invited his field to do the same. I praised him whenever he understood and oftentimes repeated that I was not attacking him but was there to help him understand his situation and help him change his reality and transform his life.

In the past-life healing sessions, he saw himself repeatedly as a warrior leaving his family for the battlefield. In one experience, he was returning home only to find his family murdered and his village plundered. In another experience, he fought furiously and died on the battlefield.

Regressing Xavier into his childhood, he saw himself as a ten-year-old boy. His family lived in a village in the Black Forest region of Germany. He was sitting by a soccer field while other kids played. He was angry at his brother who was a couple of years older and who kept beating him up, apparently for no reason. He said his parents didn't seem happy. There was a lot of screaming. His dad kept yelling at his mom. When I asked him how his mom reacted, he said that she just kept quiet.

Xavier was angry that his father kept yelling at his mom but he couldn't do anything about it because his dad also yelled at him a lot, not so much at his brother. Xavier resented his father for favoring his brother and he hated that his father kept bossing him around. Xavier started treating his younger brother the way he was treated by his older brother.

Finishing school, Xavier moved to a larger town where his girlfriend was from. He took on an apprenticeship as a carpenter. His relationship with his girlfriend lasted two years. He then had a few other relationships here and there, nothing serious and they never lasted long.

He was in his late twenties when he met his future wife. She was from the countryside and they started to hang out a lot. She was funny and had a practical side to her which he appreciated. They fell in love and made plans to move to the countryside and start a family. They married three years later and moved to a smaller town where he was hired by a Swedish furniture design producer. His wife became pregnant within the year and they had their first child, a daughter. Within five years, he became the manager of the furniture production company. They were now a family of five. And so it went on until recently when his wife left him with their kids.

Xavier stated that he loved his wife and believed he treated her well. He said he never screamed at her like his father did at his mom.

I asked him if he could discern any parallels between his mom and his wife. Reflecting deeper on the family dynamics he had grown up in, Xavier started to understand that he expected his wife to behave like his mom had.

Though he insisted that he behaved far different than his dad, he could now see some parallels. He understood that though his mom had not left his father and simply kept enduring, his wife had taken the next step and left him to himself. He also admitted that his relationships with his older son and his oldest daughter were strained. He added that he might have been too strict with them.

I didn't hear from Xavier again. Other clients of mine who were living in the same town shared that Xavier's wife ended up filing for divorce. They got shared custody of their children. His wife got a job at the local school as a school teacher.

I do hope though that Xavier, in undergoing the healing work with me, became able to access his right judgment by looking at the other side of the coin, so to speak, and start to understand that his arrogant behavior had been the instigator of the misery he now felt. I hoped for him that even though his marriage had fallen apart and was beyond repair, he would be able to better his relationship to his children and to himself, and find a degree of peace and serenity in his new life without his family.

Chapter 86

JANE & JOHN: HOW DESTRUCTIVE PATTERNS BECOME A MARRIAGE THREAT: THE PSYCHOPATHIC – MASOCHISTIC INTERACTION

Jane requested to work with me but asked if the healing work could negatively affect her unborn baby that was due in two weeks. I responded that whatever ailments came up and were resolved would be of benefit to everyone, including the baby. Upon hearing this, she signed up. Her husband John signed up as well.

In the initial interview, Jane sobbed uncontrollably as she attempted to share how at the age of six years of age, her mother had sent her down into the cellar to get a bottle of mineral water (her parents owned a restaurant). Obeying her mother, she went down and found her father dead, hanging from the ceiling.

During her first healing session, I regressed her back to her childhood. With the voice of a six-year-old child, Jane described in minute detail her childhood, how her mother constantly criticized her dad, how she yelled at him, ridiculed him, and how nothing her dad did was ever good enough for her mama. Jane felt so sorry for her papa, yet helpless as she could do nothing to protect him.

Throughout the entire session recounting everything in the six-year old's voice, Jane didn't cry a single tear.

Jane then continued describing how at the funeral a butterfly appeared in the church and kept flying around. She concluded that she knew this was her papa showing her that he was finally free, that he could now fly.

This first healing session with Jane was the longest I ever worked with a client laying on the massage table: six hours, plus the two hours prior in which she shared her story. When Jane's husband, who was scheduled next, rang the doorbell, I had to reschedule him for the next day.

During John's initial interview, he described how miserable he felt, how the relationship with his wife was beyond repair, how he couldn't go on living with things the way they were. His wife constantly criticized him, belittled him, controlled him, constantly yelled at him, and told him that nothing he did was good enough for her.

It was obvious the two of them were caught in the repetitive pattern of Jane's childhood and the experience of her parents' relationship dynamic.

John told me that he had grown so tired of this and that he could no longer bear to live this way. He told me that not long ago he made the decision to shut her mouth forever by killing her. He bought a gun but said as soon as he held the gun in his hands, he knew he could never kill another human being. But what he would be able to do is kill himself. He set the date for his suicide. It was ten days from our session, shortly before the birth of their baby.

During the healing session with Jane the next day, I guided her to look at her life with John. She described how she couldn't stand his behavior. He was clumsy and did everything wrong. She had to do everything herself in order to get it done right. She had zero respect for him, would lose patience with him, and scream and yell at him. She couldn't love him because she constantly had to control him.

In the course of their healing work, each of them realized separately the underlying patterns that had led to their current situation. Jane cried deeply as she saw that she had adopted the exact behavior patterns of her mom. The two of them could finally release their heavy burden of victimizer versus victim and begin to see each other with new eyes. Two months later, they paid me a visit to present me with their little baby daughter. They were now a happy young family.

Section 5

The Fourth Wounding

Chapter 87

THE MASOCHISTIC WOUND

When a child is stifled in their process of autonomy due to the control of one or both parents, the child's healthy development gets blocked. This wound is inflicted when a child is no longer identifying exclusively with one or both parents, is beginning to view themselves autonomously, but are made to feel guilty whenever they attempt their own freedom. Love was conditional from a dominating and sacrificing mother. The child was force fed and their bathroom excretions were controlled. As infants, they might have been led on a leash or restrained by it.

The parents' love was overprotective and experienced by the child as suffocating. The parents lived their life through their child's life. Every move the child wanted to make was controlled. Their private space, their personal boundaries, was constantly invaded and all attempts to declare freedom were crushed.

As a result, the child felt trapped, humiliated, and defeated. As a child, they were teased and humiliated, which resulted in the child learning to not share their feelings but rather hold them in. This led to stored-up anger, hatred, and rebellion. Their creativity was also controlled and stifled, thus the child wasn't able to express their creative impulses freely and unhindered.

They were also humiliated for their sexuality. They were punished and scolded when they touched their genitals, as children naturally do. Now as adults, they might be impotent and addicted to pornography. A women might feel non-organic and her sexuality viewed as unclean.

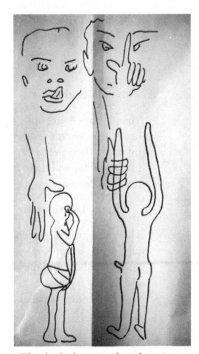

The little boy in the drawing is being punished and scolded for touching his erection.

331

As an adult, an individual with the Masochistic Wound demands independence but, conversely, it's challenging for them to become independent because they've always been controlled by others. Hence, they unconsciously seek someone who will control them again and a situation that will imprison them.

In their past lives, they didn't own their life. They were slaves and owned by someone else who ruled over them body, life, and Soul. They had to work hard in order to remain of value to their owner.

These individuals suffer, whine, and complain. They marinate in self-pity. They love negativity and do a lot of silent brooding. Because they hold their thoughts and feelings in, they feel separated from others. Their main energy is internalized. They are phlegmatic and hypoactive but boiling inside. Within themselves, they hold blocked feelings of spite, negativity, hostility and superiority. This might well result in passive-aggressive behavior patterns and words and actions that are hurtful, even harmful, to others.

- These individuals feel constantly controlled
- They provoke others to control them
- They also provoke others until they explode
- They feel imprisoned in their life situation
- They suffer, whine, and complain
- They marinate in self-pity
- Their energy is very slow moving and stagnated
- They might be impotent
- There is a heaviness about them
- They experience unexpressed hatred towards others
- When addressing others, they speak in "we" terms because as children, their boundaries were constantly violated
- They tend towards negativity and silent brooding while inwardly they are boiling
- They feel humiliated and defeated
- They feel disempowered

Body

The person's entire body is heavy with overdeveloped muscles. Their pelvis is tucked under and their head juts forward.

Energy Distribution

Their energy is stagnate (appearing unmoving) and bottled up, and they're grounded, appearing bolted to the earth, unable to move.

Physically, these people are heavy and compact with overdeveloped muscles and a short neck and waist. Their body has accumulated a lot of tissue and fat in order to create a buffer zone between themselves and the continuous invasion they initially experienced in childhood by their controlling parent, as well as life circumstances they keep creating to reinforce their control over them.

Tension is held in the neck, jaw, throat and pelvis, which is tucked under. Their buttocks are cold. Their throat area is choked and the head thrusts forward. Their energetic field is fully inflated and heavy with a lot of very slow-moving energy. Picture a lake with no inlet or outlet of water. Such is the energetic field of a person with the Masochistic Wound. Because of all the stagnated energy in their field, this wound remains the most challenging one to heal.

In communications and interactions, they express themselves politely but with a whining disgust so as to subtly manipulate others. Their constant whining complaints and negativity triggers teasing from others, which gives them the green light to become angry. Anger was already there but just held in. Now the anger has a reason and permission to be unleashed. Like an emotional pressure cooker, they feel and store a lot of tension and seek to release that tension by blowing up — but they can only do that when they are given permission. Hence, they provoke others to get angry and upset, which gives them a reason and permission to explode in violent verbal and/or physical rage.

I have observed many individuals with this wound acting like energetic parasites. For instance, when in a situation where the financial needs are met by their spouse or parents or a trust fund, etc., they gladly do not work. They happily agree to the role of the househusband staying at home while their wife or partner works. Oftentimes, the wife is not only the breadwinner but also does the household chores and takes care of the children when she comes home because such individuals tend to be very phlegmatic.

People with this wound are confident in using big words and making speeches without doing much. Often, they act entitled and with disguised arrogance. In interactions, they seem to submit, though they don't. Thus, their unconscious intention is to remain blocked by sabotaging themselves in order to remain a victim of some sort, to continually hurt themselves emotionally.

Their presenting complaint is a lot of built-up tension they're suffering from what has caused the tension — other people and their behaviors, and them feeling disempowered. They seek to release that tension but don't know how except through explosive, anger-filled outbreaks. Unconsciously, they believe that releasing tension leads to their submission and humiliation. They purposely put themselves in a position to be humiliated in order to then become submissive to someone else.

What is needed to heal from the Masochistic Wound is to learn to express feelings honestly and without holding back, and in a regulated and civilized manner. Such individuals need to free themselves from humiliation by freeing their aggression in a healthy and non-destructive way. They need to express themselves actively and whenever they want, to let go and release all their stored up and blocked energies. As children, these individuals' creativity was stifled, so their healing must be connected to their creative expression.

Once these individuals realize in healing sessions or therapy that they were controlled during their childhood and continue to be controlled as adults, they oftentimes have the need to cut relations with their parents by ending contact or moving away and starting a new life. They need to be able to build their own lives, choose their own life circumstances, and feel they are able to control their personal situations and interactions by clearly voicing their needs and their limits.

They need to feel that they are in control of their lives rather than someone else controlling it. Because they have continuously felt their boundaries disrespected and their private space invaded, these individuals need to put up strong boundaries that need to be respected above all else.

In doing so, their new-found freedom will provide them with the direct experience of empowerment, the feeling of self-worth while building their self-respect. Their caring heart for others can then be expressed in healthy ways but they should avoid mothering their children and others in a way that could lead to control just as they experienced as a child. Their healing needs to be related to creativity, bringing forth the vast landscape of stored-up creativity and sharing it with others.

Chapter 88

ANTONIA AND HER REFUSAL TO REMOVE HER CANCEROUS TUMOR

Antonia was diagnosed with a malignant tumor in her uterus that needed immediate removal — yet she refused surgery.

In the course of our work, it became clear to Antonia that her refusal was linked with rebellion. Looking deep into her childhood upbringing and its dominating factors she started to understand that all her life her parents had controlled her out of too much love and concern, which resulted in too much intervention. They had lived through her, inhibiting her process from childhood into a healthy, autonomous adult. They had invaded her private space and made every decision for her.

Now that she had finally something to herself — the cancerous tumor — she refused to let it go. She distanced herself from her parents and was no longer in contact with them. It took a number of healing sessions over several months until Antonia felt the decision to keep or remove the tumor was hers and hers alone, as well as understanding that by keeping the tumor within her body she was threatening her own life. She underwent surgery and decided to keep working with me. In fact, Antonia became a student of the HeartPath Re-Alignment.

The more Antonia started to realize how her Masochistic Wound was inflicted on her in her childhood due to the overprotective attitude of her parents, the more her desire grew to fully let go of her past, cut ties with her parents, and live her life with her husband with whom she felt very happy.

Following the surgery, her process was to explore why the cancerous tumor had manifested in her body, particularly in the uterus. In a series of healing sessions, Antonia uncovered her childhood sexual abuse by her father. She was in shock. And she decided on the spot to confront her father. Antonia requested that I be present during their meeting to facilitate the confrontation. When her parents arrived at the retreat where I was teaching, Antonia very matter-of-factly presented the reason for the meeting.

Now her parents were in shock. Her mother kept stating that this was impossible, that as her mother she would have known. Her father declared that he would immediately schedule a consultation with his doctor who would attest that he had never done such a thing. It was a ridiculous statement. While a doctor can check if a girl still has her hymen intact, a medical exam has no way of detecting sexual abuse in the genitalia of a man.

I was glad I was present because in the face of the utter denial of both her parents, Antonia lost her adult identity and became a child again. She stuttered in utter confusion. It was as if she were hypnotized under all the pressure. I asked everyone to become silent and guided Antonia to breathe deeply and calmly. Deep and concentrated breathing always has the effect of bringing a separation between the occurrence, in this case the pressure of her parent's denial and Antonia's declared truth, the sexual abuse.

By breathing deeply and remaining silent, Antonia started to feel present within herself again and came back into the present moment. She told her parents that she was deeply saddened with their denial and that as a result would cut all contact with them. Her parents silently stared at her. They were in shock. After some time passed, they made a few attempts to express to Antonia that they were sorry that she wanted to cut them out of her life. But they didn't express that they were willing to go deep within to search for any wrongdoings on their part.

We then terminated the meeting, Antonia's parents needed time to digest what their daughter had brought up. Both parents were in deep shock and pain and it would take time for them to digest and sort through Antonia's accusation.

Chapter 89

OTTO, THE BIG, FAT PARASITE

Charlotte is a former client of mine, who in the past did a number of healing sessions with me. She is a successful dentist with a busy practice. During her recent Maha Intensive, she was seeking an understanding of the dynamics in the relationship with her husband Otto. They have two young adult children. Charlotte described Otto's characteristics as someone with a very developed Masochistic Wound.

Over the years, Otto's business kept going downhill. Without Charlotte's knowledge, he attained ever-higher and larger bank loans, which she ended up having to pay off. In order to save his business from bankruptcy, he committed tax fraud behind Charlotte's back. He was caught, charged, and sentenced to prison. In order to save their kids from the shame of having their father in prison, Charlotte paid a huge sum of money to the tax department and exhausted her entire savings.

Otto's irresponsible business conduct provoked a lot of irritation in Charlotte. She had for too long endured and enabled her husband to continue his behavior. She felt great disappointment, anger, and frustration about her husband's continuous irresponsible behavior pattern for which he never took responsibility, but instead always found lame excuses and banal explanations. Though his failures were obvious to everyone, he stubbornly remained in utter denial.

For quite some time, he was happily doing nothing, spending her income, and living his life as a house husband. He drove their only car while the busy worker bee Charlotte took the train to work.

Charlotte wanted her husband to work and suggested numerous times that he seek employment but work wasn't to his taste. After all, his wife was earning more than enough for their lifestyle. But for Charlotte, Otto's parasitic behavior had become a burden. She felt it wasn't healthy to just sit around, do nothing, and live off someone else. It also set a poor example for their children. But Otto always resisted change and insisted on staying ensconced in his set behavior patterns.

Charlotte loved her husband but their marriage was in serious crisis. She wanted to change the dynamics for them in order to stay together, but whenever she tried to talk to Otto, he managed to talk her out of it.

Therefore, prior to returning home, Charlotte wrote her husband a loving but clear letter in which she stated that change needed to happen on his part in order for their marriage to survive. She left the sum of

$8,000 in a bank account set up for him so that he could temporarily move out. She cut Otto off from access to her own bank account so that he couldn't spend money as he pleased. She stated she needed a temporary separation, so in an attempt of utter transparency, she forwarded the letter to their kids, her mother, and her brothers.

As a result, all hell broke loose. Otto felt defeated and was filled with rage. He declared Charlotte responsible for his misery and threatened suicide. Charlotte's tough mom and one brother completely supported her decision. The children only felt pity for their dad whom they viewed as a coward, unable to take charge of his own life.

Their daughter fell into a deep crisis and threatened her mom that if she went ahead with her plan of a temporary separation, she would forever disappear from her mother's life. This upset Charlotte deeply and she started to experience self-doubt. She shied away from being made responsible for her husband's suicide in case he made good on his threat. Change didn't happen as Charlotte had desired because his manipulative threat of suicide lay too heavy on her shoulders.

To my knowledge, Otto's highly developed Masochistic Wound was never addressed. Though Charlotte worked deeply on releasing her role of enabler, Otto might have continued his habits of phlegmatic passivity and manipulative behavior patterns with his passive-aggressive attitude toward resisting change, remaining blocked, and controlling the family and relationship dynamics.

Section 6

The Fifth Wounding

Chapter 90

THE RIGID WOUND

The last wound inflicted on a child is during their puberty. The parent of the opposite sex is no longer comfortable with the child's changing body and begins to treat their child differently. For example, a dad might start to feel uncomfortable seeing his daughter grow into a young woman, so he no longer fully hugs her. The child can interpret this as rejection and as a betrayal of love because they aren't viewing themselves as a sex symbol. To compensate for this rejection, the child decides to control any kind of feelings. Their feelings are suppressed and not authentically expressed anymore.

As an adult, the individual with this wound holds back feelings and actions in order to not look foolish. Their inner reality is walled off from the outpouring and inpouring of feelings. Feelings cannot flow naturally anymore, they get blocked. This creates a "false mask" behavior that's presented to the world to such an extent that the person fully identifies with the image they're presenting because their original feelings have been stifled and they can no longer feel or recognize them.

It's scary for these individuals to admit and submit to feelings of love because they're afraid their heart will be betrayed. In love and sex, they manipulate indirectly through seduction to get what they need.

Vulnerability is to be avoided at all costs. These individuals are deeply afraid of being hurt, specifically, it's the rejection of sexual love that hurts their feelings. Sex is viewed with contempt, not love. At some point, they come to realize that sex without love remains unsatisfying. Though they demand love and sexual feelings from others, they seduce but remain uncommitted. This leads to competition rather than give-

and-take love. Their pride is then hurt, which causes them to become even more competitive. Thus, they remain in a vicious cycle where they never get what they want.

Individuals with the predominantly Rigid Wound are fully grounded in the material world; they identify exclusively with their body and the material world. To them, nothing else exists. They have no clue about their spiritual nature. Usually, they are atheists and agnostics. They defer to science and technology to perfectly explain matter. A higher power is not known to them.

Body

The person's body is very balanced, their pelvis is tilted backward to avoid feelings and their head is usually tilted up, which gives them the appearance of being superior.

Energy Distribution

They are well grounded, but lack connection to Spirit. Their energy is evenly distributed, concentrated on their outer image with a lack of connection to their feelings and inner core.

Such individuals are hyperactive and highly energized. They live primarily in their well-developed mind and function through willpower. They regulate themselves well, are integrated, and do not easily lose control. Their body is balanced and harmoniously proportioned with either an emotional mesh armor or steel plate for protection. When severely triggered, they might explode hysterically but they usually display power with their force of will and maintain strong boundaries. Their life is very organized, very structured, and they often possess a high level of integrity, and they demand the same high standards from others.

The focus of the person with the Rigid Wound is on their personal appearance. They identify exclusively with the physical world and thus usually have no clue to their own innate spirituality as all their energy is focused on their external presentation and expression. They are usually very worldly and with a lot of ambition and competitive drive. They continually demonstrate that they are superior and know everything. They communicate in qualifiers by setting values and enforcing rules that must be obeyed.

- Such individuals hold back their feelings to avoid appearing foolish

- They can appear cold and cut off from their feelings

- Rather than being real, they have a need to appear perfect

- They operate in inauthentic mask behavior

- Their focus is on their perfect appearance

- They identify strongly with the physical world, matter, technology, and science

- They deny the existence of a higher power

- They are unaware of their core essence and their spiritual nature

- They possess strong self-control

- They avoid vulnerability

- They behave in very rigid terms

- They function through pride and arrogance

They hold their head high and their backbone straight with pride. Their pelvis is tipped back and cold. Life is going well, all is well, they have no presenting complaints. Or even if life isn't going well, they won't admit it. Their heart is closed and their presenting issue is that they have no feelings. They want to surrender to their feelings but believe that feelings will only hurt them, so they decide it's better to live without feelings.

Because these individuals mainly operate with their mind and will, they need to open their feeling centers, allowing the energy to flow in and out, and be seen by others. Their heart needs to open and they need to allow themselves to love. Their aura needs softening. Most importantly, they need to drop their mask behavior and become authentic and real. Their feelings, thoughts, and actions need to become transparent. They need to connect their genitals with their heart by allowing true, heartfelt love into their lives while surrendering to their sexual desire and attraction.

Their inner landscape is full of passion, love, and adventure. Their past lives are filled with heroic adventures and journeys of accomplishments. They usually have a deep sense of integrity and place high demands on themselves and others. Their goals are noble and they are capable of inspiring others with their love and passion for life.

Healing happens when people no longer identify exclusively with the mundane world, the perfection of their appearance, and the presentation of mask behavior but connect to their inner nature. It is of the essence that they connect to their spiritual Self. Once they do, it will be a revelation to them as if a new and unknown Universe is opening up to them.

Individuals with the Rigid Wound are natural leaders. They are balanced in their interactions with others. Their life is well organized and structured. They communicate with mental clarity. People look up to them and seek their advice. They inspire others as role models. Once their wounding is transformed, they can become great teachers and powerful leaders in their field of expertise.

Chapter 91

HARRY: WHEN THE RIGID MASK BREAKS

While still living in Switzerland, Harry's wife Barbara first came to work with me. She shared about her life and her marriage and told me that her husband, Harry, a former high-ranking officer in the military, treated their three daughters as if they were boys when they were growing up. He called them "Giele" (boys). They were used to drills and a strict regimen of rules as if they lived in a military camp. Barbara shared that the atmosphere of the house felt just like how it must feel in the military. Breakfast, lunch, and dinner had to be punctually served to the minute in order to avoid their father's hysterical outbursts. Once seated at the table, no word was spoken, there had to be absolute silence. The radio was on and the news dominated the meal.

This kind of rigid tyranny allowed for no joy or play. Barbara said she felt miserable in her marriage and that she was slowly dying. Her husband was the patriarch and he set the house rules. During their entire marriage, Barbara had submitted to her husband and had kept her mouth shut. But she was fed up with her husband's behavior.

The day came when she brought in a large serving platter of food. Instead of putting it down on the table, she flipped it over, upside down on the table, food flying everywhere. Harry stared open-mouthed and in shock. Then he screamed at her, "Are you nuts?! You're ready for the nut house!" But Barbara had already stormed out of the room. This incident marked the beginning of a grand change to come.

Within a month of having worked with Barbara, her husband Harry signed up for a healing session cycle. He spoke of his tough upbringing in the Swiss countryside and the strict discipline of his father who Harry feared as a child. His mother was submissive and had not much of a voice. His dad controlled the household.

In Harry's regression to about age three, he saw himself playing under the table with his imaginary spirit companions. He loved to play with them more than his childhood friends. The spirit companions were much more real and fun to play with as they could do tricks his friends were unable to perform. They made him laugh with their funny behavior. For years, day after day, he was happily consumed by his fantasy world. His spirit friends all had names and he would lose himself in his play with them for hours at a time.

As I asked Harry to see himself at six years of age, he saw his parents ridiculing him for his imaginary friends, telling him they weren't real, that they didn't exist, that he must grow up and behave normally, that he must stop invoking them and talking to and playing with them.

Harry felt great sadness. His Heart was broken and he lost his innocence, all because he believed his parents more than his own experiences. He stopped calling his spirit companions to play with him. He let them go and completely forgot about them.

I asked Harry to see himself at 8, 9, and 10 years of age. He witnessed himself growing up bit by bit, losing more of his spontaneity and innocence. His spirit connection was totally lost. He turned cold to his feelings and his Heart became numb. The military, with its drills and strict rules, provided the perfect environment to distance himself further from his true self.

The healing session experiences threw Harry into a big emotional pit. After each healing session, he sobbed for many hours in his room. He shared that for three days he sobbed nonstop — a whole river — as the icy wall around his Heart broke open and he processed all the grief his adult behavior had caused himself and the damage he had invoked towards the ones he loved.

Harry underwent many healing session cycles with me. It was most challenging for him to face the acts of sexual abuse he had performed on his daughters when they were young. It was easier for him to talk about the sexual abuse of his dog. He described taking their dog on walks into the forest where he exposed his penis and held it for the dog to lick.

At some point during his healing sessions, Harry saw his father forcing oral sex on him regularly when he was a baby.

Healing sessions with Harry always started with him watching clouds of colors turning into other colors, often for an hour (he needed time before going to the core of the issue). He was in much denial about his having been the victimizer, even though his wife and daughters had sat him down and had a conversation about it all. In his conscious mind, he knew it to be true and admitted to it. But to go back to the time when the girls were small and the abuse took place was emotionally almost unbearable for him. He sobbed a lot and spoke about how lonely he had felt throughout his life.

The process was slow and heavy, like slogging through molasses, but healing was occurring. He confronted his pain, as well as his wrongdoings. He asked each family member for forgiveness — it was harder, though, to forgive himself. As time passed, that came, too, as he opened his Heart to feelings of self-love and self-compassion.

I have often witnessed that for the perpetrator of sexual abuse, it is extremely challenging to face the truth and take responsibility for their actions. For example, upon being confronted with the past for the sexual abuse of his daughter, a father of one client (see Chapter 88) was in utter denial of sexually abusing his daughter and responded that he would schedule a physical exam with his doctor who would then attest that he had never performed such acts. Another father disappeared into the bathroom and kept looking at himself in the mirror. To his image, he repeated over and over, "I didn't do this. I could not possibly have done this. Did I really do it? Is it really true? I don't remember ever having done this." — while his daughter, who had brought up the issue of sexual abuse, observed him through the open door.

Yet, healing of the past can only happen by taking an honest look at the facts. This goes for the perpetrator, as well as for the victim. Only by being willing to accept what happened can we release it into the Light, no matter how hard it is to face the truth and the unimaginable actions. Once we do, we become free of the burden that was carried.

Oftentimes, this invokes ancestral healing as well. We need to realize that we are the last link in a long chain of ancestral heritage. We are wounded because the wounds of our ancestors were passed on to us. By our being able to release the painful incidences of the past, we release the painful incidences of our ancestors. By our being able to heal and become free, our ancestors heal and become free.

Chapter 92

JEREMY'S NEED TO LEAD AND INTERFERE

Jeremy was a good looking man with a great physique dealing with a midlife crisis. Angelique, his wife of a decade, had left him after a heavy discussion in which she told him she needed to find herself and live her own life. She said she needed to find out who she was and what was right for her and needed to be on her own because her marriage felt stifling to her.

Angelique was only twenty-two when she met Jeremy, who was eight years older than she. At such a young age, eight years makes a big difference. Angelique was a sought-after model and he was proud to appear with her at his side. He fell in love with her because of her beauty and didn't mind that her personality had not yet quite developed. He enjoyed that she felt insecure and relied on him. They lived a good number of years feeling happy and content. At least, so he thought.

Jeremy confessed that he felt deeply hurt by her statements. He had always felt secure guiding their life together. He loved taking care of her. His leadership identity was strongly developed. Jeremy said Angelique had loved it and always encouraged him to do so. It had functioned well during many years, and now all of a sudden and without any warning it all fell apart.

What devastated him the most was that soon after Angelique left him, she found a new love and this was a double sword thrust to his Heart. He suspected she'd been unfaithful while they were still living together and that was in fact the reason she left him. Angelique was now with a woman, a model, and Jeremy felt there was no chance to make amends and give their marriage a second try.

Jeremy was deeply hurt. The breakup of his marriage shattered him. He was plagued by deep insecurities and self-doubt. He was also dealing with depression. His whole focus had been on their relationship and now that she was no longer there, he could not see what could possibly come after.

During the healing work, Jeremy saw himself as a boy very much adored by his mom. His dad, who had been an athlete, encouraged him to pursue athletics. His younger brother looked up to him and loved the protection his older brother provided.

Progressing further into his teen years, Jeremy experienced again the feelings of pride for being best in his school class. He also excelled in athletics and his parents had every reason to be proud of him. All was going excellently for Jeremy. He chose a career in the banking industry and was looking at a bright future.

During the next healing session, Jeremy saw himself as a conqueror during the Roman Empire. His tent was elegantly decorated with carpets and fine fabrics. He had a wife and two children at home, and a great number of concubines from his journeys conquering peoples and nations. His army was well trained, well fed, and strong. He treated his soldiers fair and well and they in return stayed loyal to him.

Returning home from battles, he was welcomed with much fanfare and high honors. But he also saw that though conquering others filled him with pride, it left his Soul empty. His emotions were centered around accomplishment rather than true fulfillment.

The next day, we talked about his childhood in this current life and then that lifetime as a conqueror. Jeremy could see how his personality consisted of a great deal of pride and honor. He now understood the deeper reasons for his intense need to lead. We also talked about the other side of conquering, the victims, the hunger, and desperation of the defeated ones.

Jeremy recognized how in this life he had practiced another type of conquest. Conquering of the heart with Angelique who became his wife. He admitted that he for too long had viewed her as his possession. He concluded that no wonder his life — as he had known it — had to end by having his heart broken. Jeremy quickly realized his circumstances and also understood that there are more important values in life than accomplishment and physical appearance, like the happiness of his Heart and being connected to God and Spirit.

Jeremy was an old and wise Soul. In his next healing session, he wanted to access a time when he had lived his wisdom. He saw himself in an exotic setting during the Mughal time in India. He was a young male whose father was a royal.

From a young age on, he witnessed the populace arriving for an audience at the court. His father had an open ear for all ailments presented and treated everyone with respect and kindness. He was so highly respected for his wisdom and fair judgment that he was revered by all. When his father passed away, Jeremy proceeded in his footsteps. He found great fulfillment in that lifetime. He loved living in harmonious synchrony with the people he guided, and his family life was a happy one.

After that, he experienced himself as a native wise woman living in the Andes a very long time ago. She was acquainted with herbs and remedies and had learned her craft from her mother. After her mother passed away, she kept living with her elderly father in the wilderness by herself. The village people knew of her healing abilities and sought her out. She never married but kept serving the village people.

Jeremy was very thoughtful the next day. He had re-connected with his deeper being.

Digesting it all, Jeremy expressed his desire for change. He admitted that ideally a relationship should be built on equality rather than control. In some ways he had been protective of Angelique, almost like a father. He also saw that while everything was seemingly going flawless in his life, he had built his personality on pride, and how as soon as he felt defeated and betrayed, he dropped into deep insecurities, doubts, and depression.

He voiced that he is looking to build a more balanced life by cultivating self-love, connecting to his inner being, and exploring his spirituality. He felt it important to find inner stability and dignity beyond outer circumstances. He said there was much transformation waiting for him and recognized the blessing of Angelique leaving him so he could start his journey of healing and transformation, which he needed to do on his own and not while in partnership.

Two Choices of Living Your Life —

The Wrong Pillar and the Right Pillar

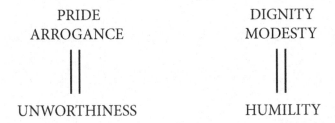

PRIDE   DIGNITY
ARROGANCE   MODESTY

UNWORTHINESS   HUMILITY

Chapter 93

WEARING THE MASK OF PERFECTION: ALEXA, IN FEAR OF AUTHENTICITY – A HARD LESSON LEARNED LATE

Alexa signed up as a paying volunteer to work with one of my trainees during their supervised internship. A young woman in her late twenties, she had recently become engaged to a man her age. All looked perfect. Her life was going perfectly. She had found the perfect mate and they were looking to build a perfect life together. Alexa's priority was to have her life and her image appear perfect.

They had the same interests, the same hobbies, the same viewpoints, and they were in love. The two were planning to start a family. They had recently moved into a new home. The wedding date was set and both parents had given their blessings to the marriage. Alexa worked as a manager in a retail store. Her fiancé had just finished his studies graduating cum laude, and was hired by a respected law firm. In short, both had great jobs and their lives looked very rosy.

But, Alexa had one issue she wanted to clear and overcome. She shared that the only problem was that neither one of them had ever been able to say to the other, "I love you." This was a big missing stepping stone for Alexa.

It might sound like a minuscule issue but for Alexa it was a huge problem. In their so-called perfectly appropriate behavior, neither one of them had ever been able to express their true and authentic feelings of love for each other. She so longed to be able to declare her love, not just in actions but also in words. Plus, she yearned to hear those words from her fiancé. This was the reason why she had signed up for the 4-day session intensive.

During the next four days, in every healing, Alexa visualized she and her fiancé together. She planned a romantic dinner as soon as she returned home where they sat together by candlelight and how these words would escape her lips. She practiced saying aloud, "I love you. I love you," over and over again. She couldn't wait to get home and put her efforts into action. She wanted to tell him that very night because the next morning her fiancé would leave for a ski weekend with his friends.

Our group was still in the training class when Alexa called three days later. She needed to talk to me. There was uncontrollable sobbing on the other end of the line. I gave Alexa a long time to allow her tears to flow.

Once she composed herself, she spoke. She had just received the tragic news that her fiancé and his friends had been buried under an avalanche. All were dead, no survivors. Oh my God, how truly heartbreaking. What a tremendously huge shock for Alexa and her fiancé's family.

After a long pause, her tears running freely, I asked her if she had been able to tell him that she loved him. "Yes," she said, "I'm telling him now. I keep screaming it around the entire apartment. 'I love you, I love you, I love you' nonstop!"

Sadly, Alexa had not been able to express her feelings of love before they parted. Now that he had passed away, she had missed her very last chance. She was devastated beyond repair.

It's typical for the person with the Rigid Wound to fear expressing feelings of the Heart. Inside, they know of their love and attraction but they fear to be ridiculed by exposing their feelings of love. She had attracted a man with the same wound who was dealing with the exact same issue. Rather than surrendering to love and expressing authentically, such individuals hide behind their false mask of in-authenticity. For Alexa, this was an extremely painful lesson learned too late.

> For beautiful eyes,
> look for the good in others;
> for beautiful lips, speak only words of kindness;
> and for poise,
> walk with the knowledge that you are never alone.
>
> ~ Audrey Hepburn

Section 7

The Sixth Wounding

Chapter 94

THE LUCIFERIAN WOUND

My observations during the course of my more than thirty years of working with individuals in my healing practice have brought me to the conclusion that there is a sixth wounding, which I have termed the "Luciferian Wound."

According to my studies, the Luciferian Wound is a combination of the first wound, the Schizoid Wound and the last wound, the Rigid Wound. If we envision a circle and place the five wounds I described in previous chapters around that circle, the Schizoid Wound would be at the two o'clock position, the Oral Wound at the four o'clock position, the Psychopathic Wound at the six o'clock position, the Masochistic Wound at the eight o'clock position, and the Rigid Wound at the ten o'clock position.

Like a circle closing, I have observed the development of the Luciferian Wound to be a combination of the first wound, the Schizoid Wound and the last wound, the Rigid Wound.

But before I explain in detail the development of this wound, I would like to explain my reason for naming it the Luciferian Wound.

According to Wikipedia, "satan, the devil, sometimes called Lucifer, is an entity in the Abrahamic religions that seduces humans into sin and falsehood."

Lucifer, the fallen angel, goes by many names. In the Christian faith, we know him as the devil, satan, the prince of demons, the father of lies. Other religions have other names for the devil or evil, the counterpart of the benevolent beings of the heavenly realms.

In Hebrew, he is called Abbadon (destroyer); in Islam he is Iblis (cast out of heaven) or Shaytan; in Hinduism it is Raksasah / Asuras; in Buddhism it is Mara (death); in ancient Egypt it was Seth (who killed his brother Osiris).

The devil is the personification of evil. He has been a part of the lore of horror stories for so long that many people think he's a fictional character, made up to scare children and movie audiences worldwide. In reality, the Devil has a story that predates humanity's creation, and it may surprise many to learn that, before his banishment from heaven, his story had angelic beginnings, not just in the Christian faith but also in Islam and Judaism.

Michael C. Thomsett, in his book, *Heresy in the Roman Catholic Church: A History*, states that "Lucifer was a glorified angel but fell from heaven to establish his own kingdom and became the Demiurge[28]. Therefore, he created the material world and trapped souls from heaven inside matter. Jesus Christ descended to Earth to free the captured souls."[29]

But now to the main concern: How is the Luciferian Wound created by the combining of the Schizoid Wound and the Rigid Wound?

I described the person with the predominantly Schizoid Wound as very connected to the spiritual world and not connected to Earth. They have a deeply spiritual nature but are ungrounded. Because the person with a severe Schizoid Wound is completely ungrounded and life on Earth feels alien and dangerous, in order to find security in their body and here on Earth, they develop their mental capacities to an extremely high degree to provide safety for themselves. They only feel secure in their own mental structures. Scientists like Albert Einstein are a great example of individuals with the Schizoid Wound.

In contrast, the individual with a predominantly Rigid Wound is unaware of the spiritual world and hence has zero clue of their spirituality. But they are so well grounded in the material world that for them nothing else except materia / matter exists. They are atheists and agnostics denying the existence of God. They are cut off from their Heart and feelings and from their inner core. They rely exclusively on science and technology. To them, the great mystery of life is non-existent, even ridiculed. The material world is their god.

---

[28] In the Platonic, Neopythagorean, Middle Platonic and Neoplatonic schools of philosophy, the demiurge is an artisan-like figure responsible for fashioning and maintaining the physical universe, though not God the Creator.
[29] McFarland, March 2011, p. 71.

In their extreme expression, they seem to have no Heart, act without a Heart, and can easily be cruel and without scruples and consideration for others. Good examples of people in their Rigid Wound are military leaders, dictators, and politicians. Extreme examples are Adolf Hitler, Joseph Stalin, Pol Pot, Heinrich Himmler, Idi Amin, Genghis Khan, etc., as well as cruel scientists torturing animals and performing horrible experiments on humans.

The heartless behavior of the person with a profoundly Rigid Wound, in combination with their denial of God / Source and the exclusive identification with the material world can develop to such high extremes that such individuals are capable of defining who has a right to live and who does not. Most mass murderers and cruel dictators are consciously serving the dark powers of destruction, evil / satan.

The combination of the two of these wounds, the Schizoid Wound and the Rigid Wound in their extremes, develops into the Luciferian Wound. Furthermore, since the Rigid Wound is inflicted during the last stage of childhood development, adolescence, we also cannot name the Luciferian Wound a childhood wound anymore. Rather, the Luciferian Wound progresses into an approach to life with the denial of the spiritual nature of mankind and God / Source and the exclusive focus on materia, technology, and science as the basis of existence.

THE LUCIFERIAN APPROACH TO LIFE WITH THE DENIAL OF GOD / SOURCE / SPIRIT AND THE EXCLUSIVE FOCUS ON MATTER, TECHNOLOGY, AND SCIENCE AS THE BASIS OF EXISTENCE IS THE DOWNFALL OF HUMANITY

The Danger of the Luciferian Approach to Life

Again, we must remember that Lucifer, the former glorified angel fell from heaven to establish his own kingdom and became the Demiurge. In doing so, he created the material world and trapped Souls from heaven inside matter. In each and every way, Lucifer / the Devil / Satan is the polar opposite to the Forces of the Source of Light / God and thus embodies the anti-Christ.

Just to clarify, my use of the term "Luciferian" is not to be confused with Rudolph Steiner's description found in his book *Lucifer and Ahriman: Human Responsibility for the Earth.*

Therefore the choice of the Luciferian approach to life it is a very concerning disease of our times. I personally believe it is THE most dangerous disease because it threatens humanity and it jeopardizes our very existence.

THE LUCIFERIAN APPROACH TO LIFE IS THE MOST CONCERNING AND DANGEROUS DISEASE OF OUR TIME

The threat to humanity by aligning with Lucifer is deeply concerning because it leads astray from our core essence — the feeling Heart and the conscious awareness and importance of our Soul — by seducing individuals into living their lives from their mind and thus deny their core essence. In doing so, they abandon their Heart, Spirit, and Soul.

As we witness the upheaval of our current global situation, each and every one of us — to a higher or a lesser degree — is forced to look beyond the symptoms served to us by the media and governments. We must question what is really going on. Let's face it, humanity has fallen victim to the self-created demons of chaos by disrespecting, interfering and destroying nature, by allowing corporate magnates to control our lives, and by worshiping materialism, technology, and science.

Since ages past, texts from various wisdom traditions speak of the coming of the anti-Christ. I suggest the anti-Christ is already living among us as an energized, cold apparatus and mechanical system aiming to deprive us of our own personal freedom and the feeling capability of our Heart. It's seducing us towards becoming controlled by an overruling entity that will take residence in our minds and it aims to take over the world. The anti-Christ is alive and thriving, striving and threatening to take over planet Earth.

The Luciferian approach to life, with the misuse of technology and science, has led a large number of our human family to align with the anti-Christ. The devil has seduced humans into misusing science and technology to create this version of the anti-Christ.

THE ANTI-CHRIST IS LIVING AMONG US AS AN ENERGIZED, COLD APPARATUS AND MECHANICAL SYSTEM

AIMING TO DEPRIVE US OF OUR OWN PERSONAL FREEDOM AND THE FEELING CAPABILITY OF OUR HEART

IT'S SEDUCING US TOWARDS BECOMING CONTROLLED

BY AN OVERRULING ENTITY
THAT WILL TAKE RESIDENCE IN OUR MINDS
AND IT AIMS TO
TAKE OVER THE WORLD

With free will, there is free choice. It's the responsibility of every human to choose and decide whether they want to live their life in the awareness and consciousness of their Spirit and Heart / Soul or whether to focus on matter, materialism, and the newest advances of technology and science.

In Part III, Section 1, Chapter 8, I spoke of the great shift around 5,000 BC from the Matriarchate to the Patriarchate. Currently, the human race is undergoing another critical turning point that will forever impact life on Planet Earth and alter our reality. It started with the Industrial Revolution taking place between 1760-1840. It brought about sweeping changes in economic and social organization as it transformed economies that had been based on agricultural and handicrafts into economies based on large-scale industry, mechanized manufacturing, and the factory system.

It also impacted how moving devices and machines were powered and the way goods were transported. This developed further to form the big corporations of this world that control our economy nowadays. The Industrial Revolution was followed by the age of science and mass production, and then the digital age.

When technology was introduced, it became the first stepping stone toward a future of artificial intelligence (AI). It's clear that technology and science have brought us many advances that are highly beneficial. Yet, technology and science used in the absence of God, the denial of the Source of Light as the ultimate truth and reality, in combination with the denial of our Heart and Soul, and the overruling of Nature will lead to what will ultimately become the downfall of humanity.

TECHNOLOGY AND SCIENCE USED
IN THE ABSENCE OF GOD AND
THE DENIAL OF THE SOURCE OF LIGHT —
IN COMBINATION WITH THE DENIAL
OF OUR HEART AND SOUL
AS THE ULTIMATE TRUTH AND REALITY
AND THE OVERRULING OF NATURE —
WILL LEAD TO WHAT WILL ULTIMATELY BECOME
THE DOWNFALL OF HUMANITY

Therefore, it's not the use of science and technology but the abuse of it with an arrogant and narcissistic mindset that could turn this planet into a man-made domain absent of God and its creative Source.

IT IS THE ABUSE OF SCIENCE AND TECHNOLOGY WITH AN ARROGANT AND NARCISSISTIC MINDSET THAT COULD TURN THIS PLANET INTO A MAN-MADE DOMAIN ABSENT OF GOD AND THE CREATIVE SOURCE

We must face the fact that in our current age and time, it has become evident that the world population at large is falling victim to the Luciferian approach to life. One such trap is how deeply we've become embedded in matter and regard technology and science as the ultimate truth.

There is simply no way we can deny the importance materialism, science, and technology have gained such prominence in our lives. (Compare with the "Dark Powers of Evil": Part V, Section 5, Chapter 53 where I'm outlining the dangers of dealing with evil).

HUMANITY HAS FALLEN VICTIM TO THE LUCIFERIAN APPROACH TO LIFE THE POPULATION AT LARGE HAS BECOME EMBEDDED IN MATTER AND REGARDS TECHNOLOGY AND SCIENCE AS THE ULTIMATE TRUTH

An example everyone can relate to is the computer.

According to Quora, less than a hundred years ago, the first programmable computer, the Z1, was built in 1936 by German Konrad Zuse and "Is considered to be the first electro-mechanical binary programmable computer and the first functional computer."[30]

---

[30] From 1939 - 1944, Aiken, in collaboration with IBM, developed the first fully functional computer, the Harvard Mark 1. It was more than fifty feet long (15 meters), weighed five tons, and consisted of approximately 750,000 parts, mostly mechanical.

The fast development from its monstrous size to a small office desk model is being argued as the result of information gained by the capture of aliens from the Zeta Reticuli star system[31] (Part V, Section 10, Chapter 64 "Galactic Experiences and Encounters," on the alien beings of the star system Zeta Reticuli) known as "The Greys / The Grey Aliens" that possess extremely highly developed minds but crippled feeling centers, according to Harvard professor / psychiatrist / Pulitzer Prize winner, John Mack.

Computer technology is so quickly advancing and the percentage of humans whose lives depend on their computer, for professional purposes or for private use, is overwhelmingly high. Cell phones came into use less than forty years ago and by now, almost every adult even in the remotest areas of the globe has a cell phone.

Computers, though extremely helpful in many ways, are also throwing our lives out of balance. For one, we rely on computers for information, communication, research, on-line shopping, storing and processing data, calculations, and more. Apparently, it's been proven that computers are more reliable than humans when driving cars. Though I doubt this, especially with pedestrians or someone in a wheelchair crossing the street.

ENIAC (Electronic Numerical Integrator and Computer), the world's first supercomputer

Artificial Intelligence "doctors" can already analyze medical images with superhuman accuracy and speed. According to *Forbes* magazine, there is "no doubt AI has fundamentally changed and enhanced our lives. Our cities are connected, our homes are smarter, and the way we do business is more efficient."

Where is the inherent respect for our Heart / Soul and God / Spirit? Where is the love for our planet and Nature? Has humanity so deeply forgotten that we fail to remember our very origin?

Again and again, the Luciferian approach to life denies the existence of our inherent Soul, the existence of Source / God / Spirit and thus we have fallen victim to the devil and ignited the technological age that might well burn us all into non-existence.

The global workforce is undergoing a massive technological shift that many are calling the "fourth Industrial Revolution." According to a recent World Economic Forum report, nearly a third of the most important skill sets in 2025 will be comprised of technology skills not yet considered imperative to the job today and which are just beginning to emerge. Could we wake up one morning dumbstruck that a super-powerful AI has emerged, with disastrous consequences?

Andrew Ng, one of the world's most prominent AI experts, has said, "Worrying about AI turning evil is a little bit like worrying about

[31] The inhabitants of the Zeta Reticuli.

overpopulation on Mars." Yet, books like *Super-Intelligence: Paths, Dangers, Strategies* by Nick Bostrom ("If machine brains surpass human brains in general intelligence, then this new super-intelligence could replace humans as the dominant life form on Earth.") and *Life 3.0: Being Human in the Age of Artificial Intelligence* by Max Tegmark argue that malevolent super-intelligence is an existential risk for humanity.

AI might well take over the world. Super-intelligence is quickly emerging and sooner or later, AI technology could turn us from masters into slaves. We are already enslaved — and this is by choice — by computer technology.

The computer, with its seemingly endless qualities and capabilities, may lead to overuse and easily to addiction. We've turned computers into an addiction. Children and adolescents, if not monitored, become automatically entranced with the Internet, virtual reality, and all forms of technology. Steve Jobs had his reasons for forbidding his kids' use of the iPad. I have witnessed this with my two small grandchildren who would throw a fit if their time spent on their computer was cut short.

We Are Enslaved by Computer Technology Computer Technology Has Turned into An Addiction

Our global population needs to become aware of the dangers involved in the misuse of computers. Our human family needs to return to the true values of life because — sadly — our chosen path is leading humanity into a cul-de-sac from where there is no exit to escape.

Experts warn that the overuse of computers and technology by children can lead to behavioral problems because of less time spent in physical and interactive play with others, which results in the loss of social and communication skills. Human contact and communication is all too often exchanged for spending time surfing the web and engaging in computer games, even while in the company of a friend, loved one, or group.

With all this constant immersion in technology, there are some very real concerns about how this tech impacts childhood development. We are wandering into unknown territory as past generations have never had this same kind of constant technological immersion. The American Academy of Pediatrics published in November of 2013 an article based on research that states "The average eight to ten year old spends almost 8 hours a day with a variety of media, and older children and teenagers spend around 11 hours per day with media. Indeed young people are spending more time with technology than they do in school."

"Children and teenagers around the country aren't cutting down their media consumption either. Some teenagers say they send thousands of text messages each month, stay up until 2 AM scrolling social media, and spend hours each day playing video games. And this has continued to get more intense over time, as more apps and options arise to distract kids." In addition, the pressure of peers and negative role models are adding up to the serious problem we're facing.

Some of the effects of spending a lot of time on computers are:

- **Lower attention span.** Teachers, parents, and students themselves find that technology can have a direct impact on attention spans. The immediacy of technological interactions make waiting harder for children. With technology, they aren't forced to wait. They can have their TV show immediately, they don't get bored because they always have something to entertain them. Technology moves fast, instant responses, and instant gratification are impacting attention spans for young children and teenagers alike.

- **Increased risk and lack of privacy.** Children and teenagers have grown up in a technological world, and the idea of privacy is somewhat foreign to them. Cybersecurity is a huge element of tech today, but it isn't always perfect. Hackers and criminals can utilize technology to steal identities and harass children.

- **Risk of depression.** Teenagers and children who report more time using media are more likely to also report mental health issues. Depression is a key issue that is correlated with more media use. This has increased suicide rates and has led to more youth needing mental health interventions like medicine and counseling. Experts believe time spent on social media or using technology can directly be tied to increased depression.

- **Obesity.** Children who spend more time inside on their phones or tablets don't spend as much time running and playing outside. They establish habits of technology use that don't involve exercise. This can lead to increased obesity rates in children and young adults.

- **Falling grades.** Many students today can see their grades take a hit when they spend more time with technology. Increasing technology usage means less time spent on homework, and the kind of developmental changes technology can bring can make students struggle with homework like reading and writing.

- **Bullying.** As technology flourishes, so does bullying. Children and teens are using technology and social media to bully other kids, without having to face them. Often called cyberbullying, this trend is increasing and getting more popular with even younger students.

- **Social interaction issues.** With more time spent on technology, younger children are having issues with face-to-face social interactions. Many seem to prefer to text or talk on social media as opposed to talking to each other in-person. Even when children spend time together, they may spend more time texting or on their phones than actually being together.

It is also a proven fact that too much screen time can lead to cybersickness with symptoms of nausea, oculomotor issues, and general disorientation due to the absence of physical motion. Furthermore, it can lead to isolation. The right measure and balance is required when using computers.

Is it becoming clear to you why I keep emphasizing the dangers involved with the Luciferian approach to life? It is high time for all of us to open our eyes to the evident dangers our global family is facing, or we might be forced to wake up to a nightmare we've created by forgetting our true heritage and aligning ourselves with the devil.

While AI and computer science are clearly almost indispensable tools for this time and age, there is another tremendous danger we must consider. The more we rely on technology, the further we move away from our human inheritance of Spirit / God / Source and our Heart / Soul.

THE MORE WE RELY ON TECHNOLOGY, THE FURTHER WE MOVE AWAY FROM OUR HUMAN HERITAGE OF SPIRIT / GOD / SOURCE AND OUR HEART / SOUL

- We're becoming an emotionally deadened society, yet at the same time swinging to extreme emotional reactions. We're devolving into a one-dimensional, low-level consciousness; becoming a nation of ADD narcissists hell-bent on immediate gratification, self-indulgence, constant distraction, and feeding our egos to the point of losing all perspective about ourselves and life.

- We're using computers as a substitute for relationships with other human beings, we've become out of balance and that's causing all sorts of social problems, for adults and children alike.

The Globe Newswire in September 2021 published that the "global virtual reality in gaming market size was US $6.26 billion in 2020. In 2020 there were more than 57 million VR users in the US and 90.9 million AR users. The market is projected to grow from US $7.92 billion in 2021 to US $53.44 billion in 2028."

The Wakeup Call

What is happening to humans?! Is real life too challenging to show up and engage in true and authentic values? Large groups of individuals are falling for artificially created universes rather than explore the real and true life we were gifted with by Nature, God, and the universe. The boredom with life and the need for escapism due to lack of connection to God / Source create an ignorance of the higher creative forces. Clearly, the absence of Soul / Spirit and, on the deepest level, the profound confusion as to the true purpose of life leads individuals further astray from their Heart and Soul. And in doing so are selling their Soul to the devil.

THE ABSENCE OF HEART / SOUL / SPIRIT AND THE PROFOUND CONFUSION AS TO THE TRUE PURPOSE OF LIFE

LEADS TO THE FACT THAT LARGE GROUPS OF INDIVIDUALS ARE FALLING FOR ARTIFICIALLY CREATED UNIVERSES

RATHER THAN EXPLORE THE REAL AND TRUE LIFE OF NATURE, GOD, AND THE UNIVERSE

Where is the wonder of the miracle of life, where is the sacredness of respecting the values of God's creation, where is the importance of virtues and the core essence of who we truly are: Spirit, Heart, and Soul?! Do we seriously consider becoming half humans with a highly developed mind but with an absence of Spirit and crippled in the awareness of our Heart and Soul?!

With the deadening of emotions due to lack of Heart / Soul / Spirit the arrogant, narcissistic mind is ruling life, and there is no place for the Heart, Soul, and Spirit. The Heart has become empty and the connection to one's innermost self and God residing in the Heart is lost.

THE CONNECTION TO ONE'S INNERMOST SELF AND GOD RESIDING IN THE HEART IS LOST

Where does it lead when the negation of Heart, Soul, and Spirit is combined with a brilliant mind curious to get absorbed in science and technology, ready to invent in labs artificial life forms that mimic the work of the Creator Source? The brilliant Albert Einstein admitted that the more he learned, the less he knew.

> "There are only two ways to live life:
> Either as if there is no Miracle or
> as if everything is a Miracle."
>
> ~ Anonymous

Indeed, this is a time of great change for our planet and humanity. More and more, it's becoming evident that we, the inhabitants of planet Earth, are obviously splitting into two categories. One group being those who believe in God / Spirit and the Heart / Soul, and the other group denying and rejecting such a reality and aligning with materialism, technology, and science. And by doing so, they are loosing their true identity and become half-humans, slowly shifting from a purely human existence towards an artificial intelligence that ultimately will threaten to rule over us.

HALF-HUMANS POSSESS A HIGHLY DEVELOPED MIND AND A CRIPPLED HEART AND SOUL

Note: According to Austrian philosopher, mystic and clairvoyant Rudolf Steiner (1861-1925), the founder of the spiritual movement called Anthroposophy, the human being is a threefold being of Spirit, Soul, and body whose capacities unfold in three developmental stages on the path to adulthood: early childhood, middle childhood, and adolescence. Steiner worked to establish various practical endeavors, including Waldorf education, biodynamic agriculture, and anthroposophical medicine. Steiner advocated a form of ethical individualism, based on a belief that there is a spiritual dimension to the human being and to all of life.

The Waldorf philosophy departs from traditional education in that it seeks to educate not only the child's mind but also their heart and body. Waldorf education works on the basis that children's creative, spiritual and moral dimensions need as much attention as their intellectual ones. Steiner was also a man of artistic talent as a sculptor and architect who saw the arts as a vital bridge between the material and spiritual worlds,

Steiner, in 1917, predicted the following:

"The time will come — and it may not be far off — when quite different tendencies will come up at a congress like the one held in 1912 and people will say: It is pathological for people to even think in terms of spirit and soul. 'Sound' people will speak of nothing but the body. It will be considered a sign of illness for anyone to arrive at the idea of any such thing as a spirit or a soul.

People who think like that will be considered to be sick and — you can be quite sure of it — a medicine will be found for this. At The Council of Constantinople the spirit was made non-existent. [The doctrine of reincarnation]. The soul will be made non-existent with the aid of a drug. Taking a 'sound point of view,' people will invent a vaccine to influence the organism as early as possible, preferably as soon as it is born, so that this human body never even gets the idea that there is a soul and a spirit.

The two philosophies of life will be in complete opposition. One movement will need to reflect how concepts and ideas may be developed to meet the reality of soul and spirit. The others, the heirs of modern materialism, will look for the vaccine to make the body 'healthy,' that is, makes its constitution such that this body no longer talks of such rubbish as soul and spirit, but takes a 'sound' view of the forces which live in engines and in chemistry and let planets and suns arise from nebulae in the cosmos. Materialistic physicians will be asked to drive the souls out of humanity."[32]

Different religions and wisdom traditions have prophesies about the end of the world as we know it. According to the Hopi, we are about to the enter the fifth world. The time of plenty is ending precisely because governments around the world are eliminating Indigenous Tribes. The devastation unfolding is incalculable. Hopi prophesies speaks of the "Powateoni – Day of Purification," described as an apocalypse or a "world-engulfing cataclysm" that will "lead to the destruction of planet Earth as we know it." Hopi elders warn about Western man's way of life being out of balance with the Creator's Law.

Today, forces are being unleashed that will challenge the very foundations of society. The Hopi foresaw the "talking cobwebs" (Internet) and "flying villages (virtual reality) generations before these things came into being. Theirs is the knowledge from deep within, long before the computer that is causing us to lose clarity and the pollution that is killing life itself.

According to the Hopi elders:

"Science can dismiss these prophecies as mere superstition, as mere coincidence that cannot be proved or disproved. But to the Hopi, the psychic pattern of the mind lives connected to its counterpart, the events of the worlds that unfold in the physical realm.

The elders warn we're facing a more radical change in civilization than has ever occurred in the human time frame. The dominant society so very bent on subjugation and extraction of resources has 'stirred the underground serpent,' which is bound to wreak future military and ecological havoc.

The elders of the Hopi emphasize that the contest today is between those who subscribe to such prejudice and those

---

[32] October 7, 1917. Rudolf Steiner, 1861-1925. *The Fall of the Spirits of Darkness*, p.85. Rudolf Steiner Press, 1993.

who recognize the human family as a balancing influence within nature.

If the mentality that rules the modern world wins, and the true caretakers of land and life lose charge of their trust, the human sojourn in this world will come to a painful conclusion, along with almost every other life form."

~ According to an interview of
Cyril Christo / Marie Wilkinson with Hopi Elders

The Aztecs, and before them the Maya, also foresaw the end of the world as we know it.

The planet's major religions each have their own beliefs about the end of the world, the triumph of good over evil and Judgment Day. In Christianity, the Book of Revelation, the last chapter of the Bible's New Testament, mentions Armageddon, the final battle on Earth between the forces of God and satan.

In Islam, the end of the world is referred to as "the Hour" and involves Jesus returning to Damascus to slay an anti-Christ who has put the planet in peril. With the anti-Christ out of the picture, a period of perfect harmony will ensue. Jesus will later die a natural death, which will usher in a time of destruction that leads directly to "the Hour."

In Judaism, there is no term for Armageddon, but there are references in the Hebrew bible to events that could be compared with Armageddon, including the "Day of the Lord."

In <u>Hinduism</u>, there is the story of the god Vishnu coming back in the last cycle of time as a figure called Kulki, who rides a white horse, carries a sword that looks like a comet and destroys the forces of evil.

In some Buddhist prophecies, the equivalent of Armageddon is Shambhala, in which good triumphs over evil. However, the planet is restored rather than destroyed so people can pursue enlightenment.

The Vedas speak of the four Yugas (Seasons of the Universe) that keep repeating themselves on planet Earth / Gaia:

- Kritya / Satya Yuga: most harmonious and beneficial season lasting 1,728,000 years

- Treta Yuga lasts 1,296,000 years

- Dvapara Yuga lasts 864,000 years

- Kali Yuga: worst cycle of the universe lasts 432,000 years before Kritya Yuga returns. Kali Yuga began 5,122 years ago and has 426,878 years left as of 2021. Kali Yuga will end in the year 428,899 CE.

The Remedy

Each of the prophesies state that after the great battle of evil versus Light, peace and harmony will return to Earth.

The Hopi elders say,

> "'Have we begun the period of the third and final world shattering event, WWIII, the separation from nature?' The elders believe that if the US government continues to impose its jurisdiction and its way of life, not only will the traditional Hopi way of life and a covenant with the Creator be compromised, but mankind's very survival will be jeopardized. Caretaking is at the center of Native peoples' concerns for millennia. 'They hold the universe in their hands,' as the elders exclaim. But today, they have lost the power to fulfill their 'true role.'
>
> The people of Indigenous tribes know that any empire built on conquest must inevitably crumble. That is what we are seeing today. True title [to take care of Life rather than destroy Life] was implemented by the forces that give life. As we can plainly see today, America and the world are reaping the results of conquest, extraction and subjugation of the land, its first peoples and other species on whom we depend for our survival. The results will be played out in our lifetime. 'In a world where rulership can be seized by the strongest army, fulfillment of our trust as caretakers requires that we learn how to place wisdom in power.'"

~ According to an interview of
Cyril Christo / Marie Wilkinson with Hopi Elders

The Hopi prophesies also say that after having passed this period of apocalypse, of social and ecological disruption, the time will come that will eventually bring a time of lasting peace over the world's people. But before that, we will have to go through the eye of the storm. Languages are fading away. And with them knowledge or rather a far-reaching wisdom about how the world actually works that is far more radical than what science understands and what the dominant society is trying to find with the search for the most minute particles and black holes.

Not long ago, Davi Kopenawa, an elder of the Yanomami of the Amazon, whose people have suffered invasions of their land, killings by foreign gold miners and unprecedented fires, told the world, "Whatever is happening to us, will happen to you." Listening, respecting, and acting on the wisdom of the first peoples of the world may save civilization.

The over-chemicalization of our planet, pharmaceuticals, opioids, recreational drugs, in short the malaise that plague humanity can be tied in with how we're de-naturing ourselves. According to Von Holstein,

"A human being is a part of the whole, called by us a 'Universe' …

The delusion of separation is a kind of prison for us …

Our task must be to free ourselves from this prison by widening our circle of compassion

To embrace all living creatures

And the whole of Nature in its beauty."

~ Albert Einstein

author of *Nature Spirits and What They Say: Messages from Elemental and Nature Beings* says,

> "The huge problem with genetically modified food and cloned animals is that there is no Soul. They are artificial. Plants represent the forces of life. When humans change the life of plants, they change the whole world. A genetically engineered change is a violent change. Something gets cut. With every genetically modified plant, you change the etheric body of the Earth. Eating such food results in the quality and thus in the deterioration of the etheric body of the human energy field. Many more metabolic disorders will arise as a result. But, as a result of producing it, humans have to eat such food. However, such food is not infusing them with life force but rather humans eat up their own disgrace."

According to Von Holstein, the elemental beings and nature spirits further warn, "With the ever-increasing use of radio frequency radiation and 5G, and the electro smog being produced, the energetic belt around the Earth is becoming more and more shielded off from allowing cosmic energy in, which carries with it the intelligence of the cosmos. Through the infiltration of cosmic energy, we are connected to the universe and the larger intelligence. Becoming blocked off from the rest of the cosmos is apparently what the evil powers of darkness, the devil / satan intend in order to take over control of Earth."

As revealed in interviews with elemental beings and nature spirits, chronicled by Verena Stael von Holstein in her book, all substance carries consciousness. This is the reason why all life is sacred — because all substance is infused with consciousness. From the lowest vibratory field, like that of a stone, to the highest vibratory field of a human. All possess a level of consciousness or spirit. In addition, animals and humans have a Soul.

Trees have a tree Spirit. I was once fortunate enough to see the Spirit of a tree. I was sitting in my old house here on the property in my office in front of my computer. Contemplating on I don't remember what, I stared without focusing on anything special. As I was simply lost in time, I became aware that a very elongated face was looking at me approximately sixteen inches long by six inches wide. It had eyes, a nose and even a mouth. It wasn't smiling, but was more on the serious side. The expression was one of utter benevolence.

It is time humanity chose either the path of annihilation or the path of everlasting life.

I realized I was seeing the Spirit of the nectarine tree I had planted a couple of years ago. That was when the face vanished. At the HeartPath Retreat Center, we have three huge cottonwood trees that are a few hundred years old. I can only fathom how extremely large the faces of those tree Spirits must be if the trunk of my nectarine was two inches in diameter and had a face 16 x 6 inches.

The Hopi prophesies predict that if the wisdom of the Ancient World prevails, our peaceful tenure could last indefinitely. It is time humanity chose either the path of annihilation or the path of everlasting life.

It is clear that our beautiful and magnificent planet, mother Gaia, the Earth has become a battleground. The Hopi elders are right, we are in WWIII. We're fighting a battle of bio weaponry between evil and Light, between the cold mind / materialism / technology / science and Spirit / Heart / Soul. At present, the Luciferian approach to life has the upper hand.

Light	Evil
Universe	Cold Mind
Source	Materialism
Spirit	Technology
God	Science
Nature	Artificial Intelligence
Heart / Soul	Half Humans

Yet, as it often is in battles, the large masses of soldiers have zero clue as to the deeper reasons for the fight while the handful of war leaders are delegating the battle from a safe spot at the top. Except in this battle, there are going to be no losers and winners. This battle is so serious that unless it does come to a stop, we all go under together.

It is high time Humanity wakes up. Our Human Family is in this battle together. We must unite towards the common goal to save our planet. We still can. We must find the right measure of using technology and science yet also become fully aware of our inherent human heritage: Nature, Spirit / God / Source, and our Heart and Soul. It must become clear to each one of us that these — and not materialism — are our everlasting possession that we cannot risk to lose.

The documentary, *Islands of Faith*, presents a number of small communities in Southeast Asia that help themselves by helping Nature and living in accord with Nature through the means of faith, saying that Nature is the most concrete proof of God's Glory. In all the holy scriptures, the idea of Heaven is described with elements of Nature.

"Nature is the most concrete proof of God's Glory."
~ Anonymous

"We are neither born into the world without suffering the pain of birth nor pass through adolescence without experiencing doubt and heartache. Humanity as an entity has just passed through puberty and stands on the threshold of adulthood. Like a teenager, we have suffered for a time and been subject to our weaknesses and impulses, but now we are growing up. As we enter the third millennium of the Common Era (more than the fourth millennium of recorded history) humanity is indeed ready to become a responsible adult."
Kosta Danaos
The Magus of Java

A community leader in Bali explains that their Hindu "Festival of Nyepi" / Day of Silence, a very sacred and important Hindu holiday and national holiday of the New Year, falls on the day following the dark moon of the spring equinox. The whole island community observes this festival over the course of one day and night by not leaving their homes, living without electricity, observing silence, fasting, meditating, and reviewing their values. The streets are off limits to everyone.

It's a 24-hour period that allows Nature to restore itself. The community leader says, "The impact is incredible on the macrocosmos and the microcosmos. Whether we realize it or not, the vibration is aligning itself in Nature's breath. Because balance is the key. And we achieve balance through control."

"It is to the holistic viewpoint afforded by Eastern Mysticism (and modern Western Science) that we must turn to if we wish to survive as a species. For most of us, the common people, the lessons of the East are simple. We need not indulge in consumerism or blindly follow the directives of special interest manipulators. We are each capable of thinking and deciding for ourselves. The road of life is one of balance, consequence, and simplicity."
Kosta Danaos
The Magus of Java

The system will collapse,
if we refuse to buy what they are selling —
their ideas, their version of history, their wars,
their weapons, their notions of inevitability.

Remember this: We be many and they be few.
They need us more than we need them.

Another world is not only possible,
she is on her way. On a quiet day,
I can hear her breathing.

~ Arundhati Roy

Chapter 95

CASPAR IN HIS OWN UNIVERSE

Caspar's upbringing was in an upper-middle class family with two siblings. His parents observed the common values of their community and participated in social aid programs. Caspar was a brilliant child who spent much time poring over reference books like the encyclopedia. It was clear to his parents that Caspar wanted to learn and excel. He also possessed a competitive mind.

Around the age of puberty, Caspar's parents became concerned about him. Although he did well in school and excelled in math and science, Caspar seemed bored and withdrawn. When asked what was happening for him, he admitted that he spent his time in the large underground city of mice. He was their ruling king and he would draw for hours the intrinsic passageways of the mouse city and their complex social activities. Caspar was living in a parallel universe with the mice.

His parents had Caspar psychologically tested and evaluated and had him in psychotherapy for a year. As a result, there was no more mention of the underground city of mice.

As soon as his parents allowed him a bit of regular computer time, Caspar withdrew from his peers and spent all his free time at the computer. He started to live in his own universe and was unable to identify with his classmates and their lives. Now even more concerned, his parents took him out of public school and enrolled him in a private school. There, he blossomed in nearly all his subjects and again excelled in math and science. But it became more and more evident to all, that Caspar had started to isolate himself and became a loner.

For certain, Caspar was entranced with what a computer could do and kept spending all his free time on the device. Peers were joking that Caspar wasn't looking for a girlfriend, he already has one to whom he devoted all his time. Caspar wrote a number of computer programs while continuing to score high in intellectual achievements. He also learned to hack computer systems and started to sell his expertise. He was a youth with a brilliant mind who sold his knowledge of computer technology to corporations.

At age seventeen, Caspar got accepted into MIT University to study computer science and electrical engineering with a focus on algorithms and data structures. He got his Masters after five years. Caspar was fascinated by sci-fi movies and deeply interested in the possibilities of artificial intelligence. He had found his field and saw it as the future's most profitable industry. He was hired by Boston Dynamics and worked there for five years. He was a firm believer that everything humans could do, robots could do, only better.

Caspar lived on his own, a very solitary life. Occasionally, he engaged in sex with call girls. At one point, he spent a bit of time with a young woman he found attractive but she ended the relationship on the basis of zero compatibility. Caspar admitted that he might not have any feeling centers in his brain.

Ever since his youth, he had always denied the existence of angels and deities. He even joked with statements like, "In case a God exists, that God must be so stupid as to have created the imperfection called 'man.'" Caspar went on to state that he would develop a robot much more advanced than any human ever could be. In short, Caspar was a firm atheist and agnostic, ready to lecture anyone willing to listen to his intelligent arguments that God doesn't exist and why. He believed that science clearly rules God out.

The Luciferian Wound in Caspar was evidenced by his exclusive focus on his brilliant mind and complete lack of awareness of the Heart / Soul / Spirit by worshiping technology, AI, and science as the most advanced strategy for life. Casper's arrogance and ridicule of God / Source of Light and his idolization of "man" in creating evermore advanced technology can be considered as evil due to the lack of his feeling center (the Heart), his inability to connect with others from the Heart, and his ignorance as to the higher order of God / Source, and regarding Nature and the Universe as sacred.

Chapter 96

A Dangerous Responsibility of Scientists Creating a Universe in the Lab

According to the journal *Nuclear Physics B*, physicists and cosmologists are currently in the process of creating universes in labs with the possibility of creating a whole new cosmos that might one day evolve its own stars, planets, and intelligent life. Some go as far as to state that our universe could have been made by an alien scientist. Others declare that scientists are aiming to "steal the feat of universe-making out of the hands of God."

Cosmogenesis, the evolution of the universe, is occupying the minds of scientists who also look into the consequences of creating universes in case this is truly possible. Where could it lead if scientists are taking on the role of cosmic creators? Humans are prone to failure and, in such a case, what would the repercussions involve? Would humanity be capable of handling the moral responsibilities?

What Moral Responsibilities Would Come with Fallible Humans Taking on the Role of Cosmic Creators

Alexander Vilenkin, the Leonard Jane Holmes Bernstein Professor of Evolutionary Science and director of the institute of Cosmology at Tufts University in Massachusetts, has been doing research on cosmic inflation, dark energy, cosmic strings and monopoles, quantum cosmology, and the multiverse for thirty-five years.

A theoretical physicist, he has written over 150 papers that were featured in the US, Europe, Russia and Japan and published books like *Many Worlds in One* and *Cosmic Strings and other Topological Defects*. He is responsible for introducing the ideas of eternal inflation and quantum creation of the universe from nothing. His work on cosmic strings has been pivotal. His findings state that the laws of quantum mechanics could have generated an inflating universe from a state in which there was no time, no space, and no matter.

The established principle in quantum theory is that pairs of particles can spontaneously, and momentarily pop out of empty space. But

Vilenkin argues that quantum rules could also enable a minuscule bubble of space itself to burst into being from nothing with the impetus to then inflate to astronomical scales. This means that our cosmos could thus have been burped into being by the laws of physics alone.

To Vilenkin, this result puts an end to the question of what came before the Big Bang. According to him, there was nothing before the Big Bang, which brought peace of mind to many cosmologists in regard to a universe without a prime mover, divine or otherwise.

Contrary to Vilenkin's philosophical beliefs, other theoretical scientists such as Don Nelson Page, a physicist at the University of Alberta in Canada and an evangelical Christian, noted for his early collaboration with Stephen Hawking on the nature of black holes, are firm in their belief that God created the Universe ex nihilo — from absolutely nothing. Page is a firm protagonist in asserting there is no way that even the most advanced physics hackers would be able to create a cosmos in a lab.

Yet other theoretical physicists on cosmogenesis, like Andrej Dmitriyevich Linde, a Russian-American and the Harald Trap Friis Professor at Stanford University, is one of the main authors of the inflationary universe theory, as well as the theory of eternal inflation and inflationary multiverse.

His vision of scientists creating a universe in a lab would require highly technical laboratory like the Large Hadron Collider (LHC), which is the world's largest and highest energy particle collider. It was built between 1998 and 2008 by the European Organization for Nuclear Research (CERN) in collaboration with over 10,000 scientists and hundreds of universities and laboratories, as well as more than 100 countries. It lies in a tunnel 27 kilometers (17 miles) in circumference and as deep as 174 meters (574 ft) beneath the France-Switzerland border near Geneva.

Creating a universe in a lab would require a seed particle called a "monopole." In particle physics, a magnetic monopole is a hypothetical elementary particle that is an isolated magnet with only one magnetic pole. It is hypothesized to exist by some models of physics, but has not yet been found. The theory is that with enough energy imparted into a monopole, it will start to inflate. Rather than growing in size within our universe, the expanding monopole would bend space / time within the accelerator to create a tiny tunnel leading to a separate region of space. Within the lab, one would see a tiny black hole looking very insignificant. Yet traveling through the tiny gateway, there would be a rapidly expanding baby universe created by scientists.

It appears that Linde's concept of cosmogenesis might still be essentially technological and therefore theoretical. Because of that, scientists who believe in God are not concerned about having their faith tested because cosmogenesis is not disturbing existing theological views.

Yet, what if scientists are even considering creating a universe one day that provides conditions for being inhabited by intelligent life? The consequences are too far out to even fathom.

The author of the book, _A Big Bang in a Little Room,_ by Zeeya Merali asks, "What if you could become God with the ability to build a whole new universe in the lab?" As startling as it sounds, modern physics suggests that within the two next decades, scientists may be able to do so. It also addresses the theoretical fact that once human scientists have created a universe in a lab, there would be little ability to control the evolutionary process of that universe. Since scientists are playing God, there are many ethical questions arising.

Eduardo Guendelman, a physicist at Ben Gurion University in Israel, conducts experimental and theoretical research programs in many cutting-edge areas such as creating baby universes in a lab. Apparently, Guendelman has no scruples and remains ignorant about the possible ramifications.

Other scientists are concerned and admit that cosmogenesis is a risky plateau to get involved with. Nobuyuki Sakai of Yamaguchi University in Japan, who proposed among other theories that a monopole could serve as the seed for a baby universe, admitted that cosmogenesis is a very concerning issue for humanity's future. At the same time, he also finds that ethical issues are not of immediate concern because the experiments are not yet realized.

The question of ethics versus scientific glory remains very concerning and many scientists are hesitant to comment. Philosopher Anders Sandberg, at the University of Oxford, questions the ethical implications of creating artificial sentient beings in computer simulations. To him, cosmogenesis is a moral obligation because "the rapid reproduction and proliferation of intelligent life, regardless of form, can be taken as something that has inherent value." In that case, cosmogenesis might actually be a moral obligation requiring moral responsibility.

The Significance of the Number "108"

According to the Himalayan Yoga Institute, "Astronomer, mathematician, and physicist Galileo Galilei said that the universe is written 'in mathematical language.' He maintained that the mysteries of creation itself could be solved through numbers and mathematical equations. Mystics of all traditions around the world, found that numbers offered more than scientific insight — they offered a secret language for awakening, a key to our own intuition and higher aspects of our being. Yogis found the number 108 to be such a key."

According to the mathematician Leonardo Fibonacci, who was born around A.D. 1170, it is believed that the number 108 "represents the unity and wholeness of existence." The well-known numerical "Fibonacci sequence" is also related to the golden ratio. The spiral arrangement of leaves or petals on some plants follows the golden ratio. Pinecones exhibit a golden spiral, as do the seeds in a sunflower, according to "Phyllotaxis: A Systemic Study in Plant Morphogenesis" (Cambridge University Press, 1994).

The number 108 has been called "nature's secret code," and "nature's universal rule." It is said to govern the dimensions of everything from the Great Pyramid at Giza to the Nautilus seashell.

Considered to be the most auspicious number of all, the number 108 has always been a highly revered number for thousands of years, sacred in many spiritual traditions, and given special significance in meditation and prayer. Additionally, the number 108 has significance in regard to the distance between the Earth and the Moon and between the Earth and the sun.

In yoga, the number 108 refers to spiritual completion. Pranayama cycles are often repeated in 108 cycles and sun salutations are often completed in nine rounds of the twelve postures, which when multiplied, equals 108. Ancient yogis believed we can attune ourselves to the rhythms of creation by completing practices in rounds of 108.

This number seems to connect the ancient world to the modern world, as well as the physical realm to the metaphysical realm. The number 108 is sacred in mathematics, geometry, astrology, numerology, and in many world religions and spiritual traditions.

CONCLUSION

Whan on May 3rd of 2021 I started my task of writing *When the Soul Calls*, my known purpose was to present a large variety of different case studies to the reader. I had zero clue that soon enough the Spirit of the book would take over and guide me to bring to paper so much more than a repertoire of my vast 30+ years of work experience. By July 24th of the same year I had completed 99 chapters.

While David, my editor, worked on those, I received from Spirit chapter titles which I was to fill with content. I obeyed and now, within nine months, *When the Soul Calls* is finished and contains a total of 108 chapters, the most sacred number in the universe.

Recounting all those sacred stories of deep healings entrusted to me has not only been deeply humbling but also truly rewarding. There is hope for a healthier world to arrive for us all — given that everyone contributes in their own way — by healing our personal lives from the inside out.

If each and every human became fully conscious of the importance of their Soul, what a world this could become. We would all live as it was intended for us to live. Indeed, we'd enjoy a life in paradise. Truly, together, we could establish Heaven on Earth. We could eliminate hatred, fear and separation and would live without famine, wars, social conflicts, and sickness.

If our lives as individuals and life as a whole become infused with the right values —God / Spirit / Source present in our everyday lives and our focus on our Hearts and Souls — we could all become healthy, happy, and whole.

> "Most people do not want freedom, because freedom involves responsibility, and most people are frightened by responsibility."
>
> ~ Sigmund Freud

Every single one of us would live in abundance, joy, and inner peace. We would all have enough, in fact much more than we would need because there is more than enough for everyone. All that matters is that power and resources be distributed fairly and justly holding the intention of the wellbeing of every sentient being.

> "When we heal the Earth,
> we heal ourselves."
>
> ~ David Orr

BOOK TWO

THE PATH OF SOUL

PART VIII

DEEP REFLECTIONS

INTRODUCTION

The more the following deep wisdom reflections were revealed, the clearer it became to me that this content needed to be separated into a second book. Because both books are closely related due to the personal healing content of Book 1 with all the different case studies, the following material concentrates on universal truths and ethics principles that become the base of personal inner healing for which we are all held personally responsible.

In many ways, the material of Book 2, *The Path of Soul*, is the matrix upon which we grow our inner awareness and raise our consciousness to higher levels of Soul growth. Here is a short summary of the book's content.

Part VIII is a series of discussions, "Deep Reflections," comprised of ten chapters focusing on spiritual teachings.

The opening chapter covers "The Two Opposing Forces: Good and Evil / Destiny and Fate" and ends with a description of "The Two Pillars of Living Your Life: The Wrong Pillar and the Right Pillar."

In Curses and Blessings," I introduce information on corresponding entities that are called into existence by either curses or blessings.

The chapter "Morals vs. Ethics / Religion vs. Spirituality" is an elaboration on the meaning and common understanding of morals and explains the fundamental difference between morals and ethics. Likewise, it continues on to explain the differences between religion and spirituality.

"Heaven / Hell and the Purgatory In Between" looks at these terms from the vantage point of various world religions, beginning with the beliefs of the ancient Egyptians, and moving on to Buddhism, Christianity, Judaism, and Islam.

"The 42 Ideals of Maat" lists a code of ethics and virtues that were practiced by the ancient Egyptians and out of which the Ten Commandments were formed at a much later time.

'The Universal Law of Expansion and Contraction' explains the natural flow of the universe and the value for our personal life by understanding and working with that law.

"The Evolutionary Path of the Soul" describes in detail the journey Soul undergoes in its countless incarnations, from primitive organism to enlightenment, and to the perfection of the Soul.

"Metta: The Responsibility of the Soul" includes many explanations and examples on the importance of this concept, and what it means to be of service to another's Soul while serving one's own Soul in the highest Light of Divinity.

"The Tao / Sufi / Tantric Path: Seeking Union with the Divine" is a comparison of these three wisdom traditions as a paradigm for living in alignment with the Universal laws and Nature while seeking the merging of the Human Soul and the Divine.

"Life as a Spiritual Path: A Reason, a Time and a Season" is an elaboration of my personal life experience of letting go of the HeartPath Retreat Center, as seen from the level of the Soul, and introduces the concept of impermanence and the perfect natural law and order underlying all deeper truths.

The final chapter, "Full Circle: When the Soul Calls," pays homage to the HeartPath Retreat Center and the region of Santa Fe, New Mexico, which I call home.

Section 1

Chapter 97

GOOD & EVIL / DESTINY & FATE

A ll too often, I hear in my healing practice phrases such as, "There is nothing I can do. It is just meant to be. I cannot fight my destiny."

Many of us have heard or even used those phrases. But there is a huge misunderstanding as to what destiny actually is. We all know the difference between good and evil. Destiny and fate are simply other terms for good and evil. The best description I know of for destiny versus fate comes from the book *Chronicles of Tao by Deng Ming-Dao*, in which the grand master explains to his disciple the following:

> "Good and Evil exist as Destiny and Fate. Destiny is that which you must fulfill in this lifetime. During your life, you must continually strive to identify it and complete it to its last detail. This is a terribly intricate and unique enigma for each person that must slowly be brought to fruition. The issue at stake is nothing less than transcending the consequences of past lives in order to be reborn in a higher state or escape the cycle of rebirth altogether. That is Destiny.

> "Fate is an active agent that exists solely to deter you from fulfilling your destiny. It struggles against you, impedes your progress. Fate functions through illusion. It is responsible for mirages that lead you astray. It is temptation. It tricks you, fills your mind with grand notions and proud thoughts. Fate would like nothing better than to deter you from your goal. Whenever you think of doing wrong or playing a trick, and you become aware of yourself, you have found fate. Give in and fate has won. Resist and it has lost. But it will be there, tirelessly waiting to distract you once more."

Fate is an active agent that exists solely
to deter you from fulfilling your Destiny.

"This is what 'Heaven and hell are right here on Earth' means. Don't look outwardly for heavenly beings and hellish denizens. Look within you. Pursue your destiny and you are closer to heaven. Yield to fate and you slip toward hell. If you ultimately fulfill your destiny, you transcend human existence. If you fall to Fate, you suffer in a quagmire of delusion and ignorance."

Pursue your destiny and you are closer to heaven.
Yield to fate and you slip toward hell.
If you ultimately fulfill your destiny,
you transcend human existence.
If you fall to fate,
you suffer in a quagmire of delusion and ignorance.

"If you understand good and evil as destiny and fate, you understand that your actions alone move you toward one or the other. Nothing else enters into your life equation. Solve a bit of your Destiny and you triumph. Give in the slightest to delusion and your vision is all the more obscured."

Your actions alone
move you toward destiny or fate.

"All your actions have consequences. Put water over fire and it boils. Jump up and you will come down. Action and reaction.

In a person's life the strands of consequence can become hopelessly tangled, imprisoning him in a matted and thick web. Such a person will be reborn a thousand times. But a net can also catch fish. The strands can be knotted into a net of good.

This is the consequence of the devout person: The net of his past good actions continues to grow and generates more good, but he will still have to be reborn. The highest level is to transcend good and evil and erase one's consequences all together. Then one leaves the Wheel of Life. So there is such a thing as divine retribution. Divine retribution is your simple interaction of destiny, fate and consequence. That is all."

> The highest level is to transcend
> good and evil and erase one's consequences all together.
> Divine retribution is your simple interaction of
> destiny, fate and consequence.

Each and every human is born with a task, our personal life task.

- For many, this might be to find their voice and speak their truth. For some, this might be to leave their victimhood and scarcity behind and come into their own personal power where they take the reins of life into their own hands and live life with abundance.

- For others it could be to use power in constructive and creative ways instead of abusing their personal power and sabotaging their life.

- Yet for others, it could be to accept their life on Earth fully and ground themselves securely in their own being and start to feel safe from within and happy in their life.

- Yet again, others might need to find the right expression for their bottled-up creativity.

- Some might need to drop their mask of perfection and connect to their feelings and express themselves authentically and become transparent in who they are.

Our personal life task is unique to each individual and never easy to complete. It might feel like having to jump over our own shadow, something that's impossible to do. And yet, how glorious when we muster the courage and face the challenge to do so. It feels like we're given a new life, as if we gifted ourselves with real life to live for the first time.

Living your destiny is the greatest blessing you can give to yourself and your Soul. Apparently, Mother Theresa encouraged Princess Diana to accept her role in life. If it is your Destiny to live in a palace, then live in a palace. If you are meant to be a street sweeper, then be a content street sweeper for as long as you are meant to do it.

Most often, overcoming our greatest personal challenge is the very reason why our Soul keeps reincarnating into different bodies. What we don't accomplish in this lifetime, we carry over to the next life and so forth. Many individuals pass on to the afterlife without having been able to resolve their biggest challenge. They might be successful entrepreneurs, scientists, doctors, engineers, mothers, artists, musicians, therapists, etc., and share their gift with the world without being able to transform their biggest issue, their own personal life task.

When life is challenging, many give in to fate. We fall and stay lying on the ground. We give up and don't try to rise again. We behave like birds whose wings have been trimmed. It's much easier to give in than to stand up and face our challenges. It's much easier to live as fate dictates. It's much easier to live a life of compromise. It's much easier to choose the path of least resistance.

At some point, we were all aware of our dream and true purpose. Some of us dreamed big and were filled with conviction, to seek out Destiny and live our dream. Some dreamt of starting a family with the person of their dream at their side. They met someone they truly liked, someone with whom they felt in complete resonance with. But when that person was not available or they couldn't be with them for other reasons, they started to look around and laid eyes on someone who was quite nice, quite wonderful, quite capable. So it made sense and was logical to the mind to start a life with that person even if their Heart wasn't at all or only partially involved.

Others' dreams might have been to shine in the world as an actor, a musician, mathematician, doctor, or whatever. But then the road of life took a curve and behind it waited Fate. We accept that we might not make it as an actor, musician, mathematician, or doctor. We accept a job that is not our dream job knowing that our potential is far bigger and we could do so much more — but we accept the lesser and give in to Fate.

I most often observe the living of a compromise when it comes to matters of the Heart. How easily do we compromise and lose the shining luster our Soul had for our dream. How effortlessly do we allow ourselves to be lured into the trap of a small life where the light within us is dimmed to only a minute speck. How often do we let go of our passion for love and life and settle for comfort and financial security? How often do we allow our Heart to die?

When we are not living our dream and true life purpose, we are also not living our Destiny. And with that, Fate settles in and has won. The definition of living a fateful life is living a life where we are not meeting up with our Destiny. I need to make it clear that the big life we are dreaming of living doesn't have to big in terms of position or status or finances. When I speak of the big life of our Destiny, I refer to living the role our Soul wants us live. This can be as simple as escaping civilization and going to live a very ordinary life in the jungle.

LIVE THE LIFE
YOUR SOUL WANTS
YOU TO LIVE

It takes courage, perseverance, and faith to keep pursuing our dream and Destiny for our lives. Resist Fate and it has lost and with it, Destiny has won. But the grand master warns:

"Fate will remain there, tirelessly waiting to distract you again and again from your Destiny. This is what 'Heaven and hell are right here on Earth' means. Look within you. Pursue your Destiny and you are closer to Heaven. Yield to fate and you slip toward hell. If you understand Good and Evil as Destiny and Fate, you will also understand that your actions alone move you toward one or the other. Nothing else enters into your life equation. Solve a bit of your Destiny and you triumph. Give in the slightest to delusion and your vision is all the more obscured. So there is such a thing as divine retribution. Divine retribution is your simple interaction of destiny, fate, and consequence."

Pursue your Destiny and you are closer to Heaven. Yield to fate and you slip toward hell.

Solve a bit of your Destiny and you triumph. Give in the slightest to delusion and your vision is all the more obscured.

Since all our actions have consequences, we might well find ourselves living in hell when we're giving in to fate by living a life filled with compromise. When we live life as a compromise, our Heart begins to die. The mind might argue that it's the right choice to make for ourselves and for others involved but that so-called "right choice" will ultimately produce a negative backlash in our lives.

"You either get bitter or you get better. It's that simple.
You either take what has been dealt to you
and allow it to make you a better person,
or you allow it to tear you down.
The choice does not belong to fate,
it belongs to you."

~ Josh Shipp

CAUSE OF PAIN

Confusion Lack of conscious intention No awareness of purpose	Clarity Awareness and conscious intention Clarity of purpose
⬇	⬇
Off track from Source Lost	On track with Source In alignment
⬇	⬇
Pain	Joy
⬇	⬇
Confusion about life purpose	Clarity of life purpose
⬇	⬇
Block: Life purpose missed	Life purpose lived
⬇	⬇
Fate	Destiny

Chapter 98

TWO CHOICES OF LIVING YOUR LIFE — THE WRONG PILLAR AND THE RIGHT PILLAR

This theme is oftentimes addressed in my healing practice. Whenever relevant, I draw these two different pillars:

Two Choices of Living Your Life —

The Wrong Pillar and the Right Pillar

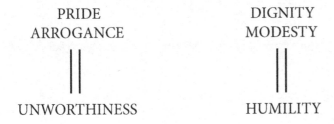

PRIDE   DIGNITY
ARROGANCE   MODESTY

UNWORTHINESS   HUMILITY

As we saw in the story of Jeremy, Part VII, Section 6, Chapter 92, the fall from pride into unworthiness is always a very painful one. To live life from pride and arrogance is never advisable because what we achieved today — and what makes us proud — we could lose tomorrow. We are dependent on our achievements and what we have and therefore define ourselves according to those. Much ego is attached to it.

When we have much and feel self-content, it's a good practice to view ourselves as having nothing and ask ourselves if we would still feel like the same person. Or if we would drop down the left pillar into unworthiness, self-doubt and insecurity given the situation that we've lost all our possessions, position, and status. If we have to admit that this would be the case, cultivating sincere self-love and respect for Self will provide a good remedy.

Living life in the Pillar of Dignity will never bring such defeat, despair, and pain. Dignity involves love of Self. With dignity, we view what we have achieved. With dignity we count our blessings. With dignity we face what is taken from us. We are not dependent of who we present ourselves to be to the world. We know internally who we are. We do not identify with our possessions. We feel secure whether we have or have not. Money is a means, a comfortable commodity, nothing more. The more we have, the more we are reminded to share and serve others.

We are not dependent of who we present ourselves to be to the world. We know internally who we are.

Section 2

Chapter 99

ON CURSES AND BLESSINGS + THE CORRESPONDING CREATION OF ENTITIES

"Whatever you're thinking about
Is literally like planning a future Event
When you are worrying, you are planning
When you're appreciating, you are planning …
What are you planning?"

~ Abraham Hicks

In my opinion, there are only curses and blessings in the Universe. Everything we feel, think, say, or do — in regard to ourselves and others — is either leaning towards a curse or a blessing. Therefore, it is to our benefit to become aware of our intentions in all of our behaviors in order to understand the full spectrum of what we are creating when we feel, think, speak, and act.

There are corresponding entities attached to curses and blessings of which very little is known. Curses create malicious entities while blessings create benevolent entities. Depending on the heaviness of the curse or the importance of the blessing, those entities correspond in size. When a whole group is involved in a curse or a blessing, whole groups of demon entities or blessing entities come into existence.

Curses create malicious entities while blessings create benevolent entities.

IT IS IMPORTANT
TO BE AWARE
OF OUR INTENTIONS
IN ALL OUR THOUGHTS, FEELINGS,
AND ACTIONS

We can best understand this by accepting the fact that matter always carries its energetic mirror. Much like for a photo to exist, there has to be the negative of the photo. For the human body to exist, there has to be its energetic counterpart. The energetic counterpart is the blueprint upon which we create ourselves. In each and every sense, we BECOME what we create.

WE BECOME
WHAT WE CREATE

What you do unto others,
you do unto yourself.

In our various roles as human beings, whether it be friend and companion, lover or spouse, parent or teacher etc., in private, in business and in public, we hold great responsibility to the physical, mental, emotional, and spiritual parts of ourselves and what we express in the world.

"A happy person is happy not because everything
is right in his life.
He is happy because his attitude towards everything
in his life is right."

~ Buddha

We are the creators of our environment. For example, a person who primarily communicates in negative ways such as "accusation mode" or "whine and complain mode" certainly spreads more curses than blessings. Likewise, it's the same with calculating individuals who continuously manipulate others by constantly reminding them of all they've done for them.

How we communicate is a direct mirror of how we treat ourselves. If my expression and language contains cuss words, what kind of mirror am I holding up for myself? Why do I keep using the "f" word and the "s" word and say, "Oh, it's just a habit." Seriously?! Is this what I intend to spread in my environment?

"Be mindful of your Self-Talk
It's a conversation with the Universe."

~ Anonymous

In the east of Switzerland, where I grew up, cursing and cussing is used by some in everyday discussions and seems to belong to a part of the population. As well, I have observed this phenomena around the world. Oftentimes, people aren't even aware of how many of those cuss words they constantly use. They remain ignorant of the fact that they are polluting the energetic environment with their behavior.

Proper use of language is very important[33]. Practicing language hygiene is imperative because it relates directly to what we create. If we constantly use meaningless word fillers, we manifest confusion because our thoughts are not clearly formed and aligned, and therefore they become a meaningless and wasted expression of ourselves.

MEANINGLESS WORD FILLERS
MANIFEST CONFUSION
AND BECOME A MEANINGLESS AND WASTED
EXPRESSION OF OURSELVES

In each and every way, we participate in manifesting evil if we speak lies. In the book of the *Nature Spirits*, it says that "If we speak lies, we create a demon of lies. If it's a white lie, it's a little demon. If it is a serious lie, a huge demon is created. Those demons become destructive forces around us. They work in favor of the dark powers of evil. Demons of lies can become so big that they possess humans. If a whole group of people spread the same lie, or dedicates itself to certain lies, larger demons are created."

It's important to become aware that every single thought creates an entity on the energetic level. It becomes an imprint. This is a very serious fact. Every thought corresponds to a being. Evil thoughts create evil beings. On the astral level, such thoughts have a stench, much like a corpse has on the physical level. When we cuss and curse, we create an evil entity. When we think in blessing ways, we create benevolent and blessing entities.

EVERY THOUGHT
CREATES AN ENTITY

CURSING THOUGHTS
CREATE EVIL ENTITIES

BLESSING THOUGHTS
CREATE BENEVOLENT ENTITIES

[33] Part III, Section, 2, Chapter 10: Language Hygiene.

It is of benefit to ask oneself: Do I show love and respect towards myself? Do I speak my truth, regardless? Do I take care of my needs? Do I set up proper boundaries between myself and my environment? Do I live according to who I am? Do I recognize my limits? Am I primarily a positive or negative thinking person? Do I live my life primarily out of fear or in trust? There are many more questions we can ask ourselves in regard to how we choose to express ourselves in the world.

We can safely assume that if we have to admit that our thoughts in general tend more towards the negative than the positive, then our thoughts, feelings, and actions are leaning more towards the curse side of the spectrum rather than the blessing side. Likewise, if we primarily worry rather than trust, our thoughts, feelings, and actions carry that worry and lean more towards a curse than a blessing. (Referring to the chart "Curses and Blessings" below, you might want to create a list for yourself and summon up where your focus and awareness are needed.)

CURSE	BLESSING
Negative Thinking	Positive Thinking
Worries, Fears & Anxieties	Trust, Confidence, Faith
Shame, Blame & Guilt	Gratitude & Recognition
Complaining & Regret	Acceptance
Resignation & Hopelessness	Hope & Joy
Reprimanding Oneself	Loving Oneself
Closed Mindedness	Open to Life's Adventure
Condemning Thoughts & Feelings	Constructive Thoughts & Feelings
Destructive Attitude	Creative Attitude
Limiting Beliefs	Willingness to Expand
Old & Set Beliefs	New Concepts of Life
Living in a Boring Routine	Enjoying Moment to Moment
Hanging on to the Past	Living in the Present Moment
Giving in or Giving up on Life	Trusting for the best to come
Arrogance towards others	Kindness towards others
Entitlement Behavior	Servitude and Humbleness

For example, we need to question the depth to which a child is psychologically affected by being consistently reprimanded and criticized by a parent without much praise and encouragement. The child constantly feels put down and this can have devastating effects on their psyche. I remember well a friend who never referred to her children as "My son or daughter." She constantly called them, "My stupid son, my stupid daughter."

Likewise, a teacher who says to a child, "You are too lazy, nothing will ever come of you!" is expressing that they don't foresee a bright future for the child. Oftentimes, encouragement is more beneficial, especially if the child has no positive role models. Parents and teachers hold such an important position when it comes to the emotional development of children.

You might be familiar with the anecdote about Thomas Edison's mother lying to her son about his expulsion from school due to mental deficiencies.

> One day, as a small child, Thomas Edison came home from school and gave a paper to his mother. He said, "Mom, my teacher gave this paper to me and told me only you are to read it. What does it say?"

> Her eyes welled with tears as she read the letter out loud to her child: "Your son is a genius. This school is too small for him and doesn't have good enough teachers to train him. Please teach him yourself."

> Many years after Edison's mother had died, he became one of the greatest inventors of the century. When he was going through a closet he found the folded letter from his old teacher. He opened it and found that the true message written on the letter: "Your son is mentally deficient. We cannot let him attend our school anymore. He is expelled."

> Edison then wrote in his diary: "Thomas A. Edison was a mentally deficient child whose mother turned him into the genius of the century."

While the account may not be true, it is correct that Edison was described by educators as "addled" and spent only a few months in a formal classroom before being taken out of school and educated by his mother. She might have told her son a white lie. Being taught by his mother who supported her son's genius was for certain a grander blessing for Edison than had he been subjected to a teacher who regarded him as addled.

All wisdom traditions state that blessings are beneficial while curses cause suffering. Blessings will return a hundred-fold to the sender. Likewise, curses return and cause the sender great pain.

"Life is an echo.
What you send out, comes back.
What you sow, you reap.
What you give, you get.
What you see in others, exists in you."

~ Zig Ziglar

Yet, what we say must be authentic and true. The words must be filled with one's essence, their Heart. If we keep saying to someone, "Oh, you're wonderful" or "I love you so much," etc. and we say these words simply out of habit and without truly believing them, we do more harm than benefit to ourselves and the other person. Then, they are simply words that are empty of essence and without meaning.

WHAT WE SAY MUST BE TRUE AND FILLED WITH OUR ESSENCE

WE MUST BELIEVE WHAT WE SAY

In the above-mentioned paragraph of the teacher calling the child lazy, it might be true that the child is lazy. Usually, there is a reason for a child to behave in certain ways. Children are conductors of the energy they are receiving. Therefore, a good teacher looks deeper than at the surface evidence and gives truthful, yet constructive, feedback.

Speaking the truth while being in one's Heart can become a powerful wakeup call that might lead to transformation in the other person's life. I have experienced this many times, in my private life and in my healing practice.

SPEAKING THE TRUTH OF THE HEART CAN BECOME A POWERFUL WAKEUP CALL THAT MIGHT LEAD TO TRANSFORMATION IN THE OTHER PERSON'S LIFE

Oftentimes in life, what might first look like a curse can later turn into a blessing. In my case, when my dad kept telling me, "Think, think, think! You cannot just feel!" it seemed like a curse because I apparently only operated in feeling mode. What at the time seemed like a curse in my adult life turned into a blessing. But as a child, what I wanted was to appease my dad and make him proud of me.

What do some famous Black models like Naomi Campbell, Grace Jones, and Iman possibly have in common? As adolescents, they kept growing taller, surpassing everyone in height. They were thinner and without hips and breasts developing. They might well have been ridiculed by their peers.

In our small and limited perspective, we are not able to distinguish what only time will reveal as the true nature of events and circumstances. Oftentimes, we might perceive something as a curse that later turns into a blessing, like the following tale shows.

> There once was a poor old man who owned a beautiful white horse. Whenever noblemen passed through the village, they always noticed the horse and offered very handsome sums of money for the stallion. But the old man always declined their offers, saying, "This horse is my friend. How can I sell my friend?"

> One morning the old man awoke to find the horse was gone. The village people gathered and said, "Old man, you were a fool not to sell the horse. You could have been wealthy! Now it has been stolen, and you have nothing. It is a great misfortune!" But the old man replied, "Don't go so far as to say that. Whether the horse was stolen or not, or whether it is a misfortune or a blessing is unknown. All we know is that the horse is not in the stable."

> Some days later, the horse returned, bringing with it several beautiful wild mares. Again, the village people gathered, and they said, "Old man, you were right! The horse wasn't stolen, and it wasn't a misfortune. It was a blessing, and now you have many fine horses!" But the old man replied, "Again, you go too far. Don't say it's a good thing, don't say it's a bad thing. Just say the horse is back. Whether it is a blessing or a misfortune is unknown."

> Some days later, the old man's only son began to train the wild mares, but he was thrown and trampled, and one of his legs was badly broken. Again, the village people gathered. "Oh, old man, you were right! It was not a blessing but a great misfortune, and now your only son is lame!" With a sigh, the old man replied, "Don't say it's a good thing, don't say it's a bad thing, just say my son has

broken his leg. Whether it is a blessing or a misfortune is unknown."

It happened that a few weeks later the country went to war, and all the able-bodied young men were forcibly taken for the military. Only the old man's son was passed over because he was crippled. The whole village was crying and weeping, for they believed their sons would probably be killed and never come home to them.

In their grief, they came to the old man and said, "You were right, old man, your son's injury has proven to be a blessing. Your son may be crippled, but he is with you, while our sons are gone forever!" The old man simply shook his head and said, "Will you never learn? Only say that your sons have been forced into the military and my son has not. More than that is not known."

~ Author Unknown

The point of this anecdote is that with our limited vantage point, the future is not known to us. What might appear as very promising in the present can turn into a less appealing direction. Likewise, what seemed to be a disadvantage might reveal itself to be fortuitous. Only the future will show.

I listened to a speech Marianne Williamson gave on A Course in Miracles. She spoke of an actor whose desperate wish was to get a role on Broadway. But she said, "What if God has an even bigger plan for that actor? If a famous director saw this actor in the local theater and felt he was perfect for a particular role in a Hollywood movie, would that actor want to be tied up for years in a Broadway Show?!" I doubt it!

We do not know Spirit's ways. How it would help if we had a bird's-eye-view' perspective and could see everything from above. When we arrive late because there was an accident and traffic was jammed, or a plane we thought we must catch gets rescheduled. We easily curse and cuss for our misfortune. But could it be that Spirit actually prevented something far worse that could have happened to us had we been on time?

The famous AA quote says it well:

"God, grant me the Serenity to accept the things I cannot change,
Courage to change the things I can,
and Wisdom to know the difference."

If our attitude for our life remains in trust and confidence, and if we keep focusing on our blessings every day — even when severely challenged — then our blessings will keep growing and we'll feel guided and protected regardless of what comes our way. We then create benevolent and blessing entities. Likewise, when we think in blessing ways, we are surrounded by benevolent and blessing entities.

"Anything that annoys you is teaching you patience.

Anyone who abandons you is teaching
you how to stand up on your own two feet.

Anything that angers you is teaching you
forgiveness and compassion.

Anything that has power over you is
teaching you how to take your power back.

Anything you hate is teaching you unconditional love.

Anything you fear is teaching you courage
to overcome your fear.

Anything you can't control is teaching you how to let go."

~ Jackson Kiddard

Chapter 100

Morals vs. Ethics / Religion vs. Spirituality

"Wrong is wrong
Even if everyone is doing it
Right is right
Even if no one is doing it."

~ Anonymous

The society we live in dictates the morals, rules, and social conventions by which we must live. Different societies teach and enforce different rules. The Hindu society has very different rules and morals than Christian society. A liberal Jewish society is organized differently than a strictly orthodox Jewish society. A Muslim society in Indonesia is very differently structured than the highly religious community in Saudi Arabia.

Whatever society and religious belief system we were born into or are living in, in order to fit in, we must succumb to those rules and regulations. If we fail to do so, we become outsiders and outcasts. Depending on how strict those regulations are, our lives might even be at stake.

For example, while living in the very Muslim country of Afghanistan, some European hippies were swimming in bikinis in a lake and got shot by the Mullahs. While living in Venezuela and Ecuador, I learned that it's imperative to always lock the house and car securely and to not leave anything laying around outside because it would be stolen. Whereas, while traveling in Japan, people told me that no one would ever touch foreign property and that it was absolutely safe to leave even very large amounts of cash in your hotel room.

Rules and regulations also depend on tribes. In Afghanistan, for example, the Hazāras people and the people from the northern tribes were generally referred to as being very honest, whereas employees from the nearby Istālif district were generally considered not so trustworthy. In general, Asians are known as hard working, Japanese as very clean, Chinese not so clean. Italians are considered as chaotic, Swiss as correct, and French as charming. These are generalizations and there are plenty of exceptions to the prescribed rules, morals, and social conventions of any group, community, or country.

In my practice as a counselor of the Soul, I don't follow the rules and regulations set by the American Psychological Association (APA). I never studied psychotherapy and never had a personal therapist. I was sent to a therapist for three or four sessions due to daydreaming as a child. When I became pregnant as a minor, an assigned state psychiatrist attested that I was capable of raising my child and didn't need a pro forma adopting agent assigned by the state.

When I studied with Barbara Brennan at her School of Healing on Long Island, NY, regular therapy sessions in Core Energetics was a requirement.

Apart from the above-mentioned experiences, I am quite unfamiliar with the regular set of rules for psychotherapists.

When I grew up in Switzerland, no one had a therapist. Psychotherapy was not viewed as a field of expertise to understand oneself better. People only sought out the aid of psychotherapy when something was seriously wrong, like a prolonged depression or suicidal thoughts. It is good that much of that has changed. In the US, especially, many individuals benefit from psychotherapy sessions, so much so, that it's an integral part of their life.

Whereas morals are rules and regulations devised by humans, ethics follow individual inner guidance. Ethics are inner principles such as knowing how to differentiate between right and wrong, good and bad. No outer authority is needed for that. But, ethics also differ depending on one's individual character, inner beliefs, and life experiences as influenced by such things as gender, age, wealth, ethnicity, ancestry, politics, education, and religion. They might have nothing or little to do with the common practice of certain social regulations. Ethics are based on deep inner convictions and are not necessarily in accordance with common morals, rules, and social conventions.

ETHICS ARE INNER PRINCIPLES BASED ON DEEP CONVICTIONS OF TRUTH AND INNER GUIDANCE

For example, even nowadays it's still common practice in many societies that the father chooses the bride's future husband. Oftentimes, what is considered a good match financially, politically, and socially doesn't necessarily serve the girl being married. Family clans are bonded in marriage for profit and other privileges. And a father might reject a man as his son-in-law due to a different ethnic background or religion.

But what about if the girl has zero attraction to the guy she is supposed to marry? What if her Heart has chosen somebody different? What if, at some point in the marriage, the woman who was forced into a marriage she never wanted meets a man and falls in love with him? And they consummate their love, which — according to her inner principles and ethics — is the right thing to do, but she is now condemned by society and family? She might even be killed for it, as often happens in strictly orthodox communities. Is it ethically right to take another person's life because that society's morals allow it? And what about laws that bind women but not men? Or laws that apply to one gender but exclude the other from any wrongdoing?

We are living in a strange world indeed. People are taught to simply settle for a living, to compromise. They are discouraged from listening to their inner voice, to do what they truly want, much less tune in to what feels right for them. Even more so, most individuals are conditioned to remain unaware that there is an inner voice, an inner authority that is perfectly capable of telling them what to do and what is right for them.

> "Learn well how to think right and then be your own shepherd, otherwise you shall be the unlucky sheep of all sorts of cunning shepherds!"
>
> ~ Mehmet Murat Ildan

THERE IS AN INNER VOICE WITHIN YOU PERFECTLY CAPABLE OF TELLING YOU WHAT IS RIGHT FOR YOU

So many people have lost their connection to their inner Self. They cannot hear their inner truth anymore. Instead, they conform to the dictates of the community they're living in — even if that community is living a lie, even if that community dictates and regulates according to lies, myths, and purposeful misinformation. "Believe what you're told and act accordingly" — that is the moral framework we're supposed to think, act, and live within.

CULTIVATE YOUR CONNECTION TO YOUR INNER SELF

LISTEN TO YOUR INNER TRUTH

But in the event the information that's been spread is a lie, is it ethically right to talk people into believing it? And, if it is a lie, isn't it the great betrayal of our lives?

- What really happened in the assassinations of President John F. Kennedy and Martin Luther King, Jr. will remain sealed from the public eye for many years to come before we learn the truth — or we may never know because the powers that be want to keep the truth hidden.

- What about the OJ Simpson case? Is it morally right that the law is possibly ruling in favor of a murderer? And this, while many innocent People of Color are sitting out their time in prison or are waiting to be executed.

- The circumstances surrounding 9/11 are still obscure as well.

- More and more people are waking up to the corrupt and illegal hidden agendas that are not flattering, moral, or ethical within governments and institutions. It seems the time of blindly trusting governments and institutions is over.

We are currently gathered here in the great school of planet Earth to learn to think again with our right mind and feel with our own Heart and execute our own free will.

THINK WITH YOUR RIGHT MIND FEEL WITH YOUR OWN HEART EXECUTE YOUR OWN FREE WILL

"Unless you drop your personality, you will not be able to find your individuality. Individuality is given by existence; personality is imposed by society — a mere social convenience.

Society cannot tolerate individuality, because individuality will not follow like a sheep.

... Society wants slaves, not people who are absolutely dedicated to freedom. Society wants slaves because all the vested interests want obedience."

~ Osho

The legal history of cannabis in the US began with state-level prohibition in the early 20th century. Many people have been sentenced to years in prison, whereas now it's becoming legal in a number of states. Is it ethical to keep those people incarcerated now that the laws and morals are changing around the country?

For too long we've been in a situation where the majority of the population has been behaving like sheep. Too many are trusting blindly information given by mainstream media and governments without seeking to check on their own by doing some research and using their own critical judgment. All over the globe, societies are splitting into two categories and free will and free choice is not executed anymore. There's a lot of emotion, misinformation, misunderstanding, grandstanding, politicizing, religious propaganda, polarization, and fear surrounding the vaccination subject — it's a complex issue.

In order to protect ourselves and others, children are forced to wear masks even for sport activities and adults are threatened with losing their jobs if they don't get vaccinated. What is going on? Is it ethically right to force vaccination? Dr. Julie Ponesse, PhD in Ethics and Ancient Philosophy and professor at Huron College of the University of Western Ontario in Canada, just declared that "It is ethically wrong to impose an experimental medical procedure upon anyone who objects in doing so. It is an injection of a substance that has not been fully tested for safety. It has not yet been shown to be effective."

She is now facing imminent dismissal after twenty-two years at her job. She stated "In the Spirit of Socrates who was executed for asking questions. This will consist of only one question to my first-year students: Is this ethically right or wrong"? Dr. Ponesse was dismissed on September 7, 2021.

> " ...I think what Martin Luther King meant by freedom was the obvious. The freedom of choice. To have the individual choice to walk down whatever road you've decided to go down. Freedom is a wonderful thing that so many take for granted. There is also something else that comes along with that freedom. Responsibility. If you have that precious right of freedom of choice, you should always make sure you are not treading on your brother or sister next to you who also have that same right of choice. Do you think we really have that 100% freedom of choice in this country?"
>
> ~ Anonymous

I hope I make it clear that this is not about being pro or con for vaccination. Rather, it is a reminder to investigate for oneself prior to making a choice. It is about free choice. With free choice, one can choose to get vaccinated or not. Free choice is different than being forced. What I object to is the blind belief and trust in the order being given, without questioning one's own inner authority as to what feels right and if the information given is correct or false.

Our world nowadays is at a crossroad — and like a crossroad, there are various and opposing directions to take. If one firmly arrives from within at what they feel is the right thing to do for them, then it is their right inner choice. If, on the other hand, one is acting in panic and fear due to the information that's spread or because of a threat, it doesn't serve their higher good to succumb to information that might be termed "brainwashing."

To speak in terms of morals and ethics, the current vaccination mandate might be morally right but ethically it's wrong. Why? Because it doesn't leave free choice as an option. Airline companies refuse transportation and many countries have set up strict mandates to decline entrance to unvaccinated travelers. As of late, several countries are starting to refrain from the vaccination mandate, perhaps for that very reason.

OUR WORLD IS AT A CROSSROAD
INVESTIGATE FOR YOURSELF

CHOOSE WHAT FEELS RIGHT FOR YOU
RATHER THAN OBEY AUTOMATICALLY
AND CONFORM BLINDLY

WE ARE NOT ROBOTS
WE ARE HUMANS
WITH A HEART TO FEEL AND ACT UPON
WHAT FEELS RIGHT

Chapter 101

HEAVEN, HELL, AND PURGATORY IN BETWEEN

The contemporary concepts of Heaven, Hell and Purgatory have their origin in the religious practices of the ancient Egyptians. The spiritual and religious beliefs of the ancient Egyptians are considered the basis of most later religions and definitely for Judaism, Christianity, and Islam and, arguably, even for Hinduism, Buddhism, and Taoism.

What is Heaven?

All religious belief systems and wisdom traditions agree that Heaven is a supernatural, transcendent place in another dimension, where divine beings like gods, angels, spirits, saints, and our venerated ancestors live.

Heaven is often described as having a golden gate leading into it, a place where synchronistic harmony, peace, and tranquility prevail. Celestial music is played with a choir of angels in an Eden-like setting, all bathed in diffused golden-white light.

Once, in a discussion, my dad objected to all the gold described in Heaven. He believed there are no material riches in Heaven (he had taken the description literally). I explained that what is meant is that the color gold has a very high frequency vibration just like white light. Whereas gold is associated with the divine, silver has more of a galactic energy to it. Because Heaven is a very high frequency dimension, dark colors are extinct in Heaven because darker colors have a lower frequency.

The ancient Egyptians called Heaven "The Land of the Beautiful West." I wonder if the name derives from the sun setting in the West since their religion was animistic.[34]

Every evening, their Goddess Nut swallowed the sun and in the morning gave birth the her again[35]. Amenti was the personification of the Land of the West. It was she who welcomed the deceased to their new dwelling place in the netherworld.

---

[34] Animistic: The belief in innumerable spiritual beings concerned in human affairs and helping or harming human interests; the doctrine that the vital principle of organic development is immaterial spirit and the belief in the existence of spirits separate from bodies; an attribution to conscious life to objects in and phenomena of nature or to inanimate objects.

[35] In ancient times the sun was considered female and the moon male.

In Egyptian mythology, Aaru (Field of Reeds), is the heavenly paradise where the God Osiris rules. The God Osiris was believed to be the lord of the underworld / afterworld. The parallels between Osiris and Jesus are noted in many a text. Like Jesus, Osiris was sacrificed and later resurrected and became the lord of the afterworld.

Duat is the realm of the dead in Egyptian mythology. It has been represented in hieroglyphs as a star-in-circle resembling the outline of a human being with spread legs and arms surrounded by the globe, the Earth.

According to the *World History Encyclopedia*, "… scholars claim the modern Egyptian and Arabic word for death, 'al mawt,' is the same as ancient Egyptian and is also used for 'mother,' which clearly links the death experience with birth or, more precisely, re-birth on an eternal plane." Wikipedia states that "In Islam, 'al Mawt' or Malak, is the name for the angel of death, which corresponds with the Hebrew-language term Mal'akh ha-Maweth in Rabbinic literature."

The ancient Egyptians believed in the afterlife for the blessed in Heaven. The nocturnal journey of the blessed[36] along with the Sun God through the underworld, was long, so Egyptians were buried with food, water, and wine to help them on their travels.[37]

During his life, the pharaoh was revered as the incarnation and representative of the Sun God / the God of Creation, to maintain the cosmic and social order represented by the Goddess Maat. He had to repel the forces of chaos that constantly threatened the order of the world. After his death, the pharaoh united with the sun disk and his divine body merged with his creator. In this new role, he continued to perform the task of subduing the powers of chaos.

This active role of the Pharaoh / Sun God necessitated a detailed description of the punishment of the damned, who represented the forces of Evil. The role of the dead pharaoh was to guide the blessed ones — the ones that had passed the trial of the Weighing of the Heart against Maat's Feather of Truth — through the netherworld to arrive at their resting place, Amenti, "The Land of the Beautiful West."

In this trial, called the "Weighing of the Heart" in the Hall of Two Truths, the Heart of the deceased was weighed against the "Feather of Truth" of the goddess Maat (see Part III, Section 1, Chapter 7, "Betrayal of the Heart").

---

[36] The ones that had passed the trial of the Weighing of the Heart (see PART III, Section 1, Chapter 7: "Betrayal of the Heart" were blessed with eternal life.

[37] To protect the flesh of the deceased from decay, Egyptian embalmers worked for seventy carefully scripted days to prepare a mummy. "First, by means of a bent iron instrument inserted through the nostrils, they extract the brains," a fascinated eyewitness, the Greek historian Herodotus, wrote in the fifth century B.C. The body was cleaned out, dried in a bed of natron salts, and carefully groomed. The lungs, stomach, liver and intestines of royalty were mummified separately, then sealed in jars; the heart, believed to be the seat of thought and action, stayed put.

A Heart light as a feather indicated the person had lived a pure and uncorrupted life. This was imperative because, otherwise, the beast Ammit devoured the Heart and the deceased's Soul was forever extinguished.

One difference between our modern concept of Heaven and the ancient Egyptian one is that even the blessed faced perilous obstacles in the netherworld, such as demons that guarded the gates of the netherworld, which required a knowledge of spells to overcome. It appears that they had to travel through the same hell of the damned, but conceptually, they occupied a very different space.

Hell

What then is Hell? Hell, also called Hades by the ancient Greeks, is regarded by various religions as a spiritual realm of evil and suffering. Hell is also understood as a state of utter chaos and restlessness, often traditionally depicted as a place of perpetual fire in the bowels of the Earth where the wicked are punished after death. In its archaic sense, the term "hell" refers to the underworld, a deep pit of misery or a distant land of shadows where demons come from and the sinners are gathered for all eternity to pay the penalty for their crimes in an inferno of misery, torment, and wickedness.

The recorded concept of hell in ancient Egypt predates the recorded concept of Hell in our modern religions. The principal sources for our knowledge of the Egyptian concept of Hell are the _Books of the Netherworld_, which are found inscribed on the walls of the royal tombs of the New Kingdom in the Valley of the Kings at Thebes, and then later on papyrus and other funerary objects belonging to commoners.

In every respect, the fate of the damned is the opposite of that of the blessed. When the righteous died, were mummified and buried with the proper rites, they could expect to start a new life in the company of the God Re and Osiris. The ritual known as the Opening of the Mouth[38] ensured that the blessed deceased would regain control over their senses.

In contrast, when the damned died, their flesh was torn away by demons and their mummy wrappings were removed so that their bodies were left to decompose. In the underworld, that the blessed successfully navigate, the order of things is reversed. Their heads and limbs are severed from their bodies and their flesh is cut off their bones. Their Hearts are removed and their Ba (Souls) are separated from their bodies, forever unable to return to them.

The concept of Hell in the ancient Egyptian religion is similar to those of our modern religions. Those who were judged unfavorably

---

[38] The Opening of the Mouth ceremony involved a symbolic animation of a statue or mummy by magically opening its mouth so that it could breathe and speak.

faced a similar fate to our modern concept of Hell, and perhaps even more specifically to the more Middle Ages concept of it as a specific region within the Earth.

Apep was the Egyptian deity who embodied chaos and was the opponent of light and order / Maat. For the damned, the entire, uncontrollable rage of the deity was directed against those who were condemned through their evils. They were tortured in every imaginable way and "destroyed," thus being consigned to non-existence. They were deprived of their sense organs, were required to walk on their heads, and to eat their own excrement. They were burned in ovens and cauldrons and were forced to swim in their own blood, which, Shezmu, the God of ointments, perfume and wine, squeezed out of them.

They even lost their shadows, which were considered an important part of the ancient Egyptian being. They had no air and suffered from hunger and thirst, as they received no funerary offerings. Worst of all, they were denied the reviving light of the Sun God, who ignored them, even as they cried out load and wailed when he passed them in the underworld at night.

But even more so, in the spiritual and religious beliefs of the ancient Egyptians, Hell was not even an option for the wicked. In the "Last Judgment" — described in Chapter 7 "Betrayal of the Heart" — the Heart / Soul was eaten by the beast Ammit who ate sinners who demonstrated the denial of an afterlife to the deceased. This was equal to being eliminated from existence and denied eternal life. Hell was complete destruction.

For the wicked, there is no renewal and no regeneration of life, only a second, definitive death. Rather than being the followers of Re, they are the "gang of Seth." Seth was the God who brought death into the world by murdering his God brother Osiris.

The fate of the wicked ones is described in terms similar to those used for earthly adversaries of the Pharaoh of ancient Egypt. They became enemies who were "reckoned with," "overthrown," "repelled," and "felled." The precise nature of the deeds that bought them to this fate were never stipulated, nor was there a direct relationship between their punishment and the crimes they committed during their lives. There are no separate areas in Hell for different categories of evildoers.

The crimes of those who were condemned to Hell consisted of nothing more and nothing less than having acted against the Divine World Order established at the beginning of creation as the concepts of Maat. Hence, they excluded themselves from the principles / Ideals of Maat (see Part VIII, Section 1, Chapter 102), a code of ethics for virtuous living, while at the same time revealed themselves as agents of chaos. After death, they became forever reduced to a state of non-being, which was the chaotic state of the cosmos before creation.

HAVING ACTED AGAINST
THE DIVINE WORLD ORDER
ESTABLISHED AT THE BEGINNING OF CREATION

THE DAMMED EXCLUDED THEMSELVES
FROM THE PRINCIPLES OF MAAT

AND BECAME AGENTS OF CHAOS
FOREVER REDUCED TO A STATE OF NON-BEING
THE CHAOTIC STATE OF THE COSMOS
BEFORE CREATION

Hence, they were excluded from the eternal Cosmic Cycle of Renewal and were instead assigned to the "outer darkness," the primeval chaotic world before creation, which is situated in the deepest recesses of the underworld, outside the created world. They were continuously punished by demons, who were the representatives of chaos. Indeed, the demons were often recruited from the ranks of the damned themselves, so that they could torture and kill one another.

Purgatory

Purgatory is the place between Heaven and Hell where a Soul's ultimate fate is decided. It's described as the place or state of being where Souls exist temporarily to admit their sins and receive punishment. Purgatory is also the process or condition of purification or temporary punishment in which the Souls are made ready for Heaven. It is a state of remorse. It is referred to as a place of cleansing and purifying prior to entering Heaven.

Apparently, the suffering endured by Souls in Purgatory is not physical pain. Rather, it is the process where the evil of sin is revealed to the person in order for them to totally and absolutely reject even the most venial and smallest of sins.

Often, after committing a sin, people experience regret and are remorseful. Dante Alighieri, in his epic poem *The Divine Comedy*, passes through the seven terraces of Purgatory: Pride, Envy, Wrath, Sloth, Avarice / Prodigality, Gluttony, and Lust.

According to Thriftbooks review, "*The Divine Comedy* is a landmark of world literature and tells of the poet Dante traveling through Hell, Purgatory and Paradise in search of salvation. The plot of *The Divine Comedy* is simple: a man, generally assumed to be Dante himself, is miraculously enabled to undertake an ultra-mundane journey, which leads him to visit the souls in Hell, Purgatory, and Paradise."

"In the middle of our journey of life
I came to myself into a dark wood
and found myself within the forest lost ..."

~ Anonymous

Written in the early 14th century, according to Goodreads, "It is widely considered the preeminent work in Italian literature and one of the greatest works of world literature." The main theme of *The Divine Comedy* is the spiritual journey of man through life. In this journey, he learns about the nature of sin and its consequences. And comes to abhor sin after understanding its nature and how it corrupts the Soul and draws man away from God."

In his day, Dante's book heavily influenced the population and Christian church with his description of purgatory.

Purgatory relates to what Buddhists call the bardo. Yongey Mingyur Rinpoche in his fabulous book, *In Love with the World: What a Monk Can Teach You About Living from Nearly Dying*, says that the:

> "... literal description of the bardos, in-between describes an insubstantial, nonmaterial state of being that is in the process of seeking to return to substance. It seeks to re-solidify, and to once again become some-body.
>
> From within our material forms, we already know that generally the experience of ourselves as no-thing and no-body is simply unbearable. We humans actually cannot stand this possibility - unless we wake up and realize that this transient and fluid state is our true home. Yet we are always in a state of not-knowing and of uncertainty. That's the nature of existence. As a daily life experience, the bardo of becoming expresses a heightened state of displacement, of falling apart, of not knowing what's happening."

Rather than purgatory awaiting us after death, Rinpoche refers to the Buddhist teachings of the bardo as a metaphor of dying while still in the body by renewing ourselves to new life. We must die to our old Self in order to be reborn into our new Life. We might have lived in certain ways that were serving us for a certain time period. After that cycle ends, we wake up to perhaps a larger truth that needs to be lived and experienced. In this sense, spiritual and philosophical seekers always question whether cherished values are still representing who we present ourselves to be in this world.

One thing is for certain, we don't have to die in order to experience Heaven, Hell, and Purgatory. They already exist now in our lives. And we know best in which of these three places we're living.

Heaven is a state of inner peace and truthful clarity. If we are able to live with inner peace and truthful clarity, a life of virtue, we have created a piece of Heaven here on Earth and can feel at home within ourselves.

Hell is experienced as deep confusion, restlessness, and utter chaos. It's a state of constantly seeking more and rushing from one achievement to the other, yet we're left with an inner emptiness likely producing deep confusion as to what are true and lasting values. Rinpoche says that "Running in circles describes the world of confusion." He also says that "hell is a state of mind, not a location. The horrific descriptions of the hot and cold hell did not point to the next life but to this one. Their teaching was to awaken us to the self-imposed punishment that anger inflicts."

Purgatory is the state of constant worries, fears, doubts, and self-condemnation. Purgatory in one's life is also a state of looking deeply at whatever wrongdoings were committed. In various religious traditions, it is recommended that in the last stage of life one enter a religious order to prepare for the afterlife to come.

"A saint was asked, 'What is anger?' He gave a beautiful answer. 'It is a punishment we give to ourself, for somebody else's mistake.'"
~ The Minds Journal

A source of some Christians' faith claims that in Purgatory the Soul loses the memory of its previous life, especially the Souls who committed bad acts and are in denial. That doesn't make sense. It rather sounds like the priest who after confession of whatever crimes were committed, gives the task of speaking a hundred Hail Marys and all is forgiven and the person leaves the church and continues on with their bad actions. We can only improve ourselves if we do remember our wrongdoings and atone for them.

Dementia and Alzheimer's are ailments of profound forgetting. I have not worked with these ailments but I suspect that the core cause might well be deeply buried childhood trauma, and possibly, in some cases, deep denial of wrongdoings that were performed. Of the war veterans I have worked with, the very few who never killed were at peace emotionally and mentally, whereas the ones who had taken active positions and destroyed lives suffered severe emotional and mental consequences as if they became the victims of their own actions that have been haunting them.

Daskalos, the healer of Cyprus, emphasized that the only chance we have to better ourselves is during our life in this body on Earth. He said that the chosen state we're in while living will also become the state once we pass over. He spoke of a friend of his who had died. The man had wasted his life with alcohol and gambling. After he had passed away, Daskalos psychically visited him on the astral realm he occupied. Much to Daskalos' shock, the man kept engaging in the same destructive activities as when he'd been alive.

If we performed wrong actions, our Soul will make us pay for it in the afterlife through repentance and also in the next life to come. While visiting the Hindu temple complex of Pashupatinath in Kathmandu, Nepal, I watched with great pity an elderly man sitting in a crowd of people. He had a huge, heavy tumor dangling from the side of his nose. It must have weighed ten pounds. He was oblivious to my staring in shock. It looked like the trunk of an elephant. As I contemplated his sorry fate, visions appeared in my inner eye where he in at least one past life had cut off the trunks of poor elephants and was now carrying them around with him.

I saw a man with a similar fate on the Internet. An individual in Indonesia appeared to be sitting on a huge sack of potatoes, only what he was sitting on was his testicles. Though, again, I can't prove this as fact, yet it came to me that he was carrying around all the testicles of the slaves he had castrated in a previous life at an oriental court where it was his task and duty to turn those men into eunuchs so they would guard women without the risk of sexually molesting them.

It's clear that whatever wrongdoings we've committed, we carry them with us energetically and even physically. While I worked with someone struggling with heavy alcohol consumption, I observed that the amount of alcohol he drank stayed in his field.

In German and English, another word for alcohol is "spirit." That term carries a lot of truth. The alcohol consumed is not simply released through urination. Energetically, it gets bottled up in the field of the addict and does great damage. All the pores of a heavy-duty alcoholic exude the smell of alcohol. Often, these people have earth-bound entities[39] in their field that — though dead — keep consuming alcohol with them, which makes it all the more difficult to escape the addiction because those entities have strong attachments to their host body.

It is an illusion to assume that after we die, whatever destructive forces we were battling with during life, will simply fall away. This is not the case. It does take a strong effort to leave those vices behind; they do not simply drop off. And it is of great benefit to do so while still alive and in the body because in the afterlife, those vices keep haunting and preventing us from finding peace.

"Whatever you've done before,
accept it and let it go.
You are not perfect.
You are capable of making mistakes.
Stop hiding from the shadow of the past.

---

[39] See Part V, Section 4, Chapter 50 for earth-bound entity attachments.

Don't be trapped in the darkness of shattered memories.
Let the light pass through and shine upon you.
Forgive yourself
because it's the only way to start again."
~ Anonymous

"Remember: When you forgive,
you heal — and when
you let go, you grow."

~ Anonymous

Chapter 102

THE 42 IDEALS OF MAAT

Starting with the Old Kingdom in 2700 BC, a rule and order called Maat / Ma'at came into place to regulate man's affairs to please their gods and the pharaoh, and to place the human being under cosmic order. Thus, the basic concept of Maat became the foundation of the ancient Egyptians.

According to Wikipedia, Maat / Ma'at refers to the ancient Egyptian concepts of truth, balance, order, harmony, law, morality, and justice. Maat was also the goddess who personified these concepts and regulated the stars, seasons, and the actions of mortals and the deities who had brought order from chaos at the moment of creation.

The concept of Maat opposes all enterprises that tend to destroy the cosmic order, nature, and thereby commits itself to the future / destiny of humanity. Her ideological opposite was Isfet, meaning injustice, chaos, violence, or to do evil.

The author Maulana Karenga in his book, *Maat: The Moral Ideal in Ancient Egypt*, quotes that Mubabinge Bilolo (Professor of Egyptology, Philosophy, and African Religion) considers Maat in essentially philosophical terms. He asserts that "the concept of Maat is a place of articulation of three ideals," namely:

a) The ideal of knowledge and the aspiration of knowledge, and more precisely, the knowledge of "true being" that which is true, sure, certain;

b) The moral ideal of truth, justice, and rectitude; and

c) The metaphysical ideal of love, and of the knowledge of Being, which is at the beginning of all being.

According to Theophile Obenga (a Congolese intellectual and scholar-historian, linguist, and philosopher), the Maatian ideal is:

1. the totality of ordered existence, and represents things in harmony and in place,

2. the political domain in which Maat is justice and in opposition to injustice,

3. the social domain in which the focus is on right relations and duty in the context of community, and

4. the personal domain in which following the rules and principles of Maat is to realize concretely the universal order in oneself; to live in harmony with the ordered whole.

The author continues to say that "the concepts emanate from the oldest reflective morality recorded and are key to the Maatian ethics. Maat is both a cosmic and a social principle, which sets the standard for both god and human. Maat is a divine concept, power and practice, which not only informed and aided the Creator's actions but was established as a fundamental concept, power and practice for the organization, maintenance and development of human society also."

"It is a link, which points to the Maatian concept of the need to constantly create and sustain an ethic context for good thought, emotion, speech, and conduct."

The book of Khun-Anup, commonly called "The Story of the Eloquent Peasant" is a text on social justice in which the peasant Khun-Anup pursues a grievance against a rich person and wins. Khun-Anup not only receives justice but delivers a treatise on justice and the obligations of leadership even from the masses. In his discourse of Maat, Khun-Anup urges leaders to:

"Speak Maat
Do Maat
For it is mighty
It is great; it endures
It's worth is tested
It leads one to blessedness."

The 42 Principles of Maat existed thousands of years before the Jewish Torah, the Christian Bible, and the Muslim Qur'an. In 1995, Arch-Priestess of Isis and foundress of the modern Temple of Isis, Lady Loreon Vigne, was traveling along the Nile in Egypt. She was inspired to create a modern-day version of the ancient 42 Laws of Maat, also known as the "Negative Confessions."

The ancient Egyptian Goddess Maat
with her Feather of Truth

1 – I HONOR VIRTUE

2 – I BENEFIT WITH GRATITUDE

3 – I AM PEACEFUL

4 – I RESPECT THE PROPERTY OF OTHERS

5 – I AFFIRM ALL LIFE IS SACRED

6 – I GIVE OFFERINGS

7 – I LIVE IN TRUTH

8 – I REGARD ALL ALTARS WITH RESPECT

9 – I AM SINCERE

10 – I CONSUME ONLY MY FAIR SHARE

11 – I HAVE ONLY GOOD INTENTIONS

12 – I RELATE IN PEACE

13 – I HONOR ALL CREATURES WITH REVERENCE

14 – I CAN BE TRUSTED

15 – I CARE FOR THE EARTH

16 – I KEEP MY OWN COUNCIL

17 – I SPEAK POSITIVELY OF OTHERS

18 – I AM BALANCED IN MY EMOTIONS

19 – I AM HONEST IN MY RELATIONSHIPS

20 – I ASPIRE TO HIGHER CONSCIOUSNESS

21 – I SPREAD JOY

22 – I DO THE BEST I CAN

23 – I COMMUNICATE WITH COMPASSION

24 – I LISTEN TO OPPOSING OPINIONS

25 – I CREATE HARMONY

26 – I INVOKE LAUGHTER

27 – I CHOOSE LOVE

28 – I AM FORGIVING

29 – I AM KIND

30 – I AM RESPECTFUL OF OTHERS

31 – I RELEASE ALL JUDGMENT

32 – I FOLLOW MY INNER GUIDANCE

33 – I CONVERSE WITH AWARENESS

34 – I DO GOOD

35 – I GIVE BLESSINGS

36 – I KEEP THE WATERS PURE

37 – I AM OPTIMISTIC

38 – I PRAISE THE GODDESS AND THE GOD

39 – I AM HUMBLE

40 – I ACHIEVE WITH INTEGRITY

41 – I ADVANCE THROUGH MY OWN ABILITY

42 – I EMBRACE THE ALL

Lady Loreon Vigne
Temple of Isis
isisoasissanctuary.org

Section 3

Chapter 103

THE UNIVERSAL LAW OF EXPANSION & CONTRACTION

"The first part of life is devoted to forming a healthy ego. The second part is going inward and letting go of it."

~ Carl Jung

Have you ever asked yourself how at one point your life was going smoothly, you felt in a good flow with everything — and then things changed? Or that you used to love your work and now it's just routine? Or why it is that even though you work harder than before it feels as if it's useless? How could this be?

Can you identify with any of the questions above? If so, those experiences might have puzzled you, especially if you feel that for you internally nothing changed. Life around you changed. Circumstances were different, but you kept doing the same as you always did. Yet everything became different. You might not enjoy life or work the way you used to. Quite possibly, this provoked a crisis for you.

There is a deeper reason for it all. Two universal laws are at work here:

1. EVERYTHING IS IN CONSTANT MOVEMENT. What was good before will change and become bad. In Buddhist terms, it's called the Wheel of Life.

   This does not necessarily mean "bad." Bad, in this context, is the opposite of good and in this universal principle, it's used for lack of a better term. What it means is that all is in constant change and nothing stands still. What was of value before is replaced by something that might not have been of value before. For example, a mother of three small children might not work while raising her kids but later decide to return to her career.

"It's funny how we outgrow what we once thought
we couldn't live without,
and then we fall in love with
what we didn't even know we wanted.
Life keeps leading us on journeys
we would never go on if it were up to us.
Don't be afraid. Have faith. Find the lessons."

~ Anonymous

Good

Bad

To fully understand this first law, it's helpful to envision a wheel that turns clockwise and has twelve positions on it like a clock. When we place in position twelve that which has priority in our life right now, the universal law of change says that everything is in constant movement and thus will change. As the wheel turns, and what was on top moves to position three, it loses its importance to a certain degree.

Once the wheel moves further to position six, it has reached its opposite position and in this sense, the universal law that states, "what was good becomes bad," what was of value before might not be of value anymore at a later time in our life.

We can observe this law at work in relationships, jobs, positions, and other matters that were important at one point in our lives but no longer hold priority. Everything is bound to change, and to not allow the change that needs to happen would be bad for us and others involved. This law is represented in many wisdom traditions as the "Wheel of Life."

THE WHEEL OF LIFE:
EVERYTHING IS IN CONSTANT MOVEMENT
WHAT WAS GOOD BEFORE
WILL CHANGE AND BECOME BAD

The Tao says about this law:

2. WHAT EXPANDED WILL CONTRACT. WHAT CONTRACTED WILL EXPAND.

The second Universal Law," What will expand will also contract," can be observed in our own body as our breathing rhythm, our heart rhythm, and our Cranio-Sacral rhythm[40].

---

[40] The Cranio-Sacral spinal fluid moves in cycles back and forth between the cranium and the sacrum, approximately 6-12 cycles per minute.

Our ancestors were deeply in tune with nature and the cosmos. The sages throughout the ages constantly observed the natural phenomena and the cosmic laws and they were well aware of the expansion and contraction cycles in nature.

WHAT EXPANDED
WILL CONTRACT
WHAT CONTRACTED
WILL EXPAND

Just like the macro cosmos is subjected to those laws and principles, so is the micro cosmos, the human being. The sages taught that these basic universal principles need to be taken into consideration for us to fully integrate ourselves and our human nature and understand ourselves better. Rather than working against these two universal laws and principles, we need to learn how to work with them.

DO NOT WORK AGAINST
THE UNIVERSAL LAWS

WORK WITH THEM

In nature, we observe these laws with the daily ebb and flow due to the gravitational attraction of the moon. You might be the strongest person on the planet but you will never be able to hold a wave thrashing against the shore. You cannot because the never-ending rhythm of the wave is immensely stronger. Yet in life, all too often we humans try to swim against the current of life. All too often do we humans assume that what once was has to remain forever that way. Such is not the case. We are not robots but live human beings subject to change.

The moon itself also goes through the different stages of waxing and waning during the month. These cycles are part of a universal law. Since we live on planet Earth, we humans are also subject to it.

The sages observed that for humans, approximately every seven years or so our personal cycles shift. We are moving from an expansion cycle to a contraction cycle and again to an expansion cycle. Most people might not pay attention to these cycles of expansion and contraction or even be completely unaware altogether. But it is imperative to keep this law in mind. It helps to understand ourselves better.

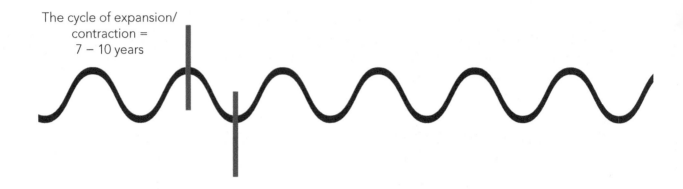

The cycle of expansion/
contraction =
7 – 10 years

AS HUMANS WE MOVE FROM
AN EXPANSION CYCLE TO
A CONTRACTION CYCLE
EVERY SEVEN OR SO YEARS

During an expansion cycle, we feel that things are going smoothly and effortlessly for us. Whatever our occupation, we perform fully. Don't we all love it when our talents and gifts are recognized and valued and we are able to express ourselves? Don't we all love it when we feel on top of our life and all is going really well for us?

We have been taught to love ourselves when we shine in the world. We have been conditioned to believe that in order to have a legitimate place in this world we must be successful in our job and personal life and demonstrate the measure of our power.

We can tell we're entering a contraction cycle when things start to become more complicated and not go so well anymore. We feel hindered and even blocked in some ways, though we work all the harder to stay on top. Being in a contraction cycle feels like swimming against the current in a river, barely able to keep our head above water.

A contraction cycle can also be initiated by an accident or an illness, the death of a loved one, or another severe crisis, like the ending of an important relationship or losing a job. Your emotional wellbeing might be severely challenged. In addition, your finances, personal life, or your job position might be affected. In any case, a contraction cycle is marked as a time of crisis. There are inner doubts and deep questioning of oneself, maybe even lingering depression.

When we don't recognize that we've entered a contraction cycle, it's an even more challenging time. We might blame others or circumstances. Often, we blame ourselves, though we might see no fault on our part. We perform on the same level as we used to. When circumstances change, we feel insecure and unworthy. Deep inside, we try to hide from the world that things are not going well.

The sages taught that an expansion cycle is a time where we fully show up in the world. They also warned against doing so during a contraction cycle. They explained that the contraction cycle is for inner development and growth and they recommended using the contraction cycle to withdraw from the world and hibernate, so to speak. It's a time best spent withdrawing from the world and cultivating a relationship with oneself. Time spent by yourself; maybe in reading, writing, fishing, hiking, exploring nature. Whatever your Heart and Soul desires.

DURING THE EXPANSION CYCLE
SHINE IN THE WORLD

DURING THE CONTRACTION CYCLE
DEVELOP YOUR RELATIONSHIP WITH YOURSELF

A well-used contraction cycle is of tremendous benefit for the upcoming expansion cycle. A well-used contraction cycle might be a time of much contemplation and introspection. For instance, I'm certain that filmmaker Craig Foster forged his relationship with a wild octopus in the kelp forests of South Africa during a contraction period. The documentary *My Octopus Teacher* won the 2020 Oscar for best documentary.

In metaphorical terms, an expansion cycle is to live fully. A contraction cycle is to die graciously. Like a snake shedding the skin it's outgrown, we are shedding our old selves during a contraction cycle.

If you fully embrace this challenging time by recognizing how it's serving you, you will create a new life from within yourself. In this sense, the contraction cycle is one of "Creation in Preparation."

CONTRACTION CYCLE =
CREATION IN PREPARATION

Nature provides us with great examples of the expansion and contraction cycles. The caterpillar enjoys a full life before it locks itself in a cocoon and its old existence dies. At the right time, the cocoon breaks open and a beautiful butterfly emerges to enjoy a new life.

DURING THE EXPANSION CYCLE
LIVE FULLY

DURING THE CONTRACTION CYCLE
DIE GRACEFULLY
TO YOUR OLD SELF

The moon is another nature example. It shines brightest when it's full. Then it gradually retracts until there is seemingly no moon, the night is utterly dark. A new moon will gradually appear and the cycle will repeat itself.

None of us doubts that the moon will build itself anew even when the night is darkest. In the Indian Tantric tradition of Oti Vidya (a distillation of a mystic practice more than 6,000 years old), the moon has a different name for every night according to its cycle. The moon, with its nightly changing faces, is viewed as a life entity with many different names according to its corresponding characteristics.

In terms of the expansion and contraction cycles, the shift from one cycle to the next is a gradual one. It's not a process from one week to another. You gradually exit an expansion cycle and gradually enter a contraction cycle and stay there for a long time — approximately 7 – 10 years — before entering a new expansion cycle.

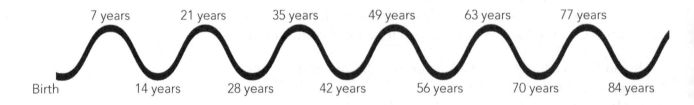

You can draw a graph of your life from birth up to now. Draw a wavy horizontal line. Divide the line into seven-year increments and then write down how your life was during those periods, those different cycles. Upon completion, the expansion and contraction cycles will become evident. They might be longer than seven years or even a bit shorter. In either case, patterns will start to appear and you will gain clarity, insight, and understanding about your life journey.

Chapter 104

THE EVOLUTIONARY PATH OF THE SOUL

"Awareness is the essence of our existence."

~ Yongey Mingyur Rinpoche

How did we evolve into who we are now? Is it true there are old Souls and young Souls? And if so, how come?

Nature provides us with perfect examples to elaborate on such questions. Usually, when we eat an apple, we are not thinking that the very seeds at the center contain the information to become a fully grown apple tree. Yet, the seed, in order to grow into an apple tree, has to undergo a long evolutionary cycle before it becomes a tree and produces apples. Nevertheless, the seed contains the essence of the apple tree and vice versa.

An even more dramatic example of the different stages of metamorphosis is the butterfly and the frog. They both start out as eggs and undergo various other life cycles before they transform and evolve into their end result, so to speak.

There is a universal law that states, "WHAT WAS SMALL WILL BECOME BIG. WHAT WAS BIG WILL BECOME SMALL." We see a baby being born and growing into a child, then an adolescent, and later into an adult. At the end of life, the cycle reverses itself and the old and frail become helpless like a baby again. Everywhere in nature we can observe this constant cycle of life, death, and rebirth.

As already discussed in a previous chapter, another universal law refers to the ever-turning Wheel of Life and states that "What was good becomes bad. What was bad becomes good." What was the right thing to do at one point might not be the right thing anymore. Everything is in constant movement and therefore changes.

In regard to the child and adolescent, it's healthy to engage in sports activities but in old age with frail bones the same activities might have an undesired effect. For example, while still living in Switzerland, I visited a dear family friend of ours. He was short of seventy years of age and had participated in a skeleton bobsled race on Lake St. Moritz. He broke a dozen bones and his legs and arms were in casts when I visited him in the hospital.

WHAT WAS GOOD SHALL BECOME "BAD"
THE WHEEL OF TIME IS EVER TURNING

WHAT WAS THE RIGHT THING TO DO
AT ONE POINT
WILL BECOME THE WRONG THING
AT A LATER TIME

LIFE IS IN CONSTANT MOVEMENT
AND THEREFORE CHANGES

When I work with victims of severe trauma, it is usually very difficult for such individuals to imagine that at some point in their Soul evolution they did wrong as well. It's hard for them to look at the suffering they caused and grasp that they did what they should not have done, that they were in circumstances of power and they abused their power.

Abuse of power is generally the reason why the Soul chooses to undergo the cycle of victimhood in this current life. Rather than abusing power again, the role of the victim is chosen by the Soul to yet again avoid the abuse of their power and, even more so, to gain a greater perspective of what it feels like to suffer. Compare Part VII, Section 2, Chapter 79, "Mary: A Story of Deepest Transformation," where Mary underwent a profound healing process during which she understood that her severe suffering in her past lives had been chosen by her Soul in order to compensate for the suffering she had caused others.

Another universal law, states, "WHAT WAS LIGHT BECOMES DARK, WHAT WAS DARK BECOMES LIGHT." The day with its light would not be day if it were not followed by the darkness of night. The moon shines brightest when full and becomes invisible during a new moon.

Humans beings are subject to the same law. We are made of light and darkness. We are half beast and half angel. Composite paintings of the Mughal period in India oftentimes depict a winged angel sitting on a horse that carries within it many different animals, which illustrates how our higher, divine nature must rein in our lower nature.

"How can I be substantial
If I do not cast a shadow?
I must have a dark side also
If I am to be whole."

~ Anonymous

Composite miniature painting, Mogul period, India. The Divine aspect of the human being is represented by Shah Jahan, with a halo, riding a horse. :The lower personality aspects and animalistic nature are represented by the animals and various humans in the horse.

We are all the self-inflicted victims of our identity.

~ Yongey Mingyur Rinpoche

In order for us to become whole, it's delusional to assume that throughout all our past incarnations we have always been good and used our power constructively. Many wisdom traditions warn of the seven vices — greed, envy, wrath, sloth, lust, pride, and gluttony — and advise that we must strive to conquer our lower nature and cultivate what the Buddhists call the ten virtues: wisdom, kindness, patience, compassion, courage, proper conduct, humility, generosity, honesty, and discipline.

As long as we only look at the light part within ourselves, we will only grasp one perspective. The other side of the coin — the polar opposite — also exists and is waiting to be recognized and reconciled.

Our shadow can only be transformed by becoming aware of it. We need to be fully looking at the dark part within ourselves and let it tell its story of how it came into existence. Then — and only then — we can release it. The energy that was held and blocked by denial and ignorance can then flow again with full and powerful force.

"All there is has its polar opposite" is another universal law. We instantly grow a huge amount if we apply this universal principle for ourselves and accept that fact. If we want to be so good, we have to be just as bad as well.

The Seven Vices
Greed
Envy
Wrath
Sloth
Lust
Pride
Gluttony

The Ten Virtues
Wisdom
Kindness
Patience
Compassion
Courage
Proper Conduct
Humility
Generosity
Honesty
Discipline

Again, I'm referring to the Soul that over lifetimes has learned the hard lesson of what not to do and how not to live. This doesn't at all mean that we have to do terrible things in order to be just the opposite.

It is only natural and healthy to aim to be a good person, but it doesn't serve us if we're in denial about our wrongdoings. No Soul growth is in that. It's an important part of anyone's healing process to look at those dark parts of ourselves as well. Not for punishment, but for insight and enlightenment.

here is the "good"

here is the "bad"

here is the "bad"
that is in the "good"

here is the "good"
that is in the "bad"

here is life

"Here is the 'bad'
Here is the 'good'
Here is the 'bad' that is in the 'good'
Here is the 'good' that is in the 'bad'
Here is life."

~ Tao

To look at our deepest pain is like placing your hand onto a hot plate and staying put. Naturally, everyone will want to pull their hand away. This is the reason why healing on the deepest level needs assistance. It cannot be done alone because our natural defense mechanisms would interfere and prevent what ails us most from surfacing.

Within everyone there is light and shadow, good and evil, love and hate, like the wise Native American who spoke to his grandson of the two wolfs living in his chest, one blood thirsty and the other friendly. In order to be truthful, you must embrace your total being. A person who exhibits both positive and negative qualities, strength and weaknesses, is not flawed, but complete. Being desirable means being comfortable with your own ambiguity. The most ambiguous reality is that we are flesh and spirit at the same time.

"The sage battles his own ego.
The fool battles everyone else's."

~ Sufi saying

If we deny the so-called negative aspects, we remain only half of who we are. We then live only half of our potential. In order for us to become whole, we need to look at all aspects, transform them, and integrate them.

TO BECOME WHOLE
WE NEED TO LOOK AT ALL ASPECTS
OF OURSELVES AND
TRANSFORM THEM
AND INTEGRATE THEM

Especially if we consider ourselves spiritually awakened and at least partially conscious, some forces of deep understanding had to evoke that realization. Wrongdoing does bring realization.

WRONGDOING EVOKES REALIZATION

I always point out that in order for the Soul to learn, we have to do wrong. There is no way around it. People of the New Age community have a hard time with that fact. I had a friend who thought herself highly evolved spiritually, but who couldn't imagine that in order to get where she currently was spiritually, she had to travel the road of life experiences like everyone else. She had to fail miserably as a human in order to learn and arrive at where she thought she was.

> "If you want to be good at something,
> you must first be willing to be bad at it."
>
> ~ Anonymous

Some religions firmly insist that their deity fell enlightened from the sky, so to speak. I happen to disagree. To me, this is a man-made declaration. I happen to believe that a universal law applies to all, without exemption. Jesus and Buddha and all the Masters of Light had to undertake the same path everyone else has had to take. This is the true sacrifice of a bodhisattva[41] — to become fully human and submit oneself to the same cycle of spiritual growth like everyone else and then remain in the cycle of death and rebirth to release the suffering of others.

Buddha is said to have experienced re-birth 400,000 times.

Apparently, the beloved Tibetan saint Jetsun Milarepa was able to turn from a master of the black arts into a saint in one lifetime. But this doesn't mean he didn't have countless lives before in order to spiritually grow and evolve.

A universal law states that "To THE SAME DEGREE THAT THE PENDULUM SWINGS IN ONE DIRECTION, IT WILL SWING IN THE OPPOSITE DIRECTION." I have often pondered what became of Hitler. Or what were today's fanatical animal protectors doing before in a past life to bind them to such a degree to the rights of animals in this lifetime. Or who Mother Theresa was before.

EVERYTHING HAS ITS POLAR OPPOSITE LIKE THE SWINGING OF A PENDULUM

---

[41] Bodhisatva is a person who is able to reach nirvana but delays doing so out of compassion in order to save suffering beings.

Buddha apparently saw how beings rise and fall through the cycle of rebirth as a consequence of their past deeds.

In order to spiritually grow, each and every one of us has to undergo a long process of purification from lifetime to lifetime. It always amuses me when individuals state in earnest that this is their fifth lifetime and that they have learned enough and certainly will not return here — and they fully believe it. If this were their fifth life, they would be existing as a very low life form. Just becoming able to inhabit a human body is the peak of evolution. Becoming a somewhat evolved human being involves thousands of lifetimes.

I previously mentioned the book about conversations with elemental beings and nature spirits. It's a worthwhile read (*Nature Spirits and What They Say: Messages from Elemental and Nature Beings Interviews* by Verena Stael von Holstein). Those beings and spirits know much. According to them, all substance has consciousness and starts low, first as elemental beings of fire, mineral, water and air; then as nature spirits: the plant kingdom and animals. Only after having undergone all those lower cycles, the substance and its consciousness will be entering the so-called human monad[42] (a single unit) by inhabiting a human form.

The Hindu concept of the evolutionary path of inhabiting first the various animal forms before evolving into human form is closer to that consciousness principle than other recognized religions. Hindus also state that failure and power abuse will result in a regression into a lower life form with low consciousness again, rather than a progression into an ever-higher form of consciousness.

The more we wake up and evolve spiritually, the more we are challenged by the tasks Spirit has in store for us. And the more tests we pass, the more challenging those tasks and trials become. And the steeper the risk of failing and falling lower again. It's like walking on the blade of a knife. The more we become actively and consciously engaged in our spiritual path, the more we will be tested.

THE MORE WE EVOLVE SPIRITUALLY THE MORE WE ARE CHALLENGED BY THE TASKS OF SPIRIT

I'm not speaking of meditation, yogic practices, or similar traditions. I'm speaking of inhabiting our body temple fully and committing to one's Soul and the life it is commanding us to live.

On our journey, it will seem as if we're stepping from one spiritual exam into the next one. The lessons successfully learned will drop away. We can mark them off. The lessons we fail will continue repeating themselves until they are also learned. Life is all about learning. Seemingly never ending is the Evolutionary Path of the Soul.

---

[42] Terminology used by Gottfried Leibniz, a German polymath active as a mathematician, philosopher, scientist, and diplomat.

LIFE IS ALL ABOUT LEARNING AND PERFECTING THE SOUL

UNTIL WE BECOME FREE TO LEAVE THE CYCLE OF DEATH AND REBIRTH

At some point on our path, we as Souls have the choice to leave the cycle of death and rebirth. Or to return again and again to serve. Until we reach that point, we have no choice. Life keeps calling us back, to learn and to atone. The more we understand this, the more we let go of the wrong assumption that to be in the body is a curse. Being in the body is a blessing for it is only in the body where we can rapidly grow and evolve — if we choose — and we always have choice.

BEING IN THE BODY IS A BLESSING

IT IS ONLY WHILE IN THE BODY THAT THE SOUL CAN GROW AND EVOLVE

In my work, I have countless times accompanied individuals to the realm of Spirit. When we are in Spirit, we have no form, there is only pure consciousness. When we entered our body, we acquired Soul consciousness. While we're in Spirit form, we remain on the level of consciousness we acquired when we were in our most recent body form. The level of consciousness we acquired represents the sum of all we learned while in our present body, plus over lifetimes. The amount we can grow while in Spirit is very limited.

"When the Buddha described how long humanity has been on the journey, as he spoke of reincarnation, he talked about a mountain six miles wide, six miles high, and six miles long. Every hundred years, a bird would fly with a silk scarf in its beak and run it over the mountain once. The length of time it takes the scarf to wear away the mountain, is the length of time you have been on the path."

~ Ram Dass
Promises and Pitfalls
of the Spiritual Path

WHEN IN SPIRIT WE HAVE NO FORM WHILE IN SPIRIT WE DO NOT GROW WE CAN ONLY GROW AND EVOLVE WHILE IN OUR BODY FORM

When our essence is in Spirit form, the sensation is ideal, harmonious, and peaceful. It feels like having the sun shine pleasantly upon us and all our needs being comfortably provided.

And there is no friction. When there is no friction, the Soul that aims to learn gets bored. The Soul wants to keep experiencing itself in form. The Soul wants to express itself in ever new forms — all for the purpose of learning and evolving. Such is the evolutionary path of the Soul.

THE EVOLUTIONARY PATH OF THE SOUL IS TO EXPERIENCE ITSELF IN EVER NEW FORMS FOR THE PURPOSE OF LEARNING AND EVOLVING

Right leadership aims to serve truth and free humanity.

History presents us with countless examples of individuals who incarnated with a particular Soul purpose. Martin Luther King, Jr., Harriet Tubman, and Mahatma Gandhi are some key figures of the recent past who incarnated with a very important Soul purpose. In doing so, they became beacons of light.

To rise up against wrong and injustice takes tremendous courage, faith, and conviction. More than anything else, right leadership carries a huge amount of responsibility to serve a larger good. Sadly, most politicians and individuals in leading positions fall victim to corruption, exploitation, and their inflated ego to accumulate riches, power, status, and control. Right leadership is not a power trip but rather a shouldered responsibility towards fellow human beings. Right leadership aims to serve truth and free humanity.

Some of the rightful leaders of this world claim they developed their courage, integrity, humility, perseverance, and genuine care for others through the fire of suffering. Uncorrupted leaders, like the former Uruguayan president, José Mujica, stated that he would never have turned into the human being he became had he not served a long-term prison sentence. The movie, *A Twelve-Year Night*, tells the story of his imprisonment as a political prisoner.

Nelson Mandela served twenty-seven years in prison. He claims that "Prison — far from breaking our spirits — made us more determined to continue with this battle until victory was won."

Civil rights activist Martin Luther King, Jr. was sentenced to prison twenty-nine times for his acts of civil disobedience and on trumped-up charges.

"Our lives begin to end the day we become silent about things that matter."

~ Martin Luther King, Jr.

When in 1988, Aung San Suu Kyi left her quiet family life in Oxford, England to visit her dying mother in Burma, she became witness to the brutal military regime that tyrannized her people. She decided to stay and put all her efforts into bringing democracy to Burma. Decades earlier, in 1947, her father, Aung San had freed Burma from British rule and on the day of his inauguration, was assassinated. A 1991 Nobel Peace Prize laureate, Aung spent fifteen years under house arrest and refused to travel to Britain to see her dying husband because she would not have been allowed entry into Burma again.

Mahatma Gandhi threatened the South African government during the first and second decades of the twentieth century like no man had done before by establishing the first anti-political organization in the country. It reached its climax in 1913 with the epic march of 5,000 Indian workers indentured in the coal mines of Natal, the former province of South Africa. This marked the beginning of the marches to freedom and mass stay-away-from-work movement, which became characteristic of the freedom struggle against apartheid. During his twenty-one years in South Africa, Gandhi was sentenced four times to prison.

Many heroes of long ago are still celebrated nowadays and have become legends. Some are revered as prophets, gods, and saints. We all know them. In the animal kingdom, animals that live in packs have behavior patterns that help them survive in nature.

"The x-factor of great leadership is not personality. It's humility."

~ Jim Collins

"How we treat the vulnerable
is how we define ourselves as a species."

~ Russell Brand

"The true price for leadership is the willingness
to place the needs of others above your own.
Great leaders truly care about those
they are privileged to lead
and understand that the true cost
of the leadership privilege
comes at the expense of self-interest."

~ Simon Sinek

LEADERSHIP IN THE ANIMAL KINGDOM

Since apes are the closest mirror we have in the animal kingdom, our political, religious, and business leaders should all be aware of this ancient "social contract" we have regarding leadership and act accordingly. Acknowledging and delivering upon these expectations can help humans to lead more naturally and effectively.

Erna Walraven, the author of _Wild Leadership: What Wild Animals Teach Us about Leadership_ (New Holland), says: "I've observed wild animal societies in the field and in human care for more than three decades. This has given me a unique perspective on leadership in nature. I have looked at leadership characteristics in lions, elephants, African wild dogs, meerkats, hyenas, gorillas, chimpanzees, bonobos, and many more species. I've watched generations of animals live their lives with the intrigue and the ups and downs of all communities. My conclusion is that animal societies, and the individuals within these, thrive or fail by the quality of its leadership."

Political chimps, like leaders in our society, have negative and positive traits, but there are many constructive traits. Being a good chimpanzee leader is hard work. There are many demands on this individual who has to nurture his relationships in the clan to keep the top job. Chimp troops are reciprocal societies: favors are exchanged and a good alpha male is the hub of this, making sure he includes everyone.

It appears that the most advanced leadership in the animal kingdom happens in the Bonobo society where females dominate but males are not excluded.

Researchers studying bonobos find it much harder to establish who the alpha female is as there is not as much reason to display dominance in a more peaceful community. The top position is gained through respect for the knowledge of the leader, not through aggression.

Male bonobos are arguably "under the thumb" but they have a significantly better quality of life than female chimps do under male leadership. Perhaps on reflection, male bonobos have what many males desire: devolved responsibility, little conflict, and lots of sex.

Bonobos and chimps represent the yin and yang of human nature, like having two first cousins, equally closely related but very different from each other. **Together, the leadership behavior of these two great apes seems to reflect our own aggressive side (chimps) and our more egalitarian, peace-loving natures (bonobo). Both leadership styles tell us something about leadership models that work in nature. Which of the positive qualities in those models could or should we emulate?**

The negative traits in those leadership styles speak for themselves: examples of animal leaders who monopolize resources (food and sex) and use violence and intimidation to seize or stay in power are plentiful. In my three decades of animal behavior experience, it never ended well for those types of leaders. It's far more instructive to focus on the positive traits that animal leaders display that result in long-lasting and thriving animal teams.

Erna Walraven is the emeritus senior curator at Taronga Zoo in Sydney
(Note from Silvana: highlighted segments are my own.)

Chapter 105

METTA: THE RESPONSIBILITY OF THE SOUL

"If you avoid conflict to keep the peace,
you start a war inside yourself."

~ Cheryl Richardson

It was in the 1990s that I saw a movie called *Beyond Rangoon* and was captured by the personality of the Burmese Democratic leader Aung San Suu Kyi. Upon reading Aung San Suu Kyi, *The Voice of Hope: Conversations with Alan Clements*, I was introduced to the concept of Metta.

In the book, Sui Kyi often refers to the word "Metta" as a spiritual discipline. She explains that the Buddhist practice of Metta is the action of serving another's Soul. More than loving kindness towards others, it encompasses serving not the ego personality of others, but rather serving them Soul to Soul.

I find this a very important principle that involves sometimes speaking a truth that's painful to the ears but beneficial to the Soul. With "telling a truth," I'm definitely not referring to an opinion coming from one's own judgmental position. Instead, I am referring to an objective truth that is in alignment with the higher reality of what is really going on. This might sound complicated but it's not.

What makes it difficult is that most people are unfamiliar with speaking truth. They might observe a friend's or family member's abusive behavior and be very familiar with their destructive attitude but they only think about it. They only register a behavior by observing and leaving it alone.

Most people have never considered speaking their objective heartfelt observations to the person who needs to hear it. Suicides and any kind of abuse could be avoided if people only took an active role. But what they usually do is either keep it to themselves or share it with someone else. Sadly, this doesn't serve the person involved. And sometimes, in today's world, to speak your truth could backfire and you could be attacked yourself.

Much abuse and self-abuse could be avoided if people only learned to speak their truth. Like the mother and grandmother of Mia, the child in Part IV, Section 2, Chapter 29 who kept enduring enormous physical abuse that could have killed her.

Years ago, I became witness to a friend who kept complaining about her husband's lack of sex drive. She was an attractive woman and obviously sexually frustrated. But what escaped her awareness was that she constantly criticized her husband and nagged him. After having heard her complaints countless times, I sat her down and brought her behavior to her awareness. I explained that if she wanted her husband to desire her, she needed to stop emasculating him with her constant complaints. As she started to bring a more positive attitude into their relationship, they became romantic again.

I also remember a friend who was struggling with alcohol. She did her best to hide it, perhaps due to the fact that she was an active member of a spiritual community. But when she came to visit after I had not seen for a long time, her whole body reeked of alcohol. Over tea, I shared my observation very lovingly. I know it helped.

Oftentimes, what another Soul needs is to be truly seen by someone else. Becoming a heartfelt witness to someone else's flaws or foibles should not make us judgmental but rather compassionate. Being compassionate does not mean to pardon a friend's behavior but rather to speak truth and let the person sit with it.

From personal experience, as well as my observations in my healing work, I can assure you that a well-spoken truth leaves the listener not defensive but rather contemplative. What was spoken must be digested. That's the reason why a well-spoken truth coming from a sincere Heart does not need to be repeated again and again. A well-spoken truth sinks in and evokes consciousness growth in the recipient.

With this said, speaking truth involves pointing out when a dear one falls off the track and behaves in ways not beneficial to their highest being. What is most important is to listen to your Heart and speak from your Heart. When this is done, the truth you speak will be received with the other person's Heart. We speak from Heart to Heart.

IN ORDER TO SERVE OTHERS
WE SOMETIMES MUST SPEAK A TRUTH
PAINFUL TO THE EARS BUT
BENEFICIAL TO THE SOUL

While living in Switzerland during the 1980s, I became best friends with a married man. Dimitri and I were kindred spirits and developed a strong bond. We met for dancing, meals, skiing, or strolling through the city and the countryside.

One day, I burst out with, "Dimitri, you are such a talented goldsmith and very successful. Your work is in museums all over the world. Your display windows are the most creative ones in the whole town. You are deeply sensitive and gifted and also a fantastic gardener and cook. Tell me, why do you smoke? This is a contradiction I don't understand."

Dimitry just looked at me but didn't answer. I must add that during the '80s, all over Europe the majority of the population heavily smoked. Restaurants and other public places were in a constant fog of smoke.

A couple of years later, Marina, a goldsmith Dimitri had trained in his studio, came to work for me at my store in Zurich. I was surprised that Marina didn't smoke anymore and remarked on it. She answered that some time ago, Dimitri stopped smoking — cold turkey. As a consequence, the entire crew in his studio also stopped smoking.

Upon meeting Dimitri again, I brought up the subject. He responded that my words had sunk deep, so he decided to quit smoking.

In her book, *Kitchen Table Wisdom: Stories that Heal*, Rachel Naomi Remen tells the story of how when her daughter was a small girl, she watched her mom one day go through quite an ordeal to carefully prepare dinner for her boss who was visiting that evening. When the arrogant woman arrived, she was dismissive of Rachel's efforts and kept talking about herself. Rachel's daughter observed her silently for a long time and with big eyes. After a while, Rachel's boss addressed the little girl and asked why she kept staring at her.

The little girl answered, "My mom says you are a self-made woman."

"Yup, that's me, a self-made woman," answered the woman.

The little girl then said, "Why did you make yourself this way?"

The woman stared at the little girl with an open mouth. Rachel wrote in her book how embarrassed she was about her little daughter's question. But, apparently, her boss' behavior at the office changed after that. She came down from her snobbish and arrogant high horse.

This little girl's comment caused a shift in the behavior of that woman. Children who are still innocent haven't yet been distorted by their parents as to what "right behavior" is. They haven't edited their thoughts yet and burst out with their feelings. They are still pure and read the energies around them accurately and unprocessed.

A TRUTH WELL SPOKEN
EVOKES CONSCIOUSNESS GROWTH

When a friend of mine from Switzerland was staying in Santa Fe, she started an affair with a man living here. Abigail was originally from New York, Jewish and married to Frank, a Swiss banker. They had two children whom she had brought with her to Santa Fe. Abigail introduced to me the man she was having an affair with, and said she was toying with the idea of having a life here with him.

She confided to me, "You know, of course I could never tell Frank. He would flip out."

I responded with, "Whether you regard this possibly as something serious or just an affair, you must tell your husband. It's not fair that your children, though small, are brought into this and are witness to you living with this man, and you living a double life here. Frank is Swiss, he will not have the reaction that you expect."

Soon after, Frank arrived to visit his wife and kids. Abigail trusted my advice and confessed to her husband that she was having an affair.

Frank's response blew her away. He said, "What you and I have is of the Heart. Live out your affair and you shall see."

Abigail told me that right then and there, she fell newly in love with her husband. Frank left soon after, due to work commitments. He had shown a reaction Abigail could never have imagined. She had been thinking within the American context of her upbringing, and hadn't taken into consideration that Europeans handle matters of the Heart very differently. Soon after, Abagail terminated her affair and returned to Switzerland and life with her husband.

Serving Soul to Soul certainly requires selfless and non-egotistical action. It also involves sacrifice, oftentimes a tremendous amount because quite possibly, we're running the risk of losing the one we love upon speaking our Truth.

This is challenging, especially when we deeply care about the person and regard them as an important part of our life. We must consider that what we might say is not pleasing for the other to hear. We could very well lose their love in the course of things.

SERVING ONE'S OWN SOUL
WHILE SERVING ANOTHER'S SOUL

REQUIRES NON-EGOTISTICAL ACTION
AND SELF-SACRIFICE

My future husband Peter and I had our first test two months into our relationship. One morning, after we made love, he confided that his Heart is in conflict. He shared that the only woman he ever cared for before me, had called him yesterday and wanted to get back together with him. It was confusing for him because she had been the only woman who had terminated any of his relationships and it hadn't felt complete for him. Peter confessed he felt split.

Without a moment's hesitation I responded, "Peter, let's interrupt our relationship for one month. That should give you enough time to be with her and figure out what you want for your future, a life with her or with me." Peter was speechless — and grateful. He left, only to return in the same evening.

He said, "What you did for me, she would have never done. I have chosen, I don't need more time. I want to live my life with you."

Likewise, to speak our Truth is challenging for the deliverer as well. Abigail and Peter were both running the risk of losing the person they loved. How much easier it often seems to keep one's mouth shut and work out the conflict within oneself. But we can't do that. It would be dishonest to one's own Soul, as well as the Soul of the other person. The conclusion is that we can only serve someone in their highest being and equally serve our highest being if we are able to express ourselves authentically regardless of the possibility of loss.

WE CAN ONLY SERVE SOMEONE
IN THEIR HIGHEST BEING
AND EQUALLY SERVE OUR HIGHEST BEING
IF WE EXPRESS OURSELVES AUTHENTICALLY
REGARDLESS OF A POSSIBLE LOSS

Most of us have been in the unpleasant situation where we can clearly see a friend or family member getting off track by some destructive behavior patterns. It's clear to us that their behavior is not beneficial to their wellbeing. What we see pains us, it might even shock us, and our first impulse might be to shut them out of our life by turning our back on them so that we don't have to directly confront and feel our pain.

How many of us choose to keep our mouth shut, even in the face of what we see is highly toxic and destructive behavior? How can we tell a dear one that they're battling an addiction problem when they're doing all they possibly can to hide or minimize it? Or that they're lying and cheating and are trying to get away with it? Or that they're earning some easy money by degrading themselves?

To effectively reach someone by speaking Truth, we must never be in a reactive mode. When someone's behavior triggers emotions in us, what we say will come across as a judgment. And for our words to have a beneficial effect, there cannot be any judgment on our part because a judgment will always result in defensiveness on their part.

We need to be present in our Heart and detached from the Truth we speak. Only then will our words reach the other person in their Heart and Soul and lead to the desired result of growth in consciousness and serving their Soul.

UPON SPEAKING TRUTH WE MUST BE IN OUR HEART AND FREE OF JUDGMENT

The #1 factor why people do not speak their truth is that they fear to lose love, affection, and connection.

How come most people would rather keep their mouth shut than summon the courage to speak their truth? I have often seen that the need to be loved is the #1 factor as to why individuals deny speaking their truth. People cannot bear to lose love, affection, and connection. It's a huge fear for most people and they'd rather stay inauthentic than run the risk of losing love. Additionally, not speaking up fits so well with the common belief system of pleasing others because that's what "good people" do. Right? Is this truly the case? Don't we show much more love by being willing to point out distortions rather than keeping our mouth shut?!

A few years ago, a very dear friend to whom I was very attracted at the time, asked me if I find it important to act upon an attraction we feel. Since he was equally attracted to me, I knew he asked in terms of us. And due to the depth of the question, I had to answer what came to my Heart. I responded by saying,

> "When getting involved in a relationship, we must take into consideration the level of hurt we might produce by doing so. In every involvement of the Heart, someone in the end is going to get hurt. If we're willing to carry that burden, then we should do it. But the consequences we carry as a result, must be known to us and worthwhile.

> It's a benefit to become aware of this fact before entering any relationship. Once we're aware, and if we're willing to include the

karma of hurt in the equation, then and only then, should we act and allow our physical impulses full exploration."

This beloved man looked at me with his serious and loving eyes. Though my response might not have been what he expected, I could see his resonance. We stayed very dear friends and never got involved. I knew that ours was, more than anything, a kindredness on the level of Soul.

I learned a long time ago that by speaking my Truth, I'm not less loved. The opposite is the case. I'm more loved, I'm also more respected. The first successful experience of speaking truth allowed me to become bolder until all fear of losing love was lost. I'm at the point in my life where in the event I do lose love, I don't care because I've observed that people come into one's life for a particular reason and possibly only for a season. Once that reason is accomplished and the lesson learned, the season is ended and the person drops away from my life. This has happened a good number of times.

People come into one's life for a particular reason and possibly only for a season.

"When I feel stuck on repeat with a person, place of thing,
I'm realizing it's usually because they were meant to be
a temporary teacher.
The broken blender doesn't have a deeper message for me
other than replacement.
The neglectful friend doesn't have a deeper message for me
than boundaries and loyalty adjustment.
It's ok to leave after the lesson's been taught.
Did you learn the lesson?
Then why haven't you left the classroom?"

~ Shade Ashani

Many of us also never ask ourselves questions regarding our Soul, much less the responsibility of our Soul. For most people, these questions are likely of no concern. But what if we become fully conscious and aware that the only thing we take with us when we leave planet Earth is our Soul and the sum of what we learned during our lifetime? If this fully dawned on us, would we then still be so concerned with matters of the mundane kind? Or would the Soul become the focal point?

Let's become fully conscious and aware that the only thing we take with us when we leave planet Earth is our Soul and the sum of what we learned during our lifetime. Our Soul needs to become the focal point.

"You've got to learn to leave the table
when love's no longer being served."

~ Nina Simone

447

True self-love involves listening to the truth of our Heart and acting in accordance with it. It involves speaking Truth rather than keeping it in. This might come across as harsh, especially for people who are used to suppressing their authentic thoughts and feelings, rather than expressing them. But if we are able to speak Truth while staying in our Hearts, it doesn't come across as criticism and judgment.

Speaking the Truth of the Heart also invokes growth of the Soul for the other person. This is Metta — serving one's Soul while equally serving another's Soul — Soul to Soul.

SELF-LOVE MEANS SPEAKING YOUR TRUTH AND ACTING ACCORDING TO IT

Chapter 106

THE TAO / SUFI / TANTRIC PATH: SEEKING UNION WITH THE DIVINE

THIS MAKES ME WONDER
IF YOU ARE IN ALL THERE IS
FROM THE SMALLEST PARTICLE
TO THE LARGEST GIANT
WHERE IS IT THAT YOU STOP AND I BEGIN?
FOR — I AM NOT WITHOUT YOU.
THERE IS NO LIFE, UNLESS YOU

The Tao (or Dao) refers to the order of the universe. Taoism teaches that all living creatures ought to live in a state of harmony with the universe, and the energy found in it, Ch'i or Qi.

Taoism has been connected to the philosopher Lao Tzu, who around 500 B.C.E. wrote the main book of Taoism, the *Tao Te Ching*, or "The Way and Its Power." Taoists believe in spiritual immortality where, after death, the spirit of the body joins with the universe.

The *Tao Te Ching* is a collection of poetry and sayings from around the third and fourth centuries B.C.E. that guides Taoist thought and actions. While the author is traditionally believed to be the philosopher Lao Tzu, there is little evidence that Lao Tzu existed at all. Rather, the *Tao Te Ching* is a compilation of earlier sayings from many authors. This book was said to be authored by the philosopher Lao Tzu for cultural and political reasons. Lao Tzu is sometimes understood as the representative of the Tao, or a god, and given legendary status.

The *Tao Te Ching* and other Taoist books provide a guide for behavior and spiritual ways of living in harmony with the energy of the universe. However, Taoists do not believe in this energy as a personified "god." Rather, there are gods as part of the Taoist beliefs, often introduced from the various cultures found in the region known now as China. These gods are part of the Tao, like all living things. Taoism has temples, monasteries and priests who make offerings, meditate, and perform other rituals for their communities.

Life Force (in Sanskrit: Prana) is the energy present in and guiding everything in the universe.

Sanskrit	→	Prana
Chinese	→	Chi
Greek	→	Pneuma
English	→	Spirit
Tibetan	→	Rlung

The Tao is the many thousands of years old ancient teaching of justice and right order. The Taoist doctrine states that the universe is comprised of Heaven, Earth and man, and that all embody a part of the Tao. Everything begins in and returns to the Tao.

The modern Yin-Yang symbol

The original, archaic Yin-Yang symbol

One of the main principles of Taoism is the belief in balancing forces, or yin and yang. These two forces represent matching pairs, such as light and dark, hot and cold, action and inaction that work together toward a universal whole. Yin and yang reveal that everything in the universe is connected and that nothing makes sense by itself.

Taoism became well known in the eighth century C.E. as the religion of the Tang dynasty. In the following centuries, it existed alongside Confucianism, another philosophical religion, and Buddhism. However, during the Communist takeover in 1959, Taoism, Confucianism, and other religions were banned. This caused a decline in the practice of Taoism in China. Many modern Taoists live in Taiwan, although recent reforms in China have increased the number of Chinese Taoists.

Sufism

Sufism is the <u>mystical</u> <u>Islamic</u> belief / high path, and practice for spiritual seekers to find the truth of divine love and knowledge through direct personal experience of God, a spiritual dimension of God-man union. Some scholars on religion and spirituality believe Sufism is a mystical concept that predates history, long before organized religion came into existence.

Since in Sufism the ecstatic union with the Divine is ignited by the internal passionate fire of the Heart, could it be there is a link to the very ancient Zoroastrian external fire worship and the Parsis (Parsees), who left Persia when the Muslims conquered Persia? Parsis still practice fire worship with an eternal flame in their temples (called Agiyari).

Sufism consists of a variety of mystical paths designed to ascertain the nature of humanity and God and to facilitate the experience of the presence of divine love and wisdom in the world. The Sufis are also generally known as "the poor" (fuqarā," plural of the Arabic faqīr, in Persian darvīsh, whence the English words fakir and dervish).

The Sufi Path has been described by some as primarily "a path of love," one in which "the human Soul searches out God, and if the grace of God falls upon the searcher, then he or she finds *fanā* (annihilation) in God and ultimately *baqā* (abiding) or eternal existence in the consciousness of God."

The Iranian-born Islamic philosopher, Seyyed Hossein Nasr, explained, "According to Sufism, the supreme goal of human life is to attain Truth, which is also Reality, the source of all reality, and whose attainment, as also stated by Christ, makes us free, delivering us from the bondage of ignorance. Although deeply involved with love, and also on a certain level with action, Sufism is at the highest level a path of knowledge (*ma'rifah* in Arabic and *'irfān* in Persian), a knowledge that is illuminative and unitive, a knowledge whose highest object is the Truth as such, that is, God, and subsequently the knowledge of things in relation to God. ... The knowledge of the Truth is like the light of the sun while love is like the heat that always accompanies that light."

Here's what Matthew Kelly wrote in an article for *Fountain Magazine*, "Rābiʿa's poetry illustrates the fact that the 'Early Sufis were mystics and philosophers first and poets second.'"

> O Lord, if I worship You
> because of fear of hell,
> then burn me in hell.
> If I worship You
> because I desire paradise,
> then exclude me from paradise.
> But if I worship You
> for Yourself alone,
> then deny me not
> your eternal beauty.

The poem, "If I Worship You," is virtually identical to a prayer attributed to St. Francis Xavier, which I discovered in reading James Kellenberger's discussion of motives for religious belief in The Cognitivity of Religion: Three Perspectives (1985: 125). Unfortunately, Kellenberger doesn't provide us with a reference. Another version, much longer, but containing the same religious sentiment regarding heaven and hell, is found here.

Many of the poems of Rābiʿa have not been authenticated, so it's possible that this is properly attributed to St. Francis Xavier, although he lived and died in the sixteenth century (and visited parts of the Islamic world in his extensive missionary travels) and Rābiʿa in the ninth, so perhaps the borrowing runs in the other direction! I've yet to come across any discussion of this in the scholarship on Rābiʿa."

Sufism has been defined in many ways. Some see it as God's annihilating the individual's ego, will, and self-centeredness and then reviving him / her spiritually with the light of His Essence. Such a transformation results in God's directing the individual's will in accordance with His Will. Others view it as a continuous striving to cleanse oneself of all that is bad or evil in order to acquire virtue.

Junayd al-Baghdadi, a famous Sufi master, defines Sufism as a method of recollecting "self-annihilation in God" and "permanence or subsistence with God." Shaykh Abu Bakr Shibli, an important Sufi of Persian descent, and a disciple of Junayd Baghdadi, summarizes it as always being together with God or in His presence.

There are some who describe Sufism as seeing behind the "outer" or surface appearance of things and events and interpreting whatever happens in the world in relation to God. This means that a person regards every act of God as a window to "see" Her / Him, lives his life as a continuous effort to view or "see" Her / Him with a profound, spiritual "seeing" indescribable in physical terms, and with a profound awareness of being continually overseen by Her / Him.

Some of the principles of Sufism are listed as follows:

- Reaching true belief in God's Divine Oneness and living in accordance with Its demands.

- Discerning and then obeying the commands of the Divine Power and Will as they relate to the universe; the laws of creation and life.

- Overflowing with Divine Love and getting along with all other beings in the realization (originating from Divine Love) that the universe is a cradle of brotherhood.

- Giving preference or precedence to the well-being and happiness of others.

- Acting in accord with the demands of the Divine Will, not with the demands of our own will, and living in a manner that reflects our self-annihilation in God and subsistence with Her / Him.

- Being open to love, spiritual yearning, delight, and spiritual intoxication of ecstasy.

- Struggling continuously against worldly ambitions and illusions, which lead us to believe that this world is eternal.

In 13th and 14th century-old Persia and Afghanistan, some Sufi poets achieved divine madness / spiritual intoxication and were highly revered for their wisdom. Their love poems have survived into the present time, like Mevlana Jalal al-Din Rumi, Hafiz, Layla, Mirabai, Kabir, Omar Khayam. Rumi is nowadays considered America's #1 poet. Sufi poems are a testimony to achieving divine bliss and spiritual ecstasy.

How do Sufis understand love? How does their poetry reflect love as a spiritual teaching? It is upon the human love for God, wherein there is always a duality between the human lover and the Divine Beloved.

"Not a single lover would seek union
if the beloved were not seeking it."

~ Mathew Kelly for *Fountain Magazine*

When love for God is described in terms of passion, then the language of romantic love is readily accessible to be adapted as the metaphoric language of the spiritual journey. In Sufi poetry there is a convention of the spiritual supplicant being called the lover of God, while God is referred to as the Beloved. Throughout Sufi poetry we read verses that elaborate ideas about the relationship of the lover and the Beloved.

Another poem of Rumi's that can be read as secular love poetry uses less recognizable references to God:

> In one sweet moment
> she burst from my heart.
> There we sat on the floor,
> drinking ruby wine.
>
> Trapped by her beauty,
> I saw and I touched –
> my whole face became eyes,
> all my eyes became hands.

Through the use of the conventional poetic symbols of his era, for example, drinking wine as a symbol for spiritual intoxication, the poet again expresses both secular and spiritual meanings simultaneously. Translator Jonathon Star says that Rumi, like other Sufi poets, at "the deepest level" of his poetry "tells only one story: the Soul's search for the Beloved." Historian and religious scholar Michael Sells writes:

> "For Rumi, passionate love, *ishq*, has two expressions. The first is love in the material world, 'like the love between male and female,' and the second is 'real love,' which is the 'love felt toward God.' In Rumi's spiritual masterpiece, *Masnavi*, the poet seeks to show that 'God is known primarily through love.'

> > Love came and it made me empty
> > Love came and it filled me with the Beloved
> > It became the blood in my body
> > It became my arms and my legs.
> > It became everything!
> > Now all I have is a name,
> > The rest belongs to the Beloved.

The verse describes the progressive, experiential knowledge of love. First came abandonment of the ego. Then, came submission whereby one no longer acts according to the ego, but in submission to the Beloved who now becomes '... his hearing with which he hears, his seeing with which he sees, his hand with which he strikes, and his foot with which he walks ...' as in the well-known hadith qudsi. When we use the metaphor of the spiritual journey, we know from Sufi poetry that love is the vehicle par excellence for the traveler.

The Arabic world abounds with poetry festivals. Iran's heritage of great love poetry is close on the lips and in the hearts of a large percentage of Iranians. Throughout much of the classical Islamic world, poetry is at the center of cultural life."

Tantra

The word Tantra means continuum and is related to the Sanskrit word for weaving. Just as in weaving a pattern is continuous, the nature of mind of ordinary beings has a continuum with the mind of enlightened beings or Buddhas. In essence, the nature of mind is the same, the union of luminosity and emptiness.

Mantra is a sacred utterance, numinous sound, a syllable, a word or group of words that has religious, spiritual or magical powers. Some mantras have literal meaning, others do not).

Tantra denotes esoteric traditions of Hinduism and Buddhism that developed in India in the first millennium AC. The term "tantra" in the various Indian traditions also means any organized, broadly applicable text, theory, system, method, instrument, technique, or practice. A key use of these traditions is the use of mantras.

Particularly in the West, Tantra is much misunderstood and is seen merely in its sexual aspect. I suggest Tantra to be an alchemical approach of transforming evil into merit, human love into Divine Love. It is the Law and Order of the Universe and Nature, much like the Tao.

Starting in the early centuries of the common era, newly revealed Tantras centering on Vishnu, Shiva or Shakti emerged. There are tantric lineages in all main forms of modern Hinduism, such as the Shaiva Siddhanta tradition, the Shakta sect of Sri-Vidya, the Kaula, and Kashmir Shaivism.

In Buddhism, the Vajrayana traditions are known for tantric ideas and practices, which are based on Indian Buddhist Tantras. They include Indo-Tibetan Buddhism, Chinese Esoteric Buddhism, Japanese Shingon Buddhism and Nepalese Newar Buddhism.

Tantric Hindu and Buddhist traditions have also influenced other Eastern religious traditions such as Jainism, the Tibetan Bön tradition, Daoism, and the Japanese Shintō tradition.

Certain modes of non-Vedic worship such as Puja are considered tantric in their conception and rituals. Hindu temple building also generally conforms to the iconography of tantra. Hindu texts describing these topics are called Tantras, Āgamas or Samhitās. In Buddhism, tantra has influenced the art and iconography of Tibetan and East Asian Buddhism, as well as historic cave temples of India and the art of Southeast Asia.

Tantra is a spiritual practice in which all aspects of earthly life, including sex, can be a path to spiritual realization. The essence of the practice is approaching everything as completely and as consciously as possible.

In his book, *Tantric Quest, An Encounter with Absolute Love*, the French author Daniel Odier travels to India and finds a female Tantrika in the wilderness. She becomes his guru and initiates him into ever-higher sexual practices combined with mental exercises for cleansing purposes. But it is only by being sent to the leper colonies that the author learns to open his Heart in compassion.

Mother Theresa found her spiritual rescue in her devotion to her Beloved, Jesus Christ. In her actions of serving the poorest-of-the-poor, she represents the epitome of compassion. So is the Little Angel of

Colombia who, since a young child, has made it his mission to take care of the poorest elderly in his city, Bucaramanga, Colombia.

In his first book, *Kali's Odyia*, author Amarananda Bhairavan describes his childhood initiation into a matriarchal Tantric tradition where he and his cousin were subjected to altered states of reality that involved shapeshifting and secret rites to transcend physical reality.

> "Important encounters are planned by the Souls
> long before the bodies see each other."
>
> ~ Paulo Coello

In terms of finding true love, I have always believed important relationships are decided while still in Spirit. The two Souls agree to incarnate at the same time, find each other, and express their lives through devotion of their love for each other. In the book, *The Shared Heart: Relationship Initiations and Celebrations*, authors Barry and Joyce Vissell tell the story of a hunchbacked man who fell in love with a beautiful maiden. But when her father introduced her to him, she had no attraction for him and kept her eyes averted.

In his attempt to win her Heart, the hunchback told her that he recognized her as his Beloved while they were both in Heaven. God said to him that she would be a hunchback, so he requested, "Let her be beautiful and give me the hunchback instead." The maiden then looked at him with an open Heart.

Adam is an Atom. Eve is an Electron. The story is mythology based on life beginning with "Splitting of the Atom," as electrons are the "rib" of the atom. God is the "Good" of your higher mind, the Cerebrum. Devil is the "Evil" of your lower mind, Cerebellum. Heaven is your "Head," the highest "heaved up" place of your body and higher nature. Hell is your "Heel," the lowest place of your body and lower nature. The tree is your spine. The apple is consciousness. Kundalini energy means activating your pineal gland; hence, conquering your own dragon.

~ Unknown

> "An invisible red thread connects those
> who are destined to meet
> regardless of time, place, or circumstances.
> The thread will stretch or tangle
> but it will never break."
>
> ~ Chinese Proverb

Love has the ability to raise us to Heaven but it can also cast us to hell. Losing the one we most love causes a death of the Heart. Yet love is like having the most beautiful butterfly landing on the palm of your hand. You cannot close your hand or the butterfly will be crushed and die. It's the same for love. Control and grasping will kill love, yet most people are so used to doing just that. Love becomes trapped with soft manipulations and hidden hooks. Once a couple has committed, it is all the harder to get out of the relationship. So people give in to an arrangement that is not true love and raise their children in a relationship that is not truly alive, vibrant, and synchronistic.

Sadly, most people fear to lose control when their Heart is getting involved. They tighten up out of fear and choose to keep their Heart protected and closed. They fear to give themselves away, loose control and fall apart. Though they seek love, they are not willing to give their All for love. What a strange concept this is.

> The risk of love is loss and the price of loss is grief. But the pain of grief is only a shadow when compared with the pain of never risking love."
>
> ~ Hilary Stanton Zunin

Many people also fail to see what true love means. True love for the Self and true love for another. We feel incomplete until we meet someone we're attracted to, and then, all we want is be with that person. We think this person makes us full where we were empty before. We view the object of our attention as the fulfillment of our dreams, and put on our rose-colored glasses and see everything as if it were a fairytale. Together, we project the "happy ending" with the "happily ever after" and think what started gloriously should forever stay that way.

"Life will break you.
Nobody can protect you from that,
And living alone won't either,
For solitude will also break you with its yearning.
You have to love.
You have to feel.
It is the reason you are here on Earth.
Your are here to risk your Heart.
You are here to be swallowed up.
And when it happens that you are broken, or betrayed,
or left, or hurt, or death brushes near,
Let yourself sit by an apple tree
And listen to the apples falling all around you in heaps,
Wasting their sweetness.
Tell yourself you tasted as many as you could."

~ Louise Erdrich

But most times, we get into a relationship due to some karmic debt and lessons needed for learning purposes. Things might not stay rosy but rather become rocky. I have often seen how people invest much effort into acquiring what they want — in this case, the desired relationship — but once they have it, they put it in their pocket, so to speak. They relax into their old habits. They lack the awareness that even if all is sweetness and light, work on the relationship has just started and is going to require a lot of attention because it's a work in progress.

It seems weird to say that for committed love, love is not enough. And yet, this is the case. Unless both partners are in service to their highest Self and committed to the consciousness growth of their Soul, love is not enough to make a relationship work successfully. If only one partner does the inner work of purification, but the other partner stays comfortable within their limited self, the relationship is doomed to fail.

BE IN SERVICE TO YOUR HIGHEST SELF AND COMMITTED TO THE CONSCIOUSNESS GROWTH OF YOUR SOUL

It helps to become aware of our intentions for the relationship we're seeking. How can we serve our Soul to the highest, while serving the other Soul equally as high?

If our intentions for the relationship are safety and security, then we are sub-consciously seeking a very different partner than if our intentions are romance and passion. I liken a "safety and security guy" more to a teddy bear father figure rather than a prince charming who, like a proud cat turned into a dog in heat, passionately takes us to cloud nine.

As for me, my primary intention in any relationship is inspiration. This applies to not only friendships but also romance. I want to be inspired by the man I love, and likewise inspire him to ever-greater heights. I want to be able to explore new universes and build visions that will become reality. With him, I want to climb Mount Everest in a sexual union of merging — not just hike a lovely hill.

"Surround yourself only with people who are going to take you higher."

~ Oprah Winfrey

We are lucky when our Soul guides us to find love. I agree with Deepak Chopra who said that "All love is based on the search for Spirit. To fall in love is definitely an act of the Soul." Yet, the English term "falling in love" feels weird. In my opinion, it should be "rising in love." After all, love raises us to Heaven. What is more exhilarating and vibrant in this world than true love, to experience synchronicity with someone as if they were an extension of the Self — in body, Heart, and Soul?!

What a mirror image of confirmation. We all want it, we all crave it. Yet we must first learn to fully love and embrace our own Self and serve our Soul above all else, for when we serve our Soul, we're also serving God / Source / the Universe.

Furthermore, it's also necessary to find the right balance in the relationship so that we're not subsumed by the other person, become co-dependent, or lose sight of ourselves.

I'm always surprised to learn how many people are concerned with how much they can get out of a relationship. But true love is being in

In the Fiji islands, nature provides an example of the Tubular Lace Coral, which stays open on one end and closes up once a female and male shrimp find their way into the tube. As it closes, the couple is protected, as well as caged forever.

service to another. True love involves sacrifice. José José puts it nicely in his song title "Amar y Querer," "To Like and to Love." Rather than being concerned with how much we can get out of a relationship, we should be concentrating on how much we can put into it — any kind of relationship.

TRUE LOVE IS SERVICE AND INVOLVES SACRIFICE

I'm definitely not referring to material goods nor speaking about accommodating a wounded personality in their distortions. What Julia Roberts said bears repeating, "Women, you are not rehabilitation centers for badly raised men. It's not your job to fix him, change him, parent, or raise him. You want a partner, not a project." Of course, the same goes for men concerning women.

"Do not commit to someone based on their potential!
They may not have a desire to reach it."

~ Pastor Marcus G

I'm speaking of the investment of the Soul. What then does it mean to be in service of another's Soul and at the same time serve your own Soul?

True loving is a highly evolved art form. Perhaps the highest spiritual art form there is. This can happen in the context of teacher and disciple, parent and child, lovers or friends. According to the ancient Greeks, there are eight types of love:

- Agápē or "selfless love" is the highest and most noble form of love. It's given without any expectation of receiving anything in return. It's the universal love for mankind.

- Eros is passionate and romantic love.

- Philia is intimate and authentic friendship among equals.

- Philautia is the term for self-love.

- Storge is the unconditional parental or familial love.

- Pragma is enduring love based on commitment, understanding, and long-term best interests.

- Ludus is flirtatious, playful, or uncommitted love.

- Mania is obsessive love.

"To love someone is to learn the song in their heart
and sing it to them when they have forgotten it."

~ Anonymous

True love can become a highly evolved spiritual art form involving great awareness and high consciousness from both participants. Ideally, both partners are on similar levels of consciousness, and must live their highest truth and wisdom in clarity and authenticity.

Serving each others' Soul requires maximum honesty towards the Self and towards the other. There is no sweet talk when it comes to speaking one's Truth. Divinity realized in an utterly human body temple.

"People think that intimacy is about sex.
But intimacy is about truth.
When you realize you can tell someone your truth,
when you can show yourself to them,
when you stand in front of them
and their response is 'you're safe with me'
— that's intimacy."

~ Anonymous

Whether the relationship is purely platonic or involves sexual engagement is to be decided between the parties involved. As described in the Sufi / Tantric tradition, spiritual seekers find the truth of divine love and knowledge through direct personal experience of God, a spiritual dimension of God-man union.

Dying to Love
Die! Die!
Die in this love!
If you die in this love
Your Soul will be renewed

Die! Die!
Don't fear the death
Of that which is known
If you die to the temporal
You will become timeless

Die! Die!
Cut off those chains
That hold you prisoner
To the world of attachment

Die! Die!
Die to the deathless
And you will be eternal

Die! Die!
And come out of this cloud
When you leave the cloud
You will be the effulgent moon

Die! Die!
Die to the din and the noise
Of mundane concerns
In the silence of love
You will find the spark of life

I Am Yours
Because the idol is your face
I have become an idolater
Because the wine is from your cup
I have become a drunkard
In the existence of your love
I have become non-existent
This non-existence linked to you
Is better than all existence

Surrender

In love, nothing is eternal but drinking your wine
There is no reason for bringing my life to you
Other than losing it
I said, "I just want to know you and then disappear"
She said, "Knowing me does not mean dying."

My Beloved

Know that my beloved is hidden from everyone
Know that she is beyond the belief of all beliefs
Know that in my heart she is as clear as the moon
Know that she is the life in my body and in my soul.

Defeated by Love

The sky was lit
by the splendor
of the moon
so powerful,
I fell to the ground.

Your love
has made me sure

I'm ready to forsake
this worldly life
and surrender
to the magnificence
of your being.

~ Excerpts from *The Love Poems of Rumi*
Edited by Deepak Chopra
Translated by Deepak Chopra
and Fereydoun Kia

Chapter 107

LIFE AS A SPIRITUAL PATH: A REASON, A TIME, AND A SEASON

"Being on a spiritual path does not prevent you
from facing times of darkness.
But it teaches you how to use the darkness as a tool to grow."

~ Anonymous

For various personal reasons, I do not regularly meditate as a spiritual practice. One reason is that I am simply too busy with my daily tasks here at the HeartPath Retreat Center. But this is a lame excuse. The other, more prominent reason is that I saw myself in a series of lifetimes, where from childhood on I left my parents and home and went into the wilderness to sit under a tree and meditate. I lost all connection to my body and the physical plane, and constantly sat in a lotus position reaching Samadhi.[43]

> "The essence of meditation is awareness."
> ~ Yongey Mingyur Rinpoche

Villagers came to feed me, but I wasn't even aware of them — and I couldn't have cared less. Mastering the ability to stay in Spirit, experiencing the all-encompassing union with the Divine, and dissolving the ego personality while having a physical body was all I cared for. It always resulted in a kind of spiritual suicide[44].

Seeing those lifetimes lost in the ether had a strong impact on me. I was shocked. Knowing that we are primarily spiritual beings with limited physical incarnations, I decided my current life should be focused on the here and now and inhabiting my body to the fullest of my capabilities.

"We are not human beings having a spiritual experience.
We are spiritual beings having a human experience."

~ Pierre Teilhard de Chardin

---

[43] Samadhi = a state of intense concentration achieved through meditation. In Hindu Yoga, this is regarded as the final stage, at which union with the Divine is reached (before or after death).
[44] When yogis focus intensely on reaching Samadhi and disregard their body's needs, they will eventually die, which is termed "spiritual suicide."

Paramahansa Yogananda in his book, *Autobiography of a Yogi*, tells of a Hindu saint who was lost in Samadhi for many hours. When he came out of it, he felt pain in his leg and saw that ants were eating away at a wound on his leg. He was conflicted because he felt the pain and at the same time, he also felt sorry for the ants who needed something to eat. So he went into Samadhi again. When he emerged again after spending many hours in Samadhi, his wound was bigger and even more ants were feasting on his leg. It hurt a lot but, again, he felt so sorry for the ants. So he kept dropping into Samadhi again and again so that the ants could eat his leg.

To me, life in itself is a constant spiritual practice and meditation. A prayer of gratitude to the Divine. I feel strongly guided and spend much time by myself, though I never feel alone. Long ago, my Soul took over.

LIFE IS A PRAYER OF GRATITUDE

Challenges are plentiful and I am certain if it were not for Spirit, I would not have the strength to proceed; to be able to remain calm, happy, and focused regardless of challenges; to remain trusting no matter what is a spiritual practice.

"No one saves us but ourselves.
No one can and no one may.
We ourselves must walk the path."

~ Buddha

Life is a constant giving and taking, a never-ending surrender to Spirit and a forever flow of receiving — a true communion. How did I get there? I didn't. It was my Soul's choice.

LIFE IS A NEVER-ENDING SURRENDER TO SPIRIT AND A FOREVER FLOW OF RECEIVING

A TRUE COMMUNION

I remember well when once in class with Les Brown I was given the assignment of listing the ten most important events of my life. I wrote down my ten most significant dreams of guidance. When the others in the class shared their most important events like graduation, marriage, children born and dear ones who died, my mouth stayed sealed in shock that once again my experience and evaluation of life was so utterly different.

We come into this life with free choice. Free choice for our ego personality is our God-given birthright. We are free to create our life anew every moment. At least, this is the way it should be. Free choice is what sets us apart from other lifeforms. To be able to execute free will is a marvelous thing indeed.

Not all people are born into circumstances where they can make use of this right. What comes to mind are people born into slavery. It still exists. Or babies born with life-altering birth defects and illnesses. Or children living in a war zone. These are just a few examples. There are many more circumstances that can inhibit this birthright of free choice. Therefore, though we are all born with free choice and free will, what we choose might be influenced and dictated by the limitations of our circumstances.

For the majority of us, however, we are "free" to exercise our free will and free choice. So the aim should be to take advantage of our free will and live it fully. Perhaps something beyond just catching up with old familiar connections and paying old karmic debts of past-life actions.

What if — while alive and in a body — we made it a priority to align ourselves with our Soul? What if — while we're alive — we constantly remember that we came into our body to learn? The more we learn, the more we grow spiritually. The more we grow spiritually, the more we advance spiritually. The more we advance spiritually, the more we experience freedom from the entrapments of the material world.

The priority is to align ourselves with our Soul.

THE MORE WE LEARN
THE MORE WE GROW SPIRITUALLY

THE MORE WE GROW SPIRITUALLY
THE MORE WE ADVANCE SPIRITUALLY

THE MORE WE ADVANCE SPIRITUALLY
THE MORE WE EXPERIENCE FREEDOM

However, I do believe there is a space beyond free will. There comes a time on Soul's evolutionary path when free choice no longer exists. If

I were fortunate enough to be able to ask His Holiness the Dalai Lama one question, I would ask, "Your Reverence, do you still have a choice?" The reason I'd ask this question is that I believe that when Soul has fully taken over in expressing our essence, there is no more need for free choice. There is only one path to choose from, only one path for us to take: the path our Soul has chosen for us. I am talking about a path no longer bound by Karma, a freely chosen path leading to utter fulfillment of body, mind, and Heart.

When we leave this earthly plane, Soul is all we are, all we leave with. Once back in Spirit, we look at a summary of our Soul growth. As I mentioned already in Part III, Section 2, Chapter 14, I compared the human energy field with an immense bio computer that stores everything — all our experiences, every emotion, our thoughts, and actions — in the Akashic Records[45]. They represent the summary and essence of who we are as Soul while in Spirit.

The center building with the Temple of the Living Goddess

Council of the Wise Elders

Moon Lake

We look at what we've learned. Observing a life is very much like watching a movie or reading a book. Sometimes we watch a movie or read a book waiting for just one meaningful sentence. One meaningful lesson learned is often all we take from each life and incorporate it into the next life. Hence our next life is the sum of all past lessons learned.

I moved from Switzerland to New Mexico in June of 1993 with the plan of building a healing retreat and training facility for my clientele and trainees. During 1995, with twenty-two crew members, we built the "La Hacienda" lodging facility and the center building with its "Temple of the Living Goddess." The oval shape of the building is reminiscent of the ancient goddess temples in the Mediterranean.

After completion, we terraced the sloping hills surrounding the center building. We connected the center building with La Hacienda via a stairway I named "Stairway to Heaven." We did this to prevent flash floods from inundating the house and so we could eventually put in a vineyard. Additionally, we improved the pond, Moon Lake, by adding bentonite to the soil to retain water and create an island in the middle for the ducks and geese to be safe from predators.

[45] A compendium of all universal events, thoughts, words, emotions, and intent ever to have occurred in the past, present, or future in terms of all entities and life forms, not just human.

Once finished, I focused on building the "Casa del Alma" guesthouse for my son Marc and my dad, Emilio.

Only when all of the above was completed, did I build my own residence. It took two years to finish. I had arrived in Santa Fe in 1993 and brought with me two 20-foot containers filled with my personal collection of artifacts from my previous life on various continents. There were also antique architectural items like doors, pillars, and windows I had purchased in India, Thailand, and Indonesia.

While building my home, I lived in the casita with my white Golden Retriever, Dreamer, the First, and my fourteen cats. La Casita had been the only existing structure when I purchased the property. I lived there for eight years and loved it so much that I had a hard time imagining ever moving out. But then, in November of 2002, I moved into my newly built home. The first time my dad walked into my new house, he commented that I had built a temple. He was right, only I had been completely unaware of it.

The entire building project was a declaration of pure love. I gave my very all. The architects were in the heavenly realm and I followed their clear and precise instructions. I was certain I would live here on the premises until the end of my days. I had zero clue that this was not to be. This beautiful and magical sanctuary represented my essence.

Up to that point, my schedule had been full with travels abroad for my work and also with receiving my students here for their training courses, as well as a full schedule of healing work and summer camps consisting of individual healing work, group meditations, physical exercise, and excursions to the Four Corners region of the Southwest.

This changed drastically with the tragedy of 9/11. I ended my last training cycle with European students and took a one-year break. There was much fear during the Bush regime. It was a gray time. Europeans didn't want to travel to the US anymore.

With 9/11, my dad got increasingly worried for me and insisted I sell the Retreat and return to Switzerland. To me, this was never an option. I had chosen my home and this was it. I had grown roots here like never before in my life. My living here was meant to be. Spirit had sent me here, for what deeper reason, I didn't yet know. When my practice slowed down considerably and finances became sparse but the maintenance and utility bills stayed high, my attitude of "giving up is not an option" remained my mantra.

But I had physically exhausted myself and was challenged with severe vitamin deficiency, mainly B12 and Folic Acid. Mysteriously, I ate ice by the bucket until a clerk at the post office pointed out that I was severely iron deficient. I felt that if I didn't take care of myself it might develop

The buffalo herd on the sacred Pojoaque Pueblo land that borders my property. Notice in the bottom picture the female white buffalo.

into something further and more challenging. It was a good time to take a break. Basically, for all of 2002, I didn't concentrate on my healing practice. Instead, I did my first pilgrimage to Santiago de Compostela.

That was the first time I walked the 500-plus miles. In subsequent years, I completed the pilgrimage two more times, but by bicycle.

With the crash of the stock market in 2008, the situation went from pretty bad to worse. The drastic cut of income made it financially challenging to maintain my Retreat Center. It broke my Heart to let go of my livestock. I owned ten Scottish Highland cattle, two paint horses, a miniature donkey, and fifteen Churro sheep. They had been living happily and peacefully together down in the barn out in the field.

During a conversation with an old friend of mine, I compared the Retreat with having a small child: We love that child and it brings only joy to us. And when the child is entering puberty and might turn rebellious, we love it all the same. My friend responded with, "It's a thing, it's not a child."

Those words sank deep. For a whole day, I saw the image of the biblical Abraham walking his son to the sacrificial place. Abraham's arm rested heavy on his young son's shoulder. In silence, they walked steadily uphill on a stony narrow trail. The image left me deeply pondering my attachment to the HeartPath Retreat Center. It had been my life work — my identity was tied to it. A life beyond the Retreat Center was unimaginable to me.

I was in too much of a shock to be able to cry. For fourteen days, I was a zombie. I didn't see or talk to anyone. I cut myself off from the world. I couldn't talk to anyone about the death process I was undergoing.

During those fourteen days, it became clear to me that I needed to let go and put my beloved Retreat Center on the market. It took me three weeks to pack up my personal sacred art collections and move out the furniture I was going to take with me. Once done, I felt my Soul had left even though I remained living there.

THERE IS A REASON, A TIME, AND A SEASON FOR EVERYTHING

ALL HAPPENS AT ITS OWN RIGHT TIME

DO NOT INTERFERE WITH THE TIMING OF THE UNIVERSE

I wrote a closing letter to my friends and clientele.

"This decision has been the most painful one I have faced in all of my life. My whole identity, my Heart and Soul, have been tied to this place I have built to grow and love with all my Being. Such an unimaginable decision I had never wanted to face!

Though as soon as I let go of my resistance to the change that needs to happen, a liberating feeling has become my constant companion. I can now joyfully say that mine is a peaceful Heart and a clear mind, trusting fully that in due time it will be revealed to me why this sacrifice was necessary in order to bring me to where I need to go in my life."

I owe the deepest gratitude to all my clients and students for their trust — in me and the work — and for their innermost commitment to themselves and their spiritual growth. I am more devoted than ever to my work and mission to transform this world into a better place, one person at a time."

All of you who have visited the HeartPath Retreat Center in Pojoaque might have a clue of the challenging task of running an operation of this size — all by oneself. The costs of building and maintenance, and the constant workload have seemed like a bottomless pit, certainly more that I would want to handle in the long run.

Powerful transitions call for tremendous sacrifice, change, and transformation. A little more than a year ago, I had a life-changing realization. In a moment of absolute clarity, I understood that during the years serving the ministry[46], I had again become the high priestess from long ago living alone in a temple within a temple complex serving the populace. Just as in the past, individuals young and old, from near and far arrived to attain advice; heal their body, Heart, and Soul; and restore their lives.

No matter where the future carries me, I will continue to serve the Goddess in this way until my parting day. This is my role. Yet I will cease to sacrifice my personal life for it. That has become very clear to me.

Where I will go from here is still a mystery. My existence will become a blank white canvas upon which I can paint in rich, bright, vibrant colors my life anew. Where Spirit will lead me — I don't yet know. I trust, though, that what lies ahead of me is grander than what I leave behind.

As soon as you let go of your resistance to the change that needs to happen

a liberating feeling will become your constant companion

Sacrifice is necessary in order to bring you to where you need to go in your life

Powerful transitions call for tremendous sacrifice change and transformation

[46] Originally, the HeartPath Retreat Center was called the "Ministry of Angels." I changed that name because in some languages, the term is associated with governmental buildings.

WHERE YOU GO FROM HERE
IS STILL A MYSTERY

LET YOUR EXISTENCE BECOME
A BLANK WHITE CANVAS
UPON WHICH YOU CAN PAINT IN RICH,
VIBRANT COLORS YOUR LIFE ANEW

WHERE SPIRIT WILL LEAD YOU —
YOU DON'T YET KNOW
TRUST, THOUGH,
THAT WHAT LIES AHEAD
IS GRANDER THAN WHAT YOU LEAVE BEHIND

A place infused with Prayer
An oasis of Beauty
A refuge of Safety
A haven of Peace
A sanctuary of Joy

A retreat from the mundane
where all becomes sacred again

In closing, I invite you to please join me in my prayer that this place continues to live and grow in the Spirit it was intended and built, a place infused with Prayer, an oasis of Beauty, a refuge of Safety, a haven of Peace, a sanctuary of Joy, a retreat from the mundane where all becomes sacred again.

To me, every awe-invoking moment is a prayer to the Universe. During my years at the ministry, I have been fortunate to witness countless prayers. Those prayers will continue to enrich and bless my life and the lives of those who witnessed. Rest assured, no matter where Spirit calls me, I shall continue to build Heaven on Earth — Glory Hallelujah!"

EVERY AWE-INVOKING MOMENT
IS A PRAYER TO THE UNIVERSE

From 2008 – 2011, my property was on the market with Sotheby's. We had a large number of showings. Apparently, everyone loved it and wanted to buy it. But the banks were not providing loans. When my Realtor suggested a ridiculously low price to sell the property, I took it off the market. I advertised the business and property for sale on a free German website and forgot about it.

In 2013, two fabulous real estate agents from Christie's approached me. The stock market had recovered and I decided to list with them. It almost sold in 2015 as a retreat center to a Chinese Chi Gong master.

In October of 2016, I returned home from a trip to Brazil and Argentina to visit my grandchildren and to tango (I am a passionate Argentine Tango dancer). Within a week, I received a phone call. A German-speaking man with an Indian accent introduced himself and said he had seen my ad on the German website. He inquired if it was still for sale and spoke to me of his plan to establish an Ayurvedic clinic on the premises.

He requested that I send an email with pics of the buildings and an exact description, as well as the asking price. I did so without further delay. He liked it very much and agreed on the price. We were setting up the next steps and it was considered sold. I informed my real estate agents.

Contemplating my great fortune of selling the Retreat, I felt tremendously relieved. I had the strong sensation that a huge load of heavy rocks had been taken off my shoulders. I was ecstatic. I also saw a big room filled with countless stacks of dollar bills. The thought, "You have just sold your Soul" suddenly came through. I had no clue what to do with all that money. And I trusted that with time I would know. Most of all, I felt immensely relieved at having passed this trial of financial hardship. It was October 23rd of 2016 and I went to bed and fell asleep.

The next morning, two days before my birthday, I woke up to a clear vision. In the dream state, Spirit gave me instruction to found the first "church" for Jesus Christ and Mary Magdalene (church in quote marks for lack of a better word). I was told they had never been able to teach together. Separate yes, but not together. Half awake, half asleep, I remember feeling, "How strange … this makes total sense. Why did I never think of this before?!"

Spirit also said that Santa Fe shall become the sacred city of the US, like Jerusalem and Rome, and by becoming the sacred city of the US, the country could begin its journey toward healing.

I was further told that Jesus and Mary Magdalene would become the new patron saints for Santa Fe, at which point, Mary Magdalene spoke saying that she already is the Virgin de Guadalupe.

> The renowned British author, Laurence Gardiner, who has dedicated his life to the unveiling of historical facts, states in his book, *The Magdalene Legacy, The Jesus and Mary Bloodline Conspiracy – Revelations Beyond The Da Vinci Code*, that in the old days, painters used a secret language of colors to identify the saints they were asked to paint. Mary, the mother of Jesus, was dressed in light blue and white, whereas Mary Magdalene, who Gardiner states was the wife of Jesus, was painted in red, royal blue, and gold. His book contains a family tree of the bloodline of the two of them. His book, *Bloodline of the Holy Grail*, is about the hidden lineage of the Holy Grail.

According to Gardiner's research, Jesus and Mary Magdalene were both from royalty, Jesus of the house of David and Mary Magdalene of Syrian royal heritage. All over Europe, the Black Madonna is highly revered in Catholic circles, though the ordinary populace was and still is not aware that the Black Madonna with her dark skin color represents Mary Magdalene. But within the secret esoteric circles, this is a known fact.

Many scholars say that the Black Madonna is a link to religions that existed long before Christianity. Her shrines are often in locations that were once pagan shrines to Diana, Artemis of Ephesus, Cybele, and other goddesses. Some Black Madonna figures, statues or paintings look just like the Egyptian goddess Isis with her infant son Horus, showing the influence of old ways on changing faiths. Even further back than that, she may represent the archetypal Earth Mother, the ancient, eternal power of the feminine force.

Without a single moment of hesitation, I sent an email to the buyer telling him that unfortunately my property was not for sale anymore. He responded with a letter, very upset, cursing me for joking with him. I apologized and affirmed to him that I meant no disrespect but that something had drastically changed in my life.

History keeps repeating itself. We can observe this on a universal level and also in our personal history. But we need to take care to pay attention. This is easy to do if we observe the various life cycles we are in during the course of our life.[47]

OUR PERSONAL HISTORY KEEPS REPEATING ITSELF

While living in Switzerland in 1989 and prior to my vocation as a healer, I was offered to become the business partner of the owner of a highly established archaeological art gallery in Paris. This was during the period when I already had given up my own gallery in Zurich but had zero clue what was next in store for my life.

Getting that offer from this friend was flattering. I thanked her and thought for a moment before I responded. "This position is maybe for your son or your daughter. It's not for me." She at first asked me about my future plans and I responded that I had no clue. She then cursed me and called me stupid for declining her offer.

---

[47] Chapter 104: The Evolutionary Path of the Soul.

Spiritual progress happens in a spiral. With the Indian buyer cursing me, I realized I was in the same cycle just as in 1989, only I was one level higher on the spiral.

The cycle of Life
(history repeats itself)

SPIRITUAL PROGRESS
HAPPENS IN A SPIRAL

EVERY TIME WE COMPLETE A CYCLE
WE ARE ONE SPIRAL HIGHER

But back to the current situation in 2016. I took down the Christie's For Sale sign and called my real estate agents and asked them for a meeting the same day. Upon meeting, I explained what had transpired and returned the For Sale sign to them. I had exactly $50 to my name without knowing where my next influx of income would be coming from. I bought a birthday cake with the $50 and invited all my friends for a birthday party at the Temple of the Living Goddess to share my experience with them.

Since 2016, I no longer celebrate my birthday. October 24th has become the celebration day of Jesus and Mary Magdalene. I celebrate it every year.

The next trial awaited me. How in the world would I do what I was being told to do?

Clueless on how to go about laying the foundation for the new "church," Spirit instructed me to return to the origin of sacred worship and include cleansing ritual, alignment with Spirit, movement, music/chant, contemplation time, and prayer.

In the Spring of 2017, I completely redecorated the Temple of the Living Goddess and also changed the royal blue color that had dominated the temple before to red, the color of Mary Magdalene and Jesus.

Thus, the Sacred Rite Celebration[48] came into being revering the divine feminine / divine masculine and the sacred marriage within. The focal point of the Sacred Rite Celebration is honoring one's sacred Heart, the ancient Egyptian rite of passage "Weighing of the Heart" ceremony is re-enacted.

In essence, the Sacred Rite Celebration consists of a series of music pieces, whenever possible channeled by a live musician. It's followed by

---

[48] The Sacred Rite Celebration is in celebration of Jesus and Mary Magdalene or the "Inner Male and the Inner Female & the Sacred Marriage Within." It is a personal, meditative experience where ancient Egyptian rites are being re-enacted.

short meditations, allowing sufficient time to connect and communicate with one's inner Self. Thus, the experience becomes very individual and personally intimate. During the years of 2017 and 2018, the Sacred Rite Celebration was held at the Temple of the Living Goddess.

> "Prayer is talking to the Universe.
> Meditation is listening to it."
> ~ Anonymous

During most of 2019, the Pojoaque Pueblo was planning on purchasing the property. It seemed an ideal fit with their plan of using it as a community rehabilitation center. Therefore, in the spring of 2019, I took down the entire interior decoration of the temple. The original royal blue silk curtains were put up again.

I sobbed uncontrollably. It was tremendously hard, much harder than taking down the decor of my home. In the middle of my tears flowing like a river, I was told very matter of factly, "You arrived here to build a healing retreat and training facility. That purpose has been fulfilled. You will receive a new assignment." Instantly, I became calm and serene and completed my task.

Months passed and in due time, I did receive my next assignment: I am to build a temple again. It will become a sacred temple ground consisting of outdoor space, a museum for the ancient Mother Goddess, a store, restaurant, several healing rooms, and a large room for the PowerLine workout. A very new concept the world has not yet seen. No more retreat center and lodging facility, but I am working on creating a foundation and serving both the city of Santa Fe and the world at large.

I have not yet passed the retreat center on to the new stewards. But looking back at my purpose in building, maintaining and passing it on, I fully understand. All happens for a reason, a time, and a season. And then we must move on. And if we don't, our life-force decreases and our purpose deteriorates. This is the spiritual path for everyone.[49]

> "If you bring forth what is within you
> What you bring forth will save you.
> If you do not bring forth what is within you
> What you do not bring forth will destroy you."
> ~ Jesus Christ
> Gospel of St. Thomas

---

[49] For reference, please review Part IV, Section 4, Chapter 37: "Anna in the Realm of the Nature Spirits" where Anna refuses to pass on her knowledge and life starts to bypass her.

ALL HAPPENS FOR A REASON, A TIME, AND A
SEASON

THEN WE MUST MOVE ON

IF WE DON'T, OUR LIFE-FORCE DECREASES
AND OUR PURPOSE DETERIORATES

THIS IS THE SPIRITUAL PATH FOR EVERYONE

Chapter 108

FULL CIRCLE: WHEN THE SOUL CALLS

WHAT YOU LOVE YOU WILL NEVER LOSE
WHAT YOU ARE SEEKING IS SEEKING YOU

For good reason, I am ending with this chapter titled the same as this book. In the beginning chapters, I described in detail how my Soul called me to do this work. I also elaborated on how over many years I have surrendered my life to my Soul.

In the previous chapter, I wrote of the challenging task of letting go of the HeartPath Retreat Center. In this chapter, I pay homage to this beloved place I shall soon leave. I cannot fathom how I came to be so fortunate as to have been able to manifest this sacred sanctuary of beauty, harmony, and serenity. I cannot even describe how deeply grateful I am for having created, lived, and worked for almost thirty years in this place infused with blessings and inspiration. Truly, I've built my dream that I didn't even know existed.

In this last chapter of the book, I also want to elaborate on passing my home on to the new stewards; ideally, someone who feels called to serving the community and will continue with the task for which it was intended and built. I trust for Spirit to guide this process of continuation and the new owners to feel equally blessed to live here in this beautiful setting. What better place to seek personal healing?

Tibetan teacher and master Yongey Mingyur Rinpoche, wrote in his book, *In Love with the World,*

> "To make yourself a better person is to make this world a better place. Until we transform ourselves, we are like mobs of angry people screaming for peace. In order to move the world, we must be able to stand still in it. Now more than ever, I place my Faith in Gandhi's approach 'Be the change you wish to see in the World.' Nothing is more essential for the twenty-first century and beyond than personal transformation. It's our only hope. Transforming ourself is transforming the world."

"Nothing is more essential
for the twenty-first century
than personal transformation.

We must all aim to become Whole.
Transforming ourselves
is transforming the world."

The HeartPath Retreat Center with its wide-open views to the Sangre de Christo mountains (Blood of Christ mountains) and the backdrop of the Barranca hills — untouched sacred land of the Pueblo to the West and the North reaching to the horizon — invites the Heart to expand, the mind to relax, and the body to rejuvenate. And sometimes, a grazing herd of buffalo appears. But before I continue describing my home, I want to introduce the town where it is situated. Pojoaque in Tewa translates as "water gathering place."

The green valley of Pojoaque offers such diversity. We have many hiking trails in the area. Nambe Falls, my favorite, is nearby. So is Santa Cruz Lake and various ancient cliff dwellings of the Anasazi. Pojoaque is a cross point between Santa Fe, Taos, and Los Alamos.

The lovingly built Pojoaque museum is a testimony to how Indians lived centuries ago and adapted to a modern lifestyle. Their little church sits on a hill in the pueblo and is another marvel worthwhile exploring. The Pojoaque Pueblo, though small, is progressive and creative in many ways and sets a great example of triumph over a painful, haunted past that the original inhabitants of the American continent were able to overcome.

Santa Fe is a marketplace for the creative arts and healing. Most people's take on healing is one of pleasant sensations, which Santa Fe provides in abundance, such as the marvelous authentic Japanese spa, Ten Thousand Waves. And then there is also the raw beauty of nature and the rich culture of the indigenous heritage, which is still very cultivated in this region and in some ways also integrated with the culture of Santa Fe.

I love the Northern part of New Mexico. This is the only home I've known for almost thirty years. The drive along the Rio Grande to artsy Taos and the route through the wilderness to Pagosa Springs in Colorado with its marvelous natural springs by the river is magical. The Jemez Mountains with Bandelier National Park and the Valle Grande down to Jemez Pueblo with its red rocks is another of my favorite destinations.

I have observed that people moving to Santa Fe experience that the town's energy will either spit you out or it will absorb you. And oftentimes, it's not them who will make that decision. Making a living in this town isn't for the faint of heart. Over the years, I have met so many who moved here by choice, leaving the big city and their high-dollar corporate salary behind and loving the feel of this place. But within a short period of time, they had to leave again because they couldn't make a living. This region calls for people to become creative and rely on their inner resources. Furthermore, people move here for healing their lives and finding peace in their Hearts. Whether they realize it or not, they want to build a quiet Heart.

Particularly since the upheaval and uncertainties of the last few years, people feel drawn to live in a more rural place, away from frenetic cities and immerse in the healing powers of Nature. Santa Fe has so much to offer, not only in this respect but also in its rich culture and diversity. Celebrities have chosen the area of Santa Fe for years as their residence, and many important international artists find their way here to perform at the Santa Fe Opera, some of its churches, and the Lensic Theatre.

Santa Fe living is authentic and down to Earth and reminds us of the more important values of a life with quality. Perhaps, without realizing it consciously, individuals feel drawn to healing their Soul when choosing Santa Fe and area as their new home.

Because Santa Fe is a 4th chakra place (4th chakra = Heart), one of the very few we have in the US, individuals are required to become very creative in making their living. Most places in the so-called civilized world are 3rd chakra places (3rd chakra = solar plexus = power + money). Whereas, in places of war, famine and poverty, people live under 1st and 2nd chakra conditions (1st chakra = root chakra = survival; 2nd chakra = reproductive organs = nurturance).

4th Chakra = Heart = Healing

3rd Chakra = Solar plexus = power + money

2nd Chakra = reproductive organs = nurturance

1st Chakra = root chakra = survival

How much I love my life here. Whenever I travel, after the excitement of the new place wears off, I start to miss my home and environment. Santa Fe provides such a different feel for living. It has truly become my home, I have grown roots here and unless Spirit decides differently, Santa Fe will stay my home. I feel I have arrived full circle in my dharma[50]. A big chapter of my life is closing by having written this book and introducing my work to a larger audience.

Ever since ancient times, people have used various divination methods like the Runes, the Tarot or the I Ching to provide insight to the various stages in life. According to the life cycle chart in the Tarot[51] book by Angeles Arrien, *The Tarot Handbook: Practical Applications of Ancient Visual Symbols*, I was in the "Death and Rebirth" cycle during 2021. I could feel the rebirth happening because I surrendered fully to

---

[50] In Buddhism, Dharma is the law governing one's individual conduct concerning a duty or given task.
[51] Tarot is a form of divination and guidance for life.

the death cycle. We need to be willing to die to our old life for rebirth to happen. By doing so, a whole new book with different chapters will open its new life for / to us.

Spiritual Realm

Thought + desire produces
instant results

Matter

It takes time + patience
until desire results in action

FULL REBIRTH CAN ONLY HAPPEN IF WE ARE WILLING TO FIRST FULLY DIE

When I left Switzerland in 1993, I truly had zero clue how big my life would become. My upbringing had been exotic and my life as a young woman had been vibrant with rich experiences in love and living in such different parts of the world and immersing myself in those cultures. Upon surrendering to my mission and life purpose, from the very start, my healing practice in Switzerland was very successful. Had I stayed in Switzerland, I would have been comfortable and widely acknowledged until the end of my days. And most certainly, also bored because I don't resonate much with the cold and foggy Swiss climate and rigid Germanic heritage.

But I had a dream and purpose, to build a healing retreat and training facility for my clientele and trainees. And I obeyed blindly when Spirit sent me to Santa Fe rather than Andalucia, Spain, my original plan to where I personally felt drawn.

Energetically, my life and task at my beloved retreat center were completed with my realization in 2008 that I needed to put it on the market for sale. I had fulfilled my purpose.

In the spiritual realm energy moves instantaneously. Each thought or desire produces instant results. It functions like a light switch: you flip the switch on and don't have to wait for the light to travel to the light bulb. Matter, on the other hand, is immensely slower and requires much patience until desire results in action.

The next step required a long waiting period. Indeed, letting go of the HeartPath Retreat Center has been a challenging spiritual task I can feel I've fully completed. I was only able to wholeheartedly do this because I received my new task from Spirit, which is closing my private healing practice and concentrating exclusively on training others in the HeartPath Re-alignment so that they can open their own healing practices.

I look forward to continuing to serve the community of Santa Fe and the world at large with the vision and direct transmission passed down to me. To immerse myself again in the creative process of building fills my Heart with so much joy. Creating holy ground with a temple where Soul resides and people can arrive and contemplate, come for healing or to train, or for physical fitness will bring much inspiration to the world.

I am truly grateful for the rich abundance of deep healings, transformation, realizations, and inspirations that occurred here at the HeartPath Retreat Center. They will forever stay embedded in this land. The rivers of tears I cried in letting go might well compete with the nearby Rio Grande, more accurately Rio Chico in this area. The healings, trainings, workshops, the PowerLine Workout classes, the weddings, the Sacred Rite Celebration events, and all the other gatherings of all different kinds of meditation, prayer, dance, and song have blessed the matrix of this environment.

Whenever I sit under the Mother tree down by Moon Lake, my Heart is filled with joy listening to the orchestra of the large chimes, sometimes almost silent and at times furiously loud. It's indeed healing to feel the elements clear the mind and open the Heart, to be surrounded by nature and smell the earth after a good rain. The closest hiking trail to the Barrancas hills just over the fence where the buffalo live. I shall miss it all — and especially the nights sleeping outside underneath the covered portal upstairs, watching the stars, listening to the frogs and crickets, the owls, and sometimes the peacocks.

I HEAR YOUR VOICE IN THE ROAMING WIND,
AND SEE YOUR FACE AS LIGHT ON EARTH.
I SMELL YOUR FRAGRANCE
IN THE FRESHNESS OF THIS DAY,
AND TASTE YOUR ESSENCE
LIKE HONEY OF MY LOVER'S KISS.
YOUR PRESENCE BRINGS PEACE.
WHAT ELSE COULD I WANT.
IN THE SILENCE OF MY HEART
I HEAR YOUR SONG.
IN THE SOLITUDE OF MY EXISTENCE
I FIND BEAUTY.

Will I ever be able to build such a beautiful place again? To me, it feels like a glimpse into paradise. I love the sacred temple of my home with all my Heart, the many nooks and altars, the arched corridors with stone pillars and the passageways, the glowing stucco-colored beeswax walls of cinnabar, saffron and pale olive-green color, the coved ceilings and the open fireplaces, and — so much more. My home, Shangri-La, is an architectural marvel indeed.

The warm season spent in my garden, an exotic oasis with the various fountains, is as if I were in paradise somewhere. But no, I am here in my home. And yes, in paradise. Flowing water amidst the desert, tremendously soothing to the Soul. The restless humming of the hummingbirds — it was calculated that more than a thousand return here every spring to nest and raise their young. I call them "dolphins of the air," their frequency is high and brings much joy. And dragonflies of all kinds; we have so many here.

I shall forever remember the days from May 3rd – July 26 of 2021 when — under the lower portal of my garden by the little creek — in less than three months, I religiously wrote this book from 7:00 am to 7:00 pm.

The countless meals I prepared with much love and devotion in my kitchen, alone or in the company of friends. Innumerable invites and parties with much joy, laughter, and celebration. My animal family loves it here too, Dreamer and my seven cats Pasha, Raji, Shakti, Buddha, Padma, Maat, and Shivani.

If love and joy could fill containers, I doubt that my very large cellar would be able to store all the bottles. Certainly, when I leave, I am taking countless loving memories with me. I shall stay nurtured for the rest of my days.

I'm reminded that Flamenco lyrics speak of fiery love and passion, whereas Portuguese Fado music is all about "Saudade," nostalgia-filled melancholic praises for the homeland and the hearth. Those are the feelings accompanying me.

In these past weeks, I have come to understand what is so deeply true: We can only let go of what we truly loved. It is the hardest but also the most liberating. Letting go of something we don't deeply care for doesn't require personal sacrifice. But in letting go of something we dearly loved lies liberation.

Not forced, though — we can only fully let go of what fully saturates us. I am reminded of the sacrifice of my great love, Roberto, and how by doing so, I received the greatest gift: my vocation to serve humanity.

"May you be at peace.
May your Heart remain open.
May you awaken to the light of your own true nature.
May you be healed.
May you be a source of healing for all beings."

~ Tibetan Buddhist Prayer

CONCLUSION

Writing this book has been an amazing journey of reflection of my own journey, as well as those with whom I've worked. The courageous work these individuals have done is remarkable, astonishing, and Soul lifting.

More than ever, the world needs healing now. We've lived through countless conflicts and two World Wars, but now we're looking at a possible sixth extinction, as well as the debasing of humanity to such a low level of consciousness that I foresee only intense strife on all levels of existence. We might not be able to recover either physically or with our sanity intact.

The HeartPath Retreat and the work I do is small relief from the fear, anxiety, and resultant destructiveness overtaking the world — but each person I work with is a beacon of light against the dark powers at work. That is my reward, to know that in my small way I am providing healing assistance and guidance for Souls in pain that are finding answers, relief, and even peace in their lives.

As Lao Tzu said, "The journey of a thousand miles begins with a single step." It is a step we must take anew each day: to face our challenges, both within ourselves and without, and seek higher understanding, wisdom, love, and inner peace.

Therefore, I dare say that the healing of our beloved planet Earth becomes a personal responsibility for each and every one of us. We must all aim to become whole from within and only then can the outer world reflect our image as ambassadors of our planet: Earth.

My wish and intention for all who read this book is to find hope and inspiration to improve their life and move in the direction of deep personal fulfillment, by understanding the importance of their Divine essence and by commencing a dialog with their innermost being, their Heart and Soul.

"Peace within the individual
is a step toward
Peace in the world."

~ Mildred Lisette Norman

ABOUT THE AUTHOR

Photo by Daniel
Quat Photography

Silvana Maria Pagani is a worldwide Soul counselor, teacher and visionary, and the founder of the HeartPath Retreat Center in Santa Fe, New Mexico, USA.

Originally from Switzerland, she lived on five different continents, speaks several languages fluently and calls the globe her home. In 1993, she followed her "Inner Call" to come to New Mexico to build the HeartPath Retreat Center, which she first named the Ministry of Angels. It includes the Temple of the Living Goddess, referred to by those who come to visit, as an architectural marvel. Unbeknownst to Silvana at the time of construction, it is reminiscent of the ancient matriarchal temples found on several islands in the Mediterranean.

Prior to moving to Santa Fe NM, Silvana ran a very successful healing practice on the outskirts of Zurich, Switzerland, working with her clientele on the level of the Soul during multi-day healing intensives. As a result, many "miraculous healings" occurred within a very short time span.

Silvana is a pioneering leader in her field. In the course of over 30 years, she developed her own holistic healing approach; the HeartPath Re-Alignment and its Maha Intensive, and the PowerLine Healing modality, as well as the PowerLine Workout program, and the TENSU Body Injury Trauma Release Healing.

She has worked with many hundreds of individuals, including children, leading them toward fulfillment and their true destiny. They return to their lives renewed, open-hearted, with a new level of clarity, and are deeply transformed. Her clientele arrive from all over the world and all walks of life.

During the dialog with their Soul, clientele gain profound understanding of their condition and deep insight into why their ego-personality attracted their ailment. With that understanding gained, the body system naturally has a chance to re-align itself in a healthy way; to cure and heal from all kinds of cancer and tumors, heart disease, headaches and migraines, back pain, intestinal problems, injuries of any kind, chronic conditions, addictions, stress and depressions, fears, panic attacks and phobias, all kinds of conscious (as well as subconscious) trauma, PTSD, grief, low self-esteem and sexual problems, childhood traumas, relationship issues, emotional problems, mental disorders, and spiritual conflicts.

In the earlier part of her life, Silvana was fully immersed in her responsibility as a young single mom. It was therefore only in her late twenties when she learned of the metaphysical, which immediately became her passion. This resulted in subsequent reading of ancient and contemporary literature on the subject. She began her studies with various teachers on Taoism, Tantra and Psycho-Spiritual therapy. She then studied and trained with physicist and former NASA scientist Barbara Ann Brennan, author of *Hands of Light*, *Light Emerging*, and *Core Healing*.

485

In her own healing practice, Silvana uses Barbara Ann Brennan's discoveries about the human energy field as a reference point and framework set in her own healing approach of the HeartPath Re-Alignment. Additionally, Silvana developed her own unique techniques toward healing the common developmental "Wounding" stages. She continues to refer to her clientele as her greatest teachers.

Silvana is also the founder of the First Temple of Jesus Christ & Mary Magdalene and the founder of the Temple of the Sacred Marriage Within. During the summer months, she hosts her Sacred Rite Celebration in the Temple of the Living Goddess.

Stained-glass window in the center skylight of the Temple of the Living Goddess

UNIVERSAL LAWS AND PRINCIPLES
(CONTINUED)

IF YOU WANT TO BECOME
SPIRITUALLY FREE
YOU NEED TO LET GO
OF THE NEED TO BE LOVED

WHAT YOU FEAR
YOU WILL ATTRACT

WHAT EXPANDS WILL ALSO CONTRACT

EVERYTHING HAS IS POLAR OPPOSITE
LIKE THE SWING OF A PENDULUM

DO WHAT YOU MUST DO
AND DO IT WITH LOVE

OUT OF CHAOS A NEW ORDER CAN BE CREATED

WHEN ACTING WITH LIKE-MINDED INDIVIDUALS
MORE CAN DO MORE TOGETHER
THE MULTIPLYING OF ENERGY CREATES

EACH LIFE IS AN ASSUMING
OF ANCIENT OBLIGATIONS
A RECOVERY OF OLD RELATIONS

AN OPPORTUNITY FOR THE PAYING
OF OLD INDEBTEDNESS
A CHANCE TO MAKE RESTITUTION AND PROGRESS

AN AWAKENING OF DEEP-SEATED QUALITIES
A RECOGNITION OF OLD FRIENDS AND ENEMIES

THE SOLUTION OF REVOLTING INJUSTICES
AND THE EXPLANATION OF THAT
WHICH CONDITIONS THE HUMAN AND MAKES HIM
WHAT HE IS
AND WITH MORE SOUL GROWTH
THAN PREVIOUSLY EXPERIENCED

DEATH AND THE REBIRTH
OF ALL THINGS
A CONSTANT CREATION AND DESTRUCTION
OF SUNS, WORLDS, AND GALAXIES
A RISE AND FALL OF GOVERNMENTS AND NATIONS

EVERYONE IS ENTITLED TO DECIDE
THE BELIEF SYSTEM
ONE FEELS COMFORTABLE WITH
MAKE CAREER DECISIONS FOR SELF
AND CREATE THE LIFE THAT WILL ALLOW ONE
TO FULFILL
HIS OR HER OWN BIRTH VISION AND DESTINY

SOUND HAS THE POWER TO RESTORE
PEOPLE TO THEIR HARMONIC PATTERNS

EVERY ACTION IS A PRAYER
TO THE CREATOR OF ALL
WHEN THIS IS DONE WITH SUCCESS

EVERY AWE INVOKING MOMENT
IS A MOMENT IN THE PRESENCE OF GOD

GOD'S ESSENCE IS REVEALED IN BEAUTY

SURRENDERING IS FRIGHTENING
AT THE INSTANT OF SURRENDER
THE ENTIRE BEING
MERGES INTO THE HIGHER MANIFESTATION
OF REALITY
IN RELATION TO ITS POINT OF DEVELOPMENT

THERE IS NOTHING BUT THE PRESENT MOMENT
THE ONLY MOMENT WE HAVE IS NOW
THIS IS WHERE WE CREATE
WHAT WE HAVE DONE IS DONE
AND THAT MOMENT IN HISTORY EXISTS
ONLY AS A RECORD IN TIME AND SPACE

THE LONGER PURE THOUGHT
OF ONE'S DESIRED GOAL
IS HELD IN THE MIND
THE MORE POWERFUL THE RESULT

HOLDING A PURE THOUGHT FOR
AN INCREMENT OF TIME
IS THE BEGINNING LESSON OF MANIFESTATION

THE SPAN OF LIFE IS RELATED TO THE RATE
OF BREATHING
THE AVERAGE RATE OF BREATHING IS
30 PER MINUTE
AND THE LIFE SPAN WILL BE ONLY 60 YEARS
BECAUSE OF POOR LIVING HABITS AND
NEEDLESS EXPENDITURE OF ENERGY

HOWEVER, THE SPAN OF LIFE WILL BE ABOUT
96 YEARS
IF THE RATE OF BREATHING IS 18 PER MINUTE

IF A PERSON BREATHED 15 RESPIRATIONS
PER MINUTE
THE SPAN OF LIFE WOULD BE 120 YEARS

IF THE RATE IS SLOWED THROUGH YOGIC PRACTICES
AND SELF-CONTROL
TO AN AVERAGE OF ONLY 5 RESPIRATIONS
PER MINUTE
THE LIFE SPAN WILL BE 360 YEARS

IF IT IS ONE PER MINUTE, THE LIFE SPAN
WILL INCREASE TO 1,800 YEARS

IF THE RATE OF BREATHING IS REDUCED TO ZERO
THE LIFE SPAN BECOMES INFINITY

THE SECRET OF LONGEVITY LIES IN THE TECHNIQUE
OF DIVERTING
THE BREATHING TO THE
SUBTLE CHANNELS AND CENTERS

EACH MANTRA IS A LINKAGE
TO A CERTAIN ASPECT OF THE ABSOLUTE

IN TRUE MANTRA PRACTICE
ONE FORGETS THE FACT THAT THE SELF
IS CHANTING
BECOMES THE MANTRA ITSELF
AND ATTAINS THE STATE WHERE NOTHING
BUT THE MANTRA EXISTS

489

Made in the USA
Coppell, TX
29 December 2023

26983142R10293